AACRAO Professional
Development & Education Series

The AACRAO 2001
FERPA Guide

Richard A. Rainsberger
Eliott G. Baker
Dennis Hicks
Brad Myers
Jim Noe
Faith A. Weese

AACRAO 1910 American Association of Collegiate Registrars and Admissions Officers

Library of Congress Cataloging-in-Publication Data

Rainsberger, Richard A.
The *AACRAO 2001 Guide to FERPA*/prepared for aacrao by Richard A.
Rainsberger, Faith A. Weese.
p. cm. — (AACRAO Professional Development & Education Series)
Includes index.

ISBN 1-57858-024-2

1. United States. Family Educational Rights and Privacy Act.
2. Student records—Law and legislation—United States.
3. Privacy, Right of—United States.
4. College registrars—United States.—Handbooks, manuals, etc.
5. College admission officers—United States.—Handbooks, manuals, etc.

I. Title: *Guide to FERPA.*
II. Weese, Faith A.
III. American Association of Collegiate Registrars and Admissions Officers.
IV. Title.
V. Series.

KF4156.5.A318 R35 2001
344.73'0793–DC21

2001022738

American Association of Collegiate Registrars and Admissions Officers
One Dupont Circle, NW, Suite 520
Washington, DC 20036-1135

Tel: (202) 293-9161 | Fax: (202) 872-8857 | www.aacrao.org

The American Association of Collegiate Registrars and Admissions Officers, founded in 1910 is a nonprofit, voluntary, professional association of more than 9,300 higher education administrators who represent more than 2,400 institutions and agencies in the United States and in twenty-eight countries around the world. The mission of the Association is to provide leadership in policy initiation, interpretation, and implementation in the global educational community. This is accomplished through the identification and promotion of standards and best practices in enrollment management, information technology, instructional management, and student services.

Table of Contents

Preface

THE PRIMARY PURPOSE OF THIS AACRAO PUBLICATION IS TO PROVIDE GUIDANCE AND SUGGESTED IMPLEMENTATION PROCEDURES FOR COMPLYING WITH THE FAMILY EDUCATIONAL RIGHTS AND PRIVACY ACT OF 1974, AS AMENDED (SUBSEQUENTLY REFERRED TO AS "THE ACT" OR FERPA). FURTHER, IT IS A PUBLICATION THAT (1) WILL ASSIST INSTITUTIONAL RECORDS-KEEPERS AND OTHER SCHOOL OFFICIALS IN UNDERSTANDING THEIR ROLES AND RESPONSIBILITIES FOR IMPLEMENTING THE ACT AND (2) WILL PROVIDE MANY PRACTICAL TIPS THAT CAN BE USED ON A DAILY BASIS IN TRAINING INSTITUTIONAL EMPLOYEES ON FERPA.

A Preliminary Caution

All professional publications are "snapshots in time." This publication is no exception. Subsequent federal legislation, regulations, and determinations by the Family Policy Compliance Office will clarify, amplify, and change what is included in this publication. The electronic transmission of student education record information is still in its infancy. The concept of the electronic signature stands to significantly change how we comply with FERPA. The Student Right-to-Know Act and Solomon Amendment continue to require clarification as these laws continue to develop and mature in character and intent.

These guidelines are, by definition, interpretive. They are not to be construed as the law and are intended for use along with the Act and its published regulations. While consulting this document, the reader should be aware of any applicable privacy or public information laws of a state which may complement or be at variance with FERPA (see Chapter 1.7 of this publication for additional information on this topic).

Additionally, FERPA applies to all levels of education in the United States, and there are significant differences in how the law applies to K-12 as compared to postsecondary institutions. This publication applies to postsecondary education only. A companion volume covering FERPA at the K-12 level, *FERPA and Secondary Education* (1997), sponsored by the National Association for College Admission Counseling and AACRAO, is available from AACRAO.

History and Contents of This Publication

The Family Educational Rights and Privacy Act (FERPA) was enacted by the United States Congress in 1974. The AACRAO *Guide to Postsecondary Institutions for Implementation of the Family Educational Rights and Privacy Act of 1974* was first printed in 1976.

Particularly in preparing the original edition, the American Association of Collegiate Registrars and Admissions Officers (AACRAO) was assisted by representatives of the following associations in developing a comprehensive and concise set of recommended institutional guidelines and procedures for postsecondary institutions implementing this law: the American Council on Education, the National Association of College and University Attorneys, The College Board, and the Educational Testing Service.

By 1984, the format for subsequent *Guides* had been determined. That year the *1984 AACRAO FERPA Guide* reflected the format and content found in subsequent editions.

The 1988 final FERPA regulations provided significant change. Most prominent among the changes was the identification of two types of parental status: custodial and non-custodial. The regulations outlined the role and rights of both of these types of parents under FERPA. By 1991, recognizing that there had been many significant changes to FERPA regulations, the AACRAO Board of Directors appointed a committee to revise the 1984 FERPA *Guide*. That committee included:

- Patrick R. Forte, University Registrar, University of Medicine and Dentistry of New Jersey
- Pinhas Friedenberg, Dean of Enrollment Management, Touro College (New York)
- Mary Beth Myers, Assistant Registrar, Indiana University
- Richard A. Rainsberger, University Registrar, Carnegie Mellon University (Pennsylvania)
- Joseph Roof, Dean of Admissions and Records Systems, Seminole Community College (Florida)

From its early discussions, this committee initiated a survey of AACRAO member institutions to assess current knowledge, procedures, and attitudes regarding FERPA. The questionnaire for this survey was sent to a randomly selected group of 500 AACRAO member institutions. A 51 percent response rate enabled the committee to identify key areas and topics that needed to be discussed and included in the publication being prepared. This publication eventually became the 1995 edition of *The Guide to Postsecondary Institutions for Implementation of the Family Educational Rights and Privacy Act of 1974 as Amended.*

This *1995 FERPA Guide*—particularly Chapters 1 through 4—followed the outline of the 1984 publication. Also, the 1995 edition introduced Chapters 5 through 7, expanded the appendices, and added a bibliography. The 1998 edition followed the same format, providing updated information on events, policies, rulings, and legislation that had affected FERPA since the 1995 publication of the *Guide*.

The genesis of the current publication occurred in June 2000 when the AACRAO Executive Board approved revision of the *1998 Guide*. Shortly thereafter, the chair formed a committee of records administrators who had direct responsibility for administering FERPA on their campuses and who also had extensive experience with FERPA and related issues. That committee included:

- Eliott G. Baker, Director of Academic Records and Summer School, Slippery Rock University (Pennsylvania)
- Dennis Hicks, Registrar, Indiana University East
- Brad Myers, University Registrar, The Ohio State University
- James Noe, Dean of Student Affairs, Mount Carmel College of Nursing (Ohio)
- Faith A. Weese, Registrar/Director of Academic Records, Grand Canyon University (Arizona)
- Richard A. Rainsberger, Director of Admissions and Records, Central Virginia Community College (chair)

The committee's work culminated in this publication.

What's New in This Publication?

The current publication follows the format of previous *Guides* except that Chapter 6 of the 1995 and 1998 *Guides* is integrated into Chapter 5 of this edition. The new Chapter 6 includes training materials that practitioners can use on their campuses in training others about their responsibilities under FERPA.

Significant changes have occurred with the issuance of the 2000 FERPA regulations. The major changes in or additions to the law are:

- Permitting disclosure of education records to authorized representatives of the U.S. Attorney General in connection with an investigation or enforcement of federal legal requirements of federally supported education programs;
- Permitting non-consensual disclosure of the final results of a disciplinary proceeding against a postsecondary student in specified circumstances;
- Permitting non-consensual disclosure to parents and legal guardians about students under the age of 21 regarding a student's violation of laws or policies governing the use or possession of alcohol or a controlled substance;
- Clarifying the conditions under which the institution may disclose records in defending itself;
- Clarifying of "directory information" and revising the examples illustrative of "directory information";
- More specific itemization of crimes of violence and non-forcible sex offenses;
- Clarifying what information can be disclosed from an institutional disciplinary proceeding and under what conditions;
- New definitions of dates of attendance, non-forcible sex offenses, crime of violence, alleged perpetrator of a crime of violence, sole possession records, alleged perpetrator of a non-forcible sex offense, final results of a disciplinary hearing.

These changes are included in the current publication. Additionally, with a decision in the Miami and Ohio State case on releasing disciplinary hearing records to news media, the definition of "education record" has been clarified. When the *1998 Guide* was in progress, a federal district court had issued an injunction prohibiting the two universities from releasing disciplinary hearing records to the *Chronicle of Higher Education*. The *Chronicle* was appealing the decision when the *1998 Guide* went to press. That appeal has now been resolved, and the "rest of the story" is included in this *Guide*.

Also, the committee reviewed the entire *1998 Guide* and made changes and additions to the content and added new features to make this *Guide* more effective as a resource tool. The inclusion of sidebar comments—"FERPA Tips"—throughout the publication is one example. The committee also added topics to Chapter 5 and expanded Chapter 7 by including more cases for readers to consider.

In an age when technology is changing business practices on our college campuses, we should remember that FERPA was passed when many of the high-tech concepts that are a reality today were, at best, figments of some very fertile imaginations. As a result, we must recognize that there is only one education records law, and that law applies whether we are discussing high-tech or low-tech issues. The arena may have changed significantly, but the guidelines have remained relatively the same since FERPA was passed in 1974. It is a credit to the foresight of our law-makers that this law has remained relatively unchanged since it was enacted. It not only has allowed us to comply with FERPA in our own unique institutional ways, but it also has provided a stable legal basis to provide guidance for those of us who regularly implement change.

Acknowledgments

With this current edition of the FERPA *Guide*, the author was greatly assisted by the many contributions of admissions, records, and registration professionals who work with FERPA daily, contribute their ideas to serving our institutions through better FERPA policies, and provide professional leadership in the area of records confidentiality. Without a doubt, this publication could not have come to fruition as quickly, completely, and more comprehensively than any prior editions had it not been for the efforts of the current *AACRAO FERPA Guide* Revision Committee members. They should be singled out and given a big thank you not only by the author, but by those of us who use the information found in this publication. **Eliott Baker**, steady as ever, reviewed every chapter and provided insightful suggestions for changes that clarified sections of the *Guide*. He also provided guidance in clearly identifying the differences between FERPA and the Solomon Amendment. The section on Solomon and the Final Rule found in Chapter 5 is his and his alone. **Dennis Hicks** worked on additions to the cases in Chapter 7 and provided many comments on other sections throughout the publication that simplified the wording. **Brad Myers** not only provided legal expertise, but also was very free in offering examples of documents and policies that are used at The Ohio State University and other institutions for complying with FERPA. The section on the FERPA Audit in Chapter 6 was his creative idea. It has proved to be a significant addition to the tools that we use to ensure FERPA compliance on our campuses. Many of those documents can be found throughout the publication. **Jim Noe** provided insight into many of the sections in the *Guide* in his unique position as a past registrar and current dean of students. He developed the section in Chapter 5 on distributed systems and FERPA implications. Last, and by no means least, **Faith Weese** provided the editorial expertise and knowledge of FERPA that provided the consistency this publication needed. In having to deal with an author that often did not meet deadlines and sometimes changed directions midstream, her patience, good humor, and flexibility are greatly appreciated. She never lost sight of the goal of this project and kept us all focused on what we were about.

In addition, the author is indebted to **Will Corprew** and the AACRAO **Board of Directors** for providing support for the project. AACRAO's Associate Executive Director, **Barmak Nassirian**, and Publications Manager, **Martha Henebry**, cannot be thanked enough for their efforts in taking the substance within this publication and producing a *Guide* of which we all can be proud.

Finally, the following individuals shared their time, knowledge, and talents in providing assistance with this publication. Their contributions provided the breadth and depth of FERPA coverage that education records professionals have come to expect from this publication:

- Lysbeth (Betsy) Bainbridge, Director, Postsecondary Electronic Standards Council
- Kathie Beaty, University Registrar, Bradley University
- Daniel Boehmer, President, National Student Loan Clearinghouse
- Ellen Campbell, Family Policy Compliance Office, U.S. Office of Education
- M.A. Car, Registrar, National University
- William Carr, Office of the Assistant Secretary of Defense for Force Management Policy, Department of Defense
- Dr. Sam Conte, University Registrar, University of Pittsburgh
- D. Scott Dittman, University Registrar, Washington and Lee University
- Joseph St. Hilaire, University Registrar, Western Washington University
- LeRoy Rooker, Director, Family Policy Compliance Office, U.S. Office of Education
- Steve Shablin, Registrar, Oakland University
- James H. Terry, Registrar, Salve Regina University
- Barbara Thrasher, Registrar, Randolph Macon Women's College
- All individuals on regist-l who posed FERPA questions, provided FERPA advice, and freely shared their insights on FERPA with others.

It has been my great privilege to complete an *AACRAO FERPA Guide* revision for the third time. In each of these revisions, the individuals mentioned reflected the best of what professional records administrators are all about.

We, and I personally, owe all of these individuals a great deal of thanks and praise for their contributions. This publication is another example of how the contributions, perspectives, cooperation, and insights of many produced a better document than the work of one. We should remember that principle as we work with our faculty, staffs, students, and the public.

—Richard A. Rainsberger

FERPA at a Glance

THE FOLLOWING TWO STATEMENTS SUMMARIZE THE ESSENCE OF FERPA:

1. *COLLEGE STUDENTS MUST BE PERMITTED TO INSPECT THEIR OWN EDUCATION RECORDS.*
2. *SCHOOL OFFICIALS MAY NOT DISCLOSE PERSONALLY IDENTIFIABLE INFORMATION ABOUT STUDENTS NOR PERMIT INSPECTION OF THEIR RECORDS WITHOUT WRITTEN PERMISSION UNLESS SUCH ACTION IS COVERED BY CERTAIN EXCEPTIONS PERMITTED BY THE ACT.*

THE FOLLOWING CONSTITUTES A MORE DETAILED SUMMARY OF FERPA.

What is FERPA?

The Family Educational Rights and Privacy Act of 1974, as amended, sets forth requirements regarding the privacy of student records. FERPA governs: (1) release of these records (known as education records) maintained by an educational institution and (2) access to these records. This law applies to K-12 as well as postsecondary education.

Who must comply with FERPA?

Any educational institution (school or other entity that provides educational services and is attended by students) and educational agency (entity that administers schools directly linked to it) that receives funds under any program administered by the U.S. Secretary of Education.

What does FERPA require for colleges to be in compliance?

- Notify students annually—see **Model Annual Notification to Students** (Appendix 14). Schools must notify students of their rights on an annual basis. There is no specific method that schools must use to notify students; it is up to the institution. Notice must take a form that is "reasonably likely" to notify students. Recommended and most frequently used ways include:
  - Student bulletin, handbook, or catalog
  - School or local newspaper
  - Student registration packet
- Protect students' rights to inspect and review their education records.
- Protect students' rights to request to amend their education records.
- Protect students' rights to limit disclosure of personally identifiable information contained in education records.
- Ensure that third parties do not redisclose personally identifiable information (except under a few circumstances).
- Keep records of requests for and disclosures of student education records in limited situations.

Who has FERPA rights at the postsecondary level?

A student "in attendance" (regardless of age) and former students.

- *Student* applies to all students attending—including continuing education students, students auditing a class, and distance education students.
- *In attendance* applies to and is determined by the institution. If the institution has not defined when a student is "in attendance," that date becomes the day the student first attends a class at the institution.

What are these rights given to students?

- Right to inspect and review their education records.
- Right to request to amend their education records.
- Right to limit disclosure of some "personally identifiable information" (information that would directly identify the student or make the student's identity easily traceable) known as *directory information.*

What are education records under FERPA?

Education records are defined as records that are:

- Directly related to a student, and
- Maintained by an education agency or institution or by a party acting for the agency or institution.

Education records are not:

- sole possession records,
- law enforcement unit records,
- employment records,
- medical records, or
- post-attendance records.

To whom and under what conditions can colleges disclose personally identifiable information?

- To anyone if the college has obtained the prior written consent of the student.
- To anyone in response to requests for directory information (information that is generally not considered harmful or an invasion of privacy if disclosed).
  - Institutions must identify those items it considers directory information and notify students.
  - Institutions must notify students that they can withhold release of this information.
- To authorized representatives of the following government entities if the disclosure is in connection with an audit or evaluation of federal or state supported education programs, or for the enforcement of or compliance with federal legal requirements that relate to those programs:
  - Comptroller General of the United States
  - Secretary of Education
  - U.S. Attorney General (for law enforcement purposes only)
  - State and local educational authorities
- To school officials determined by the institution to have a legitimate educational interest.
- To agents acting on behalf of the institution (e.g., clearinghouses, degree/enrollment verifiers).
- To schools at which the student seeks or intends to enroll.
- To anyone who is providing financial aid to the student ("financial aid" does not include any payments made by parents) (conditions exist).
- To organizations conducting studies for or on behalf of educational institutions.
- To accrediting organizations (for accrediting purposes).
- To parents of a dependent student.
- To parents/legal guardians when their children (under age 21) are found to have violated the alcohol or drug policy of the institution (Warner Amendment).
- To comply with a judicial order or subpoena.
- To anyone if a health or safety emergency exists and the information will assist in resolving the emergency.
- To the student.
- To an alleged victim of a crime of violence of the results of a disciplinary hearing regarding the alleged perpetrator of that crime with respect to that crime.
- To anyone requesting the final results of a disciplinary hearing against an alleged perpetrator of a crime of violence or non-forcible sex offense (Foley Amendment).
- To the Immigration and Naturalization Service (INS) for purposes of the Coordinated Interagency Partnership Regulating International Students.
- To military recruiters who request "Student Recruiting Information" for recruiting purposes only (Solomon Amendment). *Student recruiting information* is name, address, telephone listing, age (or year of birth), level of education, and major (conditions exist).
- To the Internal Revenue Service (IRS) for purposes of complying with the Taxpayer Relief Act of 1997.
- To authorized representatives of the Department of Veterans Affairs for students receiving educational assistance from the agency.

How does technology impact FERPA guidelines?

As we move toward an environment with less paper, it is important to note that the same principles of confidentiality must be applied to all media, including but not limited to electronic data, e-mail, and video- or audio-tapes.

What happens if a college does not comply with FERPA?

The Department of Education may issue a notice to cease the practice complained of and ultimately could withhold funds administered by the Secretary of Education. (However, as a practical matter, the Secretary has never withheld funds because voluntary compliance has always been secured by the Family Policy Compliance Office.)

Where can I get more information regarding FERPA?

Family Policy Compliance Office, U.S. Department of Education, 400 Maryland Avenue, SW, Washington, DC 20202-4605.

- E-mail: ferpa@ed.gov
- Web: www.ed.gov/offices/OM/fpco/

Chapter One

Introduction

The purpose of the Family Educational Rights and Privacy Act (hereafter referred to as the Act or FERPA) is to afford certain rights to students concerning their education records. The primary rights afforded are:

- the right to inspect and review the education records;
- the right to seek to have the records amended; and
- the right to have some control over the disclosure of information from the records.

Education institutions and agencies are required to conform to fair information practices. This means that persons who are subjects of data systems (i.e., students at an institution) must:

- be informed of the existence of such systems,
- have identified for them what data about them are on record,
- be given assurances that such data are used only for intended purposes,
- be given the opportunity to request an amendment or correction to their records,
- be certain that those responsible for data systems take reasonable precautions to prevent misuse of the data, and
- know that the institution will respond reasonably when an alleged misuse of, or access to, data is brought to the attention of those responsible for data systems.

Although the Act does not require it, those responsible for data systems are obliged to consider properly disposing of, or destroying, information when the conditions under which that information was collected no longer exist and there are no legal restrictions preventing such disposal.

1.1 Historical Background

On June 17, 1976, the Department of Health, Education, and Welfare issued the initial final regulations in the *Federal Register* for the Family Educational Rights and Privacy Act of 1976 (P.L. 93-568, Sec. 2), as amended (P.L. 93-568, Sec. 2; 20 U.S.C. 1232g), more commonly known as the "Buckley Amendment." An additional document relating to the Act appeared in the June 17, 1976, issue of the *Federal Register.*

When the Department of Education was established, the implementing regulations were transferred to the Department of Education and codified in Part 99 of Title 34 of the Code of Federal Regulations (34 CFR 99). Slightly modified final regulations were issued in the *Federal Register* on May 9, 1980, Vol. 45, No. 92. In 1988 revised final regulations to the Family Educational Rights and Privacy Act were promulgated. The stated purpose of that revision was to simplify and clarify the previous provisions and to reduce, where possible, the regulatory burden on colleges and universities. In 1990 the Crime Awareness and Campus Security Act modified the disclosure rules in FERPA (see Chapter 4.1.3). These changes to FERPA were published in the *Federal Register* on January 7, 1993.

FERPA was amended by the Higher Education Amendments of 1992, which excluded, under certain conditions, law enforcement records of an institution of higher education from the provisions of FERPA (*Federal Register*, Department of Education, 34 CFR 99, Notice of Proposed Rule Making, December 14, 1993, pp. 65298–65300). The final regulations regarding law enforcement records were published in the *Federal Register* on January 17, 1995. The 1996 changes to FERPA affecting higher education:

- eliminated the requirement that each institution have a FERPA institutional policy statement and substituted an expanded annual notification requirement.
- required State Educational Agencies (SEAs) to afford eligible students access to education records maintained by the SEA. This right of access is the only right

parents and eligible students are afforded at the SEA level. SEA also includes state governing bodies of higher education.

- clarified that, if an education agency or institution initiates legal action against an eligible student, it must make a reasonable effort to notify the student in advance of its intent to disclose the information from education records to a court of law.
- amended FERPA so that a school is not required to notify an eligible student before complying with certain subpoenas. A college does not have to notify the student of the existence of a subpoena if it receives a federal grand jury subpoena and the court has ordered that the college not disclose to any person the existence or contents of the subpoena. Additionally, if a court or other issuing agency issues a subpoena for a law enforcement purpose and orders the school not to disclose the existence or contents of the subpoena to the student, FERPA does not require notification before compliance with the subpoena.
- clarified that a college may include information in a student's education records concerning disciplinary action taken against the student for conduct that posed a significant risk to the safety or well-being of that student, other students, or other members of the college community.
- clarified that a college may disclose, without prior consent, information contained in a student's education records concerning disciplinary action taken against the student, described above, to teachers and school officials who have legitimate educational interests in the behavior of the student. FERPA was amended to allow this type of disclosure to teachers and school officials in other schools who have legitimate educational interests in the behavior of the student.
- added a provision that, if a third party rediscloses personally identifiable student information in violation of FERPA, the college which disclosed the information to the third party shall be prohibited from permitting access to education records to that third party for a period of not less than five years.
- clarified that persons filing complaints under FERPA with the Department of Education must have legal standing. That is, a complainant must be an eligible student affected by an alleged violation. This is consistent with other laws affording specific rights to persons.

The 2000 changes and additions to FERPA as found in the new final regulations include:

- permitting disclosure of education records to authorized representatives of the U.S. Attorney General in connection with an investigation or enforcement of Federal legal requirements of federally supported education programs;
- permitting non-consensual disclosure of the final results of a disciplinary proceeding against a postsecondary student in specified circumstances;
- permitting non-consensual disclosure to parents and legal guardians of students under the age of 21, regardless of their dependency status, of information regarding a student's violation of laws or policies governing the use or possession of alcohol or a controlled substance;
- clarifying the conditions under which the institution may disclose records in defending itself;
- clarifying of "directory information" and revising the examples illustrative of "directory information";
- more specific itemization of crimes of violence and non-forcible sex offenses;
- clarifying what information can be disclosed from an institutional disciplinary proceeding and under what conditions; and
- new definitions of dates of attendance, non-forcible sex offenses, crime of violence, alleged perpetrator of a crime of violence, sole possession records, alleged perpetrator of a non-forcible sex offense, final results of a disciplinary hearing.

Copies of the original 1974 Act as amended and the new 2000 final regulations are included in the Appendix section of this publication.

The reader should always check to see if the Department of Education has issued any regulations subsequent to July 6, 2000 (*Federal Register*, pp. 41852–41853) through the web page of the Family Policy Compliance Office (the office in the Department of Education that has responsibility for administering FERPA) at:

- http://www.ed.gov/offices/OM/fpco; or
- the AACRAO web page at: http://www.aacrao.org.

1.2 Essence of the Act

FERPA deals specifically with the education records of students, affording them certain rights with respect to those records. For purposes of definition, education records are those records which are (1) directly related to a student and (2) maintained by an institution or a party acting for the institution.

FERPA gives students who reach the age of 18 or who attend a postsecondary institution the right to inspect and review their own education records. Furthermore, students have other rights, including the right to request amendment of records and to have some control over the disclosure of personally identifiable information from these records. Institutions may grant students more rights than those guaranteed in the Act.

FERPA applies to all schools that receive funding under most programs administered by the Secretary of Education (c.f. 34 CFR 99.1). Almost all postsecondary institutions, both public and private, generally receive such funding and must, therefore, comply with FERPA.

Institutions must annually notify students currently in attendance of their rights by any means that are likely to be read by students. The most common examples are the student handbook, catalog, or student newspaper. This notice also applies to any students pursuing education via distance education or any other nontraditional educational delivery processes. (See Appendix 14 for a sample of a model annual notification statement provided by the Family Policy Compliance Office.)

The regulations do not specify the means to be used for annually notifying students of FERPA rights. Schools are not required by FERPA to notify former students of their FERPA rights. Although it is highly recommended that each institution publish its annual notification on its website, this method is only acceptable for fulfilling the annual notification requirement if all students are required to have personal computers and those computers have connectivity to the institution's website.

Institutions may not disclose information contained in education records without the student's written consent except under conditions specified in the Act. An institution is not required to disclose information to the parents of dependent students but may exercise its discretion to do so. It is the responsibility of an institution to ensure that information is not improperly disclosed to the parents of students.

1.3 To Whose Records Does the Act Apply?

FERPA applies to the education records of persons who are or have been in attendance at postsecondary institutions, including students in cooperative and correspondence study programs and in any nontraditional educational delivery processes, such as distance learning.

FERPA does not apply to the records of applicants for admission who are denied acceptance or who, if accepted, do not attend an institution. Furthermore, rights are not given by FERPA to students enrolled in one component of an institution who seek to be admitted to another component of the school (e.g., a student admitted to one college within a university but denied admission to another does not have any FERPA rights in the college which denied him or her admission).

1.4 To What Records Does the Act Apply?

The Act applies to all education records maintained by a postsecondary institution, or by a party acting for the institution, which are directly related to a student and which are maintained by the institution. Records containing a student's name, social security number, or other personally identifiable information, in whatever medium, are covered by FERPA unless identified in one of the Act's excluded categories (see "Education Records" in Chapter 2 for excluded categories).

1.5 To Which Institutions Does the Act Apply?

The Act applies to all institutions that receive funds administered by the Secretary of Education. This funding can either be in direct grants to the institution or to students attending the institution (financial aid). The Act applies to the entire institution even though only one component (e.g., department or college) of the institution receives such funding.

1.6 Enforcement and Penalties

Responsibility for administering the Act has been assigned to the Family Policy Compliance Office within the Department of Education. This office reviews and investigates complaints and attempts to bring about compliance through voluntary means. The penalty for noncompliance with federal regulations can be withdrawal of Department of Education funds from the institution, but action to terminate funding generally will be taken only if compliance cannot be secured by voluntary means.

1.7 Conflict with State Law

FERPA may be more permissive than the privacy and public information laws of some states. If a conflict exists between the Family Educational Rights and Privacy Act of 1974 and state or local law, and if an institution determines that it cannot comply with the requirements of the Act, it should advise the Family Policy Compliance Office, U.S. Department of Education, 400 Maryland Avenue, SW, Washington, DC 20202-4605; (202) 260-3887; fax: (202) 260-9001, within 45 days of that determination, giving the text and legal citation of the conflicting law. These guidelines, therefore, should not be interpreted to reduce the stringency of such state laws. They counsel common sense, good judgment, perspective, and integrity for compliance by postsecondary institutions in the implementation of the Act.

During the 1990s several challenges to FERPA were made based on various states' open records/meetings laws. For more information, see Chapter 5.31.

1.8 The "Musts" and "Mays" in FERPA

Throughout the Act, the words "may" and "must" are used. These words usually are used in connection with sections of the Act that either permit or require an institution to perform an act to comply with FERPA. In the former case, the institution has control over a decision; in other words, it **may** do something. In the latter case, the institution has no choice; in other words, it **must** do something.

There are many "mays" and a few "musts" in FERPA. The reader should be aware of these words and not make an incorrect decision that an institution is required to release education record information when FERPA actually states that the institution **may** release education record information. For example, FERPA states that each institution may identify certain items as directory information; however, this is an institutional decision. By deciding not to identify any items as directory information, the institution would be making a decision that would have a major administrative impact on all offices. After all, what would be required to produce a commencement program listing the names of all the graduates and their degrees?

Chapter Two

Definitions of Terms

UNDERSTANDING KEY TERMS IS ESSENTIAL TO THE INTERPRETATION OF THE ACT AND THE FINAL REGULATIONS FOR ITS IMPLEMENTATION. SOME DEFINITIONS AND EXPLANATIONS WHICH CARRY SUBSTANTIVE MEANING FOR UNDERSTANDING THE ACT ARE LISTED HERE FOR THE CONVENIENCE OF THE READER. THE REGULATIONS (SEE APPENDIX 2 OF THIS GUIDE) PROVIDE ALL LEGAL DEFINITIONS.

Act: Refers to the Family Educational Rights and Privacy Act of 1974, as Amended, enacted as Section 438 of the General Education Provisions Act (20 U.S.C. 1232g).

Agency: An organization, company, or bureau that provides a service for another; a company having a franchise to represent another.

Agent: A person or business formally authorized to act on another's behalf.

Alleged perpetrator of a crime of violence: A student who is alleged to have committed acts that would, if proven, constitute any of the following offenses or attempts to commit the following offenses: arson, assault, burglary, criminal homicide (manslaughter by negligence), criminal homicide (murder and non-negligent manslaughter), destruction/damage/vandalism of property, kidnapping/abduction, robbery, forcible sex offenses.

Alleged perpetrator of a non-forcible sex offense: A student who is alleged to have committed acts that, if proven, would constitute statutory rape or incest.

Attendance: Includes but is not limited to (a) attendance—in person or by correspondence study (program) and (b) the period during which a person is working under a work-study (cooperative) program.

CFR: Code of Federal Regulations. The annual cumulation of executive agency regulations published in the daily *Federal Register*, combined with regulations issued previously that are still in effect. The CFR contains the general body of regulatory laws governing practice and procedure before federal administrative agencies. The regulations pertaining to FERPA are found in 34 CFR 99 (see Appendix 2).

Crime of Violence: Any of the following: arson, assault, burglary, criminal homicide (manslaughter by negligence), criminal homicide (murder and non-negligent manslaughter), destruction/damage/vandalism of property, kidnapping/abduction, robbery, forcible sex offenses.

Dates of Attendance: The period of time during which a student attends or attended an institution. Examples of dates of attendance include an academic year, a spring semester, or a first quarter. The term does not include specific daily records or a student's attendance pattern at the institution.

Directory Information: Information contained in an education record of a student that generally would not be considered harmful or an invasion of privacy if disclosed. It includes, but is not limited to, the student's name, address, telephone listing, electronic mail address, photograph, date and place of birth, major field of study, dates of attendance, grade level, enrollment status (e.g., undergraduate or graduate; full-time or part-time), participation in officially recognized activities and sports, weight and height of members of athletic teams, degrees, honors and awards received, and most recent education agency or institution attended.

FERPA TIPS

ITEMS THAT CAN NEVER BE IDENTIFIED AS DIRECTORY INFORMATION ARE A STUDENT'S SOCIAL SECURITY NUMBER, CITIZENSHIP, GENDER, RELIGIOUS PREFERENCE, GRADES, AND GPA.

Note 1: It was determined in 1996 that class rosters and student schedules could be directory information items. They are not included in the above list. Although class rosters and student schedules can still be identified as directory information by an institution, the Family Policy Office is currently reviewing their status as directory information based upon concerns that have been expressed since 1996.

Note 2: Items that can never be identified as directory information are a student's social security number, citizenship, gender, religious preference, grades, and GPA.

Disciplinary Action or Proceeding: The investigation, adjudication, or imposition of sanctions by an education agency or institution with respect to an infraction or violation of the internal rules of conduct applicable to students of the agency or institution.

Disclosure: To permit access to, or the release, transfer, or other communication of, personally identifiable information contained in education records to any party by any means, including oral, written, or electronic.

EDI (Electronic Data Interchange): Utilizes standard data formats for transmitting data from one computer to another.

Education Institution (or Agency): Generally means (1) any public or private agency or institution (including governing boards which provide administrative control or direction of a university system) of postsecondary education that (2) receives funds from any federal program under the administrative responsibility of the Secretary of Education. The term refers to the institution as a whole, including all of its components (e.g., schools or departments in a university).

Education Records: Those records directly related to a student and maintained by the institution or by a party acting for the institution.

The term "education records" **does not** include the following:

- records of instructional, supervisory, administrative, and certain educational personnel which are in the sole possession of the maker and are not accessible or revealed to any other individual except a substitute who performs on a temporary basis (as defined in the institutional personnel policy) the duties of the individual who made the records.
- records maintained by a law enforcement unit of the education agency or institution that were created by that law enforcement unit for the purpose of law enforcement.
- records relating to individuals who are employed by the institution which are made and maintained in the normal course of business, relate exclusively to individuals in their capacity as employees, and are not available for use for any other purpose. (Records of individuals in attendance at an institution who are employed as a result of their status as students are education records, e.g., work-study, graduate assistants.)
- records relating to a student (see the definition of "eligible student" below) which are (1) created or maintained by a physician, psychiatrist, psychologist, or other recognized professional or paraprofessional acting in his or her professional capacity or assisting in a paraprofessional capacity; (2) used solely in connection with the provision of treatment to the student; and (3) not disclosed to anyone other than individuals providing such treatment, so long as the records can be personally reviewed by a physician or other appropriate professional of the student's choice. (Appropriateness may be determined by the institution.) "Treatment" in this context does not include remedial educational activities or activities which are part of the program of instruction at the institution.
- records of an institution which contain only information relating to a person after that person is no longer a student at the institution (e.g., information gathered on the accomplishments of alumni).

Eligible Student: Refers to a student who has reached the age of 18 or is attending an institution of postsecondary education. Because these guidelines are specifically for postsecondary institutions, "student" as used in this document is presumed always to refer to an eligible student. In non-postsecondary institutions, parents of students have additional rights not covered in this *Guide*. (For additional information, see Chapter 5.20.3 of this publication.)

Enrolled Student: For the purposes of this publication, this term refers to a student who has satisfied all of the institutional requirements for attendance at the institution. The Family Policy Compliance Office has stated that each institution may determine when a student is *in attendance* in accordance with its own enrollment procedures (*Federal Register*, July 6, 2000, p. 41856).

Family Policy Compliance Office: The office within the U.S. Department of Education that is responsible for enforcing/administering the Family Educational Rights and Privacy Act of 1974, as Amended. This office has responsibility for FERPA at all levels of education (K-12, postsecondary).

"Final Results" of a Disciplinary Proceeding: A decision or determination, made by an honor court or council, committee, commission, or other entity authorized to resolve disciplinary matters within the institution. The disclosure of final results must include only the name of the student, the violation committed, and any sanction imposed by the institution against the student.

Financial Aid: A payment of funds to an individual (or a payment in kind of tangible or intangible property to the individual) which is conditioned on the individual's attendance at an education agency or institution.

"In Attendance" (or when is a student "in attendance"?): See "enrolled student."

Institution of Postsecondary Education: An institution that provides education to students beyond the secondary school level. "Secondary school level" means the educational level (not beyond grade 12) at which secondary education is provided.

Law Enforcement Unit: Any individual or other component of an institution, including commissioned police officers and noncommissioned security guards, officially authorized by the institution to enforce any local, state, or federal law and to maintain the physical security and safety of the institution. (Although the unit may perform other non–law enforcement functions, it does not lose its status as a law enforcement unit.)

Law Enforcement Unit Records: Those records, files, documents, and other materials that are (1) created by a law enforcement unit, (2) created for a law enforcement purpose, and (3) maintained by the law enforcement unit. Law enforcement records do not include: (1) records created by a law enforcement unit for a law enforcement purpose other than for the law enforcement unit; (2) records created and maintained by a law enforcement unit exclusively for non–law enforcement purposes, such as a disciplinary action or proceeding conducted by the institution.

Legitimate Educational Interest: The demonstrated "need to know" by those officials of an institution who act in the student's educational interest, including faculty, administration, clerical and professional employees, and other persons, including student employees or agents, who manage student record information. (Although the Act does not define "legitimate educational interest," it states that institutions must establish their own criteria, according to their own procedures and requirements, for determining when their school officials have a legitimate educational interest in a student's education records. This is a recommended definition. Sample institutional statements on legitimate educational interest are found in Appendix 11.)

Non-Forcible Sex Offense: Statutory rape or incest.

Parent: Includes a natural parent, a guardian, or an individual acting as a parent in the absence of a parent or a guardian. (For additional information, see Chapter 5.20 of this publication.)

Party: Refers to an individual, agency, institution, or organization.

Personally Identifiable: Data or information which include (1) the name of the student, the student's parent, or other family members; (2) the student's address; (3) a personal identifier such as a social security number or student number; or (4) a list of personal characteristics or other information which would make the student's identity easily traceable.

Record: Any information or data recorded in any medium (e.g., handwriting, print, tapes, film, microfilm, microfiche, any form of electronic data storage).

Regulations, The: Final revised regulations related to FERPA, approved in 1988, amended in 1990, 1992, 1994, 1995, and 1996 and found in Appendix 2. Also cited in this publication as 34 CFR 99.

School Officials: Those members of an institution who act in the student's educational interest within the limitations of their "need to know." These may include faculty, administration, clerical and professional employees and other persons, including student employees or agents, who manage student education record information. (Although the Act does not define "school officials," it states that institutions must establish their own criteria, according to their own procedures and requirements, for determining them. This is a recommended definition.)

Sole Possession Records: Records that are kept in the sole possession of the maker, are used only as a personal memory aid, and are not accessible or revealed to any other person except a temporary substitute for the maker of the record.

Any record that is made in conjunction with a student or other school official is not a sole possession record.

FERPA TIPS

IF THE INSTITUTION DOES NOT MAKE A DETERMINATION OF WHAT "IN ATTENDANCE" MEANS AT THAT COLLEGE, THE STUDENT IS CONSIDERED "IN ATTENDANCE" WHEN HE OR SHE BEGINS ATTENDING CLASSES. ALTHOUGH FERPA IS SILENT ON WHETHER A STUDENT IS "IN ATTENDANCE" DURING VACATIONS AND SUMMER BREAKS, FERPA APPLIES TO ALL STUDENTS PAST AND PRESENT. THEREFORE, "IN ATTENDANCE" ESTABLISHES THE TIME WHEN A STUDENT'S FERPA RIGHTS BEGIN INITIALLY AS A COLLEGE STUDENT OR "ELIGIBLE STUDENT."

Solomon Amendment: Sometimes referred to in this publication simply as "Solomon." This 1996 amendment to three appropriations bills proposed to withdraw funding from institutions that have been certified to have an anti-ROTC policy or practice that prevents Department of Defense representatives from obtaining, among other things, student information for military recruiting purposes.

Student: Any individual for whom an education institution maintains education records. The term does not include an individual who has never attended the institution. An individual who is or has been enrolled in one component unit of an institution and who applies for admission to a second unit has no right to inspect the records accumulated by the second unit until enrolled therein.

Student Recruiting Information: That information identified in the Solomon Amendment that institutions are required to provide military recruiters upon request once a term. Those items are: student name, addresses, telephone listings, date and place of birth, level of education, academic major, degrees received, and the most recent previous educational institution at which the student was enrolled.

Student Right-to-Know Act of 1990: Referred to in this publication as SRTK, the act requires colleges and universities to report graduation rates to current and prospective students.

Subpoena: A command from a court to require the person named in the subpoena to appear at a stated time and place to provide testimony or evidence. There are two main types of subpoenas: *duces tecum* (requires the production of documents, papers, or other tangibles) and *ad testificandum* (requires person to testify in a particular court case).

U.S.C.: United States Code. A compilation of all federal legislation organized into 50 titles. Revised every six years with supplementary volumes issued in intervening years. The legislation related to FERPA is found in 20 U.S.C. 1232g (see Appendix 1).

Chapter Three

Requirements for Compliance

Students have three primary rights under FERPA. They have the rights:

❶ to inspect and review their education records,
❷ to have some control over the disclosure of information from their education records, and
❸ to seek to amend their education records.

To comply with these rights and all of the provisions of the Act, its regulations, and disclosure provisions, each education institution must notify students annually of their FERPA rights and provide students access to their education records.

3.1 Notice to Students of Their Privacy Rights

Each institution is required to notify students annually of their FERPA rights. To assist each institution in complying with the annual notification requirement, the Family Policy Compliance Office provides a model annual notification of FERPA rights in (see Appendix 14).

The annual notification must specify student rights covered by the Act, including the right to:

- inspect and review information contained in education records (see "Students' Access to Their Education Records," Chapter 3.2).
- request the amendment of the student's education records to ensure that they are not inaccurate, misleading, or otherwise in violation of the student's privacy or other rights (see "Challenge of the Contents of Education Records," Chapter 4.2).
- consent to disclosure, with certain exceptions specified in the Act, of personally identifiable information from education records (see "Disclosure of Education Record Information," Chapter 4.1).
- file complaints with the Department of Education concerning alleged failures by institutions to comply with the Act. Written complaints should be directed to The Family Policy Compliance Office, U.S. Department of Education, 400 Maryland Avenue, SW, Washington, DC 20202-4605; (202) 260-3887, fax: (202) 260-9001.

Former students do not have to be notified. The Family Policy Compliance Office has indicated that the method of notifying students annually is left to the discretion of the institution, as long as the means employed are reasonably effective to communicate those rights. For example, means may include individual student notification or publication in college catalogs, schedules, or student newspapers. A 1997 survey of the registrars of member universities of the American Association of Universities (AAU) found that the most frequently used methods of annual student notification were the college catalog, student handbook, and schedule of classes (Turner-Dickerson 1997, p. 34).

As mentioned in Chapter 1, although it is highly recommended that each institution publish its annual notification on its website, this method is only acceptable for fulfilling the annual notification requirement if all students are required to have personal computers and those computers have connectivity to the institution's website.

3.1.1 Notification to Students of the Institution's Public or Directory Information Category; Student's Right to Non-disclosure of Public or Directory Information

Although not required to be included in the institution's annual notification to students, FERPA requires institutions to give public notice to students of the categories of personally identifiable information which the institution has designated as public or directory information.

Although this notification is not required to be made annually, it is recommended that the annual notification include:

- Types of information which may be designated as public or directory information as listed in "Definition of Terms" (Chapter 2) of this *Guide*.

  These items of directory information may be "grouped" into categories for release to the public for specific purposes. In such cases, institutions may restrict the dissemination of an entire category if the student requests exclusion of any items of directory information.

- Specific procedures to inform students how to withhold categories of public or directory information. Students must be given a specific period of time within which they must inform institutions, in writing, that such categories of information are to be withheld (see "Disclosure of Education Record Information," Chapter 4.1). Although not a FERPA requirement, institutions should alert students to the possible undesirable consequences of withholding directory information. Institutions are advised to formulate procedures that will permit students to make informed decisions when they exercise their right to exclude directory information (see Chapter 5.33).

  Institutions may disclose directory information about former students without meeting the notification requirements. However, if a student, at his or her last opportunity as a student, requested that directory information not be disclosed, the institution must continue to honor that request until informed to the contrary.

FERPA TIPS

STUDENTS HAVE THE RIGHT TO ACCESS THEIR EDUCATION RECORDS. THEY DO NOT HAVE THE RIGHT TO COPIES OF THOSE RECORDS UNLESS GEOGRAPHIC DISTANCE PRECLUDES PERSONAL INSPECTION.

Assistance with the preparation of an annual notification statement to students can be found in Appendix 14.

3.2 Students' Access to Their Education Records

Students and former students have rights to inspect and review their education records.

Procedures must be developed to permit students to inspect and review their education records (except as limited in Chapter 3.2.1, below) within a maximum of 45 days after they request to do so. The right of inspection and review includes:

- the right to access, with an explanation and interpretation of the record, and
- the right to a copy of the education record when failure to provide a copy of the record would effectively prevent the student from inspecting and reviewing the record. A copy may be refused, but only if, in doing so, the institution does not limit the student's right to inspect and review that record.

3.2.1 Limitations on Students' Right to Inspect Their Education Records

Limitations exist on students' rights to inspect and review their education records. The institution is not required to permit students to inspect and review the following:

- financial information submitted by parents.
- confidential letters and recommendations placed in their files prior to January 1, 1975, provided these letters were collected under established policies of confidentiality and were used only for the purposes for which [they were] specifically collected.
- confidential letters and statements of recommendation, placed in the records after January 1, 1975, to which the student has waived his or her right to inspect and review and that are related to the student's admission, application for employment or job placement, or receipt of honors (see Chapter 3.2.2, below).
- education records containing information about more than one student; however, in such cases the institution must permit access to that part of the record which pertains only to the inquiring student.

3.2.2 Student's Waiver of Right to Review Confidential Letters of Recommendation

Students may waive any or all of their rights to review confidential letters and statements of recommendation under the Act. The right of waiver is subject to the following conditions:

- that institutions do not require waivers.
- that no institutional service or benefit be denied students who fail to supply waivers (although institutions are free to request waivers).
- that the documents to which students have waived the right to access are used only for the purposes for which [they were] collected. If used for other purposes, the waivers are void and the documents may be inspected by students. Institutions would be well advised to assure all parties concerned that the instruments used for soliciting recommendations and evaluations contain the specific purposes for which they will be used and the timeframe in which such forms will be destroyed.

- that the waivers are in writing and signed by the students. Students may waive their rights to inspect and review either individual documents or classes of documents (e.g., part or all of an admission or job placement file). They may revoke the waiver in writing; however, by revoking it, they do not have the right to inspect and review documents collected while the waiver was in force.

Note: When "applicants" who waive their rights to access documents become students, they may specifically request and be given the names of all individuals who submitted letters and statements of recommendation for them.

3.2.3 Destruction of Education Records

The regulations contain only one restriction pertaining to the destruction of education records. This is that once students have requested access to their education records, such students' records cannot be destroyed until inspection and review have been provided.

Two additional items must not be destroyed unless the records to which they pertain are destroyed: (1) "explanations" placed in the records by students as a result of a request for amendment that has been denied, and (2) records of disclosures and requests for disclosures.

FERPA TIPS

ALTHOUGH THERE IS NO RECORDS RETENTION POLICY IN FERPA, EACH INSTITUTION IS ENCOURAGED TO HAVE A RECORDS RETENTION POLICY THAT FOLLOWS THE GUIDELINES IN "AACRAO'S RETENTION OF RECORDS: GUIDE FOR RETENTION AND DISPOSAL OF STUDENT RECORDS 2000 UPDATE"

Chapter Four

Procedures and Strategies for Compliance

TO FULFILL THE BASIC REQUIREMENTS FOR COMPLIANCE WITH THE ACT, EACH EDUCATION INSTITUTION MUST (1) PREVENT IMPROPER DISCLOSURE OF PERSONALLY IDENTIFIABLE INFORMATION FROM EDUCATION RECORDS, (2) PROVIDE OPPORTUNITY FOR CHALLENGE OF THE CONTENTS OF EDUCATION RECORDS AS REQUIRED BY FERPA AND THE REGULATIONS, AND (3) MAINTAIN ADEQUATE RECORDS OF REQUESTS AND DISCLOSURES AS DETAILED IN THIS CHAPTER.

4.1 Disclosure of Education Record Information

4.1.1 Institutions must obtain written consent from students before disclosing any personally identifiable information from their education records (with exceptions as noted in Chapter 4.1.2, 4.1.3, 4.1.4, and 4.1.5, below). Such written consent must:

- specify the records to be released,
- state the purpose of the disclosure,
- identify the party or class of parties to whom disclosure may be made, and
- be signed and dated by the student.

4.1.2 Institutions must disclose education records or components thereof without written consent to students who request information from their own records and to representatives of the Veterans Administration to determine compliance with educational assistance provided to eligible veterans or other persons.

4.1.3 The next section, referred to as the "exceptions" section of the regulations, outlines the conditions under which an institution may release personally identifiable education record information about a student without first obtaining the student's written permission. This is formally found in 34 CFR 99.31 (see Appendix 2). New items added in the 2000 regulations are shown **in bold lettering.**

Institutions may disclose education records or components thereof without written consent of students to:

- authorized representatives of the following for audit and evaluation of federal and/or state supported programs, or for enforcement of or compliance with federal legal requirements which relate to those programs (see 34 CFR 99.35 for additional conditions that must be met).
  - the Comptroller General of the United States
  - **the Attorney General of the United States**
  - the Secretary of the Department of Education
  - state and local educational authorities.
- state and local officials to whom disclosure is specifically required by state statute adopted prior to November 19, 1974.
- Veterans Administration officials (not covered by FERPA but specified under Title 38, Section 1790 (c), United States Code; see Appendix 7).
- other school officials within the institution determined by the institution to have a legitimate educational interest (see Chapter 5.16).
- officials of other institutions at which a student seeks or intends to enroll, on the condition that the issuing institution makes a reasonable attempt to inform the student of the disclosure, unless the student initiates the transfer or the annual notification of the institution (discussed in Chapter 3.1) includes a

FERPA TIPS

THE WORDS "MAY" AND "MUST" HAVE DIFFERENT MEANINGS. PAY ATTENTION TO THESE WORDS THROUGHOUT THIS PUBLICATION. THEY HAVE A SIGNIFICANT IMPACT ON HOW EACH INSTITUTION DEVELOPS ITS ANNUAL NOTIFICATION AND POLICIES IN COMPLYING WITH FERPA.

notice that the institution forwards education records to other institutions at which the student seeks or intends to enroll that have requested the records (see 34 CFR 99.34 for additional conditions that must be met).

- persons or organizations providing financial aid to students or determining financial aid decisions, on the condition that the information is necessary to: (1) determine eligibility for the aid, (2) determine the amount of the aid, (3) determine the conditions for the aid, or (4) enforce the terms and conditions of the aid.
- organizations conducting studies for, or on behalf of, education agencies or institutions to develop, validate, and administer predictive tests, to administer student aid programs, or to improve instruction. Those organizations may not disclose personally identifiable information on students, and information secured must be destroyed when no longer needed for their projects. Institutions are advised to obtain such assurance in writing.
- accrediting organizations carrying out their accrediting functions.
- parents of a student who have established that student's status as a dependent according to Internal Revenue Code of 1986, Section 152 (see Appendix 7 and Chapter 5.20).
- persons in compliance with a judicial order or a lawfully issued subpoena, provided that the institution makes a reasonable attempt to notify the student in advance of compliance (see Chapter 5.40.7 and Appendix 15).

  Note: The institution is not required to, and should not, notify the student if a federal grand jury subpoena, or any other subpoena issued for a law enforcement purpose, orders the institution not to disclose the existence or contents of the subpoena.

  An institution is not required to obtain a subpoena to produce education records of a student if the institution is sued by the student or takes legal action against a student. The records produced must be needed by the institution to proceed with legal action as plaintiff or to defend itself.

- persons in an emergency, if the knowledge of information, in fact, is necessary to protect the health or safety of students or other persons. (According to 34 CFR 99.36, the wording of this section "shall be strictly construed.")
- **a victim of an alleged perpetrator of a crime of violence or a non-forcible sex offense, subject to the new definitions in new section 99.39 (see Chapter 2 and Appendix 2, section 99.39). The disclosure may include only the final results of the disciplinary proceeding conducted by the institution with respect to that alleged crime or offense. The institution may disclose the final results of the disciplinary proceeding, regardless of whether the institution concluded a violation was committed.**
- **interested individuals (the public), subject to the requirements in new section 99.39, in connection with the final results of an institutional disciplinary proceeding.**

  The institution must not disclose the final results of the disciplinary proceeding unless it has determined that:

  - **the student is an alleged perpetrator of a crime of violence or non-forcible sex offense; and**
  - **with respect to the allegation made against him or her, the student has committed a violation of the institution's rules or policies.**

  The final results must include only: the name of the student, the violation committed, and any sanction imposed by the institution against the student.

  The institution may not disclose the name of any other student, including a victim or witness, without the prior written consent of the other student.

- **parents regarding the student's violation of any federal, state, or local law, or of any institutional policy or rule governing the use of alcohol or a controlled substance if**

  - **the institution has determined that the student has committed a disciplinary violation with respect to that use or possession; and**
  - **the student is under the age of 21 at the time of the disclosure to the parent.**

  This item does not supersede any state law that prohibits an institution from disclosing this information.

This section (4.1.3) does not forbid an institution from disclosing, nor does it require an institution to disclose, personally identifiable information from the education records of a student to any parties.

4.1.4 Institutions may release without written consent those items specified as public or directory information for students who are currently enrolled, provided the following conditions are met prior to disclosure:

- that the institution inform the students of information or categories designated as public or directory information;
- that students be given the opportunity to refuse disclosures of information for any or all categories of directory information; and
- that the students be given a reasonable period of time in which to state such refusals in writing.

4.1.5 Institutions may release without written consent those items designated as public or directory information on any student not currently enrolled unless that student, at his or her last opportunity as a student, requested otherwise.

4.1.6 Institutions may also disclose to a third party personally identifiable information from a student's education records if the eligible student has signed and dated a written consent form which is presented to a school official by the third party.

4.1.7 Institutions are responsible for informing parties to whom personally identifiable information is released that recipients, as a general rule, are not permitted to disclose the information to others without the written consent of the students. An example of such wording follows.

The attached information has been forwarded to you at the request of the student with the understanding that it will not be released to other parties. The Family Educational Rights and Privacy Act of 1974, as Amended, prohibits release of this information without the student's written consent. Please return this material to us if you are unable to comply with this condition of release.

In certain circumstances, found in Section 99.33 (34 CFR 99.33) of the regulations, the recipient of the information may legally redisclose that information. However, the 1996 final regulations added a provision that, if a third party rediscloses personally identifiable student information in violation of FERPA, the college that discloses the information to the third party shall be prohibited from permitting access to education records to that third party for a period of not less than five years.

4.1.8 Terms under which institutions may disclose information to parents of students are:

- by obtaining the student's written consent, which institutions must do if the student is independent, or
- by establishing the student's dependency as defined by Internal Revenue Code of 1986, Section 152 (see Appendix 7). An explicit institutional policy covering "dependency" determination should be available if release is to be made to parents under this provision (see Chapter 5.20). That policy might include:
  - advising each student during the registration process that their records may be disclosed to their parents upon request if their parents claim them as dependents for income tax purposes **and** the institution has verified that fact. Students should be asked to indicate if they are claimed as a dependent by their parents, or by one of their parents in cases of divorce, and to sign an acknowledgment that they were provided the opportunity to notify the school that they are not dependents for income tax purposes. Thereafter, if a parent of a student who has indicated that one or both of the parents claims the student as a dependent requests access, the school may give access to either parent (custodial or non-custodial) unless there is a court order, state statute, or other legally binding document prohibiting such.
  - requiring a certified copy of the parents' most recent Federal Income Tax Form.

4.2 Challenge of the Contents of Education Records

The Act and regulations do not provide details about required grievance and hearing mechanisms to be employed, but institutions should have clear channels of appeal which (a) are stated in the written institutional policy, (b) involve disinterested institutional personnel, and (c) take the following provisions of the regulations into account:

- Institutions must provide students with an opportunity to challenge and amend the contents of education records which the students consider to be inaccurate, misleading, or otherwise in violation of their privacy or other rights (see 34 CFR 99.20, 99.21, 99.22 for additional information).
- Officials who receive challenge requests must decide within a reasonable period of time whether corrective action consistent with the student's request will be taken. The student must be notified of the decision. If the decision is in agreement with the student's request, the appropriate record(s) must be amended.
- A student who is not provided full relief sought by his or her challenge must be informed by the appropriate official of the decision and of his or her right to a formal hearing on the matter.
- A student's request for a formal hearing should be in writing (see Appendix 9). Within a reasonable period of time after receiving the requests, the appropriate official must inform students reasonably in advance of the hearing of the date, place, and time of the hearing.
- The student must be afforded a full and fair opportunity to present evidence relevant to the issue raised. The student may be assisted or represented at the hearing by one or more persons of his or her choice, including an attorney, at the student's expense.
- The hearing may be conducted by any individual, including an official of the institution, provided such person does not have a direct interest in the outcome of the hearing.
- Decisions of the colleges and universities must be in writing, must be based solely on the evidence presented at the hearing(s), and must include a summary of the evidence and the reasons for the decision. The

decision should be delivered to all parties concerned who have a legitimate educational interest.

- The institution will correct or amend the education record in accordance with the decision of the hearing if the decision is in favor of the student and will inform the student of the amendment in writing.
- Should the education agency or institution decide not to amend the record in accordance with the student's request, the appropriate official must inform the student that:
  - the student has the opportunity to place with the education record a statement commenting on the information in the record or a statement setting forth any reason for disagreeing with the decision of the hearing.
  - the statement placed in the education record by the student will be maintained as part of the record for as long as the record is held by the institution.
  - this record, when disclosed to an authorized party, must include the statement filed by the student.

4.2.1 An Institutional Policy and Procedures Related to a FERPA Hearing Request

As an example of how an institution can comply with a student's request to change or delete education record information, the following information will be helpful.

FERPA TIPS

FERPA WAS NOT INTENDED TO PROVIDE A PROCESS TO BE USED TO QUESTION SUBSTANTIVE JUDGMENTS THAT ARE CORRECTLY RECORDED. THE RIGHTS OF CHALLENGE ARE NOT INTENDED TO ALLOW STUDENTS TO CONTEST, FOR EXAMPLE, A GRADE IN A COURSE BECAUSE THEY FELT A HIGHER GRADE SHOULD HAVE BEEN ASSIGNED. FERPA IS INTENDED TO ENSURE THE FACTUAL AND ACCURATE NATURE OF THE INFORMATION IN STUDENTS' EDUCATION RECORDS AND STUDENTS' RIGHTS TO VERIFY THAT INFORMATION.

Found below are the relevant sections of Ohio State University's FERPA policy related to complying with a student request to challenge the contents of his or her education records:

Right to Challenge Information in Records

Students have the right to challenge the content of their education records if they consider the information contained therein to be inaccurate, misleading, or inappropriate.

This process includes an opportunity for amendment of the records or insertion of written explanations by the student into such records.

Note: The right to challenge grades does not apply under the Act unless the grade assigned was inaccurately recorded, under which condition the record will be corrected.

Procedures for Hearings to Challenge Records

Students challenging information in their records must submit, in writing, a request for a hearing to the appropriate office maintaining the record, listing the specific information in question and the reason(s) for the challenge.

Hearings will be conducted by a university official who does not have a direct interest in the outcome of the hearing.

Students shall be afforded a full and fair opportunity to present evidence relevant to the reasons for the challenge.

The hearing officer will render a decision, in writing, noting the reason and summarizing all evidence presented within a reasonable period of time after the challenge is filed.

Should the hearing decision be in favor of the student, the record shall be amended accordingly. Should the request be denied, an appeal may be made, in writing, and submitted to the university registrar within 10 days of the student's notification of the decision of the hearing officer. The appeal shall be heard by an appeals board of three disinterested senior university officials and a decision rendered, in writing, within a reasonable period of time.

Should the appeal be in favor of the student, the record shall be amended accordingly. Should the request be denied, the student may choose to place a statement with the record commenting on the accuracy of the information in the record and/or setting forth any basis for inaccuracy. When disclosed to an authorized party, the record will always include the student's statement and notice of the board's decision, as long as the student's record is maintained by the university.

4.3 Records of Requests and Disclosures

All institutions subject to the provisions of the Act are required to maintain records of requests for and disclosures of personally identifiable information. The records of requests, whether granted or not, shall include the name(s) and addresses of the person(s) who requested the information and their legitimate interests in the information. Records of requests and disclosures do not have to be maintained for:

- those requests made by students for their own use,
- those disclosures made with the written consent of students,

- those disclosures made to school officials under the conditions that allowed such disclosures, or
- those disclosures made to a party seeking directory information.

The records of disclosures and requests for disclosures are considered a part of the students' education records; therefore, they must be retained as long as the education records to which they refer are retained by the institutions.

The records of requests and disclosures must include:

- the parties who have requested or obtained personally identifiable information from the education records of a student, and
- the legitimate interests these parties had in requesting or obtaining the information.

These records must be made available for inspection to students, responsible institutional officials, state and federal auditors, and others, as prescribed by law.

4.4 Institutional Records and Recordkeeping

Reference is made throughout these guidelines to various documents. Among them are forms documenting waiver of rights and consent for disclosure, subpoenas, requests for and notices of hearings, and summary proceedings of the hearings. Neither the Act nor the regulations for its implementation stipulates procedures for retention of such written documents. Most questions about the accuracy of education records have been and will continue to be settled informally.

Nevertheless, it is clear in both the Act and the regulations that, if a complaint regarding violations of the Act should be filed against an institution, the institution's defense will depend largely upon documentation of its procedures and practices in any individual case. Therefore, these guidelines advise institutions to take necessary precautions to retain all documentation pertaining to compliance with the Act. The manner in which these records are kept is at the discretion of the institution. As mentioned earlier in this publication, it is recommended that the institution establish a records retention/management policy according to the guidelines found in AACRAO's "Retention of Records: Guide for Retention and Disposal of Student Records 2000 Update."

The reader of these guidelines also should note that in several places, it is implied that institutions may choose to inform students about certain aspects of the Act either orally or in writing. The foregoing paragraph should be kept in mind when exercising this discretion.

Finally, the reader's attention is directed specifically to the definition of "education record" in Chapter 2, where the records which are not subject to the provisions of the Act are specified. There will be instances where institutional files will contain records which are covered by the Act, as well as those which would not be if they were separate. For example, notes that a school official makes for his or her own use are not "education records" if they are created solely by the maker with no assistance from anyone else and are only revealed or made accessible to a temporary substitute.

FERPA TIPS

GENERALLY, AN INSTITUTION IS ONLY REQUIRED TO KEEP RECORDS OF DISCLOSURES OF NON-DIRECTORY INFORMATION TO THIRD PARTIES WHO ARE NOT SCHOOL OFFICIALS, AND ONLY IF THE STUDENT HAS NOT GIVEN WRITTEN CONSENT. THE MOST PREVALENT EXAMPLE OF THIS TYPE OF DISCLOSURE WOULD BE IN COMPLIANCE WITH A LAWFULLY ISSUED SUBPOENA OR IRS SUMMONS.

However, if a school official places his or her notes in a file to which other school officials, or the student, have access, or if the notes were prepared with the assistance or participation of others (e.g., interview notes), the notes could be considered "made accessible to" other persons and therefore would be considered "education records" subject to FERPA requirements.

Chapter Five

Issues

SINCE THE PASSAGE OF FERPA, A NUMBER OF ISSUES HAVE ARISEN AS A RESULT OF CHANGES IN TECHNOLOGY, INTERPRETATIONS OF THE ACT BY THE FAMILY POLICY COMPLIANCE OFFICE, INSTITUTIONAL PRACTICES, AND AN INCREASING INTEREST IN, AND PRESSURE FROM, A SOCIETAL "NEED TO KNOW." THIS SECTION COVERS SOME OF THESE ISSUES. THE DISCUSSION OF THESE ISSUES IS BASED ON THE MOST RECENT INFORMATION AVAILABLE AND SHOULD NOT BE CONSIDERED LEGAL INTERPRETATION OR LEGAL GUIDANCE.

5.1 Academic Standing

A student's current academic standing (such as "in good standing" or "eligible to return") should not be designated as directory information under FERPA. By process of elimination, those who are "not in good standing" could be identified, and this would be considered an invasion of privacy under FERPA.

5.2 FERPA Rights Accorded Admitted vs. Enrolled Students

Persons who applied for admission but were not accepted have no rights under FERPA. Admitted students are covered by FERPA only within the component unit to which they are admitted once they have enrolled at the institution. The institution should have a definition of "enrolled" since that determines when a student's FERPA rights begin.

Individuals who are denied admission to a program of study or component unit are not entitled by FERPA to have access to materials relating to the denied application, even if the individual subsequently is admitted into and enrolled in another course of study as an auditor. However, these individuals may have access to these records under a state's open records laws.

Each institution can identify the time when a student's FERPA rights begin after being admitted. If the institution does not identify this period, the student's FERPA rights begin on the first day the student begins attending class.

5.3 Anecdotal Notes on a Student

All anecdotal notes made about a student that an institution maintains and shares with school officials, regardless of the medium, are included in the definition of education records. Therefore, they are subject to FERPA. Unless the notes are kept in the sole possession of the maker, and have not been created with the assistance of anyone else, and are accessible only to a temporary substitute, they are part of the education record, subject to review by the student. This includes all shared paper files as well as notes made about the student on a shared computer record. If a student has requested access to his or her education record, none of these notes may be destroyed prior to student review.

Student admissions files for any admitted students should be reviewed in order to remove any items which have fulfilled their admissions-related purpose and will no longer be required in the student's academic career. Although an institution can decide which records to keep and which to destroy, each institution should establish a regular process to accomplish this task.

One category of items which should be considered for removal, especially at selective institutions, are notes written by admissions counselors during the admissions process and any voting records found in students' files on which a decision of admission has been based. This information, if not removed from students' files, becomes part of the students' education records and can be reviewed by the students.

5.4 Annual Notice to Student

An institution is required by FERPA to notify students annually of their rights under FERPA. The annual notice must include certain statements. However, a letter or specific form is not required. The notice must inform students of their specific rights as noted in Section 99.7 (34 CFR 99.7) of the regulations (see Appendix 2). This notice can be included in the registration instructions, student handbook, student newspaper, or other medium which is available to all students. (See Appendix 14 for a sample annual notification statement.)

Although the sample annual policy in Appendix 14 does not identify all of the valid FERPA exceptions to releasing education record information without the student's written permission found in 34 CFR 99.31 (see Chapter 4.1.3, the institution may exercise its rights to do so on any of these exceptions on a case-by-case basis.

5.5 Campus Security/Police

Although law enforcement records are not considered education records, they must be kept separate from students' education records. If a copy of a law enforcement record is given to a school official and that copy is placed in a student's folder or in another location within the institution but outside the law enforcement office, that copy becomes an education record subject to FERPA.

5.6 Requests from Census Officials

Every ten years when the official census is taken, many colleges and universities have had census takers request information about students who failed to submit completed census forms. Questions arise as to what information can be released to these individuals.

Officially, the Family Policy Compliance Office encourages each institution to cooperate with the census takers within FERPA guidelines. Therefore, without students' written permission, institutions may only provide directory information.

Census takers have no special privileges. They are to be treated as any other third parties requesting information from students' education records.

For the 2000 census, census takers asked campus officials for lists of student directory information, including race and gender. Census Bureau Officials indicated that they did not need the students' names in order to generate the information necessary to complete the census survey.

In response to many inquiries from campus officials regarding these requests, LeRoy Rooker, director of the Family Policy Compliance Office, responded to census and school officials that institutions may release race and gender information to census takers if names are not included in reports.

In his words to the Census Bureau,

...[I]nstitutions may disclose directory information items without student names, provided that the institution is disclosing the directory information (without names) of a minimum of several students, and include the additional information on race and gender.... In sum, this Office has advised postsecondary institutions that they may—to the extent allowed by FERPA—provide information to and cooperate with 2000 census takers. This may include disclosing properly designated directory information on those students to census takers, as well as distributing census forms to the student population.

Therefore, institutions also may disclose directory information items and include the additional information on race and gender, without student names, provided that the institution is disclosing the directory information (without names) of a minimum of several students.

The full text of the letter is included in Appendix 4.

5.7 Computer Access to Records

Initially, it is advisable to provide training to potential users regarding FERPA before access to education record information via computer terminal is given. After training, users should be required to sign a form indicating they have been made aware of the issues relating to student privacy, particularly legitimate educational interest, and the subsequent implications of a violation on their part. (A sample is found in Appendix 12.) Only then should system access codes be assigned or renewed. Subsequently, whenever one logs on to the system, a statement of alert cautioning users regarding student privacy rights should be displayed. It also should be reasonably easy to determine that a student has placed a block/non-disclosure on his or her directory information.

Data release via tape or other means is prohibited unless use is authorized in accordance with law, i.e., student release or legitimate educational interest, court order, etc.

5.8 Crisis Situations/Emergencies/ Disciplinary Notifications

If non-directory information is needed to resolve a crisis or emergency situation, an education institution may release that information if the institution determines that the information is "necessary to protect the health or safety of the student or other individuals" (34 CFR 99.36). This includes releasing information to school officials at another institution. A record must be made of the disclosure (see Chapter 4.3).

Factors to be considered or questions to be asked in making a decision to release such information in these situations are (1) the severity of the threat to the health or safety of those involved; (2) the need for the information; (3) the time required to deal with the emergency; and (4) the ability of the parties to whom the information is to be given to deal with the emergency.

The institution may want to develop some procedures that balance the student's privacy with the emergency situation. For example, rather than releasing a student's schedule to a third party, a representative of the institution could deliver an emergency message to the student and the student could respond accordingly.

As a clarification to this section, the Family Policy Compliance Office, in its November 21, 1996, final regulations, stated that an education agency or institution "may include information in a student's education records concerning disciplinary action taken against the student for conduct that posed a significant risk to the safety or well-being of that student, other students, or other members of the school community." It further stated that an institution may disclose, without prior consent, information contained in a student's education records concerning disciplinary action taken against the student, described above, to teachers and school officials who have legitimate educational interests (see Chapter 5.16) in the behavior of the student. Furthermore, the Family Policy Compliance Office stated that FERPA was amended to allow this type of disclosure to teachers and officials in other schools who have legitimate educational interests in the behavior of the student.

This means that institutions may disclose, without the student's prior written consent, information about certain disciplinary actions taken against the student to other institutions, regardless of level (K-12 to K-12, K-12 to postsecondary, or postsecondary to postsecondary), and that the student does not have to be either (1) in attendance at the other institution or (2) seeking or intending to enroll at another institution (see 34 CFR 99.36, Appendix 2).

5.9 Deceased Students

Under common law regarding privacy rights, the privacy interests of an individual expire with that individual's death. Accordingly, the disposition of records held by an institution and pertaining to a deceased individual is not a FERPA issue but a matter of institutional policy. Because FERPA would no longer apply, the institution may exercise its own discretion in deciding whether, and under what conditions, information should be disclosed to survivors or other third parties.

5.10 Developing FERPA Policy on Campus

No institution is required to have a FERPA policy.

FERPA does, however, require institutions to notify students annually of their FERPA rights. This annual notification must include several specific items: (1) the right of students to access their education records, (2) the right to request a change to an education record to prevent any inaccuracy or misleading information, (3) the right to a hearing if the request to correct an alleged inaccuracy is denied, (4) the right to consent to certain disclosures of information, and (5) the right to file complaints with the Family Policy Compliance Office. Additionally, the institution, if it has a practice of releasing education record information to third parties without the student's written permission, must notify students of the conditions under which this information will be released, identify those "school officials" who will have access to students' records, and note the "educational interests" that permit these school officials to gain access to these records (see Chapter 3.1).

Thus, the annual notification provides a means whereby the institution can include many significant items that reflect the institution's direction in complying with FERPA. (A model annual notification to students is included as Appendix 14.)

It should be a regular practice for the registrar or administrator responsible for institutional compliance with FERPA to convene a group of key administrators from both academic and non-academic offices to discuss any changes that need to be made to the institution's annual notification to students or to clarify any items that may be confusing or misunderstood.

FERPA TIPS

EACH INSTITUTION SHOULD DEVELOP A POLICY ON RELEASING INFORMATION ON DECEASED STUDENTS. SUCH POLICY MIGHT INCLUDE A PERIOD OF TIME DURING WHICH ONLY THE EXECUTOR/EXECUTRIX OF THE ESTATE OR NEXT-OF-KIN COULD AUTHORIZE THE RELEASE OF EDUCATION RECORD INFORMATION ON THE DECEASED STUDENT. BEYOND SUCH TIME, INSTITUTIONAL POLICY MIGHT PERMIT ACCESS TO ANYONE WITHOUT PERMISSION.

5.11 Electronic Transmission of Student Data (SPEEDE)

Today's technology permits the electronic transmission of student data to institutions and government agencies through the use of diskette, magnetic tape, direct connection, value-added network, or the Internet. The use of electronic data interchange (EDI) is growing for a number of applications, such as the exchange of student academic records, test score reports, enrollment reporting, and applications for admission. EDI employs standard data formats for carrying data from one computer to another. The printing and mailing of student information and re-keying of these data into another computer are not necessary when the sender and receiver both utilize EDI.

A standing committee of AACRAO, SPEEDE (Standardization of Postsecondary Education Electronic Data Exchange) has developed a number of EDI standards related to student data. Approved as Draft Standards for Trial Use by the American National Standards Institute Accredited Standards Committee X12 are:

- Transaction Set 130 Student Educational Record (Transcript)
- Transaction Set 131 Student Educational Record (Transcript) Acknowledgment
- Transaction Set 138 Testing Results Request and Report
- Transaction Set 146 Request for Student Educational Record (Transcript)
- Transaction Set 147 Response to Request for Student Educational Record (Transcript)
- Transaction Set 189 Application for Admission to Educational Institutions
- Transaction Set 190 Student Enrollment Verification

FERPA requires institutions to prevent the unauthorized release of personally identifiable, non-directory information from student education records without the permission of the student. When student data are transmitted electronically, the sender must require the same written authorization from the student as it does for a paper document (see Chapter 4.1). Current policies and procedures for release of protected student data on paper are maintained and even enhanced by the use of EDI.

An example of improved privacy and confidentiality with electronic transmission is the sending and receipt of a student academic record, according to the SPEEDE Committee. The confidentiality of the record and its authentication are certified by the sender's and receiver's adherence to the following measures:

- Use encryption to eliminate unauthorized access while the document is in transit.
- All participants agree to send transcript/credential information to the published address appearing in the AACRAO-approved Participant Table or to the address of the receiver with whom there is a formal trading partner relationship.
- All participants in the electronic data exchange agree to acknowledge to the AACRAO-approved address of the sending institution all receipts of transcript/credential information. Using Transaction Set 131 as an acknowledgment of receipt of Transaction Set 130 serves to inform the institution sending the student record of checkpoint items on the transcript, such as the number of courses included, highest degree earned, and final GPA.
- All participants are encouraged to devise an automated system of comparing acknowledgments received against credentials transmitted in order to be alerted to any misuse or failure of the system. If the checkpoint items on Transaction Set 131 do not match what was sent in Transaction Set 130, a second transmission can override the first.
- All participants in the exchange make a commitment to educate their own staff as to the need for careful handling of all access information in order to protect all users of these systems. "The greatest threats to privacy/confidentiality [with electronic transmission of data] are similar to the greatest threats to security of any correspondence or information," according to Robert Morley, past SPEEDE Committee Chair. "The greatest threat is not in the transmission or interception of the information/correspondence but rather with the particular level of integrity and commitment of staff in the originating and receiving offices" ("Killing the Electronic Messenger," *CAUSE/EFFECT*, Spring 1996).

5.12 Facsimile Records (Fax)

The use of fax technology involves two issues. The first revolves around the use of fax machines to receive student requests (the student's consent) to release information from his or her education records to third parties. FERPA requires that the student's written permission, under most circumstances, be obtained before releasing a non-directory education record (for example, a transcript) to a third party. The receipt of a written request to release an education record via fax satisfies this requirement of FERPA. According to the 1991 "Survey of AACRAO Member Institutions on FERPA Policies and Practices," 62.5 percent of respondents honored fax requests to send official transcripts to third parties.

The Family Policy Compliance Office recommends that institutions have "sufficient information to convince the responsible official at the institution that the signed document is a bona fide copy of an original consent." (Rooker, Family Educational Rights and Privacy Act [FERPA] Paper presented at the Annual Meeting of the American Association of Collegiate Registrars and Admissions Officers, Chicago, Illinois, April 18, 1989.) Furthermore, the Family Policy Compliance Office requires that "an institution have a student's written consent before it discloses or releases (non-directory) information pursuant to the student's telephone request." (Letter from LeRoy Rooker, Director, Family Policy Compliance Office, to Richard Rainsberger, Registrar, Carnegie Mellon University, October 4, 1993.)

The second issue involves the actual sending and receiving of student transcripts or other education records via fax. According to the SPEEDE Committee, the transmission of records via fax is less secure than the transmission of electronic records via SPEEDE/EDI.

Institutions must make their own decisions, following their own procedures, as to whether to send and accept faxed records. According to the 1991 "Survey of AACRAO Member Institutions on FERPA Policies and Practices," most institutions which accept fax transcripts will accept them for advising purposes but require that the student subsequently provide an official copy.

Table A: Recommended List of Faxed Documents to Be Sent or Received*

Document	Recommended (R)/ Institutional (I) Decision	Official (O)/ Unofficial (U) Copy
Application for Admission	R	O
Application for Scholarship	R	O
Correspondence	R	O
Credit Card Authorization	R	O
FERPA Request Release	R	O
Financial Aid Application	R	O
Financial Aid Transcript	R	O
Financial Statement (Foreign Student)	R	O
Foreign Transcript	I	U
Good Student Discount	R	O
Housing Application	R	O
Immunization Information	R	O
Letter of Degree Completion	R	O
Letter of Good Standing	R	O
Letter of Intent to Enroll	R	O
Letter of Recommendation	R	O
Letter of Verification	R	O
Military Document (Early Release Form)	I	U
Orientation Application	R	O
PC Fax	I	O
Signature	R	O
Test Scores (AP, CLEP, ACT/SAT, IB)	R	U
Third-Party Document	I	U
Transcript (High School and College)	R	O
Transcript Request	R	O

*Subject to institutional policy, security measures, and validation procedures.

Upon the recommendation of the Fax Guidelines Task Force, the AACRAO Board of Directors in March 1996 approved the practice that allows institutional prerogative to establish fax policies that address the use of fax technology and delivery of services. *Recommendations and Suggestions for Incorporating Fax Technology* is a publication available from the AACRAO office and at http://www.aacrao.org/about/faxguide.html. Table A lists recommendations as to what could constitute an official faxed document (either sent or received), subject to institutional security measures and validation procedures.

Instrumental to the extensive use of fax technology is the position of the Family Policy Compliance Office, which states, "FERPA would not preclude the disclosure of information for a student's education records based on a telefaxed consent provided the consent is bona fide" (Letter from LeRoy Rooker, October 12, 1990).

AACRAO Transcript Directory

The AACRAO Transcript Directory recommended by the Fax Guidelines Task Force is available at http://www.aacrao.org/transcript_directory/tdindex.html. The indexed Transcript Directory lists institutionally maintained information concerning transcripts, including frequently asked questions (FAQs) of address, cost, process, and fax and EDI capabilities. Colleges and universities are encouraged to establish and maintain their Transcript Directory on the AACRAO home page.

5.13 Charging a Search/Retrieval Fee

The final regulations allow for the assessment of a fee unless its imposition "effectively prevents a parent or eligible student from exercising the right to inspect and review the student's education records" (34 CFR 99.11). Such fees are limited to copying/postage charges. The institution cannot charge the student a search fee to retrieve his or her records.

The regulations are silent on charging fees for valid third party requests for students' education records.

The Family Policy Compliance Office has stated that nothing in FERPA prevents an institution from charging a search and retrieval fee along with other administrative fees to third parties that request information from students' records.

5.14 IRS Summons

For purposes of FERPA, an IRS summons should be treated as a "lawfully issued subpoena." Information from a student's education records can be disclosed without the student's written consent to comply with the summons. A reasonable attempt to notify the student is required prior to releasing the information (see Chapter 5.40.7 and Appendix 15).

5.15 Law Enforcement Records/Medical Treatment Records

Law enforcement agencies and health offices requiring access to student records are bound by all of the conditions of accessibility stipulated by FERPA. Congressional legislation passed in 1992 exempts from FERPA's definition of education records those "records maintained by a law enforcement unit of the education agency or institution that were created by that law enforcement unit for the purpose of law enforcement." Thus, law enforcement unit records are not covered by FERPA and could be released without written permission of the student involved. Certain medical treatment records have always been exempt from the definition of education records under certain conditions specified in the Act and the regulations.

FERPA TIPS

INSTITUTIONAL LAW ENFORCEMENT AND MEDICAL TREATMENT RECORDS SHOULD ALWAYS BE KEPT SEPARATE FROM EDUCATION RECORDS.

Institutional law enforcement and medical treatment records should always be kept separate from education records. Such separation of records not only further protects the privacy of the student's education records but facilitates timely and appropriate access to personal and sensitive information by authorized school officials.

Although law enforcement unit records are not considered to be education records if kept separate from other institutional education records, a law enforcement unit record will become an education record, subject to FERPA, if the original or a copy is shared with another school official outside of the law enforcement unit or if it is placed in an area where it could be reviewed by other school officials.

FERPA TIPS

"LEGITIMATE EDUCATIONAL INTEREST" IS THE TERM THAT IS USED IN FERPA TO DESCRIBE A SPECIFIC CONCEPT BY WHICH "SCHOOL OFFICIALS" MAY OBTAIN ACCESS TO EDUCATION RECORDS. HOWEVER, IN DISCUSSIONS ON FERPA AMONG EDUCATION PRACTITIONERS, THE TERMS "NEED TO KNOW," "LEGITIMATE NEED TO KNOW," AND "EDUCATIONAL NEED TO KNOW" HAVE BEEN USED.

Additionally, law enforcement officials of the institution or others contracted to perform a law enforcement service for the institution can be identified as "school officials" in the institution's annual notification to students of their FERPA rights.

5.16 Legitimate Educational Interest

One of the main emphases of FERPA is that personally identifiable information in an education record may not be released without prior written consent from the student. However, the Act does provide several exceptions to this consent requirement which allow institutions to disclose personally identifiable information from a student's education record without prior written consent.

FERPA TIPS

IT IS NOT A LEGITIMATE EDUCATIONAL INTEREST FOR FACULTY TO REVIEW A STUDENT'S PREVIOUS ACADEMIC HISTORY IN OTHER CLASSES PRIOR TO ASSIGNING A FINAL GRADE.

It is important to note that through these exceptions, FERPA does not require an institution to disclose education record information to any party. FERPA does set forth conditions under which an institution may disclose such information without a student's written consent.

One of the primary exceptions is that an institution may disclose personally identifiable information without the student's written consent to school officials whom the institution has determined have a legitimate educational interest. The regulations implementing FERPA, however, do not establish criteria for determining the limits of what may be considered a legitimate educational interest.

There are several important factors to consider if an institution is to exercise prudence in releasing education record information under the aegis of legitimate educational interest:

- Although FERPA makes it clear that an institution may release personally identifiable information to school officials, an institution must state its intention to utilize this practice in its annual notification to students on FERPA.
- The criteria for determining who is a "school official" must be specified in the annual notification.
- Criteria must be formulated for determining legitimate educational interest.

5.16.1 "School Officials"

In most cases, an institution's policy will include faculty members in its definition of school official. A faculty member performing a task or function specified in the institution's policy as constituting legitimate educational interest then could gain access to a student's education record. Certain contracted individuals who are not employees of the institution but who provide a service that the institution normally would perform itself also may be covered as school officials in the institution's FERPA policy. Such individuals may include an outside attorney providing legal services to the institution, an insurance representative, or a collection agency.

Similarly, it would be relevant to include "agents" as "school officials" if the nature of the agency relationship is to provide a service that otherwise could or would be performed by the institution. For example, many institutions have established an agency relationship with the National Student Loan Clearinghouse (NSLC) to provide student loan verification to loan servicers, including the federal government. In this case, the NSLC is acting in place of the institution. Other examples include outsourcing enrollment and/or degree verification information to an agency such as Credentials, Inc. The agent, whether an individual or an organization, must operate within the same parameters as would the institution, and only for a relevant business purpose. Therefore, it would be a violation of FERPA for the agent to release any personally identifiable information to such a third party. It also would be expected that an agent should either return or destroy any student data when the business service function is completed. (See Figure 5.16.1 for an example of an agency agreement.)

Fig. 5.16.1: Sample Agency Agreement

AGENCY AGREEMENT
Office of the University Registrar

The University agrees to provide the following student information: ____________________

____

to ___(Agent)____ for the sole purpose of ____________________
and for the time period of ____________________.

In the course of performing this function for the University, _____(Agent)_____ is acting as a legal agent ("school official") of the University and will release information only in the following circumstances: ____________________

____________________,

and only to the following persons/organizations: ____________________

The student information submitted to _____(Agent)______ by the University is confidential information and shall be used only for the purposes stated in this agreement. ______(Agent)_______ agrees not to share or disclose this data with any third-party outside of the purposes stated in this agreement, unless required to do so by law or other agency regulations. Failure to comply with the requirement not to release information, except for the sole purpose stated above, will result in cancellation of this agreement and the eligibility for _____(Agent)_______ to receive any student information from the University for a period of not less than five (5) years. In addition, ______(Agent)_______ agrees to indemnify and hold the University harmless for any loss, cost, damage or expense suffered by the University as a direct result of _____(Agent)______ failure to comply with the requirement not to release information, except for the sole purpose stated above.

_____(Agent)______ agrees to either destroy the student information in a manner that completely protects the confidentiality of the student information or return the information to the University upon the expiration of this agreement.

____________________	__________	____________________	__________
Agent Representative	Date	University Representative	Date

An institution's policy also may include student workers within the category of "school officials." A student worker performing a task or function covered under the institution's definition of legitimate educational interest may then be given access to other students' education records. It is advisable to (1) familiarize student workers with FERPA guidelines and policies, (2) explain the importance of preserving the confidentiality of education records they encounter in their tasks, and (3) require student workers to sign an agreement (similar to that shown in Appendix 10) prior to their employment to emphasize the importance of education record confidentiality and to minimize the chance that FERPA will be violated through the unauthorized release of non-directory information.

It would be impractical to list, in specific terms, who might be considered a "school official." The institution's criteria should be broad enough to include anyone who may reasonably fall within that category. Sample criteria for determining a "school official" might be:

- a person employed by the institution in an administrative, supervisory, academic or research, or support staff position;
- a person serving on an institutional governing body;
- a person employed by or under contract to the institution to perform a special task, such as an attorney or an auditor;
- a person or organization acting as an official agent of the institution and performing a business function or service on behalf of the institution (the function or service must be one that the institution normally would perform itself);
- a student serving on a committee; or
- a student assisting another school official in fulfilling his or her professional responsibilities (work study).

Although a person may be designated a "school official," he or she does not have inherent rights to any and all education record information. The school official must demonstrate to the records keeper a legitimate educational interest (as opposed to a personal or private interest), and such a determination must be made on a case-by-case basis.

5.16.2 Articulating Legitimate Educational Interest

A sample policy outlining what constitutes legitimate educational interest might include:

A school official is determined to have legitimate educational interest if the information requested is necessary for that official to (a) perform appropriate tasks that are specified in his or her position description or by a contract agreement; (b) perform a task related to a student's education; (c) perform a task related to the discipline of a student; (d) provide a service or benefit relating to the student or student's family, such as health care, counseling, job placement, or financial aid.

FERPA TIPS

THE CONCEPT OF "LEGITIMATE EDUCATIONAL INTEREST" APPLIES ONLY TO INDIVIDUALS OR GROUPS IDENTIFIED BY THE INSTITUTION AS "SCHOOL OFFICIALS."

An institution also should make clear in its annual notification to students that disclosure to a school official having a legitimate educational interest does not constitute authorization to share that information with a third party without the student's written permission. Such information, when it has fulfilled its originally specified purpose, should be destroyed or returned to the originating office for appropriate disposition.

The custodian of the education record requested must decide the legitimacy of each request for information. If there is any doubt or question regarding the request, the custodian should withhold disclosure without either written consent of the student, concurrence of appropriate institutional officials, or approval of the immediate supervisor. Employees in offices containing education records must be instructed to determine legitimate educational interest first, before an education record is released, in all cases. This also means that all school officials must be aware of the requirements for determining legitimate educational interest and be prepared to demonstrate their need to know upon request. This will eliminate needless confrontation and provide a better working environment for all concerned.

FERPA TIPS

IT IS RECOMMENDED THAT PRIOR TO PROVIDING ANY ACCESS TO EDUCATION RECORD INFORMATION IN ANY MEDIUM, THOROUGH FERPA TRAINING BE GIVEN TO ANY PROSPECTIVE USER. AT THE END OF THE TRAINING, IT IS ALSO RECOMMENDED THAT THE USER SIGN AN AGREEMENT ACKNOWLEDGING THAT HE OR SHE WILL HAVE ACCESS TO CONFIDENTIAL EDUCATION RECORDS AND THAT SUCH ACCESS WILL ONLY BE USED IN FULFILLING HIS/HER PROFESSIONAL RESPONSIBILITIES. THE CONSEQUENCES OF ANY DISCLOSURE NOT IN ACCORDANCE WITH FERPA SHOULD BE INCLUDED IN THIS AGREEMENT. SEVERAL EXAMPLES OF SUCH AGREEMENTS ARE FOUND IN APPENDIX 11.

If asked to investigate a controversial disclosure to a faculty member regarding a letter of recommendation, the Family Policy Compliance Office would seek answers to the following questions to determine whether FERPA had been violated:

- Has the institution established a criterion in its FERPA policy that appears to address disclosures for the purpose at issue?
- What does the faculty contract, job description, or other similar document specify regarding the duties and responsibilities of faculty?
- Does or did the faculty member teach the student in any course?
- What is the practice regarding recommendations at the institution?
- Does the faculty member otherwise have personal knowledge of the student's abilities?
- Was the faculty member asked by the student to provide a recommendation?
- Is there any state law on this issue?

Representative institutional policy statements on legitimate educational interest appear in Appendix 11.

5.16.3 Computer Access and Legitimate Educational Interest

The ability of computer systems to provide education record information to an increasing number of institutional personnel presents distinct challenges in complying with the FERPA requirement that school officials access education record data only for a legitimate educational interest.

In this era of distributed computing, dial-in access, and administrative management systems that bring student database information to all parts of the campus and beyond, it is essential that database administrators institute guidelines and policies for restricting access and ensuring that access to education record information is only for a legitimate educational interest. Policies and procedures establishing appropriate security guidelines which ensure proper and responsible use of education records must be developed and enforced.

Institutions should establish computer access policies and procedures for all of the following:

- Initial instructing of prospective users in FERPA confidentiality requirements.
- Online, initial access warning which cautions users and reminds them of the responsibilities they are agreeing to by accessing student education records.
- Periodic review and update of approved users of all confidentiality protocols.
- Full use of the institution's software security assignments to control access to various levels of online users, depending on the user's need to know and maintenance capabilities.
- Periodic monitoring and system tracking of user access by system officials to guard against abuse.

- Efficient systems to remove user access immediately upon the user's leaving the institution or position.

The institution also should emphasize the importance of instructing school officials of FERPA's confidentiality requirements before it gives them access to the student information system. These school officials should also be informed of the institution's criteria for determining legitimate educational interest and their responsibility for ensuring that access is not abused.

As mentioned above, each institution should provide a warning whenever a user logs on to the student information system. Sample messages appear below:

Sample Log-On Message #1

NOTICE

YOU ARE ATTEMPTING TO ACCESS INFORMATION THAT IS PROTECTED BY FEDERAL PRIVACY LAW. DISCLOSURE TO UNAUTHORIZED PARTIES VIOLATES THE FAMILY EDUCATIONAL RIGHTS AND PRIVACY ACT (FERPA). YOU SHOULD NOT ATTEMPT TO PROCEED UNLESS YOU ARE SPECIFICALLY AUTHORIZED TO DO SO AND ARE INFORMED ABOUT FERPA.

WHEN ACCESSING THE SYSTEM, YOU MUST ACCESS ONLY THAT INFORMATION NEEDED TO COMPLETE YOUR ASSIGNED OR AUTHORIZED TASK. YOU MAY COMMUNICATE THE INFORMATION ONLY TO OTHER PARTIES AUTHORIZED TO HAVE ACCESS IN ACCORDANCE WITH THE PROVISIONS OF FERPA.

IF YOU HAVE ANY QUESTIONS ABOUT THESE PROVISIONS, PLEASE CONTACT THE OFFICE OF THE REGISTRAR.

ENTER (D) IF YOU DISAGREE OR (A) IF YOU AGREE.

Sample Log-On Message #2

I UNDERSTAND THAT I HAVE ACCESS TO STUDENT RECORDS WHICH CONTAIN INDIVIDUALLY IDENTIFIABLE INFORMATION, THE DISCLOSURE OF WHICH IS PROHIBITED BY THE FAMILY EDUCATIONAL RIGHTS AND PRIVACY ACT (FERPA). I UNDERSTAND THAT THE DISCLOSURE OF THIS INFORMATION TO ANY UNAUTHORIZED PERSON COULD SUBJECT ME TO CRIMINAL AND CIVIL PENALTIES IMPOSED BY LAW AND COULD BE CAUSE FOR DISCIPLINARY ACTION INCLUDING TERMINATION OF MY EMPLOYMENT. I UNDERSTAND THAT BY MY SIGN-ON (NAME AND PASSWORD) I ACCEPT FULL RESPONSIBILITY FOR COMPLYING WITH THESE REGULATIONS.

Sample Log-On Message #3

WARNING * * * * * * WARNING * * * * * * WARNING

STUDENT RECORDS ARE STRICTLY CONFIDENTIAL, PROTECTED UNDER FEDERAL LAW KNOWN AS THE FAMILY EDUCATIONAL RIGHTS AND PRIVACY ACT OF 1974, AS AMENDED (FERPA). UNDER FERPA YOU MAY ACCESS THIS INFORMATION ONLY IN THE LEGITIMATE EDUCATIONAL INTEREST OF THE STUDENT. YOU MUST KEEP ALL INFORMATION CONFIDENTIAL. YOU ARE GIVEN ACCESS TO THESE SCREENS ON THE CONDITION THAT YOU DO NOT SHARE YOUR ACCESS WITH ANY OTHER PERSON. IF YOU DO NOT AGREE TO THESE CONDITIONS, TYPE "S" & PRESS THE ENTER KEY.

5.17 Letters of Recommendation

Statements made by a person making a recommendation that are made from that person's personal observation or knowledge do not require a written release from the student who is the subject of the recommendation. However, if personally identifiable information obtained from a student's education record is included in a letter of recommendation (grades, GPA, etc.), the writer is required to obtain a signed release from the student which (1) specifies the records that may be disclosed, (2) states the purpose of the disclosure, and (3) identifies the party or class of parties to whom the disclosure can be made. (See Chapter 6.5, Slide 42, for an example of a "permission to disclose" letter.)

If kept on file by the person writing the recommendation, it would be part of the student's education record and the student has the right to read it unless he or she has waived that right of access. (See 34 CFR 99.12 (b)(3) in Appendix 2.)

5.18 The Media

Nothing in FERPA allows an institution to discuss a student's education records publicly—even if a lawsuit has made the information a matter of public record. A school

Sample Log-On Message #4

TERMS OF USAGE

REVISED JANUARY 28, 2000

YOU ARE ENTERING A SECURE INFORMATION AREA. ANY INFORMATION YOU ENTER OR CHANGE WILL BE EFFECTIVE IMMEDIATELY UNLESS OTHERWISE NOTED, AND YOU ARE RESPONSIBLE FOR SUCH ENTRIES.

PLEASE DO NOT SHARE YOUR ID OR PIN WITH OTHERS AS YOU WILL BE HELD RESPONSIBLE FOR CHANGES MADE USING YOUR ID WITH YOUR KNOWLEDGE AND PERMISSION.

FOR MORE INFORMATION, REFER TO OU POLICY.

ALL UNIVERSITY EMPLOYEES ARE REMINDED THAT THE FAMILY EDUCATIONAL RIGHTS AND PRIVACY ACT (FERPA) PROHIBITS THE RELEASE OF ANY INFORMATION ABOUT A STUDENT (EXCEPT INFORMATION CLASSIFIED AS DIRECTORY INFORMATION) TO ANY PERSON OUTSIDE THE UNIVERSITY COMMUNITY OR TO ANY UNIVERSITY PERSONNEL WITHOUT A LEGITIMATE EDUCATIONAL REASON TO KNOW.

IN ADDITION, SOME STUDENTS HAVE REQUESTED THAT EVEN DIRECTORY INFORMATION NOT BE RELEASED ABOUT THEM. THESE STUDENTS WILL APPEAR IN BANNER WITH THE MESSAGE, "WARNING: INFORMATION ABOUT THE PERSON IS CONFIDENTIAL." ALSO, THE WORD "CONFIDENTIAL" APPEARS IN THE UPPER LEFT-HAND CORNER OF BANNER FORMS RELATED TO THE STUDENT. FOR DETAILED INFORMATION CLICK ON FERPA. IF YOU AGREE TO THESE TERMS OF USAGE, CLICK ON THE "CONTINUE" BUTTON BELOW. OTHERWISE, CLICK ON THE "EXIT" BUTTON.

official may not assume that a student's public discussion of a matter constitutes implied consent for the school official to disclose anything other than directory information in reply. The school official who wishes to respond to the media under these circumstances should ask the student for a properly executed consent form.

5.19 Parent Address

While local and permanent addresses could be considered directory information under FERPA, the addition of a separate parent address should be considered very carefully before including this as an item of directory information.

Especially at larger institutions, where access to a large cache of information is available, unscrupulous vendors may obtain this information for mailing lists.

While it is true that permanent and parent addresses are often the same, in many cases these two addresses differ. Therefore, it is recommended that parents' addresses not be disclosed without prior written consent from the student.

5.20 Parental Access to an Eligible Student's Education Records

At the postsecondary level, parents have no inherent rights to inspect their son's or daughter's education records. The right to inspect is limited solely to the student.

Records may be released to parents only if one of the following conditions has been met: (1) through the written consent of the student, (2) in compliance with a subpoena, and (3) by submission of evidence that the parents declared the student as a dependent on their most recent federal income tax form (see Appendix 7, Internal Revenue Code of 1986, Section 152). An institution is not required to disclose information from the student's education records to any parent of a dependent student. However, it may exercise its discretion to do so. It is strongly recommended that a statement of the institution's policy regarding parental access and disclosure be clearly stated in its FERPA policy.

FERPA TIPS

FERPA APPLIES TO EDUCATION RECORDS AT ALL LEVELS OF EDUCATION: PRIMARY, SECONDARY, AND POSTSECONDARY. UP TO THE TIME THE STUDENT ATTAINS THE AGE OF 18 OR BEGINS ATTENDING AN INSTITUTION OF HIGHER EDUCATION, REGARDLESS OF AGE, FERPA RIGHTS RESIDE WITH THE PARENTS. ONCE THE STUDENT ATTAINS THE AGE OF 18 OR BEGINS ATTENDING AN INSTITUTION OF HIGHER EDUCATION, REGARDLESS OF AGE, FERPA RIGHTS TRANSFER TO THE STUDENT. THE TERM "ELIGIBLE STUDENT" IS USED IN THE LAW TO DENOTE THIS TRANSFER OF RIGHTS TO THE STUDENT. (SEE DEFINITION IN CHAPTER 2.)

5.20.1 Biological, Custodial, and Non-Custodial Parents

In cases of divorce, separation, or custody when only one parent declares the student as a dependent, an institution may grant equal access to information from the student's education records to the other parent unless there is a court order, state statute, or legally binding document stating otherwise. The institution is not, however, required to provide such information to either parent.

State law, however, may require that such a disclosure be made. This disclosure would not be a violation of FERPA since FERPA does not prevent disclosure based on state law as long as the state law is in compliance with FERPA in every other respect. For example, if state law requires an institution to provide parents with information that is identified as directory information by the institution the student is attending, the institution would be required to provide it to the parents. However, if the state law required that the institution provide the parents with grades of their son or daughter at the end of each grading period, FERPA requires that the institution must not release this information without the student's written permission or first determining that the student is a legal dependent of the parent.

Even if written permission were granted by the student and/or dependency were determined, the institution is under no obligation to release the grades under FERPA. Where the institution finds that a state law and FERPA are in conflict, it must notify the Family Policy Compliance Office within 45 days of the finding. (See Chapter 5.31—Conflict with State Law.)

When access is granted, based upon demonstration of dependency, the file should note that the determination to authorize access was based upon appropriate documentation.

5.20.2 Student Permission to Send Grades to Parents

Because many institutions have established traditions of notifying parents of their children's academic progress at the institution, does FERPA preclude the institution from notifying parents about such academic progress?

The answer is "no." However, FERPA does require that students provide written permission for the institution to release any non-directory information to parents or that the institution determine that the student is legally a dependent of the parents before releasing the information. (See Chapter 4.1.3.)

The latter is time consuming. As a general rule, if the institution decided that it wished to notify parents about their children's academic progress or to share any non-directory information with the parents, it must obtain the written permission of the student to do so. This written permission should be obtained in an uncoercive environment without the parents present. This could occur during a new student orientation session when students and parents were in separate sessions. The institution's administrators could briefly explain to the students FERPA and the institution's policy/practice regarding sharing information with parents. Each student could then decide whether his or her parents should receive any non-directory information. The choice to provide written permission should be obtained in an controlled environment very early in the student's academic career at the institution to permit the organized integration of this information into the student information system. (Sample release forms are found in Appendix 3.)

5.20.3 Parents' Access to Their Children's Education Records According to FERPA

The following four statements summarize FERPA's position regarding parental access to their children's records:

- When a student reaches the age of 18 or begins attending a postsecondary institution, regardless of age, FERPA rights transfer from the parent to the student.
- Parents may obtain directory information only at the discretion of the institution.
- Parents may obtain non-directory information (grades, GPA, etc.) only at the discretion of the institution **and** after it has been determined that their child is legally their dependent.
- Parents also may obtain non-directory information by obtaining a signed consent from their child.

5.21 Penalties for Violating FERPA Regulations

The Family Policy Compliance Office reviews and investigates complaints of violations of FERPA. If the Office finds that there has been a failure to comply with FERPA, it will notify the institution about the corrections that need to be made to bring the institution into compliance. The Office will establish a reasonable period of time for the institution to voluntarily accomplish the specified changes.

If the Secretary of Education finds, after this reasonable period of time, that an institution has failed to comply with FERPA and determines that compliance cannot be secured by any means, he can, among other options, direct that no federal funds under his administrative control (financial aid, education grants, etc.) be made available to that institution.

Although federal funding has never been withheld from any institution under these regulations, civil cases have been brought for alleged violations of FERPA.

5.22 Posting of Grades by Faculty

The public posting of grades either by the student's name, institutional student identification number, or social security number without the student's written permission is a violation of FERPA. This includes the posting of grades to a class/institutional website and applies to any public posting of grades for students taking distance education courses.

Even with names obscured, numeric student identifier numbers are considered personally identifiable information. Therefore, the practice of posting grades by social security number or student identification number violates FERPA.

Instructors and others who insist on posting grades should use a system that ensures that FERPA requirements are met. This can be accomplished either by obtaining the student's uncoerced written permission or by using code words or randomly assigned numbers that only the instructor and individual student know. The order of posting should not be alphabetic.

Another method of notifying students of their final or other grades prior to official institutional notification is to have any interested students provide a self-addressed, stamped envelope to the instructor. The student writes the course and section on the front of the envelope. The instructor records the grade on the inside flap of the envelope, seals the envelope, and mails it to the student when grades have been determined.

Notification of grades via a postcard violates a student's privacy.

Notification of grades via e-mail is slightly more secure than sending grades on a postcard via USPS. However, there is no guarantee of confidentiality on the Internet. The institution would be held responsible if an unauthorized third party gained access, in any manner, to a student's education record through any electronic transmission method.

5.23 Postsecondary Feedback to High Schools

Under normal circumstances, personally identifiable, non-directory information from education records may not be released to a student's high school without the written consent of the student. Aggregate data that do not personally identify students may be submitted without a release. While some institutions include a statement of consent in their admissions application which will permit the institution to provide personally identifiable information to high schools, this practice could be challenged if it were perceived as coercive or as a requirement for admission to the institution. The institutional statement of consent must specify the records/information to be disclosed and the purpose of the disclosure. The statement of consent should give the student the option of consenting or not consenting to the release.

There may be conditions under which personally identifiable information can be released for postsecondary feedback purposes without students' written permission.

Florida, for example, passed the Postsecondary Feedback Act in 1991. This act requires postsecondary institutions in Florida to supply certain personally identifiable information from students' education records to the Florida Commissioner of Education. The commissioner is then required to organize the student records by school district and public high school at which the students were enrolled and to report the information to each school district.

The Florida Board of Education rules implementing this provision require each postsecondary institution to "report to the school district on the performance of the school district's public high school graduates who are enrolled at the (institution)." The following information must be reported for each student: name of school and county number; student name, social security number, and specified demographic information; date of birth; reporting institution; term of first enrollment; reading, writing, or mathematics courses; test scores below a specified level; enrollment in certain remedial courses; credits attempted and earned toward graduation; grade point average; and courses taken.

In response to a 1992 question to determine if the Florida Postsecondary Feedback Act was in conflict with FERPA, the Family Policy Compliance Office stated that postsecondary institutions in Florida could release personally identifiable information from student education records without violating FERPA. The office stated:

FERPA generally provides that an education institution must obtain a student's written consent before disclosing personally identifiable information from the student's education records [20 U.S.C. 1232g (b); 34 CFR 99.4 and 99.30]. FERPA does provide that an education institution may disclose education records or personally identifiable information from such records without prior written consent under certain limited exceptions [20 U.S.C. 1232g(b); 34 CFR 99.31]. Under one of the exceptions, an education institution may disclose information without consent when the disclosure is to authorized representatives of state and local education authorities in connection with an audit or evaluation of federal or state-supported education programs (34 CFR 99.31(a)(3) and 99.35).

Nonconsensual disclosure is also permissible when the disclosure is to organizations conducting studies for, or on behalf of, education agencies or institutions to improve instruction [34 CFR 99.31(a)(6)]. Both the recipients (Commissioner of Education and school districts) and the nature of the information required to be disclosed under this state statute indicate that the purposes of the disclosure include evaluation of state-supported education programs and improvement of instruction. Accordingly, we believe that disclosure without prior written consent is permissible under both sections 99.31(a)(3) and 99.31(a)(6).

FERPA establishes a recordkeeping requirement that an education agency or institution must meet in making nonconsensual disclosures from education records. Those conditions are set forth in 34 CFR 99.32.

Briefly, 34 CFR 99.32 states in paragraph (a) that an education institution (1) shall maintain a record of each request for access to and each disclosure of personally identifiable information from the education records of each student and (2) shall maintain the record with the education records of the student as long as the records are maintained. Paragraph (a) further states that the record of disclosure must include (1) the parties who have requested or received personally identifiable [information] from the education records and (2) the legitimate interests the parties had in requesting or obtaining the information.

The letter continued by pointing out that the state agencies and school districts to whom the education record information had been transferred were under an obligation to (1) use the information only for the intended purposes, (2) not release this information to unauthorized third parties outside of the organization, and (3) destroy the information when its purpose had been fulfilled [34 CFR 99.31 (a)(6); 34 CFR 99.35] (Letter from LeRoy Rooker, Director, Family Policy Compliance Office, to Joseph Roof, Dean of Admissions and Records Systems, Seminole Community College, December 3, 1993).

5.24 Purging of Requests for Access, Records of Disclosure, and Education Records

An institution may not purge any education records if there is an outstanding request to inspect and review the records. Furthermore, the institution shall maintain a record of each request for access and disclosure of personally identifiable information from education records as long as the records are maintained by the institution. It is, therefore, strongly recommended that each institution establish a records retention schedule/program following the AACRAO guidelines found in AACRAO's *Retention of Records: Guide for Retention and Disposal of Student Records 2000 Update.*

5.25 Recordkeeping of Disclosures

According to FERPA, an institution must maintain a record of each request, with the exceptions listed below, for access to, and each disclosure of, personally identifiable information from education records.

The record of each request for access and each disclosure must contain the names of the parties who have requested or received information and the legitimate interest the parties had in requesting or obtaining the information.

A record does not have to be kept if the request was made by or disclosure was made to (1) the eligible student, (2) a school official who has been determined to have a legitimate educational interest, (3) a party with written consent from the eligible student, or (4) a party seeking directory information only.

Thus, the recordkeeping requirement of disclosures of education record information without the student's written consent would include but not be limited to disclosures: (1) to the parent (either custodial or non-custodial) of an eligible student, (2) in response to a lawfully issued court order or subpoena, (3) for external research purposes where individual students have been identified, or (4) in response to an emergency.

These records must be maintained with the education records of the student as long as the records are maintained by the institution.

5.26 Releasing Non-directory Information over the Phone

FERPA does not preclude an institution from disclosing non-directory information from a student's education record to that student by telephone. Institutions are charged with implementing whatever procedures they deem necessary to verify the individual's identity. Questions such as student identification number, date of birth, place of birth, parent name and address, high school, major program, class level, recent courses taken, etc. could be asked by the school official. These questions should be correctly answered by the student calling before personally identifiable information is provided via the telephone.

Without the student's written permission, it is a violation of FERPA to release non-directory information over the phone to a third party, unless the information requested is needed to help resolve an emergency situation.

5.27 Religious Organization Requests; Religion as Directory Information

Religious organizations periodically request information such as names and addresses of any students who have indicated a religious preference related to their particular organization. Some of these religious organizations may be sanctioned by the institution. Can an institution provide this information without violating FERPA? Can a religiously affiliated school choose to classify "religious preference" as directory information?

A student's religion or religious preference cannot and can never be considered "directory information." Therefore, you should only provide that information to school officials with a legitimate educational interest. If the persons who are requesting this information do not fall under your institution's definition of school official with a legitimate educational interest, you cannot provide this information unless you obtain the written permission of the student or can justify the release under one of the exceptions to written permission found in 34 CFR 99.31 (see Chapter 4.1.3).

However, institutions may provide directory information on all students to any religious organization that requests this information. You may not, however, provide directory information to the religious organization on just those students who have indicated a religious preference for the religious organization since the selection criterion would have been based on non-directory information (religious preference).

5.28 Use of the Social Security Number as a Student Identifier—The Federal Government's Position

References in congressional legislation to the social security number (SSN) as a personal identifier are limited. The Privacy Act of 1974 states that:

It shall be unlawful for any Federal, state, or local government agency to deny any individual any right, benefit, or privilege provided by law because of such individual's refusal to disclose his social security account number [Section 7 (a)(1), Privacy Act of 1974, PL 93-579; 5 U.S.C. 552a note]; and

Any Federal, state, or local government agency which requests an individual to disclose his social security account number shall inform that individual whether that disclosure is mandatory or voluntary, by what statutory or other authority such number is solicited, and what uses will be made of it [Section 7 (a)(2)(B), Privacy Act of 1974, PL 93-579; 5 U.S.C. 552a note].

Thus, the federal government recognizes that the SSN can be used for purposes other than an individual's transactions with the Social Security Administration.

In higher education, use of the social security number was tested in a New Jersey federal district court case, *Krebbs* v. *Rutgers* (797 F. Supp. 1246; 1992). In this case, the judge upheld the use of the social security number as a personal identifier for administrative purposes. However, the judge also stated in his decision that the unauthorized dissemination of social security numbers was prohibited.

Although the Privacy Act does not directly specify public colleges and universities, it has implications for all institutions of higher education. While many colleges and universities do use the student's SSN as an ID number (and Congress is now requiring its use by any student who applies for any type of financial aid supported by the federal government, as well as for federal tax purposes), these institutions must take steps to protect the privacy of that number as required by FERPA.

Thus, colleges and universities should consider providing an alternate personal identifier at the student's request. This could be in the form of an institutionally assigned ID number. As part of the agreement to change a student's ID number, the student could be required to sign a statement of irrevocability and whatever other requirements the institution feels are appropriate, e.g., use of this ID number in any transaction with the institution (as with the offices of the cashier, dining, etc.; see Appendix 13 for a sample agreement).

5.29 Standards for Defining Directory Information

Directory information or information from a student's education record that would not normally be considered a violation of a student's privacy can be disclosed without the student's written permission. As defined in Section 99.3 of the original FERPA regulations, directory information includes:

the student's name, address, telephone number, date and place of birth, major field of study, participation in officially recognized activities and sports, weight and height of members of athletic teams, dates of attendance, degrees and awards received, the most recent educational institution attended by the student, and other similar information.

The 1988 final regulations added that directory information was that "information contained in an education record of a student which would not generally be considered harmful or an invasion of privacy if disclosed" (34 CFR 99.3; *Federal Register*, 4/11/88, p. 11944). It therefore attempted to establish a clarifying standard for assisting institutions in determining what could be included as directory information.

FERPA TIPS

STUDENT IDENTIFICATION NUMBERS OR SOCIAL SECURITY NUMBERS, RACE/ETHNICITY, GENDER, CITIZENSHIP, NATIONALITY, AND RELIGION CANNOT BE DESIGNATED AS DIRECTORY INFORMATION. GIVEN THESE RESTRICTIONS AND GUIDELINES, EACH INSTITUTION MAY BE AS INCLUSIVE OR AS RESTRICTIVE AS IT WISHES.

In recent years, the Family Policy Compliance Office has determined that an institution could include a student's photograph, class schedule/class roster, e-mail address, and enrollment status (full time or part time) as directory information. The 2000 final regulations, however, do not include class schedule and class roster as examples of directory information. This exclusion has come about as the Family Policy Compliance Office has become increasingly concerned about the release of non-directory information as part of the student's class schedule or class roster that would compromise the privacy of the student. Although these two items are still considered directory information by the Family Policy Compliance Office, their status is under review as this publication goes to press.

What have colleges and universities identified as directory information since FERPA was enacted in 1974? Two surveys have attempted to answer that question. In a 1988 survey of 56 registrars of institutional members of the American Association of Universities (AAU), it was found that all of the 46 institutions responding identified name, address, telephone, dates of attendance, and degrees received as directory information. A 1991 AACRAO survey to which 257 of a randomly selected group of 500 colleges and universities responded revealed that more than eight out of every ten institutions identified name, dates of attendance, degree(s) received, major, address, and telephone number as the most common items of directory information. A 1997 survey of the registrars of the universities of the American Association of Universities (AAU) confirmed that directory information had not changed significantly in nine years. The one significant addition to directory information (at 17 percent of the institutions responding) was students' e-mail address (Turner-Dickerson 1997, p. 38).

(The results of the 1998 and 1991 surveys can be found in Appendix 8.)

5.30 State Databases

The technological advances that have led to SPEEDE and other forms of electronic transfer of records have also led to the development of statewide databases for a variety of purposes. In many states, state laws and regulations require public education institutions to provide personally identifiable student data to the appropriate state agency. These agencies usually are charged with state research and reporting responsibilities.

The Act (Section 99.31 (a)(3) of the regulations) permits institutions to provide personally identifiable information from education records to state agencies without consent under certain conditions specified in Section 99.35. In general, institutions can provide these data in connection with audits or evaluations of federal or state-supported education programs. The Act [see Section 99.31(a)(6)] also allows disclosure to organizations, including state agencies, "for conducting studies for, or on behalf of, educational agencies or institutions to develop, validate, or administer predictive tests, administer student aid programs, or improve instruction" (Rooker, Family Educational Rights and Privacy Act (FERPA) paper presented at the Annual Meeting of the American Association of Collegiate Registrars and Admissions Officers, Honolulu, Hawaii, April 15, 1991). Paragraph (ii) of Section 99.31(a)(6) sets forth the conditions that apply to these disclosures.

Institutions that provide personally identifiable student data to state agencies, whether in electronic or hard copy format, should have procedures in place which will protect the confidentiality of this student information. State agencies should be advised of the FERPA requirements, especially Section 99.35, which require the destruction of this information once it is no longer needed for its original purpose.

In addition, state agencies should not, in turn, release personally identifiable student data to a third party, except within the provisions of FERPA. For example, one state agency could share directory information for students who have not blocked release of such data to another state agency for the purpose of tracking transfer students. However, that release must only include directory information. Non-directory information must not be included in these releases unless written permission of the students is obtained; nor should releases include any data for students who have requested non-disclosure of their directory information.

Institutions must record the disclosures in accordance with Section 99.32 of the regulations. Finally, the SPEEDE Task Force recommendations on security enhancement have applicability to this type of electronic transfer of data. Registrars and other institutional officials with responsibility for the protection of student FERPA rights should take all precautions necessary to ensure that security is maintained as the records are transferred from the institution to the state education agency. (See Chapter 7.4.3 for discussion of a related topic, "Postsecondary Feedback to High Schools").

5.31 State Law: Conflict with State Law

Often, state and local open records laws appear to conflict with FERPA. However, the open records laws of many—if not most—states provide for federal law to supersede state law when they conflict. Therefore, in most instances, state open records laws defer to federal guidelines on education records. When state open records laws are applicable, they usually cover only public institutions.

The test often reduces to a basic question: "Is the record or issue covered under FERPA?" If the answer is "yes," then resolution of the situation would fall within the regulations and requirements of FERPA. If the answer is "no," then the resolution of the situation may fall under provisions of the state open records law. Thus, if in your professional judgment you determine that the student record, or part thereof, is not covered by FERPA, then the release of or access to that record may be determined under the state open records law. This has not been any more relevant than with the issue of student disciplinary records (covered in 5.34 below).

5.31.1 States' Open Records Laws and FERPA

Should a state or local law appear to conflict with FERPA, section 99.61 of the final regulations mandates that institutions that cannot comply with the Act or regulations due to a conflict with state or local law must notify the Family Policy Compliance Office within 45 days, giving the text and citation of the conflicting law (34 CFR 99.61). Notifications should be sent to the Family Policy Compliance Office, U.S. Department of Education, 400 Maryland Avenue, SW, Washington, DC 20202-9001; (202) 260-3887; fax: (202) 260-9001.

5.32 Student Computer Access to His or Her Own Education Records

An institution may allow a student access to his or her education records by computer, provided the institution has established procedures to ensure the student will obtain access only to his or her own records. The development of guidelines for restricting access and ensuring proper security of data in computer systems is an institutional responsibility. It is suggested that the institution use at least a student identification number and a Personal Identification Number (PIN) to grant computer access (See Chapter 5.42.3).

5.33 Student Directories

Release of directory information to any group for publications such as student directories, award ceremonies, yearbooks, etc. is subject to FERPA restrictions. Any group seeking to publish a student directory at an institution that chooses to release directory information must do so through a supervising school official or office. It must give students who wish to be excluded from the listing the opportunity to notify the group within an appropriate timeframe prior to publication.

5.34 Student Disciplinary Hearing Records—Are They Education Records?

During the 1990s the question arose as to whether student disciplinary records are education records subject to FERPA. In at least five states (Louisiana, Georgia, Missouri, Ohio, and North Carolina), the question was decided in a state court. But the decisions were mixed.

The common scenario for these cases begins when a student newspaper requests the records of the campus student judicial/disciplinary proceedings with specific names attached. They cite, as their basis for making the request, the state's open records/meetings laws. The institution refuses to release the information, based on FERPA, and the student newspaper sues to obtain the information.

In Georgia and Missouri, the state court ruled in favor of the newspaper, declaring that these records were not subject to FERPA. In Louisiana and North Carolina, the court found for the university.

In 1996 Miami University (of Ohio) became involved in a similar situation: Citing the Ohio Public Records Act, the student newspaper requested records of disciplinary proceedings. In its request, the editors of the student newspaper stated:

It is not a condition to this request that the subject records contain the name, social security number, student identification number, or other information that conveys the identity of any accused or convicted party. If this identifying information cannot be deleted from the aforementioned records, however, then the record[s] should be provided in their original form.

On April 5, 1996, Miami University (of Ohio) released copies of the disciplinary board's records. However, in response to the confidentiality provisions of FERPA, the Miami officials deleted from these records the identity, gender, and age of those accused, as well as the date, time, and location of the incidents that led to the disciplinary charges. University officials also deleted certain internal memoranda, written statements prepared by students appealing adverse disciplinary board decisions, and the disposition of certain proceedings.

The student newspaper's editors believed that the response to their public records request was inadequate and that Miami University was required to provide them with complete copies of the public records requested, removing only the name, social security number, or student ID number of any accused or convicted party. Because the university also deleted other information from the requested records, the editors also brought suit against the university, seeking full disclosure of the disciplinary board records requested.

In July 1997 the Ohio Supreme Court ordered the university to provide the requested records to the student newspaper with the names deleted.

In fall 1997 Miami appealed the decision to the United States Supreme Court, which refused to hear the case.

Subsequent to the Ohio Supreme Court's decision, *The Chronicle of Higher Education* requested the campus's judiciary records containing students' names from both Ohio State and Miami Universities. In accordance with FERPA, the universities notified the Family Policy Compliance Office. In January 1998 the Department of Education brought suit in the U.S. District Court in Columbus, Ohio, to prevent the two universities from providing the requested information. It was the Department of Education's opinion that it would be a violation of FERPA to do so without first obtaining the students' written permission. In February 1998 the district court issued a temporary injunction preventing the two universities from complying with the *Chronicle's* request, stating that, by FERPA definition, the records requested were education records and subject to FERPA.

In March 2000 the Federal District Court in Columbus permanently enjoined Miami and Ohio State Universities from releasing the detailed disciplinary information, holding that disciplinary records are education records protected under FERPA. The judge therefore concluded that FERPA does not require public disclosure of disciplinary records without the students' consent. In his opinion, "The public, while certainly benefiting from laws that promote openness in public records, also benefits from the privacy accorded students through FERPA. Congress, through FERPA, has balanced the interests of privacy versus public disclosure, and the Court is in no position to second-guess it." Referencing statistics provided in response to the Student Right-to-Know and Campus Security Act, the judge stated,

The Court believes that these disclosures are adequate to inform students, prospective students, and parents about the safety of various college campuses. Releasing the personally identifiable information of the students accused or convicted of violating university regulations, as well as information about victims, would not further advance the public's interest.

The case has since been appealed to the 6th Circuit Court of Appeals in Cincinnati. At the time of this publication, no decision has yet been rendered.

5.35 Student Right-to-Know Act of 1990, The National Student Loan Clearinghouse, and FERPA

The Student Right-to-Know Act of 1990 (SRTK) requires institutions to publish and distribute graduation rates to current and prospective students.

Discussion in the 1995 edition of this *Guide* of this topic as it related to FERPA was relatively brief. It affirmed that, since data were to be reported in aggregate form (with no personally identifiable information disclosed), no conflict with FERPA was anticipated. It was assumed that institutions would collect their own data on those students who (1) completed degrees at their original institutions and (2) transferred to other institutions (transfer-outs).

While guidelines (rules) were being developed by the Department of Education for complying with SRTK, a more comprehensive set of graduation data for the IPEDS reports was prepared. These have become known as the Graduation Rates Survey (GRS). SRTK data have been included in the GRS. Therefore, if done correctly, GRS will provide the information needed to comply with the reporting requirement of SRTK. Under SRTK, the institution still will have to publish/disclose graduation information to current and prospective students. The institution also is required to notify potential scholarship athletes, as well as their parents, guidance counselors, and coaches, prior to the signing of any binding letter of intent to enroll at the institution.

The Department of Education released its SRTK regulations on December 1, 1995. According to these regulations, to calculate the completion or graduation rate,

a student shall be counted as a completion or graduation if, within 150 percent of the normal time for completion of or graduation from the program, the student has completed or graduated from the program, or enrolled in any program of an eligible institution for which the prior program provides substantial preparation... [20 U.S.C. Sec. 1092 (a)(3)]

While reporting transfer-out rates is optional for most four-year and upper-division institutions, community colleges and similar institutions that have determined that their missions include providing substantial preparation for students to enroll at another institution without first completing a program or graduating will have to report transfer-out rates.

To report these transfer-out students, the institution is required to document that the student has enrolled at another institution by obtaining:

1. a certification letter from the receiving institution,
2. an electronic certification from the receiving institution,
3. a confirmation of enrollment data from a legally authorized statewide or regional tracking system (or shared information from these systems), and
4. institutional data exchange information.

Department of Education sources have indicated that completed questionnaires from phone calls to and exit interviews with the students (although some question how useful this latter method would be) are also acceptable as long as the information verifies a student's current—and not anticipated—enrollment status.

Electronic tracking and reporting of transfers would eliminate much of the administrative burden related to accurately and completely reporting transfer-outs. However, since the method of verification involves the sharing of the student's social security number (to accurately verify all students—particularly those with common names, e.g., Robert Smith), it appears as if FERPA prevents any institution from utilizing Methods 1 through 4 above.

In early 1996 representatives of the National Student Loan Clearinghouse (an organization originally established to (1) assist colleges and institutional lenders in tracking students who transferred from one institution to another and (2) report the enrollment status of students with loans to lenders) contacted the Family Policy Compliance Office, indicating that several colleges/universities had contacted them to request assistance in complying with SRTK. The institutions would provide social security numbers to the clearinghouse, and the clearinghouse would search its database to determine which students had transferred and where. The clearinghouse then would provide the names (not the social security numbers) of those students to the original institution.

In a series of letters and discussions throughout 1996, it became clear to the two offices that FERPA and SRTK were in conflict and that FERPA did not specifically permit the release of the requested information, based upon the use of the student's social security number. The rationale was that, by requesting information via a student's social security number, the original institution would be able to obtain information maintained by the NSLC on any student. Thus, the NSLC would be opening up all of its student files to all inquiring institutions requesting information based upon an item of non-directory information, the social security number.

However, the Family Policy Compliance Office determined that, because SRTK was enacted more recently than FERPA (1990 as compared to 1974), Congress did not intend for FERPA to prevent a college from complying with SRTK.

Therefore, in late 1996, colleges and universities were given permission to utilize the resources of the clearinghouse to gather data on its transfers for the purpose of complying with SRTK. However, this ruling was challenged since it was subsequently determined that reporting transfer-outs was not required by SRTK.

This challenge led the Department of Education to reconsider its decision. On January 6, 1998, in a joint communiqué, AACRAO and the National Student Loan Clearinghouse advised institutions not to share "personally identifiable information" with the student's original institution until the Department of Education had reached a decision on its reconsideration.

On August 2, 1999, the Family Policy Office determined that it would be acceptable for the NSLC to assist institutions in complying with SRTK as long as only directory information was used.

To accomplish this task, each participating institution, as part of the basic participation agreement with NSLC, would modify its database to include a "data block indicator" for those students who requested that directory information not be disclosed. This data block indicator would be included with the other information transmitted by each institution to NSLC at regularly scheduled intervals during the academic term.

Additionally, the requesting institution would have identified the student's name, date of birth, and date of last attendance as directory information. As part of its annual notification to students of their FERPA rights, the institution would have notified students of what it considered to be directory information. As part of this notification, students would have been informed and would have had an opportunity to request that any of this information not be disclosed. (See Chapter 3.1.1.) As part of the search process, the requesting institution would submit to NSLC the names, dates of birth, and dates of last attendance of those students who had not requested non-disclosure. NSLC then would use the same information to search its database to see if there was a match.

FERPA TIPS

THE INSTITUTIONAL PROCESS OF COMPLYING WITH A STUDENT'S REQUEST TO BLOCK THE RELEASE OF PERSONALLY IDENTIFIABLE INFORMATION IS CALLED "NON-DISCLOSURE."

If a match was found and there was no block on the release of this directory information provided by the institution that submitted the information to the clearinghouse, then NSLC would provide the following directory information to the requesting (the student's original) institution:

- the student's name,
- whether a transfer record was found (Y/N),
- the student's new name (if any),
- the name of the school of first transfer,
- the Office of Postsecondary Education Identification (OPEID) code of the transfer school, and
- the starting date for the transfer term.

FERPA TIPS

THE STUDENT MAY REQUEST NON-DISCLOSURE AS A CURRENTLY ATTENDING STUDENT ONLY. THIS NON-DISCLOSURE REQUEST APPLIES TO INSTITUTIONAL DIRECTORY INFORMATION ONLY. IT MUST BE HONORED BY THE INSTITUTION. REQUESTS FOR NON-DISCLOSURE FROM FORMER STUDENTS MAY BE HONORED BUT ARE NOT REQUIRED BY FERPA. THE NON-DISCLOSURE REMAINS IN EFFECT UNTIL THE STUDENT NOTIFIES THE INSTITUTION TO REMOVE THE NON-DISCLOSURE.

The Family Policy Compliance Office also indicated that NSLC would ask participating institutions to complete a data block indicator for former students, and that if an institution was unable or unwilling to provide that information for former students, then NSLC would not release enrollment status information for those students. (Letter from LeRoy Rooker to Daniel Boehmer, August 2, 1999, in Appendix 17; the letter also can be read at http://www.ed.gov/offices/OM/Omltrs/herndova.html.)

5.36 Students' Right of Non-Disclosure of Education Record Information

According to FERPA, a student can request, while still enrolled, that the college/university not release any directory information about him or her. Colleges and universities must comply with this request.

With graduating students, the decision to request non-disclosure is particularly important as this decision may have employment, and other, repercussions. In instances where a student is considering non-disclosure, the student should be advised of the potential problems that may occur as prospective employers and other interested parties make inquiries.

Additionally, FERPA allows students the right of non-disclosure of directory information only. Institutions may disclose information, even if the student requests otherwise, under the exceptions to FERPA's written consent requirement (see Chapter 4.1; Appendix 2 (34 CFR 99.31).

It is not recommended that any institution limit how long non-disclosures remain in effect. It should not, for example, inform students that any request for non-disclosure must be renewed on a yearly basis. This can result in confusion if the student leaves the institution without renewing the request since the institution must honor any requests for non-disclosure for students who have left the institution and requested non-disclosure before doing so.

5.37 The Student's Right to Review Records

Students have the right to view their education records wherever these records are maintained on campus. Once a student has submitted a request to inspect his or her records, an institution must comply within 45 days.

When the student has an outstanding financial or other hold on the records, the student still maintains the right to review his or her education records. He or she does not have the right to obtain any copies of those records unless failure to do so would effectively deny the student the right to inspect and review the records. Also, that student does not have the right to have a transcript sent to a third party until the obligation is fulfilled.

In cases where a student is not within commuting distance (50 miles) of campus and therefore is physically unable to be present to view the record on campus, the institution must make arrangements for the student to obtain access for review of these records. The institution may do so either (a) by making copies of the requested records and sending them to the student by mail or other means; or (b) by making arrangements with an appropriate third party, such as another institution or an attorney's office located in the vicinity of the student, to act as an agent. Such individuals would agree to abide by the institution's instructions to allow the student to review but not copy the records. This method would be used particularly in instances where the student has an outstanding financial or other obligation to the college.

When providing a copy of a student record to authorized parties, a reasonable fee may be assessed. Regulations allow for the assessment of a fee unless its imposition "effectively prevents a parent or eligible student from exercising the right to inspect and review the student's education records" (34 CFR 99.11). Under normal circumstances, it is recommended that the fee assessed be based upon a reasonable determination of the cost of providing the copies, to include full administrative expenditures of materials, labor, and postage, and, at the same time, serve as a deterrent to possible frivolous requests. Colleges and universities may not charge the student a fee for searching for or retrieving their records since this is considered part of accepted and normal business (see Chapter 5.13).

5.38 The Student's Rights after Ceasing Attendance or Graduating

Students who have ceased attendance or who have graduated from an institution of higher education have the same FERPA rights as students currently attending a college or university, including the right to (1) inspect their education records, (2) have a hearing to amend an education record, and (3) have their education record privacy protected by the institution. Former students may request non-disclosure of their education records, but the institution does not have to honor the request. Institutions, however, can grant the right of non-disclosure to former students if they wish.

Institutions may limit the length of time the request for non-disclosure is in effect, as long as the student has been properly notified (possibly through the institution's annual notification). However, if a student has requested non-disclosure of directory information in his or her last term of attendance, that request must be honored until that student requests its removal.

5.39 Students as Members of Institutional Committees

Students are members of institutional committees at many colleges and universities. Quite often, the committee needs to review the education records of students. Is it permissible for students serving on these committees to view the education records of other students in conducting the business of the committee?

The answer to this question depends on what the institution's annual notification (see Appendix 14) and FERPA policy say about who "school officials" are and what "legitimate educational interests" permit these "school officials" to view education records. Often, student scholarships, for example, are awarded on the basis of the student's education record. If such review is made only by school officials who have been determined to have a "legitimate educational interest," then no student release is necessary. If, however, such a review includes a person or persons not identified as "school officials" in the institution's annual notification or FERPA policy statement, then a signed written consent from the student must be obtained before any review of his or her education record may take place. Alternately, the third party can be designated as a "school official" in the institution's FERPA policy statement for the specific purposes for which the scholarship committee is responsible.

In the case of student committee members, the institutional FERPA policy could identify a student serving on a committee as a "school official" while performing his or her responsibilities as a committee member. This would then permit the student to view other students' education records without those students' prior written consent.

FERPA TIPS

ALTHOUGH THE STUDENT HAS REQUESTED NON-DISCLOSURE, THE INSTITUTION MAY STILL RELEASE ANY PERSONALLY IDENTIFIABLE INFORMATION, INCLUDING DIRECTORY INFORMATION, UNDER ANY OF THE EXCEPTIONS FOUND IN 34 CFR 99.31.

In a very informal survey conducted on the registrars' discussion list (regist-l) in 1997, nine of 16 institutions responding indicated that students were members on a committee at their institution that acted on individual academic exceptions. All nine institutions indicated that these students had voting power, and all but one saw no legal problem with this arrangement. Comments included:

- "No problem with students judging their peers...done elsewhere: residence hall, discipline board, juries in our legal system."
- "We define committees as having legitimate educational interest and brief the members on the confidentiality of records."
- "Majority of students appearing before committee do want student members present and voting; they seem to feel more comfortable being judged by their peers."
- "They are functioning as a university official much the same as a student aide functions as an employee."
- "They are elected by the student body to sit on the committee; thus, the student body is giving them authorization for access to records."
- "We explain to student representatives FERPA regulations and the importance of confidentiality."

- "I think it inappropriate for students to sit on a committee, and a good lawyer probably could make a case for it being a violation of students' privacy rights as well."

5.40 Subpoenas

A subpoena is a command from a court to require the person named in the subpoena to appear at a stated time and place to provide testimony or evidence.

FERPA TIPS

WHENEVER SERVED WITH A SUBPOENA, IT IS ALWAYS ADVISABLE TO CONSULT LEGAL COUNSEL. HOWEVER, LEGAL COUNSEL MAY NEED TO BE INFORMED ABOUT THE NOTIFICATION REQUIREMENT IN FERPA PRIOR TO COMPLYING WITH THE SUBPOENA.

There are two main types of subpoenas: The subpoena *duces tecum* requires the submission of documents, papers, or other tangible things to the court. The subpoena *ad testificandum* requires a person to testify in a particular court case. A bench warrant issued by a judge, also considered a court order, requires a person to produce something to, or testify before, a court.

5.40.1 What FERPA Says about Subpoenas

According to the regulations (see Appendix 2), non-directory, personally identifiable information from education records can be released "to comply with a judicial order or lawfully issued subpoena" provided that the "institution makes a reasonable effort to notify the student of the order or subpoena in advance of compliance" [34 CFR 99.31 (a)(9)(i)(ii)].

Legislation passed on September 28, 1994, modified the requirement of notifying students of the receipt of a subpoena. This legislation orders institutions not to notify the student of the receipt of a federal grand jury subpoena, or any other subpoena issued for a law enforcement purpose, if specifically ordered not to do so in the subpoena [34 CFR 99.31 (a)(9)(ii)(A)(B)].

Furthermore, the 2000 regulations clarified that if an institution initiated legal action against a student, or vice versa, no subpoena for the relevant education records of a student would be required for the institution to either proceed with legal action as plaintiff or defend itself [see Appendix 2; 34 CFR 99.31 (a)(9)(iii)(A)(B)].

5.40.2 How Subpoenas Are Created

The following information pertains to the federal court system only. The *Federal Rules of Civil Procedure* state that every subpoena shall: state the name of the court from which the subpoena is issued; state the title of the action, the name of the court in which the action is pending, and its civil action number; and command each person named in the subpoena to appear and either give testimony or produce documentary evidence at a time and place specified in the subpoena.

A blank court subpoena is issued by the clerk of the court. Normally, it is signed and sealed but is otherwise blank. The subpoena is then completed by an officer of the court, usually an attorney who is authorized to practice in the court where the subpoenaed documents are to be produced (*Federal Civil Judicial Procedures and Rules, Title 28—Judiciary and Judicial Procedure*. 2000 (rev. ed.), p. 198). The subpoena must then be served by someone who is not a party to the civil or criminal action.

Any attorney can obtain these blank forms and complete them as needed. There is very little control over the distribution of these forms. Some courts do record the control numbers on the forms which have been sold or distributed and the name of the officer of the court who purchased them, but there is no universal requirement to do so. In most cases, the subpoena is not reviewed by the court before being presented. The signature is not normally that of the judge nor the clerk of court but rather a machine-printed facsimile made available for that use.

The attorney issuing the subpoena has the obligation of notifying the opposing attorney that a subpoena is being presented. Sometimes, however, this is not done.

5.40.3 Jurisdiction

The *Federal Rules of Civil Procedure* require that a subpoena be issued from the court for the district in which the hearing or trial is to be held. If the subpoena orders the production or inspection of documents, the subpoena must be issued from the court in which the production or inspection is to be made (*Federal Civil Judicial Procedure and Rules*, p. 200).

A court cannot act upon a person over which it has no jurisdiction. State courts have jurisdiction only within the boundaries of the state. However, federal district courts effectively have jurisdiction in all 50 states since attorneys who are permitted to represent a client in a federal court can issue a subpoena from any federal court for the district in which the subpoena is to be served. "In authorizing attorneys to issue subpoenas from distant courts, the rule effectively authorizes service of a subpoena anywhere in the United States by an attorney representing any party." If a subpoena is served on an individual that requires the individual to testify personally (*ad testificandum*) as opposed to providing documents only (*duces tecum*), the deposition/hearing must be conducted no more than 100 miles from the site of the hearing. The individual is not compelled to travel further (*Federal Civil Judicial Procedure and Rules*, p. 204).

5.40.4 Being Presented with a Subpoena

FERPA does not mandate that an institution of higher education automatically comply with a lawfully issued subpoena. To determine if the institution should comply with a subpoena, the following information should be considered.

- **Determine if it is a subpoena.** In many cases, the document being presented will "look" like a subpoena. Not all subpoenas are issued by a court. Some public agencies, through the statute that created them, have been given subpoena power. Many of these subpoenas do not look like a court-issued subpoena but may have the same authority. Some valid and invalid subpoenas will appear on letterhead. It is the responsibility of the person served with the subpoena, or his or her institution, to determine if the piece of paper presented has the validity of a legal subpoena (see examples in Chapter 7.2).

  How do we know an agency has subpoena power? Each state has a reference source which identifies current statutes the legislature has enacted. In Pennsylvania, for example, Purdon's "Pennsylvania Statutes" is the source. Each state has similar reference sources which will help determine if a public agency has subpoena power.

- **Determine if the court issuing the subpoena has jurisdiction.** The subpoena powers of a court—federal district, state, and county—are limited. In order for the subpoena to be binding upon the institution on which the subpoena is served, it must be issued by an officer of a court that has jurisdiction over the institution. As stated earlier, a federal district subpoena has validity in all 50 states as long as the 100 mile rule (see Chapter 5.40.3) is observed. However, at the state level, for example, a subpoena issued from a state court in Michigan has no validity in Texas.

  In many instances, colleges and universities have complied with subpoenas issued from courts which have no jurisdiction over them. The person served with a subpoena should determine whether the subpoena is valid before complying. If the court issuing the subpoena does not have jurisdiction, then the person upon whom the subpoena was served, or the institution's legal counsel, must inform the maker of this fact. It then is up to the maker to determine if the information is important enough to seek a subpoena from a court which has jurisdiction. Once served with a subpoena from a court that has jurisdiction over the institution, that institution should comply with the request rather than face possible contempt of court charges.

- **Determine what is requested.** Part of the subpoena identifies what the maker is requesting. In many instances, the wording of what is requested is very broad, suggesting that the person who prepared the subpoena is on a "fishing expedition." Whenever confronted with such wording in a subpoena, the institution has every right to request that the issuer of the subpoena be more specific with the request. In many instances, the person upon whom the subpoena has been served may comply by copying selected information from the student's education record folder located in that person's office.

- **Determine if what is requested follows the prescription within FERPA (i.e., does it conform to FERPA?).** In some subpoenas, the maker of the subpoena commands the person served with a subpoena to refrain from notifying the subject that the person served with a subpoena is complying with the subpoena. Until September 28, 1994, this would have been a violation of the FERPA requirement to, in all cases, notify the student of the receipt of the subpoena. However, according to the legislation enacted on September 28, 1994, the institution is not required to notify the student of the receipt or contents of a federal grand jury subpoena if ordered not to do so. This also applies to any other subpoena issued for law enforcement purposes.

  Under FERPA, the requirement that the person served with a subpoena notify the student of the receipt of a subpoena and the institution's probable intent to comply should override any command within a subpoena to the contrary (with the exceptions noted in the previous paragraph). In most cases in which this occurs, no judge reviewed the subpoena before it was issued. It should be quite obvious to anyone who is knowledgeable about FERPA that the issuer of the subpoena does not realize that a prior notification requirement exists within FERPA.

  When the subpoena orders the recipient not to notify the student (and the subpoena is not a federal grand jury subpoena or one issued for law enforcement purposes, as mentioned above), it is best to contact the person who issued the subpoena and notify that person of the FERPA requirement. If the issuer insists that the student not be notified, the person served with a subpoena should seek advice of counsel. He or she also could inform the issuer that he or she will only comply with that request upon receipt of a court order from a judge serving on a court that has jurisdiction over the institution served with the subpoena.

  FERPA's "prior notification" requirement regarding subpoenas is intended to alert the student to possible court action and allow him or her to determine if he or she wishes to seek counsel if he or she feels that the subpoena is unwarranted. The student's counsel can make a motion to quash the subpoena in the court from which the subpoena was issued. This was successfully demonstrated in the case of *Goldman v. Goldman*, Family Court of the State of New York, County of Rockland, v-852/91.

The judge of a court from which a subpoena was issued can order the quashing, or modification, of a subpoena if the subpoena fails to allow reasonable time for compliance or requires disclosure of privileged or other protected matter and no exception or waiver applies.

5.40.5 Rights of a Person When Served with a Subpoena

A person served with a subpoena should not feel intimidated or threatened if he or she understands FERPA and is making an honest effort to comply with the requirements within FERPA.

When a person is served with a subpoena, the party responsible for issuing the subpoena must "take reasonable steps to avoid imposing an undue burden or expense on (that person)." If the person served with a subpoena is commanded to produce, permit inspection of, and copy documents, that person does not have to appear in person, unless specifically ordered to do so (*Federal Civil Judicial Procedure and Rules*, p. 201).

Also, as indicated above, if the subpoena is issued from a federal district court having jurisdiction, the person served with a subpoena does not have to travel more than 100 miles to provide the deposition or produce documents. The person served with a subpoena may also submit a written objection (see instances below which may apply) to the issuer of the subpoena. This must be done within 14 calendar days after being served or before the time specified for compliance if such time is less than 14 days after service.

If objection is made, the party who served the subpoena is not entitled to inspect the materials specified unless an order of the court permitting inspection is issued. If objection has been made, upon notifying the person served with the subpoena, the party serving the subpoena may move to compel the production of the materials in the original subpoena.

In some cases, the institution may have legal or policy reasons for wishing to object to a subpoena. The institution should have a protocol in place for identifying any such cases. The protocol should require that the institution's attorneys be notified whenever all subpoenas or subpoenas of special types are received. The attorneys then can take responsibility for objecting to the subpoena and/or having it quashed.

5.40.6 Duties in Responding to a Subpoena

According to the federal rules of judicial procedure, the person served with a subpoena to produce documents shall produce them "as they are kept in the usual course of business or shall organize and label them to correspond with the categories in the demand" (*Federal Civil Judicial Procedure and Rules*, pp. 201–202).

When the person served with a subpoena withholds information sought in a subpoena "on a claim that it is privileged or subject to protection," that person shall do so in a way which will be supported by a description of the documents not produced "to enable the demanding party to contest the claim" (p. 202). Basically, a list of the withheld documents needs to be made.

The person served with a subpoena should always consult with his or her institution's legal counsel regarding the receipt of any subpoena.

5.40.7 Notifying the Student

The subpoena must give the person served with a subpoena a "reasonable time to respond." "Reasonable time" is normally considered 14 calendar or 10 working days.

Sometimes a subpoena is received that requires delivery of education records prior to the passage of 14 calendar days. This is usually due to the fact that the attorney who caused the subpoena to be issued was not familiar with FERPA's notification requirement. In such cases, the person served with the subpoena, or the institution's legal counsel, should contact the attorney and explain the notification requirements under FERPA.

If the institution is required to notify the student on the receipt of a subpoena, the person served should promptly notify the student of the receipt and that the institution intends to comply (if it does) on a particular date (realistically, 14 days from the date the subpoena is received). The notice should inform the student that a motion to quash the subpoena must be filed before that date, with a copy to the institution. The notice to the student should ordinarily be sent by certified mail, return receipt. A copy should also be sent to the person who caused the subpoena to be issued.

In the case of an alumnus with no current address, the institution should do its best (within reason) to locate him or her and document what was done. Best efforts to notify students/alumni whose addresses, maintained by the institution, may not be current would include: telegram, any special delivery that provides a record of receipt, fax, and telephone, with the call noted in the file with a memo. Attorneys involved in the case also may be an appropriate source for obtaining current addresses. (A sample letter used to notify students of the receipt of a subpoena is included as Appendix 15.)

5.40.8 Complying with the Subpoena

Once the person served with a subpoena is satisfied that he or she has been served with a valid subpoena from a court having jurisdiction over the institution, that a reasonable attempt has been made to notify the student of the institution's intent to comply with the subpoena, and that a reasonable amount of time has elapsed for the student to react to this notification, the person served with a subpoena can provide certified copies (never the originals) of the documents requested to the issuer of the subpoena or the agency which collects such documents for court hearings/trials. In certain jurisdictions, it may be possible to submit the requested records to the attention of the presiding judge of the court having jurisdiction in the case.

5.41 The Solomon Amendment and FERPA

The Solomon Amendment was introduced in the House of Representatives on July 11, 1996, and was enacted September 30, 1996. The regulation (interim rule) which implements the law (32 CFR 216) took effect March 29, 1997. It proposed to withdraw federal funding from institutions which are certified to have an anti-ROTC policy or a policy or practice that prevents Department of Defense representatives "from obtaining, for military recruiting purposes, entry to campuses, access to students on campuses, (or) access to directory information* on students" (*Federal Register*, April 8, 1997, p. 16691). On April 8, 1997, an Interim Rule was published in the *Federal Register* inviting comments through July 7, 1997. The final regulations were published on October 23, 1998. A second Interim Rule was published on January 13, 2000. It is expected that additional Interim Rules will be published in 2001.

Although this section of this publication covers only those items that relate to FERPA (specifically, that information which is personally identifiable directory information), the Final Rule is included in Appendix 18 of this publication.

The Solomon Amendment requires institutions to provide directory-type information on students at least 17 years of age upon request of representatives of the Department of Defense for military recruiting purposes. This information, now referred to as "student recruiting information," includes: student name, addresses, telephone listings, date and place of birth, level of education, academic major, degrees received, and the most recent previous education institution at which the student was enrolled.

Most important in this analysis of Solomon and FERPA is that (1) the definitions of the term "directory information" (FERPA) and "student recruiting information" (Solomon) are not synonymous, and (2) a request for student recruiting information under Solomon must be honored unless there is an exception in the law which precludes the institution from providing the requested information. The most important exceptions are that the school:

- has a long-standing policy of pacifism based on historical religious tradition;
- certifies that such information is not collected by the school; or
- certifies that each student concerned has formally requested the school to withhold "directory information" under FERPA from third parties.

It is important to note that even if an institution has a policy of not releasing "directory information" under FERPA, the institution still must comply with requests by the military for "student recruiting information" (except as noted above).

Institutions are obligated to provide the information only once a term to each branch of the armed services. The

* The term "directory information" is now referred to as "student recruiting information" to avoid confusion with FERPA.

FERPA TIPS

"DIRECTORY INFORMATION" UNDER FERPA AND "STUDENT RECRUITING INFORMATION" UNDER SOLOMON ARE MUTUALLY EXCLUSIVE. WHERE AN INSTITUTION HAS DISCRETION IN IDENTIFYING "DIRECTORY INFORMATION" AND RELEASING THAT INFORMATION, "STUDENT RECRUITING INFORMATION" IS SPECIFICALLY IDENTIFIED BY LAW, AND THE INSTITUTION MUST RELEASE THAT INFORMATION IF REQUESTED.

FERPA TIPS

WITH THE EXCEPTIONS NOTED BELOW, INSTITUTIONS MUST RELEASE "STUDENT RECRUITING INFORMATION" TO MILITARY RECRUITERS UNDER SOLOMON. INSTITUTIONS MAY RELEASE "DIRECTORY INFORMATION" TO ANYONE UNDER FERPA.

FERPA TIPS

MILITARY RECRUITERS CAN ONLY REQUEST AND OBTAIN "STUDENT RECRUITING INFORMATION" FROM COLLEGES AND UNIVERSITIES. THAT INFORMATION IS: STUDENT NAME, ADDRESSES, TELEPHONE LISTINGS, DATE AND PLACE OF BIRTH, LEVEL OF EDUCATION, ACADEMIC MAJOR, DEGREES RECEIVED, AND THE MOST RECENT EDUCATIONAL INSTITUTION AT WHICH THE STUDENT WAS PREVIOUSLY ENROLLED.

information must be provided in a usable form. There are no additional requirements. Institutions can charge a reasonable and customary fee for the service rendered. Sources within the Family Policy Compliance Office have indicated that institutions that comply with a Solomon request will not be in violation of FERPA. Also, these sources have indicated that if an institution discloses "student recruiting information" after a student has requested non-disclosure of information under FERPA, the school will not be in violation of FERPA. However, the Family Policy Compliance Office may investigate continuous reports of similar violations by the institution.

FERPA TIPS

THE SOLOMON AMENDMENT REQUIRES INSTITUTIONS TO PROVIDE "STUDENT RECRUITING INFORMATION" TO MILITARY RECRUITERS ON CURRENTLY ENROLLED STUDENTS WHO ARE 17 YEARS OF AGE OR OLDER. IT DOES NOT REQUIRE AN INSTITUTION TO PROVIDE ANY INFORMATION ON STUDENTS NOT CURRENTLY ENROLLED FOR AT LEAST ONE CREDIT.

Because race, gender, and veteran status are not considered "student recruiting information," institutions are urged not to release this information or provide lists for these specific subgroups. It is also important to note that because information is to be released only for students registered for at least one credit in the requested semester/term, drop-out lists should not be provided under Solomon. An institution may release drop-out lists under FERPA if all information requested by the military recruiter, including "enrollment status," is identified as directory information. However, institutions do not have to release drop-out lists under either FERPA or Solomon.

FERPA TIPS

WHETHER WE ARE DEALING WITH HIGH-TECH OR LOW-TECH EDUCATION, WE ONLY HAVE ONE EDUCATION RECORDS LAW: FERPA. WE DO NOT CHANGE OUR POLICIES OR PRACTICES SIMPLY BECAUSE OUR EDUCATIONAL DELIVERY METHODS HAVE CHANGED.

Regarding the student's right to request non-disclosure of directory information under FERPA, as part of the final Solomon regulations (1998), if a student:

- has been notified by his or her institution according to the annual notification provision under FERPA that he or she has the right to request non-disclosure of his or her directory information; and
- the student subsequently requests non-disclosure of any or all directory information (as identified by the institution under FERPA),

then the Department of Defense will honor that non-disclosure for the purposes of satisfying a request made under the Solomon Amendment.

If, however, the student has not exercised his or her right of non-disclosure under FERPA, the rules under Solomon will apply and the student recruiting information required by Solomon must be released. This includes any item of information considered "student recruiting information" (Solomon) but that may not have been identified as "directory information" by the institution under FERPA. For example, if a Department of Defense representative requests all students' places of birth as part of his or her request for information under Solomon, that information must be released even though the institution may not have identified that item as "directory information" under FERPA.

Note: As this publication was going to press, an additional Interim Rule (Frank Amendment) was to be published clarifying whether student aid will be affected if an institution does not comply with the Solomon Amendment and whether an entire institution will risk losing government funding if one of its sub-elements, e.g., a law school, is not in compliance with the Solomon Amendment.

5.42 Electronic Technology and FERPA

For more than 40 years, we have experienced the fruits and vicissitudes of a technology revolution that has become ubiquitous, influencing how we conduct our daily activities and fulfill our responsibilities. Beginning slowly in the 1970s and accelerating in the 1980s, the technology revolution entered the 1990s on a fast track.

We have been the recipients of this high-tech revolution and have found ways to utilize the products of many creative talents. It is important for us to identify and discuss some of the implications for FERPA that this revolution has spawned.

The issues listed below have become prevalent discussion topics whenever registrars discuss high-tech happenings on their campuses. These issues will continue to evolve, and new issues will emerge. This subsection therefore should be considered a "work in progress." We don't have all the answers, but we have provided as much guidance as seems currently possible. You, the reader, must keep alert to changes in any of the information presented in these sections.

5.42.1 Faculty Sending Grades via E-mail

There is no guarantee of confidentiality in transmitting information electronically via campus e-mail or through the Internet. Faculty who wish to send grades to students via e-mail need to understand that if there is an unauthorized release of grades to someone who is not a school official, the institution would be in violation of FERPA if the student whose grades were illegally disclosed filed a complaint with the Family Policy Compliance Office.

5.42.2 Electronic Signatures

With the passage in 2000 of the Electronic Signatures in Global and National Commerce Act (ESIGN), it has become legal to utilize an electronic signature in any business transaction. This means that digital signatures on the Internet have the same status as signatures on paper. It ensures that an electronic signature is valid and admissible in court.

Because a key requirement within FERPA is written permission of the student to release any non-directory information, this new legislation provides an opportunity for institutions to explore various electronic methods of obtaining written consent that will comply with FERPA.

The Family Policy Compliance Office has observed that the legislation approving the use of the electronic signature was for business transactions as part of valid contracts. The legislation did not address the validity of the electronic signature for fulfilling the FERPA requirement of a student's written permission to release education record information. Nevertheless, the Family Policy Compliance Office has indicated that guidance on the use of electronic signature technology to comply with FERPA may be available sometime in 2001.

5.42.3 PINs

In restricting electronic access to education record information, an institution usually assigns an identification number to a user (staff or student) so that the user can gain access to the information. This number is either the student's or staff member's social security number or some other unique set of numbers or letters assigned only to that user. In addition, when the user logs on to the system, a personal identification number (PIN) usually is required as a second level of security, providing additional authentication that the proper person is accessing the records.

The most acceptable scenario for utilizing the ID number in conjunction with the PIN is for the institution to initially assign a default PIN, e.g., date of birth, and to require the user to change that PIN when he or she first attempts to log on. In this case, the student controls and maintains his or her own PIN. If the student forgets the PIN, he or she contacts a particular office, and that office resets the PIN to the default. When the student logs on again, he or she is prompted to change the default PIN.

Because the student controls and maintains the PIN, it does not become an education record. Therefore, it is recommended that the institution utilize the convention above that permits the student to maintain and control his or her own PIN. This is one item that does not have to be subject to FERPA and that does not have a negative impact on systems security management.

The Family Policy Compliance Office has advised that the PIN does not meet FERPA's requirement for signed consent to disclose information to a third party. Under FERPA, the consent must be signed and dated and must specify the records that may be disclosed, state the purpose of the disclosure, and identify the party or class of parties to whom the disclosure may be made. (See 34 CFR 99.30.) For example, a student must provide written consent in accordance with the requirements of FERPA before an institution issues the student's transcript to a prospective or current employer. The Family Policy Compliance Office expects to issue guidance regarding the use of PINs or other forms of "electronic signatures" for purposes of meeting the prior written consent rule under FERPA once certain legal issues have been addressed.

FERPA TIPS

WRITTEN REQUESTS THAT PERMIT INSTITUTIONS TO RELEASE NON-DIRECTORY INFORMATION TO THIRD PARTIES ON A CONTINUING BASIS, E.G., SENDING GRADES TO EMPLOYERS AT THE END OF EACH SEMESTER OF ATTENDANCE, ARE ACCEPTABLE UNDER FERPA AS LONG AS THE REQUEST INCLUDES ALL THE INFORMATION REQUIRED UNDER FERPA. ALTHOUGH THESE REQUESTS ARE ACCEPTABLE, EACH INSTITUTION CAN DECIDE IF IT WISHES TO HONOR THEM.

The written consent requirements of FERPA do not apply, however, when a student seeks access to his or her own records. Because FERPA restricts disclosure of education records to unauthorized parties without the student's prior consent, it is incumbent upon an institution to ensure that computer databases and other systems function so that only authorized parties may obtain access to the records. In these cases, the primary considerations are identification of authorized recipients of information and security of transmissions so that records are disclosed only to authorized parties.

FERPA TIPS

"THERE IS NO GUARANTEE OF PRIVACY ON THE INTERNET." LEROY ROOKER, DIRECTOR, FAMILY POLICY COMPLIANCE OFFICE, APRIL 10, 2000, AACRAO ANNUAL MEETING, NEW ORLEANS, LA.

Where an institution provides a secure web application for a student to request that any item of his non-directory information (most likely a transcript) be released to him personally, the Family Policy Compliance Office has indicated that it would be permissible for the student to log on using his ID number and secure PIN and request that any non-directory information be released to him. The request would be transmitted electronically within this secure web application to the student information system, and the student's non-directory information (including a transcript) would be produced and sent to the student. If human intervention were needed, the school official issuing the non-directory information would have obtained the student's ID and secure PIN—which theoretically, only that student knows.

FERPA TIPS

CHANGING THE METHODS OF DELIVERING EDUCATION TO STUDENTS DOES NOT MEAN THAT FERPA RULES CHANGE. WE NEED TO ENSURE THAT STUDENTS ARE NOTIFIED ANNUALLY OF THEIR FERPA RIGHTS AND THAT WE ARE FULLY IN COMPLIANCE WITH FERPA NO MATTER HOW EDUCATION IS DELIVERED TO STUDENTS OR WHERE THESE STUDENTS ARE LOCATED.

The key word in this procedure is "secure." This means that the information required for the student's transcript and any other non-directory information to be sent to the student must not be accessible to any third parties who are not school officials and that the request be transmitted electronically within the institution's computer infrastructure.

5.42.4 E-mail Transcript Requests

If a student sends a transcript request via e-mail, the request should not be honored since FERPA requires written permission to release any non-directory information (such as the student's transcript).

Although FERPA requires a student's written permission to release a transcript, it is silent on how that permission is to be transmitted to the office issuing the transcript. Therefore, transcript requests received via fax that include the student's signature, or a scanned document attached to an e-mail message authorizing release of a transcript that includes the student's written permission on the document, are acceptable methods of providing the written permission required under FERPA.

Also, if a student has submitted written permission to send a transcript—or end-of-term grades or any other non-directory information—on a regular basis to a third party, the institution may send the requested information upon receipt of an e-mail message from the student. The institution does not have to obtain written permission every time non-directory information is to be released, as long as the institution has on file written permission from the student to release such information to a specific third party. Such written permission must include: the party to whom the information is to be released, the information to be released, the purpose for the release, and the signature of the student. Although students may submit such standing letters to release non-directory information, it remains the institution's prerogative to honor such requests.

5.42.5 Distance Education; Web Teaching

The high-tech revolution that has occurred in the past 20 years has permitted educational institutions to explore alternate ways of providing education to students.

As many institutions explore these nontraditional means of providing education, it is best to keep in mind that whether we are dealing with high-tech or low-tech issues, we have one education records law (FERPA).

This means that for FERPA purposes, it is of no consequence how education is delivered to students. Whether they are on campus attending classes in traditional classrooms or halfway around the world taking courses via the Web, students have the same FERPA rights and are to be accorded equal treatment under the law.

Therefore, institutions must plan to notify all of their students annually of their FERPA rights, no matter where the students are living or taking courses. This also applies to students' right to access their records and any other right accorded to students by FERPA.

This added dimension to providing education creates challenges for an institution in complying with FERPA in a distributed environment. However, the technological means are available to assist each institution with its task of complying with FERPA. For example, annual notification can be sent via e-mail to each student anywhere in the world who is taking courses via the Web.

5.42.6 Sharing E-mail Addresses or Other Personally Identifiable Information among Students in the Same Class

Faculty who utilize electronic teaching tools such as WebCT or Blackboard may wish to share students' e-mail addresses or other personally identifiable information in a class with others in the same class. This is permissible as long as (1) the institution has identified e-mail addresses as directory information, (2) the students have had an opportunity to request that their e-mail addresses not be disclosed, and (3) the faculty member does not share the e-mail address of any student who has requested non-disclosure.

In the latter case, an institutional procedure could be developed regarding students in these classes who request non-disclosure. The procedure would authorize, at the instructor's request, a school official (office) to identify and contact any students who had requested non-disclosure of their e-mail addresses. The students could then be notified of the implications of the non-disclosure and instructed on how to remove the non-disclosure if they wished to do so. Such notification might be made as follows:

Dear Student,

You are registered for (name of course) which is supported with Web-based activities using Blackboard. In order to take advantage of these additional resources and participate fully in this course, you will need to change your privacy status with the Registrar's Office or see your instructor to manually sign up for this course. If you have any questions concerning this, please contact the Registrar's Office.

Cordially,

Chapter Six

FERPA Training Materials

THIS CHAPTER PROVIDES HELPFUL INFORMATION THAT WILL ASSIST FERPA PRACTITIONERS IN TRAINING OTHER SCHOOL OFFICIALS REGARDING THEIR RESPONSIBILITIES UNDER FERPA.

6.1 Frequently Asked Questions

These are the more commonly asked questions regarding FERPA. Answers to all of these questions may be found in this publication. You might want to use some of these as teaser questions to stimulate interest in FERPA on your campus.

- What is FERPA? How does it affect me as a school employee?
- Are parents allowed to see their child's records?
- What rights do students have under FERPA?
- What obligations do colleges have under FERPA?
- Can the annual notification to students be posted on the institution's web page?

From Parents:

- Why can't I get my son/daughter's grades/schedule? I'm paying the bills!
- How can I pay my son/daughter's account if you can't even tell me how much he or she still owes?!

From Students:

- I want to know how I can let my friends get my address/phone number on campus, but I don't want it given out indiscriminately!
- Why am I always getting junk mail from insurance companies, credit card companies, auto agencies, etc. that want to sell me something? Can't you keep these vultures from getting my name/address, etc.?

From Faculty:

- Why can't I post grades by SSN?
- Why can't I have access to ALL our students, not just my advisees and students in my classes?
- May I include a student's GPA in a letter of recommendation if the student has asked me to write the recommendation? What can I include in the recommendation? What can't I include?
- Are examinations and term papers subject to FERPA?
- What do I have to do to comply with FERPA in returning examinations and term papers?

From Registrars:

- Can I change directory information just for my campus?
- Is it O.K. for me to not give out any student information to anybody?
- How can I comply with FERPA and at the same time be a customer service officer?
- How can I make sure that all student information users on my campus abide by FERPA?
- Can I confirm to someone (other than the student) over the phone that a student did or did not receive a degree without first getting the student's permission?
- A third party calls and wants to confirm the date of a student's degree. Can I confirm to that person that the student did not receive a degree if the student has requested that we not disclose that information? What would be the proper response?
- I have work-study students. Can they look at other students' records?

6.2 Key Terms/Concepts in FERPA

Anyone who wishes to have a working knowledge of FERPA needs to understand the following key terms and concepts. These are all discussed in this publication. (See Fig. 6.2 on the following page.)

If you have a working knowledge of these concepts and terms, you will have gone a long way toward understanding what FERPA is all about.

6.2.1 How Do You Determine What an Education Record Is?

To apply FERPA to a record, it must be identified as an education record according to FERPA. Here are some guidelines to follow to determine whether a record meets FERPA requirements for an education record.

Table 6.2: Key Concepts and Terms

Concepts	Source in the Code of Federal Regulations (CFR)	Source in 2001 AACRAO FERPA Guide (Appendix 2)
Required annual notification	34 CFR 99.7	p. 122
Written permission of student required to disclose	99.30	p. 125
Exceptions to written permission	99.31	p. 125
Student's right to access records	99.10	p. 123
The "musts" and "mays" in FERPA	throughout; notably 99.31	p. 125
Parents/parental disclosure	99.31(a)(8) (remember this is in a "may" section)	p. 126
Legitimate educational interest	99.31(a)(1)	p. 125 Note: FERPA does not define this concept; each institution determines what constitutes legitimate educational interests at that institution. Examples of institutional statements are found in Appendix 11 pp. (159–160).
Terms	**Source in the Code of Federal Regulations (CFR)**	**Source in 2001 AACRAO FERPA Guide (Appendix 2)**
Directory information	99.3	p. 120
Education record	99.3	p. 121
Eligible student	99.3	p. 121
Personally identifiable	99.3	p. 121
School official	99.7(a)(3)(iii)	p. 122

If you have a record which is

- maintained by your institution;
- personally identifiable to a student (directly related to a student and from which a student can be identified); or
- not one of the excluded categories of records (see Chapter 2);

then you have an education record…and it is subject to FERPA.

6.2.2 What Does FERPA Say about Parents?

- When a student reaches the age of 18 or begins attending a postsecondary institution regardless of age, FERPA rights transfer to the student.
- Parents may obtain directory information at the discretion of the institution.
- Parents may obtain non-directory information (grades, GPA, etc.) only at the discretion of the institution **and** after it has been determined that their child is legally their dependent.
- Parents may also obtain non-directory information by obtaining a signed consent from their child.

6.3 Written Authorization by Student to Release Information

(See Fig. 6.3 on this page.)

6.4 The Student's Right of Non-Disclosure under FERPA

- A student has the right to request non-disclosure of directory information only.
- A student does not have the right to request non-disclosure to a particular person or group of persons, but the institution may honor such a request if it wishes.
- An institution may honor a student's request to not disclose non-directory information but it does not have to.
- The student has the right to request non-disclosure only while in attendance.
- Students who have left the institution do not have the right to request non-disclosure, but the institution may honor such a request if it wishes.
- Institutions must honor a non-disclosure request for directory information.
- The non-disclosure hold remains in effect until the student directs the institution to remove it. This remains true even after the student has ceased attendance at the institution.

Fig 6.3: Permission to Release Education Record Information

I give permission for ________________ to release my
(institution)

____
(education record information to be released)

to: ____
(name, address)

for (purpose): ____________________________________

Signature: ______________________ Date: __________________

Action taken: ____________________________________
(date) (by whom)

6.5 A FERPA Workshop/Presentation

The following slide outline is designed to form the basis of a FERPA workshop/presentation in Powerpoint. Most of the slides have notes explaining what is covered in the slide. The first slides offer some suggestions on how to enhance the presentation on your campus. An electronic version of this sample presentation is downloadable from AACRAO's website at www.aacrao.org/compliance/ferpa/.

Slide 1: Training Faculty and Staff on FERPA (Title Slide)

Slide Notes: *The title you give to the presentation can be anything that describes what the presentation is about. The catchier the title, the better.*

Slide 2: Some Tips on Training Faculty and Staff on FERPA

We remember:

- 10% of what we hear.
- 20% of what we see.
- 40% of what we see and hear.
- 60% of what we see, hear, and do.

Slide Notes: *This information came from a World War II study of what teaching techniques would be most effective in training servicemen. It remains useful today as we plan training sessions for our colleagues.*

Slide 3: Some Tips on Training Faculty and Staff on FERPA (cont.)

- Limit training to no more than one hour and fifteen minutes.
- Have a timekeeper.
- Train faculty and staff separately if at all possible.
- Use illustrations/examples from your campus wherever possible.
- Don't assume something won't happen at your school.
- Use a pretest to stimulate thought.
- Take questions as they are asked.

Slide Notes: *This slide is self-explanatory and may be eliminated. (Ditto with slides 4-7.)*

Slide 4: Some Tips on Training Faculty and Staff on FERPA (cont.)

- Remember the kiss principle: "keep it simple, stupid."
- Use "ahah" and "aheh."
- Always have a handout.
- Always have enough handouts.

Slide 5: Some Tips on Training Faculty and Staff on FERPA (cont.)

- Use streaming video.
- Go for graphics.
- Borrow/steal ideas from others.
- Personalize the presentation as much as possible.

Slide Notes: *Personalizing the presentation means using examples from your own institution and examples relevant to your specific audience.*

Slide 6: Institutional FERPA Web Sites

- George Mason University, Office of the Registrar http://registrar.gmu.edu/faculty_services/ http://registrar.gmu.edu/ferpafaqs.html
- Illinois State University http://coe.ilstu.edu/portfolios/students/wjpearc/final%20project/ferpa1.htm
- New York University, University Registrar (as part of faculty handbook) http://www.nyu.edu/registrar/13faculty.shtml
- University of Connecticut, Office of the Registrar http://www.registrar.uconn.edu/ferpa.html
- University of Nebraska at Omaha http://www.ses.unomaha.edu/ppt/ferpa/

Slide Notes: *These websites have been created by individuals who wish to provide FERPA information to their constituencies.*

Slide 7: Institutional FERPA Web Sites (cont.)

- Central Virginia Community College, FERPA Workshop Presentation in Powerpoint (for downloading) http://studentservices.cv.cc.va.us/admissions/ferpa.htm also www.aacrao.org (Resource Center)
- University of Nebraska at Kearney, FERPA Quiz/ Tutorial for Faculty and Staff http://www.unk.edu/departments/registrar/home.html
- University of Puget Sound, Office of the Registrar http://www.ups.edu/registrar/
- University System of Maryland, Student Information System Project http://info.fmis.ums.edu/ferpaweb/

Slide 8: Key Concepts

- Required annual notification
- Written permission of student required to disclose
- Exceptions to written permission requirement
- Students' right to access their records
- The "musts" and "mays" in FERPA
- Parents/parental disclosure
- Legitimate educational interest

Slide Notes: *These are the important concepts that anyone needs to know if he or she is to master FERPA.*

This and the next slide are shown twice in this presentation. The first time is here, to introduce participants to the concepts and terms that will be emphasized in this presentation. The second time this slide is displayed is toward the end of the presentation, when you sum up and emphasize those key concepts and terms one needs to know to understand FERPA.

Slide 9: Key Terms

- Directory information
- Education record
- Eligible student
- Personally identifiable
- School official

Slide 10: Family Educational Rights and Privacy Act of 1974

"A federal law designed to protect the privacy of *education records*, to establish the right of students to inspect and review their education records, and to provide guidelines for the correction of inaccurate and misleading data through informal and formal hearings."

Slide Notes: *Congress enacted FERPA for the three main purposes shown in this slide. This presentation covers the first two purposes. The third has not become a major factor in our study of FERPA. Although important to the overall understanding of the intent of Congress in protecting the privacy of education records and providing for corrections to erroneous information found in education records, the hearing process has not emerged as an important part of this legislation since there have not been many hearings that have resulted from a FERPA complaint within an institution.*

Throughout the presentation, certain terms will be highlighted in italics. For example, the term "education record(s)" in this slide is in red in the Powerpoint presentation that was used to prepare this section of Chapter 6. The reader/participant should understand what these key terms/phrases/concepts are. They are important to understanding FERPA.

Slide 11: Family Educational Rights and Privacy Act of 1974 (cont.)

This act is enforced by the *Family Policy Compliance Office*, U.S. Department of Education, Washington, DC.

The Family Policy Compliance Office is the office within the Department of Education that administers FERPA and is responsible for providing technical assistance on FERPA to educational institutions.

Slide Notes: *FERPA is applicable to both K-12 and higher education. The Family Policy Compliance Office is responsible for both levels of education.*

The main difference in FERPA between these two levels of education is that the rights ascribed to the "student" at the higher education level are the parents' at the K-12 level. As will be made clear in subsequent slides, FERPA rights are granted to parents until their son/daughter reaches the age of 18 or begins attending an institution of higher education regardless of age.

The term "eligible student" found in the law (but not used in this presentation) refers to a student who has gained FERPA rights.

Slide 12: The Essence of the Act

- College students must be permitted to inspect their own *education records*.
- *School officials* may not disclose *personally identifiable* information about students nor permit inspection of their records without their written permission unless such action is covered by certain exceptions permitted by the Act.

Slide Notes: *The two statements found in this slide capture the essence of what FERPA is about. Note that the terms "education records," "school official," and "personally identifiable" are highlighted in this slide.*

Slide 13: What Is an Education Record?

- Any record, with certain exceptions, maintained by an institution that is directly related to a student or students. This record can contain a student's name, or students' names, or information from which an individual student, or students, can be personally (individually) identified
- These records include: files, documents, and materials in whatever medium (handwriting, print, tapes, disks, film, microfilm, microfiche) which contain information directly related to students and from which students can be personally (individually) identified.

Slide Notes: *This is the FERPA definition of an "education record." It is important to start with this definition since you must determine if a piece of information is an "education record." If the record can be identified as an "education record," it is subject to FERPA.*

Notice how broad the definition is not only in the information covered but also in the variety of media in which such a record can be found.

This definition states that an education record is not just a record that can be identified by a student's name; nor is it just a paper document found in the Registrar's Office.

This pervasive definition draws most—if not all—academic and administrative offices of an institution under the FERPA umbrella.

Slide 14: "Personally Identifiable"

Personally identifiable means data or information which include:

- The name of the student, the student's parents, or other family members;
- The student's campus or home address;
- A personal identifier (such as a social security number or student number); or
- A list of personal characteristics or other information which would make the student's identity easily traceable.

Slide Notes: *To determine what is "personally identifiable," FERPA provides these guidelines. Note that "personally identifiable" includes more than just a student's name; it can include a "personal identifier" such as a social security number. This is why it is illegal to post grades by ID or social security number without obtaining the student's written permission to do so.*

Slide 15: Grades Posted on Bulletin Board outside Instructor's Office

Slide 15: Grade Posting Sample 1

Instructor Summary December 15, 1999
Grade Book (Unregistered Copy)
MKT 227 Fall 99

A = 90.0 B = 80.0 C = 70.0 D = 60.0

ID	Rg Avg% 100.00	Ext Cr % 5.6	Grade
2949	93.8	2.1	A
4532	84.5	4.2	B
5599	83.1	0.7	B
1197	71	0.7	B
7463	72.6	0.7	C
6115	66.2	5.6	C
7692	66.9	4.2	C
2342	68.1	1.4	D
1543	62.9	0.7	D
6748	61.8	0.7	D

Slide 16: Grade Posting Sample 2

IST 133-02 Grade Book

Grades as of
12/18/99 3:48 PM

Last 4 SSN	Homework Assignments										HW Pts	Tests				Test Pts	Project		Grade		
	1	2	3	4	5	6	7	8	9	10		1	2	3	4		Grade	Points	Pts	%	Ltr
1523	3.0	3.0	3.0	2.6	2.7	3.0	3.0	3.0	2.9	3.0	29.2	96	94	95	98	36.3	99	24.8	97.2	97.0%	A
2313	2.4	3.0	3.0	2.9	2.9	3.0	3.0	3.0	2.4	3.0	28.6	90	96	91	85	36.2	82	20.5	89.4	89.0%	B
3380	3.0	3.0	3.0	2.9	3.0	3.0	2.9	3.0	3.0	3.0	29.8	90	87	90	80	34.7	89	22.3	91.2	91.0%	A
3566	3.0	3.0	3.0	2.5	2.9	3.0	3.0	3.0	2.2	3.0	28.6	99	96	91	100	38.6	88	22.0	93.6	94.0%	A
3576	3.0	3.0	3.0	2.7	3.0	3.0	3.0	3.0	3.0	3.0	29.7	86	71	86	80	32.3	93	23.3	89.9	90.0%	A
3690		3.0	2.5	2.9							8.4	61	0	0	0	6.1	0	0.0	–	–	–
3893	3.0	3.0	3.0	3.0	2.8	3.0	3.0	3.0	2.6	3.0	29.4	88	95	96	100	37.9	98	24.5	96.7	97.0%	A
4278	3.0	3.0	3.0	2.6	2.8	3.0	3.0	3.0	2.5	3.0	28.9	88	76	95	100	35.9	88	22.0	91.2	91.0%	A
4459	3.0	3.0	3.0	2.5	2.9	3.0	3.0	3.0	2.8	3.0	29.2	91	65	93	90	33.9	98	24.5	92.5	93.0%	A
6047	3.0	3.0	3.0	2.7	2.7	3.0	3.0	3.0	3.0	3.0	29.4	93	97	94	98	38.2	95	23.8	96.1	96.0%	A
6585	3.0	3.0	3.0	3.0	3.0	3.0	3.0	3.0	3.0		30.0	100	69	95	100	36.4	90	22.5	93.4	93.0%	A
7004	3.0	3.0	3.0	2.5	2.7	3.0	3.0	3.0	3.0	3.0	29.2	91	100	91	100	38.2	94	23.5	95.6	96.0%	A
8286	3.0	3.0	3.0	2.5	2.7	3.0	3.0	3.0	2.4		28.6	92	78	82	90	34.2	92	23.0	90.4	90.0%	A
8441	3.0	3.0	2.3	2.5	2.9	2.4	3.0	3.0	3.0		28.1	55	42	71	73	24.1	84	21.0	77.4	77.0%	C
9607	3.0	3.0	2.5	2.5	2.5	2.5	2.7	3.0		3.0	24.7	78	98	85	90	35.1	79	19.8	83.5	84.0%	B
9693	3.0	3.0	3.0	2.5	3.0	3.0	2.9	3.0	2.8	3.0	29.2	100	96	90	100	38.6	99	24.8	97.5	98.0%	A
0151	3.0	3.0	3.0	3.0	3.0	3.0	3.0	3.0	3.0		27.0	59	55	0	0	11.4	0	0.0	–	–	–
0847	3.0	3.0	2.5	2.7	2.9	3.0	3.0	3.0	3.0	3.0	29.1	97	77	93	90	35.7	82	20.5	89.4	89.0%	B

Slide Notes: *The next two slides are taken from two instructors' web pages. Both slides show the grades, etc. of their students in a section of a class they are teaching. The identifying numbers in the left-hand column show the last four digits of the students' social security numbers.*

According to the Family Policy Compliance Office, this is a legally acceptable way of publicly posting this non-directory information (grades) without obtaining the students' written permission.

Although this is acceptable, you should recommend that the alphabetical order of the list be rearranged so that students who have names beginning with A or Z cannot be personally identified.

Although this posting is legally acceptable, we do not recommend it.

One question that is asked frequently is, "Well, how can we do this if we want to?" Probably the most acceptable answer, if there is insistence on posting grades, is to have the instructor assign a personal ID code that only the instructor and the student know.

Slide 16: (Refer to graphic above)

Slide 17: What an Education Record Is Not

- "Sole possession" notes
- Law enforcement unit records
- Records maintained exclusively for individuals in the their capacity as employees
  - Records of individuals who are employed as a result of their status as students (work-study) are education records.
- Doctor-patient privilege records
- Alumni records

Slide Notes: *These are the categories of information that are not subject to FERPA. "Sole possession notes" will be covered shortly. Law enforcement unit records are those records created by a law enforcement unit for a law enforcement purpose and maintained by the law enforcement unit. Any of these records that are shared with another school official become subject to FERPA.*

Employee records: If a student is also an employee of the institution, the employment records of that person are not subject to FERPA. However, those records created for an employment purpose by the fact that the person is a student are education records. The most common examples of these kinds of records are work-study records. Doctor-patient privilege records: Those records made or maintained by a physician, psychiatrist, psychologist, or other recognized professional or paraprofessional acting in his or her professional capacity or assisting in a paraprofessional capacity in the treatment of a student. These records are only to be disclosed to those providing treatment to the student. "Treatment" does not include any remedial educational activities or activities that are part of the educational program of the institution. Alumni records are those records created by an institution after a student has left the institution.

Slide 18: "Sole Possession Notes"

Are made by one person as an individual observation or recollection, are kept in the possession of the maker, and are shared only with a temporary substitute.

- This term has always been narrowly defined.
- Notes taken in conjunction with any other person are not sole possession notes (e.g., counselor's notes, interview notes).
- Sharing these notes with another person or placing them in an area where they can be viewed by others makes them "education records" and subject to FERPA.
- Best advice: If you don't want it reviewed, don't write it down.

Slide Notes: *There has been some confusion over what constitutes a "sole possession" record, and many within higher education attribute a broader definition to a sole possession record than what is legally correct. This slide demonstrates how limited the definition of a sole possession record can be.*

(Follow this slide up with Story #1 to reinforce the limited nature of "sole possession note.")

Slide 19: "Sole Possession Notes" (cont.)

OK, folks...It's story time!!!

Story #1

Slide Notes: *Prior to reading this story, you should have reviewed the characteristics of a "sole possession note" according to the law. You could provide an example, such as a notation of a "knee-jerk observation of a student's behavior that a temporary substitute might need to be aware of."*

Story #1—At an institution in the midwest, the Affirmative Action Officer (subsequently referred to as the AAO) was investigating a complaint filed by a student with the state's Department of Human Rights. The student alleged that she had been sexually harassed by a faculty member.

In the investigation, the AAO interviewed all students who may have observed the alleged incident. The AAO interviewed each student individually and privately, and while interviewing, wrote notes of each student's observations and recollections. The AAO did not ask each student to review the notes for accuracy and did not share the notes with anyone. The interview notes were maintained in the AAO's office in a locked cabinet. No other person had access to the notes. The AAO did review the notes when preparing a response to the Department of Human Rights but did not disclose the notes themselves to anyone.

Several years later, the student who had made the accusation of sexual harassment discovered that the notes existed and asked to see them since, under FERPA, she said, a student has the right to examine education records. The AAO was advised by legal counsel that the notes were "sole possession" records and thus were not education records and not subject to review by the student. The student then filed a complaint with the Family Policy Compliance Office, claiming that her "right to access" under FERPA had been denied.

Was her "right to access" improperly denied?

The Family Policy Compliance Office determined that since the notes had been "...prepared with the assistance or participation of others, such as the students interviewed...," the notes were education records and the student must be provided access to them under FERPA. The notes in question were not sole possession notes.

Redacted to protect the privacy of the students who had been interviewed, the notes were provided to the complainant (student).

Slide 20: What Is an Education Record? (Summary)

If you have a record that is:

- maintained by your institution;
- personally identifiable to a student (directly related to a student and from which a student can be identified); and
- not one of the excluded categories of records...

then you have an education record, and it is subject to FERPA.

Slide Notes: *This is the end of the beginning of the presentation.*

This slide presents the steps in the test to determine if there is an education record. Ask the three questions below:

1. *Is it personally identifiable to a student?*
2. *Is it maintained by the institution?*
3. *Can it be excluded from all of the categories of records that are not education records (law enforcement unit records, employment records, etc.)?*

If you can answer "yes" to all three questions, you have an education record, and it is subject to FERPA.

Slide 21: Requirements for Compliance

What we must do:

- Provide *annual notification* to students of their FERPA rights.
- Provide students with *access* to their education records.

Slide Notes: *This is the beginning of the second part of the presentation: What we must do to comply with FERPA.*

There are two main FERPA requirements with which each institution must comply.

Slide 22: Requirements for Compliance (cont.)

Provide annual notification to students of their right to:

1. Inspect and review their education records.
2. Request an amendment to their education records.
3. A hearing if the request for an amendment is unsatisfactory.
4. Request that the institution not disclose *directory information* items about them.
5. File a complaint with the U.S. Department of Education.

Slide Notes: *Six main points must be included in the annual notification to students regarding their FERPA rights. The first five are self-explanatory and are easily covered; the sixth is more complex and is addressed separately on subsequent slides.*

The seventh point of this presentation—student notification regarding directory information—is not legally required to be included in the annual notification. However, since FERPA requires us to notify students of what items of information an institution identifies as directory information, we, along with the Family Policy Compliance Office, recommend that this notification be included in the annual notification to students.

Also, it would be helpful to download the Model Annual Notification from the Family Policy Compliance Office's website to study how these seven points are included in the annual notification. The URL for the Family Policy Compliance Office's website is www.ed.gov/offices/OM/fpco.html

Slide 23: Requirements for Compliance (cont.)

Provide annual notification to students of their right to:

6. Know (1) that *school officials* within the institution may obtain information from education records without obtaining prior written consent, (2) the criteria for determining who will be considered school officials, and (3) what *legitimate educational interests* will entitle school officials to have access to education records.

Slide Notes: *Point six is extensive. Within it lie three key terms that are at the foundation of understanding what FERPA directs regarding how education records should be treated by school officials within the institution. This point, intertwined with the key terms, provides the legal underpinning for establishing the necessity of demonstrating a professional need to know prior to accessing an education record. Because a person is employed by the institution does not mean that that person has an implied right to go on a "fishing expedition" among students' education records. There must be a professional need to know, and that concept is identified as a "legitimate educational interest." This is an important part of the annual notification to students. This law states that students must be informed of who within the institution will have access to their education records and the conditions under which this access will occur.*

Slide 24: Requirements for Compliance (cont.)

Provide annual notification to students of their right to:

- Know which information the institution has designated as public or *directory information.*

  Note: This notification of directory information is not required to be included in the annual notification.

Slide Notes: *As this slide indicates, notification to students of what the institution has designated as directory information is not required to be included in the annual FERPA notification. FERPA does require that each institution notify students of what it considers to be directory information. The Family Policy Compliance Office has recommended that this notification be included in the annual notification.*

Slide 25: Requirements for Compliance (cont.)

Directory Information

- Although not required to be included in the institution's annual notification, the institution **must** notify students of what information the institution has designated as *directory information.*
- The Family Policy Compliance Office has recommended that this notification be part of the institution's annual FERPA notification to students.

Slide 26: Requirements for Compliance (cont.)

Directory Information

- Information not normally considered a violation of a person's privacy.
- Students must be notified of the items of *directory information.*
- Students must be given the opportunity to request that directory information not be released. This right of non-disclosure applies to directory information only.

Slide Notes: *These are the three key points in FERPA regarding directory information. Probably the most misunderstood point is that the student's right to non-disclosure applies only to directory information. An institution may still disclose directory information under any of the exceptions to student written permission beginning at slide 45 and continuing through slide 53 (these encapsulate all of the exceptions to written permission found in the FERPA regulations at 34 CFR 99.31).*

Also, a student may request non-disclosure at any time, whether he or she is a currently enrolled or former student. The institution MUST honor the non-disclosure request of a currently enrolled student; it does not have to honor a non-disclosure request from an former student, but it may do so if it wishes.

Non-disclosures that have been honored by the institution remain in effect until students remove them. The institution may require a student to renew the non-disclosure as long as he or she is still in attendance. However, if the student has requested non-disclosure during the last term of attendance, the non-disclosure must be honored by the institution until the (now) former student informs the institution otherwise.

Slide 27: What Can Directory Information Include?

Directory information **may** include the following student information:

- Student's name
- Address
- Telephone number
- Date/place of birth
- Major
- Fields of study
- Participation in officially recognized activities and sports
- Height/weight (for athletic team members)
- Dates of attendance
- Degrees and awards received
- Most recent education institution attended
- Other similar information as defined by the institution that would not normally be considered an invasion of a student's privacy

Slide Notes: *These are examples of directory information that are specifically found in FERPA. Note the use of the word "may." In other words, institutions have a choice of selecting any, all, or none of these items as directory information.*

What would be the implications of NOT designating anything as directory information?

Slide 28: What Can Directory Information Include? (cont.)

Directory information may include the following recent additions to student information:

- Class schedule
- E-mail address
- Class rosters
- Photographs

Class schedule and *class rosters* are currently (2000) under review as to whether they will remain directory information.

Slide Notes: *These items of directory information have been added by the Family Policy Compliance Office since 1990 through determinations that have been made in response to questions from institutions. In 1996, the Office determined that class rosters and a student's class schedule could be identified as directory information as long as these items contained only directory information.*

Subsequent to this determination, the Office has received some comments regarding access to these items. The Office is currently reconsidering its position on these two items but has not excluded them from the "directory information" category.

Slide 29: What Can Directory Information Include? (cont.)

Directory information can **never** include a student's:

- Race
- Gender
- Social security number
- Grades
- GPA
- Country of citizenship
- Religion

Slide Notes: *The Family Policy Compliance Office has determined that releasing these items would be a violation of a student's privacy if released without the student's written permission.*

Slide 30: Directory Information, College XXX-Style

XXX college has designated *directory information*, according to the Family Educational Rights and Privacy Act of 1974, to be the student's:

- Name
- Local and permanent address/telephone number
- Major field of study
- Participation in officially recognized activities/sports
- Weight and height (for members of athletic teams)
- Dates of attendance
- Degrees and awards received and dates awarded
- Most recent previous educational institution attended
- Academic level
- Enrollment status (full time/part time)

Slide Notes: *You can now display what your institution identifies as directory information.*

This is a good "post-it" for future reference. Have this available as a separate handout, or advise session participants to copy it and post it close to their phones.

Slide 31: Directory Information

- It is important to remember that "directory information" be defined as such.
- If a data element isn't defined as "directory information," it isn't directory information and can be released only if the student's written permission is obtained or the release can be justified under one of the exceptions to students' written permission found in FERPA.

Slide Notes: *This slide emphasizes the importance of not releasing an item of information if it has not been identified as directory information.*

It also reinforces one of the two statements in Slide 12, "The Essence of the Act."

The exceptions to students' written permission are found in 34 CFR 99.31 (Appendix 2 of the 2001 AACRAO FERPA Guide) and in Slides 50 through 55 of this presentation.

Slide 32: Requirements for Compliance

Provide annual notification to students of their right to know:

6 (1) that *school officials* within the institution may obtain information from education records without obtaining prior written consent, (2) the criteria for determining who will be considered school officials, and (3) what *legitimate educational interests* will entitle school officials to have access to education records.

Slide Notes: *Now back to point 6. The first part informs students that "school officials" can have access to their education records without their written permission. Though this may seem obvious, it is important to have this included as part of the law. The next two slides clarify who a school official may be.*

Note the word "may" in the first line of part 6.

Slide 33: School Officials

A "school official" can be a person:

- employed by the college in an administrative, supervisory, academic, research, or support staff position (including law enforcement and health staff personnel),
- elected to the board of trustees,
- or company employed by or under contract with the college to perform a special task (such as the attorney, auditor, or collection agency), or
- a student serving on an official committee, such as a disciplinary or grievance committee, or assisting another school official in performing his or her tasks.

Slide Notes: *There is no definition in FERPA of "school official." FERPA states that each institution must specify the "criteria for determining who constitutes a school official..." (34 CFR 99.7 (a)(2)(iii); see Appendix 2.) Therefore it is up to each institution to identify the "school officials" at their institution and to include those individuals or groups in the annual notification. This slide identifies the typical individuals and groups who can be identified as school officials. Note that individuals other than the institution's faculty and staff may be included as "school officials." Also, if an institution has graduate assistants and/or work-study students or has students serving on committees that have access to other students' education records, the institutional definition of "school official" must be broad enough to include these students. It is not necessary to require these students to sign an agreement regarding the confidentiality of education records. Generally, students who are informed of the importance of their responsibilities regarding the privacy of education records under FERPA present little, if any, threat to the violation of that privacy. Train them on FERPA and then treat them as intelligent adults. Your trust will be amply rewarded.*

Slide 34: At XXX College, a school official is a person:

- employed by the institution in an administrative, supervisory, academic or research, or support staff position (including law enforcement unit personnel and health staff);
- or company with whom the university has contracted, e.g., attorney, auditor, collection agent;
- serving on the Board of Trustees;
- or student serving on an official committee, such as a disciplinary or grievance committee, or assisting another school official in performing his or her tasks.

Slide Notes: *This slide illustrates a typical institutional statement regarding who school officials are considered to be. For this slide, substitute your institutional statement on who school officials are.*

Slide 35: Requirements for Compliance

Provide annual notification to students of their right to know:

6 (1) that *school officials* within the institution may obtain information from education records without obtaining prior written consent, (2) the criteria for determining who will be considered school officials, and (3) what *legitimate educational interests* will entitle school officials to have access to education records.

Slide Notes: *The term "legitimate educational interest" is coupled with the definition/identification of "school officials." It is important for these two* *terms to be associated with each another, e.g., a "school official" must have a "legitimate educational interest" to gain access to a student's education record. In other words, a school official cannot be on a "fishing expedition" when he or she reviews a student's records. There must be a purpose and that purpose must be covered in the institution's statement on "legitimate educational interest" and included in the annual notification to students.*

Slide 36: Legitimate Educational Interest

- The demonstrated need to know by those officials of an institution who act in the student's educational interest, including faculty, administrators, clerical and professional employees, and other persons who manage student record information.
- Although FERPA does not define legitimate educational interest, it states that institutions must specify the criteria for determining it.

Slide Notes: *Like the term "school officials," FERPA is silent on what constitutes a "legitimate educational interest" (34 CFR 99.7(a)(3)(iii); see Appendix 2). Therefore, each institution must articulate what this term means and include it in its annual notification. The definition in this slide is from an early (1980s) AACRAO FERPA Guide.*

This is another way of explaining/introducing "legitimate educational interest" to the group.

Slide 37: Legitimate Educational Interest at XXX College

A school official has a legitimate educational interest if the official needs to review an education record in order to fulfill his or her professional responsibility.

Slide Notes: *This slide is similar to Slide 34 on "school officials." You will want to substitute your institutional definition of "legitimate educational interest" here. Examples of statements of "legitimate educational interest" can be found in Appendix 11 of the 2001 AACRAO FERPA Guide.*

An "educational need to know," or something similar, is sometimes used synonymously with "legitimate educational interest." The legal term used in FERPA is "legitimate educational interest." This term most commonly requires that in order to view a student's record, a "school official" must be performing a duty or service related to a professional responsibility outlined in his or her contract. This statement may be expanded to include designated agents performing duties that school officials normally would perform.

Slide 38: Legitimate Educational Interest

Time for another story:

Story #2

Slide Notes: *Story #2 is a 1988 letter addressed to the assistant registrar of a major university. If this incident can happen at one institution, it can happen at any institution.*

"Dear Ms. XXX:

I am writing concerning the release of information about my educational record to my ex-husband, xxxxxx, the director of xxxxxx at xxxxx University. I refer to the unofficial grade transcript I gave to you during our meeting last week.

I was separated from him in December 1983 and was divorced from him in October 1984. We are currently involved in a court decision concerning custody of our two children. In his answers to interrogatories filed with my attorney on February 11, 1988, my ex-husband wrote that he would submit the "educational record" of me as evidence at the trial. My attorney said that he didn't know how my ex-husband would be able to supply the court with a copy of my transcript, since that information is protected.

On March 3, his lawyer gave my lawyer several documents he intended to use as exhibits in court, including my grade transcript. The hearing date was March 4. At the hearing, his attorney did not submit my transcript itself, but he submitted a sheet showing a set of bar graphs representing my academic progress at xxxx University as opposed to his progress at Yale and Harvard. This sheet had been prepared by his new wife, a faculty member in the Statistics Department. In his testimony, my ex-husband also referred to my grades since the divorce and to the fact that I had completed the required number of hours for an M.A. but had not yet completed my thesis.

My ex-husband has obtained my unofficial transcript to further his case against me as a custodial parent. I am angry that he has gotten this personal information about me and shared it with his lawyer, my lawyer, his wife, and perhaps other people as well. I am proud of my academic record, but it is my record to disclose..."

We, of course, would agree that this is a violation of a student's FERPA rights. It is also an example of a school official (the ex-husband) obtaining an education record without demonstrating a legitimate educational interest. This violation of FERPA could have had serious legal implications for the university. The lesson to be learned is that there needs to be a continuous attempt to inform all school officials, new and old, of their FERPA responsibilities. FERPA has implications for any employee who comes in contact with education records at any institution.

Slide 39: Requirements for Compliance

- Provide annual notification to students...
- Provide students access to their education records.

Slide Notes: *This is a transition slide between this part (Requirements for Compliance) and Part 3 (providing students access to their records). In other words, we're going to consider what FERPA says about how we permit students to look at their records and under what conditions that review can take place.*

Slide 40: Requirements for Compliance (cont.)

Provide students *access* to their *education records.*

Students have the right to:

- inspect and review within 45 days of their request to do so.

Slide Notes: *This slide emphasizes one of the major rights of students under FERPA: their right to review (access) their records.*

FERPA allows an institution 45 days to comply with a student's request to review his or her records. Quite often, the institution complies in much less time.

Note: The hearing process (another FERPA right of the student) is not covered in this presentation because of time constraints and because FERPA hearings have not become prevalent on college campuses. Some general guidelines for conducting FERPA hearings are provided in Chapter 4.2.

Slide 41: Requirements for Compliance (cont.)

Provide students *access* to their education records.

Limitations on the right to inspect:

- parental financial information;
- confidential letters and recommendations to which the student has waived his or her right of inspection;
- education records containing information about more than one student.
  - The institution must permit access to that part of the record which pertains only to the inquiring student.

Slide Notes: *There are three main areas of education records that students do not have the right to view. These are shown in this slide.*

If you come from a selective institution, you may want to find out how the admissions office handles confidential letters of recommendation. Some selective institutions request applicants to indicate whether they waive or do not waive their right to inspect a confidential letter or recommendation prior to providing the form to the person asked to write the letter. Thus, the counselor, headmaster, principal, clergy, etc. knows before writing the letter if the student has waived the right to subsequently review the letter of recommendation. Remember that the confidential letter of recommendation becomes an "education record" if maintained by the institution after the student has begun attending the institution. Therefore, if the student has not waived his or her right to review the letter, or has not been given the opportunity to waive his or her right, the letter is subject to review by the student. You may want to find out if the individuals writing the letters of recommendation are assuming that these letters are confidential when, in fact, these letters may legally be reviewed by the student after the student is attending the institution.

You may want to get an example of an admissions packet if you are at an institution that requires written recommendations. You will find either that the institution is not asking applicants to waive their rights to subsequent review (therefore, the recommendations will be subject to review by the students after they are admitted) or that there is a section where applicants can indicate whether they have waived their right to subsequent review of recommendations. This slide should be included in presentations to both faculty and staff.

Slide 42: Sample Permission Letter to Write a Letter of Recommendation

I give permission for Prof. Kostal to write a letter of recommendation to:

Annie's Catering
344 Willow Dr.
Lynchburg VA 24502

Prof. Kostal has my permission to include my grades, GPA, and class rank in this letter.

I waive/do not waive my right to review a copy of this letter at any time in the future.

Signature Date

Slide Notes: *This is an example of a form that school officials (including faculty) can use with students who wish for the school official to write a letter of recommendation that includes non-directory information maintained by the institution (such as grades, GPA, class rank). If any non-directory information is included in a letter of recommendation, the student's written permission is required. This slide was added in 1998 because a student filed a complaint with the Family Policy Compliance Office alleging that a faculty member had included a grade and GPA in a letter of recommendation without obtaining the student's permission to do so. The Family Policy Compliance Office determined that the faculty member had violated FERPA.*

Slide 43: Procedures and Strategies for Compliance

Disclosure of education record information.

1. Institutions shall obtain written consent from students before disclosing any *personally identifiable information* from their education records (with the exceptions as noted in sections 2 and 3 below). The written consent must:
   - A. specify the records to be released,
   - B. state the purpose of the disclosure,
   - C. identify the party or parties to whom disclosure may be made, and
   - D. be signed and dated by the student.

Slide Notes: *This is a summary slide regarding one of several essential statements in FERPA: A student's written permission is required to release information unless the release is justified under one of the exceptions to written permission found in the law.*

Using a transcript request as an example, we typically are able to meet three of the four criteria specified in this slide: (a) the records to be released, (c). party/parties to whom disclosure is to be made, and (d) signature of student and date. We often do not obtain (b). the purpose of the disclosure. Although not obtaining the purpose for the release may be a technical violation of FERPA, we must balance legal requirements against the realities of the amount of time it might take to obtain this information from the student if it was not provided initially. The most important of the criteria specified are: (a) the records to be released, (c) to whom, and (d) the signature of the student whose records are to be released and the date of the signature.

Slide 44: Procedures and Strategies for Compliance (cont.)

Disclosure of education record information.

2. Institutions **must** disclose education records *without written consent* of students to the following:
   - A. Students who request the information from their own records.

Slide Notes: *This is the only situation according to FERPA where we MUST release information about a student. All of the other releases are in the MAY category that appears on later slides. The Veterans' Administration (VA) law authorizing payment to veterans for educational purposes requires that education records be made available to VA representatives.*

Slide 45: Procedures and Strategies for Compliance (cont.)

Disclosure of education record information.

3. Institutions **may** disclose education records *without written consent* of students to the following:
   - A. Authorized representatives of the following for audit, evaluation, or enforcement of federal and state-supported programs:
     - Comptroller General of the United States
     - The Secretary of the United States Department of Education
     - U.S. Attorney General (law enforcement only)
     - State education authorities

Slide Notes: *The following nine slides are the heart of where we spend most of our time as records keepers in interpreting FERPA. These slides show why and/or to whom education records may be released without students' written permission.*

If you are a subscriber to regist-l or scr-l, count how many FERPA questions fall into the "exceptions" category. In one survey of questions from registrar-l (regist-l) and the small-college-registrars discussion lists (scr-l) covering a period of three months in 2000, 8 of every 10 questions on FERPA focused on this section.

Note the differences in these slides between the words "may" and "must." These words have a significant impact on how institutions comply with FERPA. Institutions don't have to be consistent but instead may decide on a case-by-case basis whether to release information.

Slide 46: Procedures and Strategies for Compliance (cont.)
Disclosure of education record information.

3 Institutions **may** disclose education records *without written consent* of students to the following:

- B Personnel within the institution determined by the institution to have a legitimate educational interest.
- C Officials of other institutions in which the student seeks to enroll, on condition that the issuing institution makes a reasonable attempt to inform the student of the disclosure.

Slide Notes: *A continuation of the exceptions to written permission topic.*

Item C permits institutions to send any non-directory information to institutions where the student is seeking to enroll. Note the notification requirement.

Anecdotal: Shortly after FERPA was passed in 1974, a registrar received a call from the dean of the Marshall University College of Education. The dean said he had received a transcript from the registrar's institution for an applicant who was seeking admission to the graduate program in education at Marshall. The dean said he believed the transcript had been forged and wanted assistance from the registrar to verify the forgery. Based on exception C shown in this slide, the registrar was able to discuss the student's record with the dean. They concluded that the applicant had given herself two additional years of credit and a bachelor's degree. The registrar notified the student of the disclosure and informed her that any transcripts that she requested to be sent in the future would have to be sent directly to a bona fide third party and not to herself. The registrar never heard from the student again.

Slide 47: Procedures and Strategies for Compliance (cont.)
Disclosure of education record information.

3 Institutions **may** disclose education records *without written consent* of students to the following:

- D Persons or organizations providing to the student financial aid or determining financial aid decisions.
- E Organizations conducting studies to develop, validate, and administer predictive tests; to administer student aid programs; or to improve instruction.

Slide Notes: *Under D the definition of financial aid does not extend to parents. Institutions could, however, release grades without obtaining written permission from the student to companies providing tuition reimbursement to their employees. Remember, an institution MAY do this; it does not have to.*

The intent of E is to provide institutions with the ability to cooperate without first obtaining students' written permission in regional, state, and national standardized testing activities or studies that can be of benefit to the institution. This is the section that some registrars have used to justify the release of personally identifiable information to doctoral students working on research related to their dissertations. This may be a "stretch," but as long as the researcher understands FERPA and agrees to keep the information confidential and destroy it when finished, it is probably worth the risk. Again, this is a situational matter. You may approve one research request for personally identifiable information yet not approve another. Or, you may decide to reject all such requests.

Slide 48: Procedures and Strategies for Compliance (cont.)
Disclosure of education record information.

3 Institutions **may** disclose education records *without written consent* of students to the following:

- F Accrediting organizations carrying out their accrediting functions.
- G Parents of a student who have established that student's status as a dependent (IRS Code of 1986, Section 152).

Slide Notes: *Under F accrediting groups at times have requested a random set of records to be reviewed by an accreditation team either prior to or during the on-site visit. This exception permits school officials to provide this information to members of the accrediting team without obtaining the students' written permission as long as the release is to comply with part of the accreditation process.*

Exception G permits an institution to release non-directory information to parents. This also identifies the conditions under which parents qualify. IRS Code of 1986, Section 152, basically says that, in the last and most recent federal income tax return of the parent, the student has been identified as a dependent. Institutions must determine that dependency before releasing information to parents. If the dependency cannot be established, the parents are not entitled to non-directory information under this exception to written permission. (A subsequent slide summarizes what FERPA says about parents.)

Slide 49: Procedures and Strategies for Compliance (cont.)
Disclosure of education record information.

3 Institutions **may** disclose education records *without written consent* of students to the following:

- H Persons in compliance with a judicial order or a lawfully issued subpoena, provided that the institution first makes a reasonable attempt to notify the student.

  Exception: if the subpoena is issued by a federal grand jury, or for a law enforcement purpose, and orders the institution not to notify the student.

Slide Notes: *This is the subpoena exception. Refer to Chapter 5.40 of the 2001 AACRAO FERPA Guide for more information on responding to subpoenas. The information in light gray in this slide was added in 1996 in response to law enforcement officials' complaints that the student notification requirement in this section was hindering their law enforcement efforts (drug busts, etc.; if students are notified, they are more likely to disappear if they have broken the law).*

An IRS summons is similar to a subpoena.

Slide 50: Procedures and Strategies for Compliance (cont.)
Disclosure of education record information.

3 Institutions **may** disclose education records *without written consent* of students to the following:

- I A court, if the student has initiated legal action against the institution or the institution has initiated legal action against the student.

Slide Notes: *This is a new addition to the list of exceptions. This exception removes the necessity of an institution getting into an awkward situation* *with a student regarding presenting the student's records in court. Prior to the inclusion of this exception, the institution either would have had to obtain the student's written permission to produce the records in court or would have had to issue a subpoena upon itself to produce the records.*

Slide 51: Procedures and Strategies for Compliance (cont.)
Disclosure of education record information.

3 Institutions **may** disclose education records *without written consent* of students to the following:

- J Persons in an emergency, if the knowledge of information, in fact, is necessary to protect the health or safety of the student or other persons.

Slide Notes: *This slide includes any kind of an emergency. This includes notifying Institution X of the dangerous personal behavior of one of your previous students who has indicated an intent to enroll at Institution X.*

Slide 52: Procedures and Strategies for Compliance (cont.)
Disclosure of education record information.

3 Institutions **may** disclose education records *without written consent* of students to the following:

- K An alleged victim of any crime of violence of the results of any institutional disciplinary proceeding against the alleged perpetrator of that crime with respect to that crime.

Slide Notes: *Basically, this translates as follows: The victim of a crime of violence may be informed of the results of an institutional hearing against the alleged perpetrator of that crime.*

Slide 53: Procedures and Strategies for Compliance (cont.)
Disclosure of education record information.

3 Institutions **may** disclose education records *without written consent* of students to the following:

- L Veterans' Administration (VA) officials in response to requests related to VA programs.
- M Representatives of the Immigration and Naturalization Service for purposes of the Coordinated Interagency Partnership Regulating International Students (CIPRIS).

Slide Notes: *These two exceptions are not found in FERPA but in other laws of Congress. The wording of the VA law indicates that the release is mandatory.*

Slide 54: Procedures and Strategies for Compliance (cont.)
Disclosure of education record information.

3 Institutions **may** disclose education records *without written consent* of students to the following:

- N Parents of a student under the age of 21 regarding a violation of any law, at any level, or institutional policy or rule governing the use of alcohol or a controlled substance.

  Note: Does not supersede any state law that prohibits disclosure of this information.

Slide Notes: *This is known as the Foley Amendment and is a new (2000) addition to the exceptions to written permission.*

Slide 55: Procedures and Strategies for Compliance (cont.)
Disclosure of education record information.

3 Institutions **may** disclose education records *without written consent* of students to the following:

- O The public, regarding the final results of an institutional disciplinary proceeding, as long as the student has been determined to be the alleged perpetrator of a crime of violence or non-forcible sex offense.

Slide Notes: *This, another new (2000) addition to the exceptions to written permission section of FERPA, is known as the Warner Amendment. It permits institutions to release the final results of an institutional disciplinary hearing after it has been determined that the student is the alleged perpetrator of a crime of violence or non-forcible sex offense.*

In other words, the institution may release this information to a newspaper if it wishes. It does not have to.

Slide 56: What Do the "Final Results" Include?

- Must include only: the name of the student, violation committed, and any sanction imposed by the institution against the student.
- The institution may not disclose the name of any other student, including a victim or witness, without prior written consent of the other student.

Slide Notes: *These are two important provisions within the Warner Amendment that relate to the "final results" of a disciplinary hearing and to the protection of the privacy of individuals other than the alleged perpetrator of the crime.*

Slide 57: Procedures and Strategies for Compliance (cont.)
Disclosure of education record information.

4 Institutions **may** disclose information about students to their parents by any of three procedures:

- A By obtaining the student's written consent.
- B By having the parents establish the student's dependency as defined by Internal Revenue Code of 1986, Section 152.
- C By exercising its disclosure option on any students under age 21 regarding a violation of an institutional rule or federal, state, or local law regarding the use of alcohol or a controlled substance if state law permits such disclosure.

Slide Notes: *These next two slides relate to parents. This slide identifies what FERPA specifically says about how we can, if we wish, release information to parents. Institutions are not required to release any information to parents.*

Many faculty have questions about what to discuss with parents regarding their child's academics. They should know that they can't just talk about anything with the parents.

If this hasn't occurred at your institution already, you might want to propose a policy regarding what to say to parents, or at least how to handle parental requests, about their child's records/academic performance.

Slide 58: What about Parents?

- When a student reaches the age of 18 or begins attending a postsecondary institution regardless of age, FERPA rights transfer to the student.
- Parents may obtain directory information only at the discretion of the institution.
- Parents may obtain non-directory information (grades, GPA, etc.) only at the discretion of the institution **and** after it has been determined that their child is legally their dependent.
- Parents may obtain non-directory information by obtaining a signed consent from their child.

Slide Notes: *This summarizes what FERPA says about parents and is a good "post-it" for quick reference.*

Slide 59: Procedures and Strategies for Compliance (cont.)
Disclosure of education record information.

5 Institutions **may** release *without written consent* those records identified as public or directory information for students who are currently enrolled with the following conditions:

A That the institution inform its students of categories designated as directory information.

B That students be given opportunity to refuse disclosure of any or all categories.

C That students be given a reasonable period of time in which to state such refusals in writing.

Slide Notes: *This slide covers the responsibilities of institutions regarding directory information. Note that students must be given the opportunity to inform the institution that they don't want directory information released.*

Students do have the right to request that only one piece of directory information not be released. If this is difficult for your institution to handle, you may inform the student of this fact and tell the student that you will not disclose any directory information. The student then has the choice as to what to do. This is an acceptable alternative according to the Family Policy Compliance Office.

From here on, except for the slides on key terms and concepts, the slides probably will not be of interest to faculty attending the workshop.

Slide 60: Procedures and Strategies for Compliance (cont.)
Disclosure of education record information.

6 Institutions **may** release without written consent those items identified as public or *directory information* on any student not currently enrolled.

7 Institutions **may** release without written consent information on any student found by a campus disciplinary body to have committed a crime of violence or a non-violent sexual offense. The information that may be released is limited to the following: name, violation committed, sanction imposed by the institution.

8 Institutions are responsible for informing parties to whom *personally identifiable information* is released that recipients are not permitted to disclose the information to others without written consent of the students.

Slide Notes: *These are some additional points that staff would be more interested in than faculty.*

You can show an example of Item 8 from any transcript you have received from another institution. The "third party notification" should be found on all such transcripts you have received.

Slide 61: Procedures and Strategies for Compliance (cont.)
Records of requests and disclosures.

1 All institutions are required to maintain records of requests and disclosures of personally identifiable information.

A These records will include the names and addresses of the requestor and his or her indicated interest in the records.

Slide Notes: *Institutions are required to keep records of disclosures. However, as this and the next slides indicate, this requirement is minor and not burdensome.*

Slide 62: Procedures and Strategies for Compliance (cont.)
Records of requests and disclosures.

2 Records of requests and disclosures **do not** have to be kept for:

- Requests from students for their own use.
- Disclosures in response to written requests from students.
- Requests made by school officials.
- Those specified as directory information.

Slide Notes: *All that remains is any release of non-directory information to a third party who is not a school official. The most common example is a release based on receipt of a subpoena. While complying with the subpoena, simply make a copy of the appropriate documentation and file it in the student's folder, attach it to the student's digitized folder (if no paper folder exists), or file or digitize it within an administrative folder labeled "FERPA Releases." Create an alphabetical index of student names included in the folder.*

Slide 63: Procedures and Strategies for Compliance (cont.)
Records of requests and disclosures.

3 Records of requests and disclosures are part of the student's education records and must be retained as long as the education records to which they refer are maintained by the institution.

Slide 64: Key Concepts

- Required annual notification
- Written permission of student required to disclose
- The exceptions to written permission
- Students' right to access their records
- The "musts" and "mays" in FERPA
- Parents/parental disclosure
- Legitimate educational interest

Slide Notes: *This is the second time this slide is shown. It is presented here to begin a summary of the presentation. These are the key concepts that one has to know to understand FERPA.*

Slide 65: Key Terms

- Education record
- Directory information
- School official
- Personally identifiable
- Eligible student

Slide Notes: *These are the key terms that are important for a working knowledge of FERPA.*

Slide 66: Current High-Tech Issues and FERPA

- Faculty < e-mail > students
- Posting grades
- Distance learning
- E-signatures
- PINs
- E-mail transcript requests
- Tracking/logging
- Annual notification via the web

Slide Notes: *This is a list of recent high-tech issues that have FERPA implications. Many of these issues have yet to be resolved. For the present, however, remember that we have one education records law. This means that we do not change our interpretations of FERPA simply because we initiate new methods of educational delivery or provide more efficient administrative mechanisms for greater student convenience.*

Slide 67: The Authoritative Source

Family Policy Compliance Office
LeRoy Rooker, Director
U.S. Department of Education
400 Maryland Ave., SW
Washington, DC 20202-4605

(202) 260-9002 (fax)
ferpa@ed.gov
www.ed.gov/offices/OM/fpco.html

Slide Notes: *If all else fails, this is the information you need to obtain assistance regarding your FERPA queries.*

Slide 68: Criteria to Be Used in Determining a Legitimate Educational Interest When Writing Recommendations

- Has the school established a criterion in its FERPA policy that appears to address disclosures for the purpose at issue?
- What does the faculty contract specify regarding the duties of faculty members? Does or did the faculty member teach the student in any course?
- What is the practice regarding recommendations at the school?
- Does the faculty member otherwise have personal knowledge of the student's abilities?
- Was the faculty member asked by the student to provide the recommendation?
- Does any state law pertain to this issue?

Slide Notes: *You probably won't want to include this in the presentation, but this is a set of questions the Family Policy Office would use to determine if there was a FERPA violation in writing a letter of recommendation.*

Slide 69: A Current Dichotomy

The public's right to know
- *An individual's right to privacy*

First Amendment
- *FERPA/States' school records laws*

Student newspaper request for personally identifiable information
- *Institution required not to release without written permission of student*

A college's need to make an informed admission decision
- *High school reluctant to share negative behavior of student with college, e.g., Illinois School Student Records Act*

6.6 A FERPA Final Exam

Confidentiality and Student Education Records

This examination is designed to test your knowledge of the Family Educational Rights and Privacy Act of 1974 as Amended (FERPA). The first section is True/False. Mark either T or F on each line next to the statement. (An answer key is included at the end of this chapter.) An electronic version of this exam is downloadable from AACRAO's website at www.aacrao.org/compliance/ferpa/.

1. __ A student's degree can be confirmed to some external (outside of your college) source without first obtaining the permission of the student as long as "degree" is identified by the institution as directory information.

2. __ A student has a right to inspect information in his or her file in the Registrar's Office and in his or her department.

3. __ It is permissible for a professor to post student grades on an office door if only a student's social security (I.D.) number is used.

4. __ The registrar may release information about a student without the student's written permission upon receipt of a subpoena.

5. __ Parents may obtain confidential information from their student's academic record.

6. __ Your college must annually notify students of their rights under FERPA.

7. __ In a legal separation or divorce situation, biological parents have equal standing with custodial parents to gain access to the student's education records.

8. __ Faculty have a right to inspect education records of any student attending your college without giving a reason.

9. __ Student representatives on committees (e.g., honors, curriculum, etc.) may have the right to see other students' education records during the deliberations of that committee.

10. __ An institution which designates certain items as "directory information" must give students the opportunity to decline to have any of that information so designated.

11. __ It is permissible to distribute graded examinations by placing them on a table for students to pick up after class.

12. __ E-mail addresses can be considered directory information.

13. __ "Student recruiting information" under the Solomon Amendment is the same as "directory information" under FERPA.

14. __ It is permissible for a faculty member to include a student's grades and GPA in a letter of recommendation without obtaining the student's written permission since the student requested the faculty member to write the recommendation and provided a copy of her resume with the requested information to the faculty member.

15. __ Former students of an institution of higher education have the right to request that their education records not be disclosed, and the institution must comply.

16. __ Currently attending students of an institution of higher education have the right under FERPA to request that all of their education records not be disclosed, and the institution must comply.

17. __ A student's written permission is required before an institution releases information to a national research organization conducting a study on the advantages and disadvantages of selective admissions.

18. __ An institution must release to anyone upon request any information identified as directory information by the institution.

19. __ Grades may be released to a student's employer without the student's written permission if it has been determined that the employer will reimburse the student/employee for any grade of "C" or better.

20. __ It is permissible for an employment agency not connected with your institution to share a student's transcript with a prospective employer as long as the student has given written permission to the institution to provide the transcript to the employment agency.

21. __ A former student has the same right to inspect and review his record as a student currently attending the institution.

Multiple Choice (Place the letter of the most accurate response on the line to the right of the question number.)

22. __ An institution must permit a student to review his records within how many days from the day the student requests the review?
    a. 10 days
    b. 20 days
    c. 25 days
    d. 30 days
    e. none of these

23. __ Which of the following is not identified in the original FERPA (the Act) as being an example of "directory information"? The student's
    a. name
    b. date of birth
    c. e-mail address
    d. dates of attendance

24. __ Directory information may include all of the following except the student's
    a. photograph
    b. major
    c. class schedule
    d. country of citizenship

25. __ You receive a phone call asking to verify (1) that a currently enrolled student: attends your institution, (2) what his address was at the time of attendance, (3) his date of birth, and (4) his GPA. According to FERPA, you can verify all of these except the student's
    a. attendance at the institution
    b. address during the time of attendance
    c. date of birth
    d. GPA

Bonus: Before you respond to the caller in Question 25, what must you determine about the student?

____

____

26. __ A faculty member asks one of your staff for the names of all of the graduates in his program since its beginning in 1980. Which of the following statements is true?
    a. The faculty member can legally obtain this information under FERPA as long as he has written permission from the dean (or designee).
    b. The faculty member cannot legally obtain this information since it is excluded from FERPA.
    c. The faculty member must provide a valid reason for obtaining the information.
    d. The faculty member is not entitled to all of the information since FERPA does not permit release of this information on students not currently attending the institution.

27. __ Question 26 is an example of the exercise of:
    a. legitimate educational interest.
    b. eminent domain.
    c. permissible exclusion.
    d. informational exclusivity.
    e. non-disclosure.
    f. implied consent.

28. __ FERPA requires institutions to obtain which of the following from the student before releasing any directory information:
    a. written permission
    b. verbal permission
    c. certified permission
    d. consensual permission
    e. none of the above

29. __ A transcript request form completed by a student:
    a. must be kept by the institution indefinitely.
    b. does not have to be kept by the institution for any period of time.
    c. does not have to be kept by the institution for more than one year from the date of the request.
    d. must be kept by the institution if the transcript is sent to a third party which the student has identified in the transcript request.

30. __ "Legitimate educational interest" refers to:
    a. a school official's need to review a student's education records.
    b. a student's right to review his education records.
    c. the need to provide education records in child custody cases.
    d. the delegation of authority to the trustees to determine educational records policy for the institution.

31. __ As defined in FERPA, "legitimate educational interest" refers to:
    a. a faculty member's need to provide feedback to students in the form of grades/evaluations.
    b. the registrar's need to obtain education record information from faculty to produce a student's transcript.

(continued)

c. a school official's right to obtain information only about students he is advising or teaching during the current year.
d. a school official's need to review student education record information to fulfill a responsibility as part of her contract.

32. __ Which of the following would not be acceptable under FERPA?
a. releasing the title of a congressman's degree to the local newspaper
b. the provost having access to all students' education records
c. notifying students of their FERPA rights via the student handbook
d. a faculty member announcing to his class that they can pick up their graded term papers from the chair outside his office

33. __ "School official" is to "legitimate educational interest" as "student" is to:
a. handbook
b. directory information
c. faculty
d. social security number

34. __ According to FERPA, students may request that institutions not disclose which of the following about them:
a. directory information
b. non-directory information
c. both directory information and non-directory information
d. incidental information
e. education record information

35. __ At the K-12 level, parents:
a. have the same FERPA rights given to students attending an institution of higher education.
b. cannot review their child's records without first receiving permission from their child.
c. have no FERPA rights since FERPA applies only to higher education.
d. can only review test scores of their children.

36. __ Which of the following is not an "education record" under FERPA?
a. a student's traffic violation
b. a student's term paper
c. a student's e-mail address
d. the women soccer team's roster showing home town, height, weight, and current class of team members
e. a work-study student's work record

37. __ At the college level, FERPA states that parents:
a. have the same rights of access and review as their child.
b. can only see their child's records after receiving permission from the dean of students (or designee).
c. may receive tuition bills for their child sent directly to them from the institution.
d. may review their child's grades if they can prove that the student is legally their dependent.

38. __ FERPA rights:
a. pass from parents to student when the student attains the age of 18.
b. pass from parents to student when the student begins attending an institution of higher education.
c. are shared equally by parents and student at the higher education level.
d. apply only to parents of students attending colleges and universities.
e. apply only to students attending institutions of higher education.
f. a and b only
g. a and e only
h. b and e only

39. __ "Parent" is to "eligible student" as "K-12" is to:
a. college.
b. legitimate educational interest.
c. FERPA.
d. personally identifiable.
e. K-9.

40. __ The FERPA rights of a student begin:
a. when the application for admission is received.
b. when the student is formally admitted.
c. when the student pays his first tuition bill.
d. when the student is "in attendance" as defined by the institution.

41. __ An education record is:
a. a list of names of students in a class.
b. a copy of a student's SAT scores in his file.
c. an electronic notation of a grade in a class recorded by an instructor.
d. a recommendation of a professor that is kept in the professor's file only and not shared with anyone.
e. a and b only
f. a, b, and c only
g. none of the above
h. all of the above (a, b, c, d)

42. __ To be an "education record," a piece of information must be:

a. personally identifiable to a student.
b. maintained by the institution.
c. kept in the registrar's office.
d. made available to the law enforcement unit.
e. a and b only
f. a, b, and c only
g. a and d only

43. __ FERPA

a. permits institutions, through the "implied consent" rule, to disclose non-directory information about a student if the student has publicly disclosed non-directory information about himself.
b. permits disclosure of non-directory information to the press based on the Privacy Act.
c. permits disclosure of non-directory information to other school officials through the "implied consent" rule.
d. permits disclosure of non-directory information to a representative of an insurance company who has been designated by the institution to recommend a new student health insurance policy.

44. __ Which of the following is required from students by FERPA before releasing information about them?

a. verbal consent to release the information
b. written permission, unless the release is covered by any exception listed in FERPA
c. verbal consent from the student's advisor
d. written consent from the parents of a dependent student

45. __ Institutions may release information to parents:

a. by obtaining the student's written permission.
b. by having the parents establish the student's dependency according to the IRS Code of 1986.
c. through a legally issued subpoena.
d. all of the above
e. a and b only

46. __ Records of disclosures of student information must be kept for requests from and releases to:

a. students for their own use.
b. school officials.
c. members of the Board of Trustees.
d. individuals seeking directory information.

(continued)

e. work-study students who have a need to access other students' records as a result of their employment in an office of the institution.
f. all of the above (a, b, c, d, e)
g. none of the above

47. __ FERPA applies to the following institutions:

a. public
b. private
c. religious
d. public and private

48. __ In publishing a student directory that includes students' home addresses, is the institution in violation of FERPA?

a. yes
b. no
c. depends

If you chose c., what is your reason?

____

____

____

49. __ Upon receiving a subpoena, you must:

a. notify the student in all cases that you have received the subpoena.
b. determine if the subpoena has jurisdiction over your institution before complying.
c. notify the server of the subpoena that you will comply within ten working days.
d. notify the student's parents that you have received it.

50. __ A student has the right to review which of the following information about him that is maintained by the institution:

a. parental financial information
b. letters of recommendation
c. law enforcement unit records
d. admissions records related to the denial of his application into another college of the institution
e. all of the above

51. __ Which of the following is not a student's right under FERPA?

a. the right to request that the institution discontinue use of his or her social security number as a personal identifier
b. the right to limit disclosure of directory information

(continued)

c. the right to request an amendment to his or her education record
d. the right to inspect and review his or her education records

52. Would the following would be an acceptable release of student information without the student's written permission? *(Enter "Y" for yes or "N" for no next to each letter.)* (1 point each.)

__ a. to the student
__ b. to the state controller's office in relation to an audit of a state-funded program
__ c. to the student's advisor
__ d. to potential employers attempting to verify grades, class rank, and degree received
__ e. to a custodial parent who is paying the student's tuition
__ f. to an officer of a court in response to a legally issued subpoena
__ g. to parents of a student, regarding an alcohol violation by the student at the institution
__ h. to the student newspaper, regarding the final results of a student disciplinary hearing
__ i. to an institution at which the student intends to enroll, and the request is for the student's GPA
__ j. to the town's local law enforcement office, inquiring whether the student is in attendance this semester

53. All items below are found in various offices of the institution; would they be considered education records? *(Enter "Y" for yes or "N" for no next to each letter.)*

__ a. an examination paper of a student with his name on it
__ b. a class roster with all students' names on it
__ c. a traffic violation of a student kept in the institution's security office
__ d. the honor roll list
__ e. the annual giving record of an former student
__ f. a note made by a faculty member of an advising session with a student
__ g. notes taken by the institution's affirmative action officer when interviewing students regarding a sexual harassment charge made against a faculty member
__ h. student photographs on a department's bulletin board identifying the majors in that department
__ i. medical records made and maintained by the university's contracted doctor related to the treatment of a student

(continued)

__ j. the employment records of an individual who is a full-time employee of the institution and also a part-time student
__ k. scores of a student who took the Test of English as a Foreign Language (TOEFL)
__ l. test scores of a group of students identified only by ID# and kept in a faculty member's office files only
__ m. a faculty member's note about a student having an epileptic seizure in one of his classes and kept in his locked office files
__ n. financial information on a student's parents filed in the Financial Aid Office

Bonus: Why is it important to identify what is and is not an education record?

____
____
____

54. Would the following requests made by **currently enrolled students** be specifically granted by FERPA? *(Enter "Y" for yes or "N" for no next to each letter to indicate whether FERPA allows you to comply with the request.)*

__ a. inspect their education records
__ b. a copy of any education record
__ c. amend an education record
__ d. non-disclosure of directory information
__ e. non-disclosure of non-directory information
__ f. have a hearing to amend an education record
__ g. prevent parents from viewing education records
__ h. forward to his attorney any subpoenas received by the college for his education records

55. Would the following requests made by **former students (no longer enrolled)** be specifically granted by FERPA? *(Enter "Y" for yes or "N" for no next to each letter to indicate whether FERPA allows you to comply with the request.)*

__ a. inspect their education records
__ b. a copy of any education record
__ c. amend an education record
__ d. non-disclosure of directory information
__ e. non-disclosure of non-directory information
__ f. have a hearing to amend an education record
__ g. prevent parents from viewing education records
__ h. forward to his attorney any subpoenas received by the college for his education records

And some brain stretchers to conclude this part of the exam...
For each of the situations below, answer the questions thoroughly and completely using your knowledge of FERPA. You will be best served if you use specifics within FERPA to make your conclusions.

56. In a "Release of Student Information" policy at one institution, the following statements appear:

    "(Public information) is limited to name; address; phone; major field of study; dates of attendance; admission or enrollment status; campus; school; college or division; class standing; degrees and awards; activities; sports; and athletic information..."

    "...Public information shall be released freely unless the student files the appropriate form requesting that certain public information not be released..."

    "Public information which cannot be restricted includes the name, enrollment status, degrees earned, and dates of attendance."

What is wrong with these statements? How should the statements be changed?

---

57. The following statement appears in one university's FERPA policy:

    "The following information will be released to those requesting it unless the student specifically requests otherwise on the form provided or by submitting written notification to the Registrar's Office:

    Student's Name
    Local Address
    Local Phone Number
    Enrollment Status
    Major
    Dates of Attendance

    All other information will not be released without written consent of the student."

What would be another FERPA-acceptable way to restate the sentence in bold above to allow your institution more flexibility in complying with requests for student information? Cite the section of FERPA to which your revised statement would apply.

---

58. University A has invested in a web-based teaching aid for faculty that permits interaction among students and the professor. One of the features that has appealed to faculty is the ability to communicate with students via e-mail.

    One faculty member has suggested that she wants to provide e-mail addresses of all students in her class to every student so they can communicate among themselves.

    As the registrar, you know that e-mail addresses are not identified as directory information at your institution.

    What would need to occur for this professor to share e-mail addresses among her students?

    Your answer should include a discussion of directory information as it pertains to FERPA, non-disclosure, and the annual notification to students, as well as any other information you deem appropriate.

Short Answer, or Your Daily FERPA In-basket—
You are the registrar/director of admissions and records for your institution. You have direct daily responsibility for academic records. You are asked to provide a solution to each in-basket item and to cite the FERPA reason(s) that justify(ies) your decision. Remember: there may be more than one correct response. Your reasoning and FERPA justification are most important here. Whether directly asked to or not, you are expected to give at least one reason for your answer. A simple "yes" or "no" is not sufficient.

Short answers, please; not essays.

In-basket Item #1
The dean of the graduate school calls you and relates the following:

"I have a question about FERPA. I am familiar with the idea of the law, but I am wondering if you can give me an interpretation for the following scenario. That is, is what I'm about to describe a violation of the student's right to review records or merely bad pedagogy?

One of our Ph.D. students took the qualifying examination in January and was told shortly thereafter she had failed. Her department informed her that she would have another chance in the summer to take the examination. The student wanted to see her graded examination, since she wanted to learn from any mistakes she may have made and also because she truly believes she performed sufficiently well to pass. She informed her advisor, the department chair, and the graduate committee chair in writing of her wish to inspect the graded exam.

After a month had passed, she reminded the graduate committee chair verbally of her desire to inspect her graded exam. He acknowledged this request but was not certain that it could be granted; a couple weeks later, he suggested she try to reconstruct the exam and her responses from memory and then discuss them with her advisor.

About two months after the student's initial request (having repeated it again a couple times in the interim), her advisor informed her that the department policy is NOT to let students inspect graded qualifying examinations. Furthermore, the graduate committee has objected to her advance request to review the grading of the second examination she is to take in the summer.

At this moment, nearly three months have passed since she first asked to inspect her graded test paper. She has come to me to appeal the decision of the department. What should I do?"

What do you advise?

In-basket Item #2

You overhear a registrar from another institution saying:

"We do verification of attendance over the phone. And we will give name, year and semesters attended, degree(s) earned, and majors. For anything else, we require a written release from the student or former student. Also, if a student signed in the last semester of attendance to withhold directory information, we will never release information, even if the student later asks us to change it. It is a binding decision."

Is this a FERPA-correct statement? Why or why not?

In-basket Item #3

Currently, your Admissions Office is the owner of all the information that is on the student's application. A copy of all this information is given to you, the registrar, **after** the student has matriculated. (Admissions keeps a copy of the data for reference for reporting, etc., purposes).

a) Career Services requests these data in order to help place students in jobs. Are you in compliance with FERPA if you give Career Services access to all this admissions data? Why?
b) Do you need any waiver or header or notification to the applicant that you are doing this?
c) Can admissions share its database information with other departments/individuals without advising the applicants?
d) Without advising the student if he or she matriculates?

(continued)

e) Without providing FERPA training/reference to the individuals who are accessing the data?

In-basket Item #4

At a meeting of the college's academic administrators, the question of providing class rolls (rosters) on a timely basis comes up. One department head indicates that these class rolls are already on the web, but each faculty has access to all of the class rolls—not just his own. He thinks this isn't appropriate and asks you whether something can't be done.

You reply that "Our current system doesn't allow us to make these very specific measures a reality. If it was more sophisticated, we might consider it. We do send out an e-mail to all faculty and staff at the beginning of the year asking them to look at just their own class rolls due to privacy issues." One dean suggests, "If we put a heading on the beginning class roll page telling them about FERPA, would that be okay instead of limiting the class roll to only the faculty/staff member who teaches the course? Our academic secretaries need access to a number of different class rolls because they work for multiple faculty. Would that be OK?"

a) How would you respond?
b) Can you suggest what the heading might say?
c) If that won't work, what other suggestions might you have?

In-basket Item #5

The director of financial aid comes to you and asks for your interpretation of when parents can/cannot see a student's education record.

She says that she had just attended a financial aid workshop where FERPA had been discussed. The college lawyer who made the presentation told them that dependency "had nothing to do with it unless the student is under 18. If the student is over 18", he said, "he or she—not the parents—has the right to the educational record. If the student chooses to waive that right and let college administrators release that information, that's up to the student. Otherwise, we cannot disclose anything from the educational record without the student's permission."

How would you respond to your colleague?

In-basket Item #6

Currently, your institution does not include birthdates as directory information. There is some discussion that the students' birthdates should be added as directory information. Some on campus are reluctant to agree to include this item because they feel that students may not want this information released.

In order to resolve this problem, your dean asks you what can be done. He is the designated official at your institution that chairs the committee that decides issues related to FERPA. He has no strong feelings one way or the other but knows that this issue will come before his committee. Because he considers you the FERPA expert on campus, he asks, "If we decide to include birthdates, do we have the option of releasing birthdates on some requests but denying to release it on other requests? If it is directory information, are we obligated to release it to everyone?"

How do you respond?

____

____

In-basket Item #7

You have a foreign national over age 18 who was placed on academic probation. The father, who lives in another country, has requested a copy of the student's grades, a report from each teacher on performance in each class, and a report of dormitory activities.

Your institution's policy is to provide the student with a copy of the transcript for parents' use. The student has not given said transcript to the parent.

You believe under FERPA that the student is subject to U.S. law and you cannot, therefore, release anything but directory information without the student's written permission.

What do you tell the parent?

____

____

In-basket Item #8

A graduate from ten years back calls your office and says that she has lost many of her "educational records." While she still has her transcript from your institution, she is requesting that you send her copies of her transcripts from previous schools that are in her folder. Can you comply with her request and still be in compliance with FERPA?

____

____

In-basket Item #9

You receive a phone call from a parent for a copy of her son's transcript. She states that her son was in a car accident and sustained head injuries; she is now his legal guardian and needs a copy of his academic record for his rehab center to continue treatment. You also find out that the injured son is a former student who is now 27 years old and who last attended your institution in 1997. You ask her for a written release and a copy of guardianship papers.

After thinking about it, you realize that you are not aware of the extent of the man's injuries, and possibly, he is capable of requesting or denying a release of his records. You phone the mother. She indicates that her son is capable of issuing the release but asks again if you can comply with the request because of her guardianship.

What issues are involved? What do you decide?

____

____

In-basket Item #10

It's final grades time, and grades are due from faculty in five hours. You see a faculty member ask one of the staff members to look at some students' academic records. The staff member asks why, and he replies that all he wants to look at are the records of students in his class. Before he assigns grades to his students, he wants to get a "feel" for what grades they received in the past.

Would you do anything? Why or why not?

____

____

In-basket Item #11

The wife of one of your students hands one of your staff members a piece of paper which is written and signed permission for the wife to pick up the student's transcript. Is this permissible? Would you permit it?

____

____

In-basket Item #12

Your boss asks you what information you can release over the phone. How do you reply?

____

____

In-basket Item #13

The dean of your college has just had a discussion with the education department head. The department head had requested to see the counseling records in the counselors' office for two education majors. He was requesting this information to determine the students' fitness to become teachers. The counselor refused to provide the information, claiming that the information in the files was "privileged." The dean asks you if the counselor was correct in refusing to provide the information.

How do you respond?

___

___

In-basket Item #14

Jill from the Human Resources Office e-mails that she has just received a call from food services, and she needs some help with a "FERPA question," as she puts it. This morning an FBI agent had visited the manager of food services and had asked to see the work records of a food service employee who was hired under a work-study contract. Jill wants to know if the manager should show the records to the agent. What should you ask her first? What do you tell her?

___

___

In-basket Item #15

An officer from a police department in a nearby town calls. The officer states that they have arrested a person who claims to be a student at your college. He is calling to verify this.

You know that this police department has the policy of releasing students for minor infractions (which is what is involved in this case) if it can be verified that the person is a student.

You check your records and find that this person is a student. However, there is a signed statement from the student that he wants no information on him released.

Do you verify to the officer that this person is a student? Why or why not?

___

___

6.7 College/Registrar Websites Related to FERPA

These websites have a variety of ideas pertaining to FERPA training and information directed to faculty and staff. They are all worth a visit.

- Catholic University of America
  http://counsel.cua.edu/OC/ferpa/index.htm
- Central Virginia Community College
  http://studentservices.cv.cc.va.us/admissions/ferpa.htm
- George Mason University
  http://registrar.gmu.edu/ferpafaqs.html
- Illinois State University
  http://coe.ilstu.edu/portfolios/students/wjpearc/final%20project/ferpa1.htm
- Maricopa County Community College District
  http://www.dist.maricopa.edu/legal/ferparticle.html
- New York University, University Registrar (as part of faculty handbook)
  http://www.nyu.edu/registrar/13faculty.shtml
- University of Connecticut, Office of the Registrar
  http://www.registrar.uconn.edu/ferpa.html
- University of Nebraska at Kearney
  http://www.unk.edu/departments/registrar/home.html
- University of Nebraska at Omaha
  http://www.ses.unomaha.edu/ppt/ferpa/
- University of Puget Sound, Office of the Registrar
  http://www.ups.edu/registrar/indes.htm
- University System of Maryland, Student Information System Project http://ferpa.sis.usmd.edu/ferpaweb/
- Washington and Lee University
  http://www.wlu.edu/registrar/ferpa.htm

6.8 A FERPA Brochure

The following is the content of an institutional brochure about FERPA. It was designed to fit on a one-page, 8.5" x 11", double-sided, trifold handout to employees of the institution, students, and other interested parties. It was not designed to substitute for the annual notification to students, but with a little work and thought, it could become that.

Family Educational Rights and Privacy Act (FERPA) Guidelines for Central Virginia Community College

The Family Educational Rights and Privacy Act Informational Guidelines

What is FERPA?

The Family Educational Rights and Privacy Act of 1974 helps protect the privacy of student education records. The Act provides for the right to inspect and review education records, the right to seek to amend those records, and the right to limit disclosure of information from the records. The intent of the legislation is to protect the rights of students and to ensure the privacy and accuracy of education records. The Act applies to all institutions that are recipients of federal aid administered by the Secretary of Education.

What rights does FERPA afford students with respect to their education records?

- The right to inspect and review their education records within 45 days of the day the college receives a request for access.

  Students should submit to the Coordinator of Admissions and Records written requests that identify the record(s) they wish to inspect. The coordinator will make arrangements for access and notify the student of the time and place where the records may be inspected. If the records are not maintained in the Office of Admissions and Records, the coordinator will advise the student of the correct official to whom the request should be addressed.

- The right to request an amendment to the student's education records that the student believes are inaccurate or misleading.

  Students may ask the college to amend a record that they believe is inaccurate or misleading. They should write the Coordinator of Admissions and Records, clearly identify the part of the record they want changed, and specify why it is inaccurate or misleading.

  If the college decides not to amend the record as requested by the student, the college will notify the student of the decision and advise the student of his or her right to a hearing regarding the request for amendment. Additional information regarding the hearing will be provided to the student when notified of a hearing.

- The right to consent to disclosures of personally identifiable information contained in the student's education records, except to the extent that FERPA authorizes disclosure without consent.

  One exception which permits disclosure without consent is disclosure to school officials with legitimate educational interests. A school official is a person employed by the college in an administrative, supervisory, academic or research, or support staff position (including law enforcement unit personnel and health staff); a person or company with whom the college has contracted (such as an attorney, auditor, or collection agent); a person serving on the Board of Trustees; or a student serving on an official committee, such as a disciplinary or grievance committee, or assisting another school official in performing his or her tasks.

  A school official has a legitimate educational interest if the official needs to review an education record in order to fulfill his or her professional responsibility.

- The right to file a complaint with the U.S. Department of Education concerning alleged failures by the college to comply with the requirements of FERPA. The name and address of the office that administers FERPA is:

  Family Policy Compliance Office
U.S. Department of Education
400 Maryland Ave., SW
Washington, DC 20202-4605

Who is protected under FERPA?

Students who are currently or formerly enrolled, regardless of their age or status in regard to parental dependency. Students who have applied to but have not attended an institution and deceased students do not come under FERPA guidelines.

Parents of students termed as "dependent" for income tax purposes may have access to the student's education records. A copy of the parent's most recent federal income tax return, on which the parents declared the student as a dependent, must be submitted to the Office of Admissions and Records to document "dependency."

What are education records?

With certain exceptions, an education record is any record (1) from which a student can be personally identified and (2) maintained by the college. A student has the right of access to these records.

Education records include any records in whatever medium (handwritten, print, magnetic tape, film, diskette, etc.) that are in the possession of any school official. This includes transcripts or other records obtained from a school at which a student was previously enrolled.

What is not included in an education record?

- Sole possession records or private notes held by school officials that are not accessible or released to other personnel;
- law enforcement or campus security records that are solely for law enforcement purposes and maintained solely by the law enforcement unit;
- records relating to individuals who are employed by the institution (unless contingent upon attendance);
- records relating to treatment provided by a physician, psychiatrist, psychologist, or other recognized professional or paraprofessional and disclosed only to individuals providing treatment; and
- records of an institution that contain information about an individual obtained only after that person is no longer a student at that institution, i.e., alumni records.

What is directory information?

Institutions may disclose information on a student without violating FERPA if it has designated that information as "directory information." At CVCC this includes a student's:

- name;
- address;
- telephone number;
- major field of study;
- dates of attendance;
- current enrollment status (full time/part time);
- class standing;
- receipt or non-receipt of a degree; and
- academic awards received (dean's list, honor roll).

How does a student authorize release of his or her education record in the form of an academic transcript?

Students must authorize the release of their transcripts by written requests with signatures or by completing and signing transcript request forms available in the Office of Admissions and Records. There is no fee for transcripts. The receipt of a written request via fax with signature to release an education record is permissible.

Who may have access to student information?

- The student and any outside party who has the student's written request;
- school officials (as defined by the college) who have "legitimate educational interests";
- parents of a dependent student as defined by the Internal Revenue Code; and
- a person in response to a lawfully issued subpoena or court order, as long as the college first makes a reasonable attempt to notify the student. Normally, the college will comply with a subpoena after two weeks have elapsed from the day the subpoena was received.

When is the student's consent not required to disclose information?

When the disclosure is:

- to school officials (defined in policy) who have a legitimate educational interest;
- to federal, state, and local authorities involving an audit or evaluation of compliance with educational programs;
- in connection with financial aid (this includes veterans' benefits);
- to organizations conducting studies for or on behalf of educational institutions;
- to accrediting organizations;
- to parents of a dependent student;
- to comply with a judicial order or subpoena;
- in a health or safety emergency;
- releasing directory information;
- releasing the results of a disciplinary hearing to an alleged victim of a crime of violence.

How does increasing technology impact FERPA on our campuses?

The use of computerized recordkeeping systems is increasing at a fast pace. We can anticipate that the distribution of electronic data eventually will replace most paper documents and provide much information about students to school officials through desktop terminals. It is the responsibility of each school official to understand his or her legal responsibilities under FERPA. The same principles of confidentiality that apply to paper records also apply to electronic data.

6.9 A FERPA Audit

Do you wonder if your campus is meeting the requirements of FERPA? Use the following questions/checklist to conduct a basic self-assessment of your office and/or campus.

Who on your campus is responsible for FERPA compliance?

- Typically, this responsibility falls to the Registrar's Office, but Legal Affairs or Academic Affairs might also hold it.

If you are the "point person" for FERPA on your campus, have you received appropriate training?

- AACRAO sponsors FERPA workshops throughout the year at various locations across the country. Visit the AACRAO website (http://www.aacrao.org) for details.
- FERPA is always a topic of several sessions at national AACRAO meetings.
- Other professional organizations [e.g., state/regional divisions of AACRAO, the Center for Policy in Higher Education (CPHE)] sponsor FERPA-related sessions or presentations each year.
- Have you read this publication, and do you understand the important concepts and terms within FERPA that are discussed here?

What resources can you utilize in addressing FERPA issues on your campus?

- Do you have a Legal Affairs or General Counsel resource (with someone on staff who is knowledgeable about FERPA)?
- Professional colleagues, professional associations, e.g. AACRAO, the National Association of College and University Attorneys (NACUA), CPHE, and publications from those entities are excellent resources. For example, NACUA has published an outstanding complement to this publication: *The Family Educational Rights and Privacy Act: A Legal Compendium* by Stephen McDonald.
- The Family Compliance Office in the U.S. Department of Education—particularly given its expanding website materials—is an excellent source of information and answers to problem situations. http://www.ed.gov/offices/OM/fpco.html
- The federal guidelines (known as the regulations) regarding FERPA are also helpful. (See Appendix 2.)

Do you have a records retention plan?

- While FERPA does not include a records retention plan, it does have a direct impact on access to and use of existing records. Having an up-to-date records retention plan is good policy for any office that works regularly with important institutional records. For example, under FERPA, if students request access to their education records, you can't destroy those records, if they still exist, until after the student has seen them. You can, however, tell a student who has requested to see his education records that those records have been destroyed (if that has occurred), as long as they were destroyed in accordance with the institution's records retention plan.

What security policies and protocols do you have in place on your campus?

- This is a critical area related to FERPA, particularly in this age of greater reliance on technology.
- Who is responsible for security controls and policy decisions regarding security in your networked/electronic environment?
- Ideally, you should establish security controls which limit access to those who should/need to have access in order to do their jobs. This refers to the FERPA concept of "legitimate educational interest" or the "educational need to know." In many older systems, student database maintenance is more tightly controlled than providing users viewing access to student records; therefore, consider both viewing and maintenance capabilities.
- Perform an analysis of roles and security-related decision-making procedures on your campus. For example, you are likely to have "sets" of common security protocols for staff advisors, faculty, office processing staff, student staff, etc. Once established, such "sets" make it easier to administer and manage security issues.

What training requirements and policies do you have in place regarding FERPA and student records?

- Do you have mandatory training for persons who have access to student records—particularly via technology?
- If so, must/should that training occur prior to receiving access (e.g., the staff person doesn't receive a password until after he or she has completed training)?
- Who is responsible for training? Is it a centralized (e.g., the Registrar's Office) or decentralized function (e.g., every department that has access to student data)?
- Consider all the options available for training and education: videotapes, workshops, documentation (both for training and for reference), and use of case studies. Some examples of training materials are included in this manual.
- Consider tailoring training for the audience involved; make it relevant for them. The needs and issues for faculty are very different from those for front-line staff in the Registrar's Office.
- What steps do you take to provide ongoing training and/or updates to the campus community? There will always be staff and faculty new to your campus, and others will change roles. Reminders about FERPA, particularly for those who don't regularly deal with security issues, and as technology and other means of access evolve, are very important.

- See Fig. 6.9A for an example of a "short course" in FERPA responsibilities for faculty and staff.

What expectations of accountability do you have for those who have access to student data?

- Do you have any written "sign-off" of responsibility by staff? Such a document is useful to clarify expectations, set appropriate limits, and give notice of consequences if the expectations are not met. Be sure to include an expectation to report violations. See Figs. 6.9A and 6.9B for examples of "sign-offs" that two institutions use.
- Ensure that you tie access directly to each staff person. For example, don't structure your security access so that multiple people use the same ID/password/pass code, and actively discourage everyone from sharing their pass codes with others—even on a temporary basis.
- Do you have tracking capabilities within the system—an "audit trail"—particularly for maintenance? This capability will be very important when researching problems or alleged violations of security.

Fig. 6.9A: Sample "Short Course" and "Sign-Off" Form

FERPA FOR FACULTY AND STAFF

A short course on the Family Educational Rights and Privacy Act of 1974 as Amended

- **Faculty and staff may disclose the following directory information upon request:**
  - ⇒ Previous dates of attendance
  - ⇒ Degrees and awards received (to include honors)
  - ⇒ Previous educational agencies or institutions attended
- **At the discretion of the College, additional directory information may be released (inquire at Records Office)**
- **Other information may be released with the student's written consent. Such written consent must (a) specify the records to be released, (b) state the purpose of the disclosure, (c) identify the party or class of parties to whom disclosure may be made, and (d) be signed and dated by the student.**

To fulfill the basic requirements for compliance with the Act, each educational institution must prevent improper disclosure of personally identifiable information from education records, provide opportunity for challenge of the contents of education records as required by FERPA and the regulations, and maintain adequate records of requests and disclosures.

An institution is not required to disclose information from a student's education records to the parents of dependent students (as established by Internal Revenue Code of 1954, Section 152). It is the responsibility of an institution to ensure that information is not improperly disclosed to the parents of students. Please refer parental requests for information to the Records Office.

- **LCCC will disclose information for a student's educational records only with the written consent of the student, except:**
  - ⇒ To school officials who have a legitimate educational interest in the records
  - ⇒ To certain officials of the U.S. Department of Education, The Comptroller General, and state and local educational authorities in connection with certain state or federally supported education programs
  - ⇒ In connection with a student's request for or receipt of financial aid as necessary to determine the eligibility, amount or conditions of the financial aid, or to enforce the terms and conditions of the aid
  - ⇒ If required by a state law requiring disclosure that was adopted before November 19, 1974
  - ⇒ To organizations conducting certain studies for or on behalf of the College
  - ⇒ To accrediting organizations to carry out their functions
  - ⇒ To comply with a judicial order or a lawfully issued subpoena provided that the institution makes a reasonable attempt to notify the student in advance of compliance
  - ⇒ To appropriate parties in a health or safety emergency

My signature affirms that I have read the above document and agree to comply with the Act. The penalty for noncompliance with Federal regulations can be withdrawal of Department of Education funds from the institution.

Printed Name	Legal Signature	Today's Date

Do (or should) you have a FERPA policy on your campus?

- Recent amendments to FERPA removed the requirement that every institution have a policy.
- You are still required to annually notify students about FERPA. What must be included in the annual notification?
  - The right to inspect and review their records (and how to do that);
  - The right to seek amendments to their records (and how to do that);
  - The right to consent to disclosure (with exceptions);
  - The right to obtain a copy of the institution's policy (if there is one);
  - The right to file a complaint.

  Other elements in your notification should include:
  - Definition of "school officials" and "legitimate educational interest" (educational need to know);
  - Whether it is the institution's policy to release records information, without the student's written consent, to another school at which the student is enrolled or seeks to enroll;
  - What the institution considers directory information;
  - The option a student has to request "no release" (non-disclosure) of directory information. You are encouraged to include the consequences of choosing this option (e.g., the student's name won't appear in an institutional directory).

See Appendix 14 of this publication for a Model Annual Notification to Students prepared by the Family Policy Compliance Office. (It can also be viewed at http://www.ed.gov/offices/OM/fpco/psi1.html.)

Students must receive notification of this information at least annually.

The mechanism of distribution is not specified—therefore, it could be included with registration materials, included in a student handbook, or sent via e-mail if that is a regular means of communicating with your students.

- Why might your campus still want to have a FERPA policy?
  - It's excellent documentation for staff and faculty educational and training purposes.
  - It's excellent documentation to use when someone—particularly a student, family members, and others in the campus community—has questions about data access and security. It also provides for consistency in responding to those questions.
  - It's excellent documentation to prove institutional policies in the event that a FERPA-related problem does arise—and it helps protect institutional "memory."

Fig. 6.9B: Sample "Sign-Off" Form

CODE OF RESPONSIBILITY FOR SECURITY AND CONFIDENTIALITY OF DATA

Both federal law (the Family Educational Rights and Privacy Act of 1974 and amendments) and state law (The Ohio Revised Code Section 102) are in effect to insure the security and confidentiality of information used in our operations is guaranteed. Thus, security and confidentiality is a matter of concern for all employees within the Office of the University Registrar and any other persons who have access to our data systems or physical facilities. Each person working in the Office of the University Registrar holds a position of trust relative to this information and must recognize the responsibilities entrusted to them and this office in preserving the security and confidentiality of this information. Therefore, each employee of this department, and any person authorized access to any information through the facilities of this department is:

1. Not to make or permit unauthorized use of any information.
2. Not to seek personal benefit or permit others to benefit personally by any confidential information which has come to them by virtue of their work assignment and in accordance with University and office policies.
3. Not to exhibit or divulge the contents of any record or report to any person except in the conduct of their work assignment in accordance with University and office policies.
4. Not to knowingly include or cause to be included in any record or report a false, inaccurate or misleading entry.
5. Not to remove any official record (or copy) or report from the office where it is kept except in the performance of their duties.
6. Not to operate or request others to operate any University equipment for purely personal business.
7. Not to aid, abet, or act in conspiracy with another to violate any part of this code.
8. To immediately report any violation of this code to his or her supervisor.

While your supervisor can assist you in understanding these policies and how we must operate within them, you should become familiar with its provisions, particularly those regarding required consent to release information, the list of information which can be released for currently enrolled students without consent, and how information is designated when the student has indicated that it cannot be released.

When the student has chosen to indicate information is not to be released, the requestor should be advised "that we are unable to release any information" and be given no indication of whether or not you may have any information on the person. You are advised to refer any questions or requests for information that you are unsure of to your supervisor.

As custodians of official University records, we all share the responsibility for ensuring the security and privacy of the records and data we maintain. Please study the attached document and, after you have read it, sign the statement below. This acknowledgement will be retained in your personnel file.

A violation of this policy may lead to reprimand, suspension, dismissal or other disciplinary action, consistent with the general personnel policies of the University, and the Code of Student Conduct for student employees.

In addition, The Ohio Revised Code specifies:

"No present or former public official or employee shall disclose or use, without an appropriate authorization, any information acquired by him in the course of his official duties which is confidential because of statutory provisions, or which has been clearly designated to him as confidential when such confidential designation is warranted because of the status of the proceedings or the circumstances under which the information was received and preserving its confidentiality is necessary to the proper conduct of government business."

Conviction for violation of this statute is a first degree misdemeanor (up to 6 month imprisonment and/or $1000 fine).

I, ______________________________, hereby affirm that I have read The Ohio State University's policy statement on Student Rights Under the Family Educational Rights and Privacy Act, of 1974 as Amended, and the foregoing statement. I understand the obligations imposed by these documents and will comply with the standards and requirements contained therein. I have retained in my possession a copy of the document for future reference.

____

Signature   Date

Are you meeting the recordkeeping requirements of FERPA?

- Under FERPA, you must record certain requests for and releases of personally identifiable records information. You are responsible to collect the following:
  - the date the information was released;
  - to whom it was released;
  - what records were released; and
  - the purpose of the request.
- You do not have to keep records for releases:
  - to the student;
  - to school officials (with the appropriate "educational need to know");
  - with the written consent of the student;
  - of directory information (assuming the student does not have a "no release"/requested non-disclosure).

Do you have appropriate institutional policies and everyday practices in place?

This is a practical encouragement for you and the appropriate people on your campus to discuss, then implement, FERPA-related policies and practices related to situations/issues that might result in FERPA violations. It is always best to be proactive in minimizing the risk of a FERPA violation by providing training and identifying potential illegal releases of student information. This is particularly relevant with regard to the release of information to third parties.

Here are just a few examples:

- In a practical sense, how do you balance appropriate access to information with the legitimate protection of a student's privacy? Have you created procedures for people to get information they need to conduct their business, without compromising the student's privacy? For example, can someone in the business community easily confirm the attendance or degree of one of your students (assuming the student has not requested that you withhold directory information/"no release")?

Fig. 6.9c: Sample Exclusion Form

The State University of New Jersey

RUTGERS

Directory Information Exclusion Form

Important Information Regarding the Distribution of Your Student Directory Information

The confidentiality of students' educational records is protected by the Family Educational Rights and Privacy Act (FERPA), a federal law. However, FERPA allows the University to release student "directory information" without a student's consent unless the student has requested such information be kept confidential. Rutgers defines "directory information" as the following: name, campus address, campus post office address, campus telephone number, Rutgers e-mail address, permanent address and telephone number, school of attendance, major field of study, class year, dates of attendance, current credit load, credit hours earned, degree(s) received, and dates of degree(s).

The two most common ways in which Rutgers releases student directory information are:

1. Through the Verifications Division of the Office of the Registrar or similar offices that have access to student records. The Verification Division is called upon to verify that a student is enrolled at the University by potential employers, credit agencies, and others. Directory information as defined above may be made available through other offices with access to student records upon similar request.
2. Through the "Finding People" database available through the principal Rutgers website (http://www.rutgers.edu) and accessible worldwide via Internet. This data base does not list campus residence address, but does list many of the other categories of directory information.

Rutgers offers students the option to keep directory information confidential. However, please be advised that doing so will make this important information unavailable to all, including prospective employers, credit agencies, and others to whom you may want this

(continued on next page)

- What does your institution consider to be "directory information?" The list included in the regulations is not intended to be absolute. So long as you do not include data elements that would be considered an invasion of a student's privacy, e.g., religion, citizenship, grades, SSN, etc., you may choose additional data items. Likewise, you do not have to include everything on the list of examples in the regulations. One common misconception is that students may request that an institution block the disclosure of all information about them. This is not correct, and it is incumbent upon you to clarify this misconception.

- What are your institution's non-disclosure ("no release") practices? Can a student have some elements suppressed (e.g., a telephone number) without necessarily suppressing all directory information? How do you receive a non-disclosure ("no release") request from your students? Do they understand the ramifications of making that decision? How does a staff person know that a student has a non-disclosure request on his or her records? Is it easy to discern that within your electronic records? See Fig. 6.9c for an example of one institution's form for students to request non-disclosure of their directory information.

- How does a student gain access to his or her record (the right to inspect and review)? Will you routinely provide a copy, if requested? Will you charge for that copy (and, if so, how much)? Do you have an expectation of how quickly you will respond to such a request?

- How does a student request an amendment to his or her record? The regulations contain a very basic protocol which focuses on the issues of timing and notification, but does your campus have a more specific policy in this area?

- What procedures do you have in place for releasing information to the parents of dependent students? This is a common question, so you should have a protocol in place that can be followed consistently across campus. In this area, what is the student development philosophy of your institution? How do you balance the role of the parents with the desire to regard the students as independent adults? How do you ask parents to validate dependency? How do you build the student into the notification loop? Do you have "pre-waivers" by students—general (all records that the student would have access to) or specific (e.g., financial information only)? See Fig. 6.9D (page 77) for an example of an authorization to release specific information to parents. This illustration also points to a commonly overlooked FERPA situation: discussing tuition/receivables bills with parents without the student's written permission. Have you examined this issue at your institution?

- What do you consider to be a valid signature or authorization for release of information? A faxed signature can be considered valid—but is that in your policies? The new federal Electronic Signatures in Global and National Commerce Act may significantly alter the way we conduct business, so we need to watch the development of this area very closely.

- Do you have an established procedure to respond to subpoenas? Unless the subpoena on its face legally prohibits you from doing so, you must inform the student as part of the process.
- Do you routinely release results of disciplinary proceedings to alleged victims?
- How do you treat the records of deceased students? FERPA rights, and the right to privacy, legally end at death, so this is an institutional policy decision.
- With the most recent amendments to FERPA, we now have the authority to inform the parents of students under the age of 21 (even if they are not dependent) that their child has violated laws or rules related to alcohol or drugs. However, we are not required to do so. Does (or should) your institution routinely do that?

Fig. 6.9c: Sample Exclusion Form (continued)

information known, or verified. Thus it is recommended that students carefully consider whether personal privacy concerns outweigh the potential inconvenience of having directory information withheld. Submitting this form will make your directory information confidential until you request in writing to the Registrar's Office that this restriction be lifted. As with all confidential student records, Rutgers University will release information to specific individuals or entities only with the express written consent of the student or as otherwise required by law.

For questions about compliance with FERPA, call the Director of Compliance and Student Policy Concerns at (732) 932-7312, Extension 11.

To continue to allow the release of your directory information, do nothing. If you wish Rutgers to keep your directory information confidential, **please print out this page** and circle the **YES** below, print your name, provide your 9-digit student identification number (Social Security number), sign and date this form, and return it to:

Office of the Registrar
Rutgers, The State University of NJ
Armitage Hall, Room 143
311 North 5th Street
Camden, New Jersey 08102-1499
ATTN: VERIFICATIONS

I want Rutgers to keep my directory information confidential: YES / NO

Name (Please Print): ________________

Student Identification Number (9-digit): ________________

Signature: ________________

Date: ________________

Rev. 9/98

These are some examples of the issues you will want to address in your planning, policy making, and implementation of procedures. This manual includes examples of training materials, solutions to potential problem situations, and a wealth of other practical information. Utilize these materials to help you and your campus identify the issues you want to address as you evaluate your institution's FERPA compliance.

6.10 Family Policy Compliance Office— Vital Information in Case Everything Else Fails

Family Policy Compliance Office
LeRoy Rooker, Director
U.S. Department of Education
400 Independence Ave., SW
Washington, DC 20202-4605

(202) 260-9002 (fax)
ferpa@ed.gov
www.ed.gov/offices/OM/fpco.html

Fig. 6.9D: Sample Release Form

CENTRAL MICHIGAN UNIVERSITY

Return form to:
Receivable Accounting
Central Michigan University
Warriner Hall 103
Mt. Pleasant, MI 48859

AUTHORIZATION TO RELEASE INFORMATION

The purpose of the Educational Rights and Privacy Act of 1974 is to protect the privacy of information concerning individual students by placing certain restrictions on the disclosure of information contained in a student's university records. I understand that in order for the Receivable Accounting Office to honor a verbal or written request for information by anyone other then the individual student a signed and notarized authorization must be on file.

Therefore, I ______________________, SS#____________________, authorize the
(PLEASE PRINT CLEARLY)

Central Michigan University Receivable Accounting Office to release information to:

______________________, ______________________.
(NAME) (RELATIONSHIP TO STUDENT)

PLEASE INCUDE BOTH MOTHER AND FATHER'S FIRST NAMES

I understand that this pertains to information regarding ALL of the following: ACCOUNTS RECEIVABLE (itemized charges and credits); FINANCIAL AID (itemized charges, credits, and refunds); HEALTH SERVICES (summarized charges and insurance credits); HOUSING (charges, credits, and itemized damage charges); REGISTRATION (number of credit hours, hours added, and hours dropped); TELEPHONE (summarized charges and credits--Telecommunications Office can be contacted for detailed information).

I would / would not (please circle one) like my Receivable Accounting statements to be sent to my home address:

STREET____

CITY______________________ STATE__________ ZIP CODE __________

TELEPHONE (   ) ____________________

I understand that this mail request applies ONLY to my monthly receivable accounting statements and tuition and fee bills. I also understand that it is my responsibility to modify this form if the above address should change.

The above information will be released with my FULL CONSENT. I understand that this authorization remains in effect from today through ____________ **(Month / Year)**. It will be necessary to send a written letter to revoke this authorization prior to the expiration date I have indicated.

Signature ______________________________ Date______________

STATE OF MICHIGAN)
COUNTY OF) SS:

Subscribed and sworn to before me______________________________ this
NOTARY PUBLIC

__________ day of ______________________, 19__________.

MOUNT PLEASANT, MICHIGAN 48859

Answer Key to FERPA Final Exam

True/False Section

1.	T	5.	T	9.	T	13.	F	17.	F
2.	T	6.	T	10.	T	14.	F	18.	F
3.	F	7.	T	11.	F	15.	F	19.	T
4.	T	8.	F	12.	T	16.	F	20.	F
								21.	T

Multiple Choice Section

22.	e[1]	36.	a	50.	b	53c.	N	54b.	N
23.	c	37.	d	51.	a	53d.	Y	54c.	Y
24.	d	38.	f	52a.	Y	53e.	N	54d.	Y
25.	d[2]	39.	a	52b.	Y	53f.	Y	54e.	N
26.	c	40.	d	52c.	Y	53g.	Y	54f.	Y
27.	a	41.	h	52d.	N	53h.	Y	54g.	N
28.	d	42.	e	52e.	N	53i.	N	54h.	N
29.	b	43.	d	52f.	Y	53j.	N	55a.	Y
30.	a	44.	b	52g.	Y	53k.	Y	55b.	N
31.	d	45.	d	52h.	Y	53l.	Y	55c.	Y
32.	d	46.	g	52i.	Y	53m.	N	55d.	N
33.	b	47.	d	52j.	Y	53n.	N	55e.	N
34.	a	48.	c[3]	53a.	Y	53 Bonus[4]		55f.	Y
35.	a	49.	b	53b.	Y	54a.	Y	55g.	N
								55h.	N

[1] The correct answer would be 45 days.

[2] Whether he has requested that any directory information not be disclosed, and that items a, b, and c are considered directory information by your institution.

[3] **Reason for choosing answer c:** If a student's home address is not designated as directory information, the institution must obtain each student's written permission to include it in the student directory.

[4] **Bonus:** If it is not an "education record," FERPA does not apply or FERPA only applies to "education records."

Brain Stretchers

56. An institution cannot tell a student what items of directory information can and cannot be subject to non-disclosure. The right of non-disclosure is the student's right exclusively. The institution may identify items of directory information, but it may not place any conditions on a student's right to block any directory information.

57. "The institution may release other information on students without written permission of the student if the release can be justified under one of the exceptions to written permission found in FERPA."

    Section 34 CFR 99.31.

58. Two possibilities:

    (1) Obtain written permission of each student in the class to share his or her e-mail address with other students in the class.

    (2) A better long-term solution would be for the institution to identify e-mail address as directory information. Before doing so, however, it would have to notify students of that intent. Students then would have to be given a period of time to request that their e-mail addresses not be disclosed (right of non-disclosure).

    The institution needs to answer the question of when to notify students about adding an item to directory information to its list. If it is in the middle of the academic year, this would necessitate a special notification to all students with the attendant period for them to request that their e-mail addresses not be disclosed. If the decision to notify students could wait until the institution annually notified students of their FERPA rights, this would save the time and effort required for a special mid-year notification and would make the notification process more efficient.

    Even if e-mail addresses were included as directory information, a special procedure would have to be created to identify any student in any class wishing to use this teaching tool that shared e-mail addresses with all students in the class. This procedure would identify any student in the class who had requested non-disclosure of his or her e-mail address. The student then could be notified of the implications of his or her non-disclosure for that class and decide if he or she wished to keep the non-disclosure active.

FERPA In-Basket

#1 The student has the FERPA right to review the examination since it meets the definition of "education record," i.e., personally identifiable to the student, maintained by the institution, and not one of the excluded categories from FERPA.

(Forty-five days have elapsed from the first request to review the record, so the institution is in violation of FERPA.)

#2 Yes. The institution may release any directory information on a case-by-case basis as long as the student (while still a student) has not requested non-disclosure. Any student, current or former, may request that the non-disclosure be removed. However, the institution does not have to honor such requests.

Note: The author does not agree with institutional policies that refuse the removal of a hold on directory information.

#3 (a) Yes. At most institutions, this would be considered a valid exercise of "legitimate educational interest." However, each institution determines what constitutes a legitimate educational interest.

(b) No. This should be part of the annual notification to students required by FERPA.

(c) Yes. Same reason as above—legitimate educational interest.

(d) Yes. Students are notified annually re: legitimate educational interest.

(e) Yes. FERPA does not require any training, but training is strongly recommended for all users of "education records."

#4 (a) It is probably not a FERPA violation to continue the status quo, but all users need to be trained regarding their responsibilities under FERPA.

(b) "Federal law (FERPA) requires that you must have a valid professional reason for viewing this class roll."

(c) (Open ended.) Given the current situation, the academic administrators should take the initiative and formulate a policy regarding access to the screens and notify everyone of this policy. It is better to have something in writing than to merely make a decision and communicate it verbally to those who need to know.

#5 The lawyer is partially correct. FERPA rights pass to the student at age 18 or when he or she begins attending a college or university. Parents have only those rights of access that the student or institution gives to the parents. [Multiple choice question #45 identifies the three ways that parents can gain access to their child's records (a, b, c).]

#6 The institution is not obligated to release directory information to anyone since FERPA states an institution "may" release. It doesn't have to.

#7 Our institution's policy is to release student information directly, and only, to students. The only valid ways that we would consider releasing information to you are (1) written permission from the student, (2) proof of your child's dependency (not applicable in this case since you do not pay federal income taxes and, therefore, you cannot provide a federal income tax return), and (3) a legally issued subpoena itemizing the specific information you wish to review.

#8 FERPA only requires institutions to provide access to education records. It does not require that you make copies of any records unless geographic distance of more than 50 miles precludes personal inspection. Professional courtesy and the fact that another institution's records on that student may have changed are two reasons for not copying other institutions' transcripts for students.

#9 Dependency, legal guardianship, written permission of the student, emergency situation—probably give to the mother after her submission of legal guardianship papers. Of course, obtaining the student's written permission, if at all possible, has the highest priority.

#10 Yes. This is not, in your mind, a valid exercise of legitimate educational interest, and you should call the dean after denying access to the faculty member. Grades are independent evaluative judgments made by a faculty member regarding a student's performance in one class. They should be assigned without any intervening external variables, such as past academic performance.

#11 It is permissible. You have the student's written permission to release the transcript to the spouse, and that is what FERPA requires. You do need to verify that the signature is the student's. You may, however, deny the release to the wife if your policy indicates release to the student only or if you question the signature of the student.

#12 Without the student's written permission, you can release what we identify as "directory information"; and you can release this information at your discretion.

Non-directory information can be released without written permission of the student if the release falls under one of the exceptions to written permission in FERPA (34 CFR 99.31).

#13 The counselor's records are "education records" and subject to FERPA. They are not sole possession notes and are not being used for the "treatment" of a student medically. Therefore, the department head may have access to these records as long as the dean determines that the department head has a "legitimate educational interest" (we are assuming here that all personnel fall under the definition of "school official" under FERPA). This is a determination for the dean.

#14 First question—does the agent have a signed release (written permission) from the student indicating that the agent can see the records requested?

If "yes," the food services manager may provide the information to the agent, although FERPA does not require it.

If "no," the food services manager should not release the information (work-study employment records are subject to FERPA).

#15 No. The student has placed a non-disclosure on this information, and you are honoring this request. (This actually happened.)

Chapter Seven

How Would You Handle...?

THE CASES IN THIS CHAPTER WILL TEST THE READER'S KNOWLEDGE AND STRENGTHEN HIS OR HER UNDERSTANDING OF FERPA. MOST OF THE CASES ARE REAL AND REFLECT ACTUAL SITUATIONS THAT HAVE OCCURRED WITHIN HIGHER EDUCATION SINCE FERPA WAS ENACTED. THESE CASES, THEREFORE, HAVE TESTED MANY PROFESSIONALS' KNOWLEDGE OF FERPA AND ARE PRESENTED HERE AS A WAY OF PREPARING READERS FOR ACTUAL SITUATIONS THEY MAY ENCOUNTER. THE FORMAT FOR ALL CASES IN THIS CHAPTER IS THE SAME: THE READER IS PRESENTED WITH A SITUATION, OR DOCUMENT, WHICH REQUIRES KNOWLEDGE OF FERPA TO RESOLVE. THE RESOLUTION TO EACH CASE IS FOUND DIRECTLY AFTER THE CASE. IN READING THE RESOLUTION OF EACH CASE, THE READER SHOULD REMEMBER THERE MIGHT BE MORE THAN ONE CORRECT RESOLUTION. THIS CAN BE A RESULT OF THE VARIETY OF LEGAL APPROACHES DIFFERENT INSTITUTIONS TAKE IN COMPLYING WITH FERPA. BECAUSE OF THEIR CONTINUED UTILITY, MANY CASES HAVE BEEN CARRIED OVER FROM THE 1998 EDITION; OTHERS HAVE BEEN ADDED TO REFLECT THE MOST CURRENT ISSUES RELEVANT TO TODAY'S FERPA PRACTITIONERS.

7.1 Legitimate Educational Interest

7.1.1 Campus Ministry Request for "Students by Country of Citizenship"

1 Your institution does not consider the student's country of citizenship to be directory information.

The University Campus Ministry, an organization affiliated with your institution, requests a list of foreign students by country of citizenship. The purpose of this request is "to make them feel at home."

Do you comply?

2 This same group also requests a directory of all students listing local and permanent addresses and local and permanent phone numbers. All of these items except the permanent phone number are considered directory information.

Do you comply?

Resolution:

Question **1**—No.

The University Campus Ministry does not have official recognition on campus, and its leaders do not have FERPA status as "school officials." The ministry was entitled to directory information only and received only a list of students.

Question **2**—Yes and No.

You release directory information only for those students who have not placed a "no release" (non-disclosure) on that information. Non-directory information can be released in similar situations only if the students have signed a written authorization specifically permitting you to do so.

7.1.2 Alumni Office Wanting Access to Admissions Applications

The Development and Alumni Offices are continuously accessing students' admissions applications to determine whether potential donors (such as parents or other relatives) are listed on the applications. In accessing these files, the staff from the Development and Alumni Offices also have access to all other information in students' folders, including letters of recommendation, petitions, grade reports, etc. You have questioned this practice but were told that although this might not be a "legitimate educational interest," it was in the institution's interest to raise as much money as possible to further its educational mission.

You are concerned about the confidentiality of the information in these folders and the uncontrolled "searching," as you see it, by these two offices.

What do you do?

Resolution:

The registrar first discussed the situation with his superior, outlining the sections of FERPA that related to "legitimate educational interest." He then got his superior's support to require that each employee of the two offices who viewed these records complete a form documenting the students' records reviewed, the date inspected, and the reasons for the review.

Subsequent to this case, the Family Policy Compliance Office stated "Nothing in FERPA would prevent a college from designating individuals who work in the Office of Institutional Advancement as school officials with legitimate educational interests in its student records policy." Therefore, disclosure of these records could be made to the Development and Alumni Offices without written permission of the students under the section of FERPA that permits release to "school officials" with "legitimate educational interests." [34 CFR 99.31 (a)(1)] (Letter from LeRoy S. Rooker to Ms. Shirley LaPointe, Merrimack College, July 2, 1996.)

7.1.3 Access to Student Information to Write a Letter of Recommendation

The Liberal Arts Office at your institution receives a request from a faculty member in the History Department for a copy of a student's record to help him write a recommendation for the student. Since only the Registrar's Office and the Liberal Arts Office can access the student's record online, the faculty member is requesting this assistance.

Can he receive a copy of the record?

Resolution:

In this instance, the response depends on whether the institution's FERPA policy defines this as a "legitimate educational interest." The professor is a "school official," but if the institution has not used wording that would identify this practice as a "legitimate educational interest," the request should be denied. If this practice has been identified as a legitimate educational interest, the professor should be informed that the written permission of the student is required if any information included in the recommendation is an "education record" (grades, GPA, and other non-directory information). The professor also needs to be advised that personal observations about the student are acceptable comments that can be included in the recommendation without the student's written permission.

7.1.4 Request for Grades of Work-Study Students

You receive a call from the Financial Aid Office requesting that the grades of work-study students who are "in trouble" be sent to their supervisors.

Can you comply?

Resolution:

This depends on whom the institution's FERPA policy identifies as "school officials" and what a "legitimate educational interest" is. In this particular case, the registrar provided the information to the supervisors since they were included under the definition of "school official" in the institutional FERPA policy. The request also revealed that the institution really hadn't formulated a policy on what it considered a "legitimate educational interest." It has since done so.

7.1.5 Student Support Services Requests Information from Financial Aid Office on Low-Income Students

The Director of the Student Support Services (SSS) Office has asked the Financial Aid Office for a list of students who are low-income and/or first-generation students. He wants this list so he can notify them of the support services available to them (through a federal grant) and to offer new incoming students a "scholarship" to attend orientation. This information is contained on the financial aid application forms.

The Director of Financial Aid has declined to provide such a list to SSS because he believes it violates FERPA. The SSS director has called a meeting for Tuesday afternoon with the financial aid director, legal counsel, and you (the registrar). The legal counsel has already said that because SSS is part of the university, the director is entitled to this information.

You know that he is not entitled to it just because "he is part of the university." But, because this information is contained only on the financial aid application that is part of the student information system that only financial aid has access to, you are inclined to agree with the financial aid director.

Is this a correct conclusion?

Resolution:

At the meeting, it was determined that the information requested did fall under FERPA (personally identifiable, maintained by the institution) and that all the players involved were "school officials." However, because legal counsel did not have a clear understanding of legitimate educational interest, the decision was deferred until legal counsel could contact the Family Policy Compliance Office.

After contacting the Family Policy Compliance Office, legal counsel determined that the institution did not have a clear statement on what constituted a legitimate educational interest. It was agreed that one would be developed; in the meantime, SSS would be provided the requested information on a one-time-only basis.

7.1.6 Designating Agents

The Director of Development has asked you about FERPA regulations with regard to alumni. She is contracting with a service that will look for "lost" alumni. However, the service wants social security numbers in addition to names, last known addresses, etc. You're not concerned about the names and addresses, but you express serious concern about releasing social security numbers.

At your school, alumni are considered to be any students who were awarded a degree **and** individuals who have completed a substantial number of credits (100) at your school.

Could this information be provided?

Resolution:

In its definition of "school official," the institution could identify a third party acting for the institution that provides a service the institution normally would provide itself. Two examples of this type of agency designation are the National Student Loan Clearinghouse (certifies student enrollments to institutional lenders) and Credentials, Inc. (certifies enrollment and degrees for employer verification services).

Therefore, institutions may disclose personally identifiable information from education records to an outside contractor without prior written student consent if (1) the institution has specified criteria for determining school officials, including outside contractors who perform a service for the institution, and (2) the institutional definition of "legitimate educational interests" is broad enough to encompass the contractor as a "party acting for" the institution and the contractor is performing a service the institution otherwise would have to perform for itself (see 34 CFR 99.3 (b)(a)(2). The third party contractor, who would now be classified a "school official," must understand that its responsibilities under FERPA are no different from those of any other institutional "school official" and that releases of any student's education record information must be within FERPA guidelines. This includes not releasing social security numbers without the students' written permission to third parties that are not "school officials."

For example, a school could enter into a contract with a private company to obtain services that it would ordinarily provide for itself and disclose student education records to that company to the extent necessary for the company to provide its service to the institution. In this case, just like the institution, the alumni search company under contract would have access to student education records. It could not disclose, or redisclose, the social security numbers of students, for example, in order to locate them. This is because a party that is acting for an institution must treat all information that it receives from that institution as if it were itself an "educational institution," and therefore it may not generally redisclose any information from education records without appropriate consent. While the alumni search company could not redisclose most personally identifiable information from education records that it receives from the postsecondary institution (including social security numbers), the company could redisclose appropriately designated directory information (e.g., student names and addresses).

This legal, agent relationship with the institution is not applicable when the service that the company provides is outside what a school ordinarily would provide for itself. For example, contracting with a long distance phone service or a bank does not, in turn, allow a school to disclose student records to the phone service or the bank. That is because their services are not ones that a school would ordinarily provide for itself. On the other hand, institutions may disclose education records without students' consent to parties with which it has a contract, such as outside legal counsel, collection agents, or, in this case, an alumni search company, if a legitimate educational interest exists for the release of the student records to that company.

Note: This case was first included in the 1998 edition of this publication, just after the Family Policy Compliance Office had provided guidance on how institutions could establish agency relationships with colleges and universities. The resolution that was included in the 1998 edition caused some confusion because some readers believed that the Family Policy Compliance Office had ONLY approved the National Student Loan Clearinghouse as an agent "acting for" an institution for a specific purpose. To clarify matters, the author wrote the following letter:

October 22, 2000

To Whom It May Concern:

RE: Designating Agents; Compliance with FERPA

I have been asked to clarify the topic of "Designating Agents" as it pertains to providing non-directory information to a service provider that performs a service on behalf of participating schools.

In Chapter 7.1.6 of the 1998 AACRAO FERPA Guide (page 46), there is a case that involves a Director of Development who wishes to contract with an outside service to locate lost alumni. The outside service is requesting that the institution provide the social security numbers as well as names and last known addresses. The problem faced by the registrar, when asked by the Director of Development, is whether it is legally possible under FERPA to release the social security numbers along with the other requested information.

The answer to this particular scenario, cited on page 69 of the 1998 AACRAO FERPA Guide, is that it would be legally permissible to release social security numbers to any third party as long as the institution's FERPA-required definition of "school official" is broad enough to include a third party acting for, or having a contract with, the institution to provide a service that the institution would normally be performing itself. Therefore, the institution may provide non-directory information, e.g., social security number, to contracted agents as long as these agents can be reasonably included in the institution's definition of "school officials."

As the author of the AACRAO FERPA Guide and creator of the case in question, I referred to the National Student Loan Clearinghouse as a valid example of institutions designating a third party/agent as a "school official" to perform a service for the institution. I used this example since the Clearinghouse had asked the Family Policy Compliance Office for clarification on its legality in performing a service for colleges and universities.

There has been some misinterpretation regarding the guidelines cited in the case above. Some have interpreted the answer to mean that the guidelines only approve the National Student Loan Clearinghouse as an agent for colleges/universities, and not others.

This is to clarify that, in the resolution to the case cited, the reference to the National Student Loan Clearinghouse was only an example and does not, in any way, limit the options of the institution in designating agents or contracting with other third parties to perform functions for the institution. Since citing this example, new firms providing other services have emerged that could be included as a "Designated Agent." Firms such as Credentials, Inc. in the degree and current enrollment verification industry could be provided with this information as long as an institution enters an agreement that establishes them as an agent of the school contracted to perform a particular task for the institution. As LeRoy Rooker, the Director of the Family Policy Compliance Office, stated, "...nothing in FERPA prevents an education institution from contracting with a person or entity outside the institution to perform services that the institution would otherwise provide for itself" (McDonald, Steven J., The Family Educational Rights and Privacy Act: A Legal Compendium, NACUA, 1999, pp. 221–223; Letter from LeRoy Rooker to Daniel Boehmer, April 19, 1993).

Therefore, any institution may designate a third party firm that performs a service normally provided by the institution. This means that non-directory information can be given to the firm to perform its contracted tasks if its definition of "school official" includes a statement such as: "A school official is a person or entity that provides a service for an institution." As a "school official," the contractor is required to observe FERPA requirements just as any other "school official."

Any interested party should refer to Appendix 14 of the 1998 AACRAO FERPA Guide (p. 145) for suggested wording on "school official" and "legitimate educational interest" that can be used in the institution's annual notification to students of their FERPA rights.

If you have any questions, please feel free to contact me.

Sincerely yours,

Richard A. Rainsberger, Ph.D.

7.1.7 Faculty/Father's Need to Know

Stephanie Student attends Cole College as an undergraduate. Her father is a faculty member in the medical school there. He wants to find out how Stephanie is doing in school, so he calls the Registrar's Office to find out. How should the office respond?

Resolution:

The father does not have a legitimate educational interest in Stephanie's record since the request is not related to his professional responsibilities as a faculty member. His request is related more to his role as father. The office needs to get written permission from Stephanie or document Stephanie's dependent status to her father before releasing the requested information.

7.1.8 Sharing Grades with Another Institution

You have developed an exchange program with an institution in Russia. The president of this Russian university wants to stay current with the academic progress of all the Russian students and so would like to receive their grades each term. As the students' advisor, you hear that some of the students would prefer that you not forward the grades to the Russian school authorities. What do you do?

Resolution:

Because the person requesting the grades represents an institution that (probably) does not receive funding administered by the Secretary of Education, he, and his institution, would not be subject to FERPA and, therefore, would not be considered a "school official" with a "legitimate educational interest." He would not be entitled to received the grades without the students' written permission.

Because the students are attending an institution located in the United States that is (probably) receiving federal funding administered by the Secretary of Education, they have full FERPA rights, as does any other student attending the institution.

7.1.9 The County Scholarship Request

You work in the Financial Aid Office at Elliott Baker University (EBU). You are talking with a member of your home county's Elliott Baker alumni group. They are establishing a new scholarship to be offered to students from your county who will attend EBU. The applications will be evaluated by a scholarship board from the alumni group. The alumnus has asked you for the names, addresses, and GPAs of all currently enrolled EBU students from your county. What should you give them?

Resolution:

Because the alumni are not employees of the institution, they do not have a legitimate educational interest in, or "need to know," details of student records. Therefore, you should release only directory information to them. Alternatively, if your FERPA policy states that such scholarship committees are considered "school officials" for the sole purpose of evaluating scholarship recipients, that could provide an opportunity for access. Also, if students applying for financial aid have given written permission to release information to third parties in reviewing all their financial aid opportunities, those students would be covered.

7.1.10 Request for List of Students by Religious Preference

One of your colleagues contacts you and relates the following.

"We collect, on a voluntarily submitted basis, information regarding a student's religious preference.

However, we do not 'list' this data element as directory information.

We have a few university-sanctioned religious organizations on campus that periodically ask me to supply them with the names and addresses of any student who has indicated a religious preference related to their particular organization.

Since these religious organizations are sanctioned by the university, can I provide this information without violating FERPA? (Obviously, I would not include any student who had requested that all of their information be suppressed.)"

How do you reply?

Resolution:

"University-sanctioned" has no meaning under FERPA.

You are maintaining an education record (religious preference) that is not (and can never be) directory information Therefore, you should only provide that information to school officials with a legitimate educational interest

I am assuming that the persons who are requesting this information do not fall under your institution's definition of school official. Therefore, you should only release this information with the written permission of the student, or provide directory information on all students to all religious organizations as long as they have not requested that you restrict this information from being released.

7.2 Subpoenas

In this section, you determine the questions to ask or actions to take to determine whether you would comply with the subpoena. What steps would you take in each case to comply with FERPA requirements?

7.2.1 Subpoena No. 1

(See Fig. 7.2.1 on the following page.)

Resolution:

The registrar can comply with the subpoena after making a documented attempt, usually a certified letter, return receipt, to notify the student involved. The registrar could also call the student (if that information was recent) and inform him or her to expect the letter.

The registrar did not immediately provide copies of the information as requested in the subpoena. He informed the person serving the subpoena that he had a FERPA obligation to notify the student and that he intended to do so. He complied with the subpoena after 10 working days from receipt of the subpoena had expired.

7.2.2 Subpoena No. 2

(See Fig. 7.2.2 on page 87.)

Resolution:

Until September 1994, the registrar was required by FERPA to notify the student before complying with the subpoena, irrespective of the command in the subpoena not to inform the student for 90 days.

After September 1994, since the subpoena was issued for a law enforcement purpose, the registrar can comply with the subpoena without notifying the student, in accordance with the command in the subpoena. [See 34 CFR 99.31 (a)(9)(ii)(A)(B).]

Fig 7.2.1: Subpoena No.1

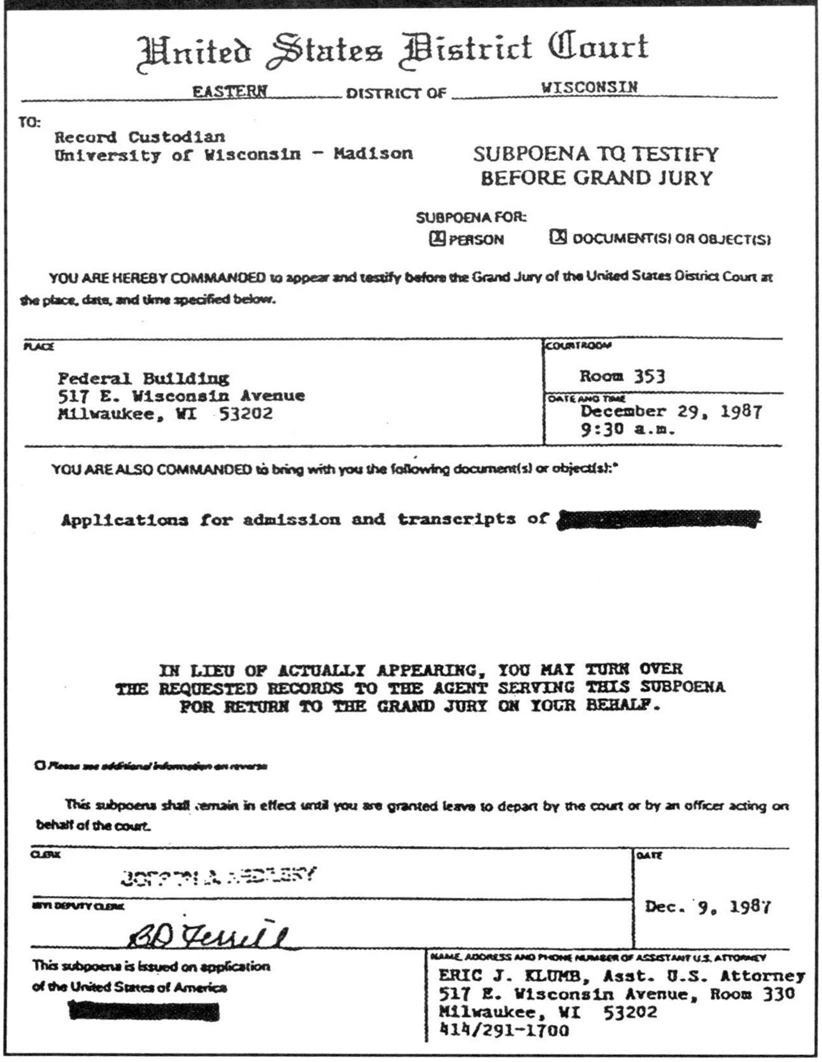

United States District Court

EASTERN DISTRICT OF WISCONSIN

TO:
Record Custodian
University of Wisconsin - Madison

SUBPOENA TO TESTIFY BEFORE GRAND JURY

SUBPOENA FOR:
☒ PERSON ☒ DOCUMENT(S) OR OBJECT(S)

YOU ARE HEREBY COMMANDED to appear and testify before the Grand Jury of the United States District Court at the place, date, and time specified below.

PLACE	COURTROOM
Federal Building 517 E. Wisconsin Avenue Milwaukee, WI 53202	Room 353
	DATE AND TIME December 29, 1987 9:30 a.m.

YOU ARE ALSO COMMANDED to bring with you the following document(s) or object(s):*

Applications for admission and transcripts of [redacted]

IN LIEU OF ACTUALLY APPEARING, YOU MAY TURN OVER THE REQUESTED RECORDS TO THE AGENT SERVING THIS SUBPOENA FOR RETURN TO THE GRAND JURY ON YOUR BEHALF.

☐ Please see additional information on reverse

This subpoena shall remain in effect until you are granted leave to depart by the court or by an officer acting on behalf of the court.

CLERK

(BY) DEPUTY CLERK

DATE Dec. 9, 1987

This subpoena is issued on application of the United States of America [redacted]

NAME, ADDRESS AND PHONE NUMBER OF ASSISTANT U.S. ATTORNEY
ERIC J. KLUMB, Asst. U.S. Attorney
517 E. Wisconsin Avenue, Room 330
Milwaukee, WI 53202
414/291-1700

7.2.3 Subpoena No. 3

(See Fig. 7.2.3 on page 88.)

Resolution:

The Bergen County Board of Social Services (a county agency located in New Jersey) has no jurisdiction over Ohio State University. The registrar did not have to comply with this subpoena and notified the Bergen County Board accordingly.

7.2.4 Subpoena for Student Record with a Hold

You receive a subpoena for a student's records. In checking, you find that there is a hold on the record because of a financial aid debt.

Should you comply with the subpoena, or does the hold take precedence?

Resolution:

Failure to comply with a lawfully issued subpoena could place the institution in contempt of court. Advice of legal counsel was sought. The subpoena took precedence over the hold since it was determined to be legally issued.

7.2.5 Subpoena: "Do I Have to Comply?"

You receive a subpoena on a preprinted form from the U.S. District Court and note that it is signed by the defendant's attorney. The subpoena is requesting the release of the plaintiff's records. Your first instinct is to deny the request because of the attorney's signature. Your institution does not have legal counsel. Using this publication as a guide, do you have to comply with this subpoena?

Resolution:

Complying with a subpoena is an institutional choice. However, if the subpoena is legally issued in all respects, failure to comply with the subpoena could lead to contempt of court charges against you and/or your institution.

The first step is to determine if the subpoena is legally issued. Legal counsel should do this, since the rules can be complex (particularly as they involve federal courts). With no legal counsel to assist you in this case, you can refer to Chapter 5.40 in this publication for assistance.

If you have determined that the subpoena has been legally issued and has jurisdiction over your institution, you should promptly notify the student [33 CFR 99.31 (a)(9)(ii); see sample notification to student in Appendix 15]. The student's attorney then could take steps to "quash" the subpoena if it is not relevant to the case. The subpoena must give you a reasonable amount of time to respond (usually 10 working days from receipt of the subpoena). If it demands a faster response, you should contact the attorney who issued the subpoena and let him or her know that you will comply on a certain date (count ten working days from the receipt of the subpoena) and that you have the obligation under FERPA to notify the student (if notification is required, depending on the content of the subpoena). Often, attorneys are not familiar with the notification requirement in FERPA.

Because the subpoena was issued from a U.S. federal district court, by an officer of the court (the attorney), it appears to be a validly issued subpoena, and you should comply. A federal district court subpoena has jurisdiction in all 50 states if issued by an attorney who is approved/licensed to practice law in the federal district court hearing the case. While you may, from time to time, find a clerk or judge signing a subpoena, it is much more common to have an attorney for one of the sides in a case signing the subpoena.

7.3 Media

7.3.1 The Release of Confidential Information to the Media

Probably one of the more publicized unauthorized releases of a student's academic information in recent years was at Syracuse University when "a documented instance of plagiarism in the law school record of a U.S. senator became a national media event." It also "contributed to the senator's withdrawal from the presidential primary race" (Letter from Peter DeBlois, Registrar, Syracuse University, June 10, 1988).

In a separate incident, a local newspaper published an article that included the grades of a celebrated university basketball player before the player had been notified of his grades. To make matters worse, the player had failed his courses that term.

Fig 7.2.2: Subpoena No.2

SUBPOENA TO TESTIFY BEFORE GRAND JURY

United States District Court	DISTRICT: SOUTHERN DISTRICT OF INDIANA
TO: Keeper of the Records: Registrar's Office Indiana University Bloomington, Indiana	SUBPOENA FOR ☐ Person ☒ Document or Object

YOU ARE HEREBY COMMANDED to appear in the United States District Court at the location, date and time specified below to testify before the Grand Jury in the above entitled case.

PLACE	COURTROOM
Room 285 United States Courthouse 46 East Ohio Street Indianapolis, Indiana 46204	DATE AND TIME October 20, 1986 9:00 a.m.

YOU ARE ALSO COMMANDED to bring with you the following document(s) or object(s):(1)

Any and all records relative to the past enrollment of DARRELL L. [redacted] ([redacted]) in undergraduate or graduate studies at Indiana University. These records are to include but are not limited to: an official grade transcript and/or any other academic record reflecting a description of courses taken, grades, semester hours passed, and GPA.

Disclosure is not to be made of this subpoena for a period of ninety (90) days for the reason that said disclosure would interfere with an investigation being conducted by federal investigative agencies and would interfere with the administration of justice.

Compliance with this subpoena can be made by delivering the requested records and/or documents to the government representative serving this subpoena. If compliance is made by turning the records over to the government representative, a receipt will be given.

☐ *Please see additional information on reverse*

This subpoena shall remain in effect until you are granted leave to depart by the court or by an officer acting on behalf of the court.

CLERK	DATE
JOHN A. O'NEAL	10/7/86 CLS/vlr
(BY) DEPUTY CLERK	

	NAME, ADDRESS AND PHONE NUMBER OF ASSISTANT U.S. ATTORNEY
This subpoena is issued on application of the United States of America by: BRADLEY L. WILLIAMS Acting United States Attorney 86-179-JJT-8-1-3	JOHN J. THAR Assistant United States Attorney Room 274, U. S. Courthouse 46 East Ohio Street Indianapolis, Indiana 46204 Phone: 317-269-6333

In addition to these instances, there have been other less well publicized cases involving the release of student information to the media.

What can you do at your institution to prevent such unwarranted disclosures?

Resolution:

In instances where members of the media seek academic or personal information concerning individuals who have attained celebrity stature or high public visibility, withholding such information may prove difficult. Media persistence and pressure can be a formidable nuisance and may even have the support of your own institution's public affairs staff. Such information should be withheld despite media or public affairs pressure. There are no inherent rights of accessibility afforded the media just because an individual is a "public" figure. Even in instances where such information has been released previously either by another party or by your institution in error, your responsibility is to adhere to your obligation to prevent further disclosure. Such high profile cases point to the need for each institution to develop a process to teach strategies for compliance with FERPA to various officials and faculty. They also point out each institution's need to develop a policy on handling requests for information on famous individuals who have attended the institution and are now deceased (since an individual's FERPA rights cease upon death). This policy could place a moratorium on releasing any information on an individual for perhaps 25 or 30 years after death or require approval of the executor of the deceased's estate before release.

7.3.2 The Scholarship Awards Winners

For many years, Midwestern University, a highly selective institution, has issued press releases identifying currently enrolled students who have won scholarships for the next academic year. Traditionally, along with the student's name, a brief description of the student's academic record is included which indicates the number of letter grades the student has earned at the university. (Obviously, most of the letter grades are As.)

Fig 7.2.3: Subpoena No.3

BERGEN COUNTY BOARD OF SOCIAL SERVICES
221 Route 4 West
Paramus, New Jersey 07652-5182
(201) 368-4200

BERGEN COUNTY BOARD OF SOCIAL SERVICES

Case No.

SUBPOENA

Ad Testificandum
and
Duces Tecum

THE BERGEN COUNTY BOARD OF SOCIAL SERVICES, To: Registrar, Ohio State University, 1659 N. High Street, Columbus, OH 43210.

YOU ARE HEREBY COMMANDED, under the provisions of N.J.S.A. 44:7-20 and 44:10-2, to attend and give testimony at the Bergen County Board of Social Services, 221 Route 4 West, and Forest Avenue, Paramus, N.J., on October 9, 1987 at xx o'clock xx.

You are also commanded to bring with you and produce at the same time and place, the following: All information as requested in attached letter.

Failure to obey this subpoena shall be punishable by the Superior Court as a contempt of court.

Dated: October 21, 1987

Edward Testa
Edward Testa - Director
Bergen County Board of Social Services

Because you are responsible for providing the academic information on these students to the Publicity Office, you indicate in your memo this year that "I believe that the press releases and announcements for these awards should not mention the grades of the recipients. FERPA protects the grades of outstanding students as well as those of average students, and I do not think we have the right to announce student grades publicly without permission of the student." A copy of this memo is also sent to the dean of the college.

Several days later, you receive a memo from the dean of the college indicating his preference for continuing the tradition of describing the academic records of scholarship winners in press releases and announcements. He bases his preference on the facts that to his knowledge: (1) no student has ever objected to a description of his or her academic record, (2) all of the students involved review the press release and approve of it orally before publication, and (3) "the audiences for scholarship announcements invariably like to hear about the academic records of the scholarship winners." Nevertheless, he does recognize your concern about the confidentiality of the academic records and he is referring the situation to the university attorney for an opinion.

Several days later, the publicity officer for the university sends you a memo in which he states, "...Vague characterizations of a student's record may be the legal safe ground, but in the news game, harder information is usually better. The student's performance in individual courses has never been used...by us in news releases... but only such aggregates as 16 As, four A minuses, and one Pass. To the best of our recollection, we have never distributed such a release without the approval of the individual student concerned. To eliminate this summary of the student's actual achievement is, in effect, to remove the news value of the release and to render it ineffective to a large degree. One could argue that all students at Midwestern are good students (by most measures) and that to say that one is more 'outstanding' without being somewhat specific is fruitless."

You phone the university attorney and ask him if you must have a student's written permission on file to release grades, or is the student's review and subsequent oral approval of a draft of a press release enough to allow public announcement and media publication of a student's academic record. How should the university attorney respond?

Resolution:

The attorney replied that uncoerced written authorization from students must be obtained before any release is made and that release needs to indicate specifically what information could be released and to whom.

7.3.3 The Newspaper Reporter

A reporter from the local newspaper calls and wants to verify some information on a famous alumnus for an article she is writing. She wants to verify the alumnus's degree, what the degree was, when the degree was received (if he did not receive a degree, she wants to know when he attended your institution), age or birthdate, and his address when he attended your institution.

How do you respond?

Resolution:

The registrar provided information on the degree received, the dates of attendance, and the address of the individual while he attended the institution since these are all identified as "directory information" in the institution's FERPA policy. The registrar cannot disclose the student's age or date of birth since this information was not identified as "directory information" by the institution. If the individual did not receive a degree, the registrar could say, "I cannot confirm the degree." If the reporter asks if the person received any degree, the registrar could simply reply that he had no comment. It is better to provide less rather than more information requested of you.

7.3.4 Publishing the Dean's List

Every semester the registrar prints a list of students who have made Dean's List and forwards it to the academic dean. Only one copy is printed, and the dean is the only one who receives it.

Would the dean be allowed to publish all the names in the local newspaper if there is no written permission from the students to do so?

Resolution:

The institutional FERPA policy identifies what items of information the institution considers directory information. FERPA permits "awards received" to be directory information. The institution would have to include it in its list of items considered "directory information." If the institution does not identify "awards received" (in this case, honors) as directory information, the institution would have to obtain each student's written permission before releasing the information to the media. If "honors" were included in the institution's directory information, all students at the institution must also have had the opportunity to request non-disclosure of any piece of directory information.

7.3.5 Student Newspaper Request for the Number of Students Dropping a Particular Course

The school newspaper has asked for the number of students who dropped a certain section of a class this term.

Do you comply?

Resolution:

This is not a FERPA question. An aggregate number is not personally identifiable to specific students. Therefore, institutional policy would prevail in this case. In the absence of an institutional policy on the request, the registrar should consult his or her superior.

A state's open records law may require the institution to provide this information if the institution is located in a state with such a law.

7.3.6 Talkative Student and the Nosy Reporter

Ted Student is an outspoken and well-known student-athlete at Barrett University. In a recent news conference he shared a great deal of information about his academic and disciplinary records. A reporter from the local newspaper calls you in the Registrar's Office to confirm the information and to get some more details. What should you tell him?

Resolution:

You can only release directory information (assuming Ted has not requested non-disclosure of his directory information). Just because the information has been made public, you still need a student release for any non-directory information. Simply because a student divulges information from his academic (education) records does not give you the right to confirm that information. There is no implied consent under FERPA. You are limited to confirming directory information (if you wish to do so).

7.3.7 Student Newspaper Request for Information

A representative from *The Lantern*, the student newspaper at Ohio State University, asks the university's Judicial Affairs Office for details about student disciplinary cases on campus. She feels it is a First Amendment right to have access to the information. Students want to know about campus crime. They've also heard that such records were recently released. Is this a FERPA issue? What should be released?

Resolution:

The federal District Court for Southern Ohio has ruled that student disciplinary records are education records and, therefore, are subject to FERPA. This means that it is up to each institution to determine whether to release this information, and to whom, as long as the institution releases the information under the requirements found in 34 CFR 99.31 (a)(14) and 34 CFR 99.39 (see Appendix 2).

The Chronicle of Higher Education, one of the litigants, has appealed the decision of the District Court; a ruling on that appeal had not yet been made when this publication went to press. (See Chapter 5.34 for additional information.)

In this case, you may release this information, though you are not required to do so. Certain prior conditions are attached to the release of this information. You should consult the above-mentioned CFR sections (in Appendix 2) before making a decision. On the other hand, you may

Fig. 7.4.1: The National Science Foundation Request

National Science Foundation
Washington, D.C. 20550

December 18, 1987

Office of Registrar
XXXXXXXXXXXXXX University

Dear Madam or Sir:

The National Science Foundation and the Department of Energy are continuing their periodic surveys to provide important up-to-date information on recent college graduates. Through mail questionnaires administered to persons who graduated from college during the academic years 1981, 1986, and 1987, we will collect data which will allow us to develop estimates of the total number of scientists and engineers in the U.S. Survey results will also be used to indicate the types of jobs being obtained by recent college graduates, the relationship between these jobs and the graduates' major fields of study, the current unemployment rate of new graduates, the proportion continuing their education, and other attributes of recent graduates. The information will assist universities and colleges as well as Federal, State, and local officials in making policy decisions and future plans.

To carry out this study, we have a nationally representative sample of institutions of higher learning of which your institution is one. This letter is to request your assistance in carrying out this study.

We are asking each of the selected institutions to furnish a list of all students to whom they have awarded a Bachelor's or Master's degree between July 1, 1980 and June 30, 1981, July 1, 1985 and June 30, 1986, and between July 1, 1986 and June 30, 1987. We need lists which include the student's name, latest available address, degree, date of graduation, and if at all possible, major field of study....We will then use these lists to draw a sample of graduates who will be sent a questionnaire requesting information on occupational and educational status subsequent to graduation. The sponsors, as well as the contractor on this project, the Institute for Survey Research of Temple University, will insure that all information collected will be treated as confidential and used for survey and statistical purposes only....

Thank you very much for your cooperation.

Sincerely yours,
William L. Stewart
Director, Division of
Science Resources Studies

always release aggregate (non-personally identifiable) information on numbers of crimes, etc., without having to comply with these sections.

7.4 Surveys/Research Requests

7.4.1 The National Science Foundation Request

(See Fig. 7.4.1 and resolution of 7.4.2.)

7.4.2 The Educational Testing Service—Graduate Record Examination Request

(See Fig. 7.4.2 on the following page.)

Note: The following resolution applies to both the NSF Request (7.4.1) and the ETS-GRE Request (7.4.2).

Resolution:

The institution complied with the request because the release of academic information to third parties conducting research "to develop, validate and administer predictive tests" or "to improve instruction" is permitted under FERPA [34 CFR 99.31 (a)(6)(i)]. Because NSF and ETS were nationally known, highly respected organizations conducting research in higher education, the institution believed its participation would benefit not only the institution but also higher education in general.

While an individual's address may be considered directory information (depending upon a school's determination of directory information), release should be guided by prudent evaluation of the purpose of the request. In most instances, it is in the best interest of students not to release their addresses unless the following can be established:

- that the requesting agency has appropriate status as an educational or research entity (e.g., a state education department, accrediting agencies, NSF or ETS, etc.); and
- that the requesting agency agrees to use the information solely for the purposes of the study or review for which it seeks authorization and that, upon completion of the project, any personally identifiable materials are returned, destroyed, or deleted from databases that may have been created.

Frequently, agencies seeking information from universities and colleges will submit their initial request to the American Association of Collegiate Registrars and Admissions Officers. AACRAO might then endorse the request and recommend your cooperation.

Although the AACRAO endorsement means that its Board of Directors has studied the proposal and has approved the request, you must be extremely careful in evaluating such requests for your institution. You may also receive independent requests for education record information for various educational (e.g., Ph.D. dissertations/studies) and non-educational purposes (e.g., addresses for a mailing by a car dealership). In general, release of addresses in the latter situation is not recommended.

Additionally, state laws may require institutions to release addresses. When in doubt, you should contact the Family Policy Compliance Office in Washington, DC. The address and phone/fax numbers are: Family Policy Compliance Office, U.S. Department of Education, 400 Maryland Avenue, SW, Washington, DC 20202-4605; (202) 260-3887; fax: (202) 260-9001.

7.4.3 Postsecondary Feedback

(See Fig. 7.4.3 on page 92.)

Resolution:

Directory information of the institution involved did not include "high school graduation." The registrar, however, wrote a letter to the counselor indicating that one of the admissions requirements to the institution was high school graduation and verified that the student was enrolled. He then forwarded the counselor's letter and his reply to the student.

Institutions may receive requests from high schools or other feeder institutions for follow-up information on their former students; some states already require this feedback. (See Chapter 5.23 for further discussion.)

7.4.4 Doctoral Dissertation Request

An employee of the college is working on his doctorate. The research project is to explore the enrollment patterns of the college's students and the relationship of these patterns to successful outcomes achievement. This person is requesting transcripts—hundreds of them—and he is willing to pay for them.

Can you comply?

Resolution:

The registrar justified the release of the transcripts under exceptions found in Chapter 4.1 of this publication [34 CFR 99.31 (a)] and under the institution's definition of "legitimate educational interest."

The individual met the definition of "school official" in the institution's FERPA policy and satisfied the criteria for having a "legitimate educational interest." The registrar also obtained a "sign-off" from the researcher, who agreed to keep the information confidential, not share it with anyone, summarize the data in aggregate fashion (no specific names would be mentioned in the final research report), and either destroy the transcripts when the research was completed or return them to the registrar's office.

Such requests can be decided on a case-by-case basis. One example of a form which assists in the process of making a decision as to whether to release non-directory information for research purposes is reproduced in Fig. 7.4.4 (page 93).

Fig. 7.4.2: The Educational Testing Service—Graduate Record Examination Request

EDUCATIONAL TESTING SERVICE PRINCETON, N.J. 08541

609 921 9000
CABLE EDUCTESTSVC
GRADUATE RECORD EXAMINATIONS PROGRAM

July 10, 1987

Dear Colleague:

On behalf of the Graduate Record Examinations Board, I would like to invite your graduate departments to participate in the GRE Validity Study Service. This free service is designed to help academic departments investigate the effectiveness of using GRE scores and other admission measures as predictors of success in graduate school.

The purpose of the service is to provide information to graduate departments to assist in the selection of applicants and for departmental self-analysis.

The GRE Validity Study Service has been redesigned for the 1987-88 academic year. It is now more accessible to smaller departments (the minimum number of students required for participation has been reduced to five) and provides more stable results through the use of statistical techniques that incorporate information from all participating departments in the analysis of each individual department. Your participation this year is especially important in establishing the statistical basis to assist in the use of the new techniques.

When possible, data needed to carry out the studies will be obtained from Graduate Record Examinations files. As you will note in reviewing the enclosed materials, participating departments are asked to supply some information about individual students. The Family Education Rights and Privacy Act of 1974 expressly permits the use of information for a validity study provided the information is destroyed when no longer needed for this purpose. The Validity Study Service will comply with this requirement by deleting personally identifiable data from our files when no longer necessary for the service. The files will be protected for as long as we retain them.

In the past, the GRE Validity Study Service has offered two cycles each year. This practice allowed departments to accumulate data over a longer period of time in order to meet the required sample size of 25 students. Since fewer students are now required for participation, there will be a single cycle in 1987-88. Enclosed is a brief outline of study procedures and the schedule of activities. If you decide to participate in the Validity Study Service, please complete the participation reply form that is included with these materials and return it to Educational Testing Service by September 15, 1987.

7.4.5 State Education Agency Requests

Your state is considering the establishment of a comprehensive statewide, multi-institutional postsecondary student database for conducting studies, tracking students, and generating reports required by the Student Right-to-Know Act of 1990 (SRTK) and the Carl D. Perkins Vocational and Applied Technology Education Act. This would require all institutions in the state to provide student information (both directory and non-directory) to the state's Board of Regents.

As a campus administrator responsible for FERPA, you wonder whether this is permissible.

Resolution:

The Family Policy Compliance Office has determined that postsecondary institutions may disclose information from education records to a state or federal agency for "audit or evaluation of...state-supported education programs." Once the education record information is

Fig. 7.4.3: Postsecondary Feedback

Andrew L. Wells
Principal
540-5300

Rick Barrett
Associate Principal
540-5356

Faith Hiller
Assistant Principal
540-5392

Steve Busch
Assistant Principal
540-5310

Richard Ceritelli
Assistant Principal
540-5325

Georgia Faubion
Assistant Principal
540-5315

Bryan Lane
Assistant Principal
540-5320

Counselors
540-5365

Fred Erdman
Head Counselor

Carol Baggett
Kay Lynch
Peggy Pickens
Barbara Vladyka
Suzan Francis

Peggy Martin
At Risk Students
Counselor

KINGWOOD HIGH SCHOOL

2701 Kingwood Drive, Kingwood, Texas 77339 (713) 540-5000

July 27, 1990

Dear Registrar,

I am requesting your assistance in locating a former student from Kingwood High School, ░░░░░░, date of birth:░░░░. ░░░░ transferred to a high school overseas for his Senior year of high school, and since the receiving school did not request that his records be mailed to them, his records are incomplete and he is considered a dropout in the state of Texas.

Considering the excellent records and grades of this student, I feel that an error has been made. Please provide me with information indicating that ░░░░ is, in fact, a high school graduate, so that his records can indicate that he is a transfer student who has continued his education.

The reputation of your fine university is well-known in the Houston area, so I am delighted that ░░░░ is continuing his education on your campus.

Thank you for your time and attention in this matter.

Yours truly,

Peggy Martin

Peggy Martin
Student Support Services

received, it is the responsibility of the agency to (1) take the appropriate steps to ensure compliance with FERPA, (2) protect the integrity of the data, and (3) ensure that it is used solely for the purposes intended and, once no longer needed, (4) the personally identifiable information should be destroyed. In general, data should be publicly released by the agency only in aggregated, generic form (see Chapter 5.30).

7.5 Deceased Students

7.5.1 Request for Information on Judith Resnik

(See Fig. 7.5.1 on page 94.)

Resolution:

FERPA rights cease upon death. Left to the institution, the request for a transcript was denied.

Because of this request and others like it, the institution now has a policy that does not permit the release of education record information of deceased students for 25 years after their death unless authorized by the executor/executrix of the deceased student's estate or parents, or next of kin, if an executor/executrix has not been appointed.

While there would have been no FERPA violation had the registrar complied, common courtesy and sensitivity prevailed in this case.

7.5.2 Request from the Utah State Police

A former student was killed in Utah and an investigator from the Utah State Police would like to interview the deceased student's teachers. Your state requires that subpoenas be issued through courts in your state. But, rather than taking the time to do that, the officer wants to know if the next of kin (i.e., parents or spouse) can authorize release of this information to the police (as he might if the student were alive).

You haven't had this question come up before. In the past, the only issue with deceased students was releasing transcripts and/or diplomas as memorabilia or for family records.

What do you advise?

Resolution:

As stated previously, FERPA rights cease upon a student's death. Institutional policy would apply. In the absence of an institutional policy, legal counsel should be consulted and a policy formulated.

Some institutions have indicated that the executor/executrix of the deceased's estate, or the deceased student's parents or next of kin, if no executor/executrix has been appointed, can grant permission if required by institutional policy.

7.5.3 The Genealogist

George is doing some family background research. He discovers that his deceased great grandmother attended your college many years ago. He asks you for whatever records you have for his great grandmother. What should you provide?

Resolution

As mentioned previously, FERPA rights and, in general, the right to privacy, end at death. State law may dictate some parameters for dealing with records of persons now deceased, but this is fundamentally an institutional policy decision. Most institutions tend to treat records for deceased students as they would live students, except that the "next of kin," or executor/executrix, is viewed as the "owner" of the record since the student is deceased. It is also appropriate to ask for proof of death if not already recorded in the institution's data files.

7.6 Fax/Decentralized Online Inquiry

7.6.1 The Fax Request #1

You receive a faxed letter from a former student requesting that her transcript be sent to IBM at an address in New York.

Can you comply? What do you need to determine first?

Resolution:

You first need to determine if the signature is valid. This is not unique to a faxed request but should be a standard business practice in processing any transcript request.

FERPA only requires the signature (signed consent) of the student to release a transcript. If the signature is valid, the transcript can be released.

Fig. 7.4.4

OFFICE OF THE REGISTRAR UW - STEVENS POINT
REQUEST FOR ACCESS TO EDUCATIONAL RECORDS FOR RESEARCH

A student may be permitted access to educational records for research purposes (according procedures established by the Registrar's Office) if the student agrees to protect the confidentiality of the information received and agrees to design the report so that it does not identify the students on whom the data was collected.

The student researcher must also either:
1. Obtain written consent from the students whose records are to be examined.

or

2. Secure written authorization, as indicated below, that the information to be gathered is for a "legitimate educational interest" and that the student is acting as a "school official" for this project only.

****

TO BE FILLED OUT BY THE STUDENT REQUESTING ACCESS TO RECORDS

Describe the purpose of the research

List the type of data needed e.g. social security number, ACT score, etc.

Describe the group to which the needed data is limited e.g. students with GPA of 3.00 or above, etc.

Signature (I agree to protect the confidentiality of the data gathered). Date

Approval to examine student records without students' consent (if applicable).

Instructor (I approve of the project described above). Date

Department chairman (I agree that the project is of legitimate educational interest). Date

Dean of the college in which the student is enrolled (I concur with the above and approve the researcher as an acting school official for this project only). Date

****

* Federal law provides that the definition of "school official" is left up to each institution. For the purposes of this authorization we have defined the term as a person approved, at the level of Dean or higher, to act as a school official for only the project described above.

"Legitimate educational interest" (for the purpose of this authorization only) means that the research in some way may help the university improve its policies or programs; i.e. it would have been done by an appropriate employee had resources permitted.

7.6.2 Online Inquiry

Many institutions now provide access to academic records through some form of computerized online access. Many have switched to online advising and transcript systems whereby approved faculty can access a student's official academic record via terminals located in their offices. The underlying assumption is that the Registrar's Office will authorize access to all of the student data traditionally available in hard copy. Protecting the confidential nature of the records and preventing unauthorized changes is a most important responsibility, especially when you have heard comments on your campus that all students' records are available for anyone to see. Although this may be overstating the problem, it is a valid concern.

What can you do to ensure that this type of decentralized inquiry into student education records will not be abused?

Resolution:

Because protecting the confidential nature of student records and preventing unauthorized release is a very important responsibility, some type of response is in order and should be carried out swiftly. If the matter is simply a lack of training, the faculty member (as well as any others who might need it) should either undergo a review of FERPA or be trained on FERPA for the first time. As "school officials," faculty and staff need to understand how broad the definition of an education record is and that FERPA's requirements apply to education records found beyond the registrar's, admissions, and financial aid offices. Any person who has access to a student's education record information should be required to sign an access form confirming their understanding of FERPA and their responsibility to uphold it. If a FERPA violation occurs after a school official has accessed the information, general computer access should be revoked, and the faculty or staff member, for all future needs, should have to demonstrate a legitimate educational need to know on a case-by-case basis before obtaining access to any non-directory information.

Many ideas throughout this publication can assist you in ensuring a FERPA-compliant campus. You might want to

Fig. 7.5.1: Request for Information on Judith Resnik

August 28, 1986

To the Registrar of C.M.U.;

I am an admirer of Dr. Judith Arlene Resnik ---who earned a bachelor's degree from Carnegie-Mellon in May or June of 1970. If I must remind you, Dr. Resnik was aboard the Space Shuttle "Challenger" on January 28, 1986. I need your help.

As a donor/member of the Oklahoma Air & Space Museum, I am very dedicated to the collection of biographical data on Judy Resnik -- I have made some very positive steps that will help to keep her memory, her work, her life and her "example" alive. Please read on.

Judy Resnik's outstanding achievements, academically and otherwise, can only serve to inspire others to great goals. She IS (not "was") a special person. As I learn more I am amazed.

If you will review the attached copy of my recent letter to the Okla. Air & Space Museum, you'll see that I am working on a special project.

I would truly appreciate receiving a copy (or copies) of Judy's transcript. I have enclosed the fee. Please send two copies:

Please, if you have any reservations on this, contact the Oklahoma Air & Space Museum for verification of my intentions.

Tomorrow, I will be contacting Washington and Houston ---
to obtain the
recently discovered flags and crew patches for the Museum. One set for each state.

When all is "said-and-done," I don't think there is anything "improper" I could do with copies of Judy's transcripts. Call if you have doubts.

Sincerely,

L. Robert Hunter
4640 Sandy Lane
Oklahoma City, OK 73116

start with the FERPA Audit found in Chapter 6.9 and then seek other tools in Chapter 6 that might help you.

7.6.3 Using the PIN to Request a Transcript

A student calls and wants you to send him a transcript. You tell the student that he can provide all the required information on the university's web page, and the transcript will then be sent within two days. All the student needs to know is his personal identification number (PIN) that was assigned when he first enrolled. The astute student asks, "What, no signature?"

How do you reply?

Resolution:

The Family Policy Compliance Office determined that a PIN satisfies FERPA's consent requirement in the case of an online request from a student for a transcript to be sent to himself. Because the information for the request is captured in electronic form on the web page and the PIN is controlled by, and known only to, the student, the PIN performs the same function as a signature, i.e., to accurately verify the student making the request. (See Chapter 5.42.3 for additional information on use of the PIN.)

7.6.4 The Fax Transcript Request via Personal Computer (PC)

A college receives a faxed (digitized) transcript request that was sent directly from the person's personal computer. The person wants the transcript to be sent to his employer. Because he was faxing from his computer, he was unable to sign the request.

Should the request be honored without the student's signature?

Resolution:

FERPA requires a student's written permission to release a transcript to a third party.

7.6.5 Releasing E-mail Addresses

The director of computer services at your institution has asked the question: Is it a violation of FERPA to release student e-mail addresses? If it is not, he wants to provide a page on the institution's website to allow students to find the addresses themselves.

Resolution:

If the institution has not designated e-mail address as directory information, the release of such information would be a violation of FERPA. If it is decided to include "e-mail address" in the institution's list of "directory information" items, the institution first must notify students of this and allow a period of time for the students to request that their e-mail addresses not be released. For efficiency's sake, this notification probably should be included as part of the next annual notification to students of their FERPA rights. (See Chapter 5.10 and Appendix 14.)

7.6.6 The Fax Request #2

Fax requests for transcripts are routine at this university. The transcript area receives a faxed letter from a nationally known, prominent journalist. The letter was sent from the broadcasting station in New York, stamped with the broadcaster's signature, and "signed" by the broadcaster's assistant. It was urgent that a transcript be sent immediately.

Do you comply?

Resolution:

While the "stamp" along with the assistant's signature is probably accepted in the everyday life of this individual, it would not hold up as a signed consent under FERPA.

Because there was such urgency to the request, the registrar's office contacted the news station by telephone and explained the procedures/requirements for issuing transcripts, including the necessity for a bona fide signature. The registrar spoke directly to the journalist, was able to verify the authenticity of the request, and asked that another request be submitted with his signature. Notes of the telephone conversation were made on the second faxed request, which was honored.

7.7 Parents and Spouses

7.7.1 Request from Father for Information on Daughter

(See Fig. 7.7.1.)

Resolution:

FERPA clearly assigns rights to students once they reach 18 years of age or enroll at a postsecondary institution. One of these is the right to authorize the release of information. In this case, the registrar's office did not provide the requested information to the father. He was told that he needed a written release from the student or had to provide documentation that his daughter was financially dependent; presenting his most recent federal income tax return could provide this documentation.

If one parent claims the student as a dependent for income tax purposes, the institution may disclose information to either parent. The institution should have a policy, as part of its institutional FERPA statement, on the release of information on dependent students to parents. The institution is not required by FERPA to release information to parents even if their child's dependency is documented.

Additional information on parental access to children's education records is provided in section 5.20 of this guide.

Fig. 7.7.1: Request from Father for Information on Daughter

The University of Iowa
Iowa City, IA 52242

To Whom it may Concern:

My daughter, , is a sophomore at the University of Iowa. My ex-wife resides somewhere in Oklahoma; I live in Illinois. Getting grade and financial information has been and is next to impossible.

As I am legally obligated to contribute to my daughter's college expenses, I feel I have a right to complete and accurate financial information. Therefore, I am requesting copies of the following documents concerning my daughter:

1) all financial aid documents, including grants, loans, etc.
2) all payment records
3) grade reports
4) her current status

If there is a charge for the photocopying of this information, please send me a bill and I will remit promptly.

Sincerely,

7.7.2 Parent Requests Transcript for Son

A parent calls the Registrar's Office requesting that her son's transcript be sent to ABC College. She indicates that her son has applied for admission to that college and is out of the country and that it would take too long for him to sign the written request that is required.

What do you do?

Resolution:

This case involves two issues: (1) the practice of accepting telephone requests for transcripts, and (2) a parent requesting a transcript for her son. The institution should have a clear policy on how to handle telephone requests for transcripts. Most institutions require a written request from the student to release a transcript to a third party. In the "1991 AACRAO Survey on FERPA," only 10 percent of responding institutions indicated they would accept a telephone request to release a transcript. Of those institutions that indicated they would honor a telephone request, most qualified this response by indicating they would release the transcript only to another institution to which the student had applied for admission. FERPA does permit an institution to provide education record information, e.g., a transcript, without the student's written permission, to an institution at which the student is seeking to enroll [34 CFR 99.31 (a)(2)]. (Certain conditions may be found in 34 CFR 99.34; see Appendix 2.)

Another option that requires foresight on the part of the student would be to assign a Power of Attorney to a parent, or other person, in order for that person to conduct business for the student whilehe is away.

The issue of whether a parent could receive the transcript of a son or daughter is addressed in Chapter 7.7.1 and is outlined in Section 5.20 of this guide. The issue of whether the student is a dependent must be resolved, and the institution should have a clear policy on how to handle requests from parents.

7.7.3 Wife Requests Information on Husband

A wife comes into your office to request a copy of her husband's grades from last semester. She doesn't want anything official, just a printout or "some copy." Her husband said it would be okay. She filled out the request form that you have in your office and gives it to you.

Would you provide the wife the copy of her husband's grades as she requested?

Resolution:

FERPA privacy and disclosure rights are assigned to the student. Only the student can authorize the release of non-directory information contained in the student's education records unless specific exceptions exist as outlined in FERPA.

There appear to be no exceptions in FERPA that address this situation. Therefore, the registrar's office should require the written authorization of the student to release this information to his wife. In the absence of any student-initiated release or legal order, e.g., court order, subpoena, or power of attorney, the registrar's office should not comply with the wife's request.

7.7.4 The Estranged Wife

(See Fig. 7.7.4.)

Fig. 7.7.4: The Estranged Wife

5/27/87
13 Hard Knocks Dr.
Down and Out, KS

President's Office
Midwestern University
Cornstalk, MO

Dear Mam/Sir:

Please route this request or let me know how to properly obtain this record.

I "worked hubby's way through college", Midwestern, from 1955-1959. His name is and we lived in Cornstalk, Mo. 1955-1959. He received a B.S. in Printing Management or what term might have been substituted.

As often with such men, has been trouble.

In Jan., 1986, I had to flee violence (mostly from our grown sons) in our home in Colo. I'm in my home town where Charles originally encouraged me to come.

Now Charles has filed for divorce. As I was a full time homemaker since 1959, I need a fair settlement. Charles went into debt, bankruptcy/ and crime in the last few years---I was party to none of this. Charles really lies so badly that I must have a confirmation regarding his college. I fled with the clothes on my back and a small bag.

Thank you,

Resolution:

The resolution to this case is similar to that of any case in which a third party is seeking access to a student's education record without the written permission of the student. Although there are specific exceptions that permit an institution to release education records without written permission (see 34 CFR 99.31), in this case the student's authorization is required since an estranged wife—or any spouse, for that matter—is not included in the exceptions. Information that can be released to the wife is limited to directory information. Because "degree" and "date awarded" were identified as directory information, the registrar provided that information.

7.7.5 The "Closed Record" Request

(See Fig. 7.7.5 on the following page.)

Resolution:

As indicated in earlier cases, the privacy rights in FERPA protect a student enrolled in postsecondary education. The student is the only person who may authorize the release or non-disclosure of student information. In this case, the request was denied with an explanation.

FERPA does permit an institution to allow parents to have access to a student's record if the parent can document that the student is a dependent as defined by the U.S. Department of Treasury "Internal Revenue Service Guidelines" (see Appendix 7) and the institution has a practice of providing information to parents. Institutions are required to annually notify students of their privacy rights and to provide them with the opportunity to prohibit the release of directory information.

7.7.6 Father Requests Grade Distribution of Son's Class

A student failed a lecture course but was given an "A" in the corresponding lab. When his father sees the grades, he calls the student's department and requests a copy of the faculty member's grade distribution for the section, suspecting, since the student said so, that a large number of students did poorly and that maybe it was not the fault of the student. As it turns out, more than 50 percent of the class got either a "D" or "F" grade. Not knowing what else to do, the department refers the father to the Registrar's Office.

Should the Registrar's Office release the information?

Resolution:

Because grade distributions do not personally identify students, the request does not fall under FERPA. Since this pertains to academic policy and procedure, the registrar consulted with the academic vice president, who refused the request and contacted the father personally.

7.7.7 Dual-Enrolled Student—Parental Access

Mary Student is a junior in high school, seventeen years old, and decides to take advantage of the joint high school/college enrollment option. She is using the coursework for both high school and college credit. Should the university release grade information to Mary's parents? To her high school?

Resolution:

FERPA is clear that a student has rights to her education records once she begins attending an institution of higher education, regardless of her age. Therefore, the parents should be treated like any other parents of a typical college student. You may release non-directory information to parents by either obtaining the student's written permission or by having the parents show that their child is legally their dependent. (See Chapters 5.20 and 6.2.2.)

To send Mary's grades to her high school, you may need to obtain Mary's written permission or find an exception to written permission in FERPA (34 CFR 99.31). For example, if the high school district is paying tuition for Mary to attend your institution (as is done in Virginia), you may release the grades to the high school based on the "financial aid" exception found in 34 CFR 99.31 (a)(4)(i)(ii).

In Ohio, public colleges and universities are required by state law to provide enrollment and grade information to the student's school district and the State Board of Education. The State of Ohio allocates the money to the college/university to support the instruction the student receives at the college/university. In turn, the high school forwards grade information to the student or the student's parents in the normal course of business. The college/university sends grades directly to the student, as to all other college/university students.

7.7.8 Divorced Parents—Access to Son's Records

Frank's parents are divorced. By agreement, his mother claims him as a dependent, but his father is required to pay his way through college. Frank and his mother have both refused to tell Frank's father anything about his academic progress at State College. Frank's father calls you, the registrar, and asks how Frank is doing in his courses. Can you give him the information?

If the son had formally requested that you honor his request for "non-disclosure" of any information to his father, would this change your decision?

Fig. 7.7.5: The "Closed Record" Request

June 21, 1989

James Cunningham
Office of Financial Aid
Frozen Slipper University
Northern Banks, AK 99999

Re: Henrietta Coldwater

Dear Mr. Cunningham:

I am writing to express Mrs. Coldwater's desire that her daughter's school records be closed to any and all persons except Mrs. Coldwater, her Attorney, Thomas A. Jones, and her daughter, Henrietta.

If you have any questions regarding this letter, please do not hesitate to contact me at the address or telephone number found in the letterhead above.

Respectfully,

Thomas A. Jones, Esq.

Resolution:

FERPA permits release of this information to either parent (34 CFR 99.4) as long as there is no legal order barring the release. The registrar involved did so after obtaining a copy of the divorce decree and determining the familial relationship between son and father.

What if the son requested that you not release any information to the father? You could honor that request if you wished. However, the student's right to request non-disclosure (as guaranteed by FERPA) applies only to directory information and not to specific individuals. You must honor the student's request of non-disclosure of directory information. You do not have to honor the son's request to block any disclosures to the father.

7.8 Emergencies

7.8.1 The University Police

You receive a visit from a university police officer. The officer tells you there has been an emergency and he needs to locate Brad M. He wants you to tell him what class the student is presently in and where that class is being held so he can go to the student and talk with him.

The officer also tells you that he has been trying to find that student for a week and has been unsuccessful.

The student's schedule is not identified as directory information by the university.

Can you assist the officer in locating the student? How?

Resolution:

If the officer expects release based on a crisis or emergency, it is important that enough information be obtained from the officer to determine if such an emergency exists. (The "tests" for such a situation are outlined in Chapter 5.8 of this guide.) However, because the officer mentioned that he had been trying for a week to find the student, it would seem unlikely that a true emergency existed. If the emergency test is not met, the information might be released based upon a school official having a legitimate educational interest. This would have to be accurately determined after having the officer provide more specifics. If the request is from a local police officer who is not a school official, the information should not be released to the officer without a lawfully issued subpoena, court order, or written permission of the student.

7.8.2 The Western Union Delivery

An officer, Jim N., from your campus police department contacts you regarding a telegram that Western Union is attempting to deliver to a student. The contents of the telegram indicate that something tragic has happened at the student's home. The officer further states that Western Union is having difficulty delivering the telegram since there are two students on campus with the same name, and the person to whom the telegram should be delivered has signed a confidentiality statement indicating she wants no information released to the public. Thus, her campus address is not in the directory the police department has. He is calling you to see what can be done.

What can you do?

Resolution:

A true emergency appears to exist in this case, and it is important that the telegram be delivered as soon as possible. Because the address information is not considered directory information by the institution, it should not be released directly to Western Union. However, it could be released to the campus police under legitimate educational interest/emergency situation, and the campus police could deliver the telegram.

If the address was identified as "directory information" by the institution, it could be released directly to Western Union.

7.8.3 Family Emergency and Access to the Class Schedule

Faith calls the Registrar's Office, looking for her husband, a student at your institution. She says it is an emergency and she needs to contact him immediately. She would like to know where he is right now. How should you respond? Does it make any difference if the student has a "no release" posted on his record?

Resolution:

This is a professional judgment call. If you haven't done so already, consider establishing a protocol for handling emergencies. Since the wife is calling, you can check the student's schedule and inform her that you will have a message sent to the next class the student is expected to attend. If your institution has identified "student's schedule" as directory information, you cannot release it under the "no release" (non-disclosure) provision in FERPA [34 CFR 99.37 (a)(2)]. You could, however, release it under any of the exceptions to student written permission found in 34 CFR 99.31. An emergency is one of the exceptions found in 99.31 at 34 CFR 99.31(a)(10) and 34 CFR 99.36. Therefore, an institution may release that information even though the student has a "no release" request in effect as long as you can accurately determine that there is an emergency and the information is required to resolve the emergency.

7.8.4 The Erratic Student

One of the counselors at your college comes to your office. She appears somewhat disturbed and asks to speak with you privately. You close the door to your office and the counselor tells you she needs your advice: A student is experiencing some mental health and drug addiction problems and required hospitalization a few weeks ago. While there is no evidence of the student being in immediate danger to himself or others, the potential for harm does exist. The college believes the parents are not aware of the situation—or at least, the severity of the situation. The counselor has two questions:

1. Since the doctors feel there is a potential for the student to harm himself, may we contact the parents concerning this matter?
2. If the student had requested non-disclosure of his education record information, could the college still initiate contact with the parents concerning this situation?

In checking your system records, you find that the student has filed a non-disclosure form with your office.

How do you respond?

Resolution:

Irrespective of whether the student has requested non-disclosure, the college could contact the parents. Because non-disclosure applies only to a student's directory information and not to particular persons, the request for non-disclosure is not pertinent to the facts in this case. Even if you determined that a student's request for non-disclosure was valid, FERPA would still permit you to release information about the student under one of the exceptions to a student's written permission found in 34 CFR 99.31.

The key question is whether a real emergency exists. Admittedly, given the facts in this case, this is a gray area since "emergency" is not specifically defined in FERPA. Under 34 CFR 99.31(a)(10), FERPA does allow the disclosure of information "in connection with a health or safety emergency." Section 99.36 of the regulations state that the disclosure is permitted if knowledge of "the information is necessary to protect the health or safety of the student or other individuals."

Based on the circumstances, the potential for harm does exist. The college has very good reason to classify this as a situation that threatens the "health and safety of the student." You suggest that the counselor document the reasons the college decided to release information to the parents (by memo and other supporting documentation).

Note: The documentation can be made available to other "school officials" who have a "legitimate educational interest" in the behavior of the student [34 CFR 99.36 (b)(2)].

7.9 Relations with Law Enforcement Units

7.9.1 The Request for Student Schedules

The Security Department at your college has had access to each student's local address and phone number since the enactment of FERPA. It has never had access to the schedules of the students. Now, that department is requesting that it regularly have access to student schedules. It claims that it would be faster to contact students in case of an emergency if the schedules were known.

Also, you have heard through the grapevine that the local police department has requested that your Security Department cooperate in the elimination of a drug ring believed to be centered at the college. The local police department has suggested that the availability of student schedules would be most helpful in apprehending the suspected ring members. You make the "intuitive leap" that these two requests may be related.

Can you comply? Would you? How might the local police department obtain the student schedules if you did not comply?

Resolution:

The request was denied for two reasons: (1) the institution did not have a clearly defined policy on what constituted legitimate educational interest, and (2) student schedules were not identified by the institution as directory information. Subsequently, the institution clarified its FERPA statement on legitimate educational interest and included security officers in its definition of "school officials." The security officers were given FERPA training and gained access to student schedules. This office was specifically prohibited from releasing non-directory information to third parties.

The local police department could subpoena the student schedules, directing the institution not to notify the students if the subpoena was for a law enforcement purpose [34 CFR 99.31(a)(9)].

7.9.2 Parking Tickets and Graduating Seniors

The spring term is winding down, culminating in a few weeks in commencement. While you are contemplating the quiet of the summer season on campus, an officer from Campus Police calls.

He would like to run their parking ticket file against the registrar's report of graduating seniors. His department wants to do this so that "holds" can be placed on the diplomas and transcripts of those who have not paid their parking fines.

What do you decide?

Resolution:

Because the report of graduating seniors includes all items that are directory information and because campus police are considered "school officials," the request was approved. Even if the report of graduating seniors was not directory information, the request still could be approved since this is an internal, administrative operation that falls under the institution's definition of "legitimate educational interest" (see Appendix 11).

7.9.3 The Arrested Student

An officer from the police department in a nearby town calls. The officer states that a person who claims to be a student at your college has been arrested. You know that this police department has the policy of releasing arrested students for minor infractions (which is what is involved in this case) if it can be verified that the person is a student.

You check your records and find that the person is a currently enrolled student. There is, however, a signed statement from the student that he wants no information released.

Do you verify to the officer that this person is a student? Why or why not?

Resolution:

You reply: "I have no information that I can release on that individual." You are honoring the student's FERPA right of non-disclosure.

7.10 Admissions

7.10.1 The "Denied" Applicant

An applicant to the engineering program was denied admission. Subsequently, he was admitted to the computer science program. This student comes to your office wishing to inspect his file. You tell him to return the next day.

Because you only have the files on admitted students, the student, upon returning the next day, is upset that the data on his "denied" engineering application are not in his file. He demands to see this information immediately. You know that this information is kept in the Admissions Office.

What do you tell this student?

Resolution:

You deny the student's request and explain that FERPA rights are provided only to applicants upon actual acceptance and subsequent enrollment into a particular component of an institution. Applicants who are denied admittance to an institution have no FERPA rights. Individuals admitted to a program have access to their own admissions records only after their enrollment. Likewise, their right of access is limited solely to their specific program—not to another. In addition, an individual who audits a course is not in the same position as one who has been granted formal admission. He is not granted the rights and obligations accorded a registered and fully admitted student [c.f. *Tarka* v. *Franklin*, 891F 2d 102 United States Court of Appeals, Fifth Circuit, 1989 (Texas)].

In *Tarka* v. *Franklin* (5th Cir. 1989), a student was not admitted as a regular student, and the University of Texas did not have to release the information under FERPA because the student was not "enrolled." (The university did, however, eventually release the records under the Texas Open Records Law.)

Records may be accessible via civil rights laws (e.g., *U. Pa.* v. *EEOC*, U.S. Supreme Court, 1990), but only as to the part of the record necessary to show bias (or lack thereof). *U. Pa.* v. *EEOC* was a sex discrimination tenure case; FERPA was not directly involved.

7.10.2 Transferring Student Request for Records

One of your students is transferring to another institution. He wants an official transcript from your institution and copies of all academic documents he submitted as part of the admission process sent to the school that he is transferring to. The student owes your institution money. Do you have to provide an official transcript of his studies to the transfer institution, or can you withhold it until his account is settled? Similarly, what about copies of documents he submitted to you?

Resolution:

You are under no obligation to provide any copies of anything to a student unless geographic distance precludes the student from viewing his education records in person. FERPA only requires you to give access (even if he owes money) to the records.

In all cases except a legal bankruptcy, you may withhold sending a transcript to another institution or third party if the student owes money to your institution. In a bankruptcy, all debts are discharged, and the student has no financial obligation to your institution.

It is questionable professional practice to send copies of another institution's records on a student to anyone outside of your institution. Tell the student that the acceptable practice is for the student to request an official transcript from the institution at which he did the work. (He may also owe them money, or something on his record may have changed since the transcript was sent to you.)

7.11 Third-Party Verification Requests

7.11.1 The Departmental Phone Call

Lynn calls from the Civil Engineering Department. She states that she has had several investigators from different federal agencies and one corporate recruiter asking for information on some of the civil engineering graduates. Specifically, they want to look into the students' files to: (1) determine American citizenship, (2) verify their Quality Point Averages (QPAS)/Grade Point Averages (GPAS), (3) determine who the students' advisor was, and (4) determine what the students' degrees and majors were. She wants to know what information she can permit these individuals to see.

What would you ask her first, if anything? Then what would you tell her?

Resolution:

The registrar asked Lynn if the investigators had signed releases from the students involved. She said, "No." He then asked her to provide the names of the students. He checked the student information system to see if any of the students had placed a non-disclosure request on his record. Finding no records of non-disclosure, he then told Lynn that she could only release information that the institution had identified as directory information. In this case, Lynn could provide to the investigators major and degree information since those two items were identified as directory information by the institution.

If the investigators had presented signed releases from the students, Lynn could have provided all the information requested, as long as the specific non-directory information was included in the signed releases of the students (34 CFR 99.30).

7.11.2 Verification of Degree #1

You receive a letter from Mr. Lee of Taegu, Korea, requesting verification of the receipt of a degree by a particular individual who claims to have graduated from your college. Mr. Lee has included a copy of what the applicant indicates is his diploma from your college and a copy of the individual's resume, which lists a bachelor's degree from your school. Upon checking, you find no record of the individual's attendance.

What can and what do you tell Mr. Lee?

Resolution:

See Chapter 7.11.3, below.

7.11.3 Verification of Degree #2

The Personnel Department of XYZ Corporation calls and wants to verify that a new employee received a bachelor of science in biology degree. The caller says the employee presented a copy of your institution's diploma that indicates he received a B.S. degree from your institution. Department policy is that all employees must provide an official copy of all transcripts of their college work. This employee indicates, however, that he cannot do so because he owes the university $2,800 in tuition and the cashier has placed a "hold" on the issuance of any transcripts for him. He claims that without a job he cannot pay the past due amount and that he is attempting to temporarily satisfy XYZ's policy by providing a copy of his diploma until an official transcript can be sent.

Upon checking, you find that the employee's academic record does not indicate receipt of any degree and that he was academically suspended six months ago after six semesters of attendance.

What would you do?

Resolution:

The registrars in both cases (7.11.2 and 7.11.3), after determining whether the former students had filed non-disclosure requests before they left the institution, replied simply that they could not verify the degree.

How would you deal with a situation in which a student who attended your institution but did not receive a degree filed a non-disclosure request and is representing to prospective employers that he received a degree from your institution?

In instances where students have barred release of information, the requester should be advised that you cannot respond without a written release from the job applicant. You can also suggest that the individual send an official transcript to the requester. It appears that fraud may have been perpetrated. You may wish to ask the requester to send you a copy of the document for your review. You may then verify the authenticity of the document, but not the information on it. You also may wish to bring this information to the attention of your school attorney to discuss possible action by the institution. Remember: the potential fraud has been perpetrated on the third party, not on the institution.

7.11.4 Releasing a List of Black Accounting Majors to a Third Party

You receive a call from a colleague at another institution. Her request is as follows:

"The Academic Vice President at my institution is interested in working with the National Association of Black Accountants (NABA) to develop opportunities for our black students. To this end, we have been asked to provide to the National Association of Black Accountants a list of students who are accounting majors who have designated their ethnicity as black. We do not list ethnicity as directory information, and I do not see how we could provide this given our published definition. Is there a way that you know of that we could adhere to FERPA and send the information they are requesting?"

What do you tell her?

Resolution:

Because ethnicity is not considered directory information under any circumstances, the request cannot be satisfied unless the written permission of the black accounting majors is obtained first. If "major" was identified as directory information by the institution, a list of all accounting majors could be provided as long as the report only included directory information. In other words, no ethnic designation would be indicated on the report.

As an alternative, you could tell your colleague that the institution could send any communication from NABA to its black accounting majors. That communication could be written so that any interested student could decide if he or she wanted to follow up. You bridged the communication gap without releasing any non-directory information.

7.11.5 Precision Engineering's Request

Precision Engineering Co. has asked you, the registrar, for a list of engineering students in the top 10 percent of the senior class and their addresses so they can send information regarding a tremendous employment opportunity. How should you respond?

Resolution:

The institution should establish a policy about release of information to third parties. You may release directory information, but the designation of "top 10 percent" is not typically directory information. You could release a list of engineering students who achieved "Dean's List" as long as "awards received," "address," and "major" were identified by the institution as directory information. This is a good example of how you could think of different ways of satisfying a legitimate request that does not initially comply in all ways with FERPA. With a little creative thought, you have probably satisfied Precision's needs and you have done so in compliance with FERPA. (You also could offer to send the letter for Precision.)

7.11.6 Embassy Request—International Student

You receive a request for information about an international student. The request comes from an official at the student's embassy asking if the student is enrolled and if so, who is responsible for paying the student's fees. You believe that providing any information to the embassy official without the student's permission would be a violation of FERPA. Are you correct?

Resolution:

You may provide enrollment information as long as your school designates enrollment status (or some such term) as "directory information." The only exception would be if the student has placed a block (non-disclosure) on the release of directory information.

If your school does not designate enrollment information as "directory information," you would have to get the written consent of the student to release it to the embassy.

You should not provide information on who pays the student's fees since this is personally identifiable, non-directory information. Such information can be released to the embassy only with the written consent of the student or through one of the exceptions to written permission found in 34 CFR 99.31.

Forms such as the I-20 have consent provisions—in particular, the release of certain information to the INS—built into them. However, releasing personally identifiable information to the embassy is not justified under this release. International students are afforded the same FERPA protection as students who are U.S. citizens.

7.11.7 Telephone Inquiry and Non-Disclosure

You are interested in knowing how your office responds to telephone queries for directory information about students who have requested that this information not be released. What is the "exact" wording of your office's standard response? (Or, at least, what is your staff supposed to be saying?)

Resolution:

- For students who have restricted their directory information, you should not even verify that the individual is a student currently attending. Say something to the effect of, "I'm sorry, but I'm unable to verify that information."
- If you say the student has requested privacy, you have "given away" the fact that he is enrolled; therefore, we say, "I'm sorry, but we cannot verify any information on that person."
- LeRoy Rooker, director of the Family Policy Compliance Office, suggests saying, "I have no information that I can release related to that individual."

7.11.8 Request for Attendance Verification Using Social Security Numbers

Institution B receives a request from Institution A accompanied by a list of students' names and social security numbers. No signed releases from the students are enclosed in the mailing. Institution A wishes to know whether any of its former students have enrolled at your institution.

Should you comply?

Resolution:

This request seems simple enough. If your institution includes "enrollment status" as directory information, why wouldn't you comply with the request?

The fact that social security numbers were included on the request complicates matters, and you could be in violation of FERPA for two reasons: First, social security numbers cannot be identified by any institution as "directory information." Therefore, if you confirm to Institution A that a student is attending your institution (Institution B), you are indirectly confirming a non-directory item (social security number) without first obtaining the student's written permission.

Second, you are technically violating FERPA because you are releasing your enrolled students' social security numbers back to Institution A without first obtaining the students' written permission.

Institution A would be in violation of FERPA because it sent you (Institution B) social security numbers (non-directory information under FERPA) without obtaining the students' written permission. No exceptions in 34 CFR 99.31 cover this situation.

In an effort to assist their colleagues, Institution B should contact Institution A and ask it to resubmit its request using just the students' names and birthdates. (This assumes that both institutions identify both names and birthdates as directory information.)

Note: Institutions requesting such information, perhaps to comply with SRTK, are strongly urged not to include students' social security numbers on their requests unless they have received written authorization from the students to release their social security numbers to the responding institution.

7.12 Students' Requests Relating to Their Education Records

7.12.1 The Phone Call for Grades

It is December. The fall semester's grades have just been processed. You receive a phone call from a person who claims to be Billy Smith. Billy states that he desperately needs to know what his fall grades are so he can complete a scholarship application that is due the next day. You tell him that the grade reports will not be sent until tomorrow. Billy asks if there is any way he could get his grades over the phone, since he cannot delay submitting his application. He is willing to provide his personal identification number and anything else you request to verify that he is who he says he is.

What do you do?

Resolution:

FERPA requires a signed release before releasing non-directory information to a third party. It does not preclude you from releasing information to the student whose record is in question. If you can verify, through a combination of PIN, student identification number, date of birth, parents' names, etc. (i.e., information that normally only the student would know) that you are actually talking with the student, then the information may be released. Otherwise, it should not be released.

As an added precaution, you could return a call to the student at one of the phone numbers on your student record file before releasing the information.

7.12.2 "Confidential References"

A freshman, Debra, comes in to see you. She is rather upset and states that she understands she has the right to look at her folder. She asks to see the references in her "admissions folder." This folder, you know, was transferred to your (the Registrar's) office after her admission, and the contents have been incorporated in her official academic folder. According to the college's policy, you tell her to return tomorrow and the folder will be available for her to review.

Upon reviewing Debra's folder, you find a form she completed as part of her admission application. By completing and signing the form, Debra waived any future right to inspect the comments from her references.

When you see Debra again, do you allow her to see the references? Why or why not?

Resolution:

By signing the form, Debra waived her rights to review those references. She cannot now change her mind. The privacy of the recommenders' comments must be protected. When she returns the following day, these letters should not be available for her review. Instead, she should be provided with an explanation and, if requested, a copy of the waiver she signed.

7.12.3 Student Request Not to Release Education Information

(See Fig. 7.12.3 on the following page.)

Resolution:

This has two correct answers.

The registrar does not have to honor the request from the student because the non-disclosure request must be made by a currently attending student, not a former student. In addition, non-disclosure applies only to directory information (see Chapter 5.36).

The registrar could honor the request since FERPA allows institutions to grant additional rights to former students if those rights are not specifically prohibited by FERPA. Thus, the institution could honor the request for non-disclosure by the former student but does not have to do so.

7.12.4 Student's Right to Access/Copy of Previous Institution's Transcript

A question has been brought to your attention concerning your institution's policy of not issuing copies of other universities' transcripts to students. For example, a student has a copy of his or her transcript from University A sent to University B. Once the student is registered at University B, the student requests a copy of the original University A transcript. What do you, as representative of University B, tell the student?

Resolution:

According to FERPA, students have the right to access their education records that are maintained by the institution. FERPA does not require an institution to provide copies of any education records unless geographic distance precludes a student from effectively having access to his or her education records.

Fig. 7.12.3: Student Request Not to Release Education Information

Monday, December 1, 1986

Office of Student Records
University of Wisconsin-Madison
Madison, WI 53706

Dear Records Department:

I am a December 1983 graduate from the University of Wisconsin-Madison with a Bachelor of Arts Degree in Communication Arts Public Address.

I am writing to require that no records of mine be sent to any one other than myself. Lately I have had to sign release of information forms for various governmental and employment agencies. If these groups contact you for release of information regarding me, you have my permission to send them a copy of my diploma only, so they have proof that I did graduate, however, in no way should you send out any copies of my other records. I do not want my transcripts or GPA sent out to anyone who has a release of informaiton form signed by me.

I hope this letter is all that is needed to legally prevent anything other than my diploma being sent to those with my signature on a release liability of information form. If not, please send to me at the above address any forms I need to fill out to comply with my request.

Thank you for your cooperation. I am enclosing a copy of one of the many Information Liability Releases that may be sent to you. They should only receive a copy of my diploma.

In response to requests for copies of other institutions' records in your possession, your reply should always be to request a copy from the original institution.

Regarding copies of transcripts from other institutions, one institution has developed the following response:

Copies of Transcripts from Other Institutions

"What is Fresno Pacific's policy on the copying of transcripts from other institutions? Transcripts and other documents from other institutions are the property of Fresno Pacific University, and, as such are under the control of the Registrar's Office. Under federal policy, the student has the right to view the documents in his or her file; the university is not required to provide (or allow the making of) copies of these documents. Transcripts submitted to Fresno Pacific University for admission or credit transfer become the property of Fresno Pacific and cannot be returned to the student or forwarded to other institutions (Academic Catalog).

Why do Fresno Pacific and most other colleges and universities have a policy that does not provide for the making of copies of transcripts from other institutions? That's a good question. On the surface, a policy that allows a person to see a document without copying it may seem odd, at best. There are, however, a number of reasons behind the policy:

- *The documents are a reflection of a student's record at the other institution at a particular time (like a snapshot), and, as such, may not be complete. In fact, the record may have been added to or changed by the issuing institution; the record may not reflect the student's most current record.*
- *The current, complete, accurate, and official record of a student's academic work is made available by the transcripting institution. Fresno Pacific is concerned that those receiving and using the record work from official documents, not copies.*
- *Fresno Pacific has no way of knowing whether a student wishes to use a copy of a transcript from another institution (with an incomplete record) to avoid having others see grades or other information which may be considered by the student to be negative (e.g., low grades, records of disciplinary actions). In other cases, students may have an account balance at the issuing institution and may therefore be prevented from obtaining an official transcript until such obligations are met. As a professional courtesy, Fresno Pacific honors the desire of the issuing institution to have official records obtained directly from that institution. Fresno Pacific expects other institutions not to make copies of FPU transcripts that may be found in its students' files.*

7.12.5 Access to "My" Advisor's Record

Joe Student is assigned to Annie Advisor. At one point during the year, he asks if he may view his education record, including everything Annie has written about him. He is concerned about what personal information Annie has included. Does FERPA allow access to all of his records? If not, can he still see his record? A year later, Joe is assigned to Bill Advisor, who "inherited" Joe (and his record) from Annie. If Joe asks to see his record again, would there be any limitations? How should the institution respond?

Resolution:

As a general rule, Joe has access to all personally identifiable information that a school official of an institution maintains on him unless that information is not subject to FERPA. This does not appear to be the case here. Even advisor's notes are education records since they were made in conjunction with another person (the student). Therefore, they are not "sole possession" notes.

What is an example of a "sole possession" note? Let's say that Annie has Joe in one of her classes. She writes a note about his behavior in class and places the note in her personal "Joe" folder that only she (or a temporary substitute) has access to. That note, since it was made as a "memory aid" and is accessible only to herself and a temporary substitute in a file that only they have access to, is an example of a "sole possession" note.

7.12.6 Victim's Access to Information

Paul Student was assaulted on campus a few weeks ago. Campus security was able to track down the alleged assailant based on Paul's description. It turned out to be another student. Paul filed charges with the local police department and with the campus judicial authorities. He knows that a hearing was held on campus, but he hasn't been able to find out what the outcome was because the hearing was confidential. Does Paul have the right to know what happened at the hearing?

Resolution:

Recent amendments to FERPA allow release to the victim of a crime the results of any disciplinary hearing regarding the circumstances and the alleged assailant [see Appendix 2; 34 CFR 99.31 (a)(13)].

7.13 Matters Financial

7.13.1 A Student Asks to See His Records

A person comes into the office and asks to look at the contents in his folder. Upon pulling the folder, you notice that he has a financial hold on his record. He owes the college $4,347.80 from the previous year.

(1) Do you show him his folder? (2) Does he have a legal right to obtain an official transcript?

Resolution:

Answer to question #1: Yes.

The student does have a right to inspect the contents of his student folder regardless of his financial status with the institution. You have 45 days to comply with the request unless your FERPA institutional policy statement indicates fewer days to comply.

Answer to question #2: No.

The institution is not required to release an official transcript if the student has a past due account with the institution and the institution has a policy to that effect. Bankruptcy, however, removes any financial obligations of the student to the institution. Where bankruptcy has been legally declared, the institution should comply with the request to send an official transcript (Tanaka, 1995).

7.13.2 The Defaulted Loan; the Withheld Transcript

As a student at Montana State University, Stanley Juras received several National Direct Student Loans (NDSLs). Following his graduation, Mr. Juras defaulted on those loans. When collection efforts proved unsuccessful, Montana State assigned the debt to Aman Collection Services for collection; the agency obtained a Montana state court judgment against Mr. Juras for the full balance. In attempting to collect the loan, Aman threatened to withhold his transcript.

Mr. Juras then filed an action against Aman in federal district court, alleging that the practice of withholding transcripts of defaulted borrowers violated the United States Constitution, the federal Fair Debt Collections Practices Act, and the (now repealed) National Direct Student Loan Act. Mr. Juras claimed that he had a "proprietary right or liberty interest in his transcripts and that Montana State was obligated to provide him with a due process hearing before it could deny him a transcript. Mr. Juras also argued that since the NDSL required universities to make student loans without 'security,' the university was violating the act by "withholding transcripts from defaulted student borrowers." (Information received from Aman Collection Services Inc., 1 South 1st Street, Box 730, Aberdeen, South Dakota; Van Tol, 1989, pp. 249–250.)

How did the court decide?

Resolution:

The court decided in favor of Aman and the university. (*Juras* v. *Aman Collection Service, Inc.*, 830 F. 2d 576 (9th Cir. 1987).

7.14 Miscellaneous Items

7.14.1 The Intern

The medical college of your university has an intern who wishes to see his records. Although he did not receive his medical training at your medical college, he claims that he has a right to review the records the medical college is keeping on him as an intern.

Can he see his records?

Resolution:

An intern is not considered a student and as a result has no FERPA right to see his record. He should be advised to obtain the desired copy directly from the institution he or she attended. Note: In many states, interns and residents are considered employees and are not accorded student status.

7.14.2 **The INS Request**

The local office of the Immigration and Naturalization Service calls and requests an official transcript of a student who is attending your institution on a student (F-1) visa.

Can you comply?

Resolution:

The registrar complied with the request since part of the I-20 form that the student signed authorizes release of such information.

All students, regardless of origin or visa status, have FERPA rights. Requests from agencies must have the written authorization of the student to release non-directory information. In some instances, the student's application for, or acceptance of, a visa automatically provides such authorization to INS (e.g., a signed I-20 or IAP-66 form).

7.14.3 **Employer Requests Information on Students**

You receive the following letter from a local employer:

D. E. Hicks Roofing Co.
PO Box 1240
4728 S. Amherst Hwy.
Skyway OH 44999

Dear Admissions Department:

Enclosed are three applications for the 2001 spring classes. These three people are employed with D. E. Hicks Roofing Co. and their classes will be paid for by the company. I would appreciate it if you could send the letters of acceptance/denial to us here at our office. I do understand if this is not possible.

Thank you for being so helpful over the phone and for answering our questions with patience. Looking forward to hearing from you.

Sincerely,

Julia G. Cyrus
Office Manager

Do you comply with the request?

Resolution:

Because the office manager indicated that the three employees' tuition would be paid by the company, you could send the requested information since FERPA permits releasing information "if the disclosure is in connection with financial aid which the student...has received..." [34 CFR 99.31 (4)]. According to FERPA, "'financial aid' means payment of funds provided to an individual...that is conditioned on the individual's attendance at an educational...institution" [34 CFR 99.31 (4)(ii)].

7.14.4 **Students as Employees—Directory Information**

Your university publishes a combined faculty/staff/student directory that for faculty and staff lists name, office address, office phone number, and home address and phone number (unless unlisted). The student portion lists the student's name, school address and school phone number, home address and home phone number, class, and major at time of publication.

To prevent directory information from being published in the directory, students can invoke their FERPA privacy right with the Registrar's Office prior to the start of classes for the fall semester. The privacy code prevents the information from being published in the student portion of the directory. However, if the student is a graduate assistant (considered an employee) or a staff member, the privacy code does not prevent school address and phone number and home address and phone number from being published in the faculty/staff portion of the directory.

Does FERPA extend to the faculty/staff portion of the directory? If so, should it be extended only if the staff member is enrolled in classes? Or should it allow any faculty or staff member to request that this information not be released, regardless of enrollment status?

Resolution:

Any currently enrolled student has the right to withhold directory information, regardless of the student's employment status at the institution and no matter where that information is published. Therefore, if a student has requested non-disclosure, the information is not to be published in any student or employee directory created by the institution.

This also applies to any employee who was once a student and who, while a student, requested non-disclosure and has not requested since that the block be lifted.

7.14.5 **A Student Request to Include in Her Record an Explanation Regarding a Grade**

A nursing student received a failing grade in a course because she made a near fatal medication error on a patient. The error was detected in time to correct the situation. The student filed a grievance with the university. The grievance committee (which could only make recommendations) recommended that the faculty member recalculate the grade. The faculty member rejected the recommendation. The department chair and dean supported the faculty member. The student engaged an attorney, reluctantly accepted the grade, but was quite unhappy. She requested that a copy of her letter explaining her side of the situation and the letter from the grievance committee chair recommending grade recalculation be made a part of her education record and that anytime a transcript was sent, copies of the letters be attached.

Should the institution comply with the request?

Resolution:

The institution is not compelled by FERPA to include the requested statement in the student's education record. The Family Policy Compliance Office has ruled that students' right of the hearing process under FERPA is not a substitute for grades accurately recorded (see Chapter 4.2 on rights of students under a FERPA hearing).

7.14.6 Student Sorority Scholarship Chair Complains about Obtaining Written Permission for Grades

You have several sororities/fraternities on campus, and each has a student scholarship chairperson. One particular sorority scholarship chairperson is requesting the grades of each of the members of the sorority so awards, etc., can be given within the sorority. This chairperson is upset because she had to go to each person in the sorority and obtain a signature on a release form, stating that the person allows the registrar's office to release the transcript to the scholarship chairperson. You are trying to make this process less cumbersome for the sorority and registrar's office staff.

Is there a better way to obtain the written consents?

Resolution:

By creating and carefully crafting a written permission form that permits the release of grades to the scholarship chairs, this permission could be completed once and used every term the student is enrolled at the college. In addition, the registrar could discuss the possibility with her superiors of identifying these chairs as "school officials" with a "legitimate educational interest" limited to performing their responsibilities as scholarship chairs. This would permit the chairs to obtain transcripts without first having to obtain the written consent of the students involved. Of course, this would involve modifying the college's institutional FERPA policy to include this procedure, as well as modifying the definition of "school official" and statement of what constitutes a "legitimate educational interest."

7.14.7 When Does a Student Have FERPA Rights?

You are asked if FERPA applies to a 14-year-old advanced high school student who is taking a college-level course. Can the parent expect/demand to get test grades from a professor? You think that FERPA does apply and the parent cannot expect/demand access to his child's grades.

What is your reply?

Resolution:

FERPA clearly gives the rights to the student when he or she begins attending an institution of higher education, regardless of age. Those rights, however, apply only to the education records of the student at the institution of higher education and not to the high school records (until the student turns 18).

The student could give written permission for the parent to receive the grades.

7.14.8 Notification of Parents of Any Alcohol Violations by Son or Daughter

Your institution recently adopted a new alcohol policy for your students. The vice president responsible for administering the policy intends to notify students' parents when any violations occur.

You know FERPA pertains to academic confidentiality, but does it also apply to this situation?

Resolution:

FERPA applies to all education records personally identifiable to students that the college maintains in whatever form. Therefore, FERPA applies to more than just the academic records of students.

With the new 2000 FERPA regulations (see Appendix 2), colleges are permitted to release this information to parents of students under the age of 21, regardless of their dependency status, without written permission of the student [34 CFR 99.31 (a)(15)].

7.14.9 Sole Possession Notes

At your institution, the Affirmative Action Officer (AAO) was investigating a complaint filed by a student with the State's Department of Human Rights. The student alleged that a faculty member had sexually harassed her. In the investigation, the Affirmative Action Officer interviewed all students who may have observed the alleged incident. The AAO interviewed each student individually and privately, and while interviewing, wrote notes of each student's observations and recollections. The AAO did not ask each student to review the notes for accuracy and did not share the notes with anyone. The interview notes were maintained in the AAO's office in a locked cabinet. No other person had access to the notes. The AAO did review the notes when preparing a response to the State Department of Human Resources but did not disclose the notes themselves to anyone.

Several years later, the student who had made the accusation of sexual harassment discovered that the notes existed and asked to see them since, under FERPA, a student has the right to examine education records. The AAO was advised by legal counsel that the notes were "sole possession" records and thus were not education records and not subject to review by the student. The student then filed a complaint with the Family Policy Compliance Office, claiming that her "right to access" under FERPA had been denied.

Was her "right to access" improperly denied?

Resolution:

The Family Policy Compliance Office determined that since the notes had been "...prepared with the assistance or participation of others, such as the students interviewed...," the notes are education records and the student must be provided access to these records under FERPA. Therefore, the notes in question are not sole possession notes.

The notes were redacted to protect the privacy of the students who had been interviewed and then were provided to the complainant.

7.14.10 Posting of Delinquent/Unfilled Requests for Student Information to Complete Student Folder

Each semester your institution admits and enrolls a few new students who haven't yet submitted all of the required admissions documents, e.g., health record, official ACT/SAT scores, measles immunization verification, etc. You give these students a one-semester "grace period" to get all of these documents to you, and at the beginning of the fall semester, you send each student a letter reminding him which documents are missing. Now, as you approach spring semester pre-registration, some students have not yet gotten all of these documents to you, and you would like to remind them once again, but this time without having to send another individualized letter.

You are considering putting a general notice (warning) in the student newspaper reminding them of this situation and directing them to check a list on a bulletin board outside your office that would indicate the following:

Student name (or ID#)	Missing Admissions Documents
John H. Jones	ACT/SAT scores, Health Record
Elizabeth Bird	High School Transcript
etc...	

Can you do this under FERPA?

Resolution:

"Missing admissions documents" are not identified as directory information by the institution. The posting would be a violation of FERPA. It also would probably be a violation of the student's privacy under any conditions. Thus, those types of documents should never be identified as directory information.

Also, any posting that includes the student's ID number without prior student approval would be a violation of FERPA.

7.14.11 The Ex-Girl Friend

Sue works in the registrar's office. She has an ax to grind with her ex-boyfriend, Ken, so she tells his fraternity brothers that he was recently placed on academic probation and is in danger of being dismissed. She knows that Ken cannot continue to hold his office position in the fraternity if they know that his grades are poor. She viewed Ken's grades while working in the registrar's office.

Upon learning of Sue's tattling, Ken and his parents have hired an attorney. Can Ken's attorney use FERPA or the state's Open Records Law to determine if any disciplinary action has been taken by the institution against Sue? Would it make a difference if the university was private or public? Would it make a difference if Sue was a regular employee rather than a student? How should the institution respond?

Resolution:

FERPA permits the institution to disclose the final results of disciplinary hearings concerning crimes of violence as long as certain conditions have been met [34 CFR 99.31 (a)(14)]. In this situation, if the institution decided to bring charges against Sue, the final results of the hearing would not be subject to disclosure since it does not involve an "alleged perpetrator of a crime of violence." Therefore, the attorney would not be eligible under FERPA to obtain any information regarding Sue's indiscretion. FERPA supersedes a state's Open Records Law, and that law would not apply to a private institution. If Sue was a regular employee, then FERPA would not apply, and the state's open records law might require release of the information. The institution should take disciplinary action against Sue if it hasn't done so already.

7.14.12 Utilizing Student Workers

Your office is moving to an integrated student information system. It has several modules in addition to student records and registration. Your human resources project team announces its intention to use student workers to create and update personal records. Although the person records these students would be creating would be for job applicants, the form that is used is the same form admissions would use to create student person records. You are concerned about security and policy issues since you don't let students update anything (except that they can enter transcript requests). This is therefore a major departure from past practice.

You aren't sure if this is permitted under FERPA, so you query regist-l and scr-l (the two listservs for registrar/records types). What responses might you get?

Resolution:

FERPA does not preclude an institution from identifying students as "school officials" with "legitimate educational interests" for specific purposes. Therefore, the practice described above would be acceptable under FERPA. The same requirements for, and responsibilities of, school officials exist for these students. Thus, they would need to be trained on FERPA just as if they were faculty or staff working for the institution.

Here are two responses that were received from two listservs in reply to the query mentioned above. These were typical of most received:

"We do allow student workers access to certain sensitive data in the Registrar's Office, more by necessity than choice. We limit it as much as possible, and of course under no circumstances would they enter grades, be privy to dismissal information, etc. When they start working in our office we have a discussion with them about privacy, the rules we exist under, information they can and cannot discuss outside of the office, and...make them sign the Student Worker Statement of Understanding of the Family Educational Rights and Privacy Act (1998 FERPA Guide, Appendix 10)."

"We allow our work-study students to do maintenance within our student records. We put them through a FERPA overview just like regular staff and inform them that they are school officials just like the rest of us and have the same responsibilities and expectations. It has worked just fine for us."

7.14.13 Records Retention Question and FERPA

You are in the process of preparing old records for microfiche. One of your assistants asks you what to do with student requests for transcripts and verifications of employment, graduation, etc. In reviewing AACRAO's latest retention of records guide, "Retention of Records: Guide for Retention and Disposal of Student Records 2000 Update," you find, under Retention Schedule C, that it indicates that transcript requests made by students can be destroyed one year after the date submitted. However, under the notes section, as well as Retention Schedule F, it specifies that "FERPA requires institutions to maintain records of requests and disclosures of personally identifiable information except for defined directory information and requests from students for their own records. The records of disclosure and requests for disclosure are considered part of the students' education records; therefore, they must be retained as long as the education records to which they refer are retained by the institution" (you assume that this would include requests for transcripts and/or enrollment and graduation verification).

You are thoroughly confused. Should you be microfilming copies of student requests for transcripts or signed authorizations for education verification from five to ten years ago, or can these be destroyed one year after the date submitted?

Resolution:

FERPA does not require an institution to keep any record of a disclosure of a student's record if that student authorized the disclosure. Also, FERPA does not require that you keep records of requests made by school officials for students' records or any request that is solely related to the release of directory information. Thus, the recordkeeping requirement for disclosures under FERPA is rather limited. Generally, an institution is required to keep records only of disclosures of non-directory information to third parties who are not school officials, and only if the student has not given written consent. The most prevalent example of this type of disclosure would be in compliance with a lawfully issued subpoena or IRS summons.

Therefore, you may keep the transcript request for whatever period you deem reasonable and destroy when you see fit. If you are employed at a public institution, you should check any applicable state laws to determine if there is a minimum time these records are to be maintained.

FERPA makes no distinction between transcript requests made by currently enrolled students and those made by students who have graduated or are no longer attending.

Records that are in the process of being reviewed or records for which a request to review has been made are not to be destroyed while the request is active. This applies primarily when the student wishes to view his or her record. Also, it is good business practice not to destroy any records which you know are being reviewed either by one of your attorneys or by an outside attorney in response to a subpoena. If you are micro-filming and destroying, place a tickler note on the student's file and revisit the situation in a month or two.

7.14.14 Power of Attorney

One of your registrar friends sends you and e-mail and needs help with a question. Here is his message:

"I have received a notarized power of attorney document that gives a former student's father the right to conduct business on behalf of his son. However, the wording of the document is specific to business transactions, and not educational records. This student is not disabled; he is just lazy, and his father is overprotective and overzealous in his son's life. Admittedly, that has nothing to do with whether the power of attorney is valid or not, but that's my two cents worth!

I can't find anything in the FERPA guidelines about power of attorney. What should I do?"

How do you respond?

Resolution:

You reply:

"First of all, you need to determine what the father is requesting. From the question asked above, it is not clear what the father wants.

Under normal circumstances, a power of attorney, if all legal requirements have been met, authorizes the person designated in the document to conduct business for the person delegating the authority. You should consult your legal counsel to determine if this is a legally binding power of attorney. If it is, you should treat the person bearing the power of attorney in the same manner as if he was the student. Although the term "business transactions" has a very broad definition, I would question whether it applies to access to the student's records. It is very questionable whether this is a business transaction. Certainly, paying for a transcript, a student's tuition, or an overdue book is a business transaction Nevertheless, if the father is requesting access to his son's education records, you have the right to question the wording in the power of attorney. That is where you need legal counsel to assist you. You are correct that laziness on the part of the student should not enter into your decision at all. The key fact is whether the power of attorney is legal and whether you are obligated under that power of attorney to grant access to the father if that is what he is requesting."

7.14.15 Student Sues College for Breach of Contract

One of your colleagues from another state calls to ask for advice. She says:

"One of our students is suing the school for what I would call a breach of contract by not fulfilling the responsibility of teaching. As I understand it, the student is claiming that the course was poorly handled, the instructor inadequate, and that many students received NC grades. (We do not have any failing grades, nor do we have a W for withdrawal; NC replaces both of those grades.)

The Business Office person testifying in court wants to take the final grade roster and show the grades. I said no, not without written consent of each student. Then I was asked if they blacked out names and ID#, could they use the grade roster. I told them via e-mail this morning that no, they cannot. Rosters are in alpha order—we ask for faculty to take attendance for at least the first two class meetings. So if the first ten grades were all As, we would have disclosed that any with a last name starting with A and B got an A grade.

I did tell them that if the course had more than seven students in the class, they could disclose the number of students who received each grade (A, B, C, and NC). Or better yet, if the same course has been taught more than once recently by the same instructor, they could add all sections together and give the grade distribution.

The student suing the school is the only student who received an NC grade. The student's academic record has not been subpoenaed by anyone. Can our Business Office person get on the stand and disclose that only one person received an NC grade? Is that person disclosing personal information on this student without consent or subpoena? Or does the fact that the student is suing the school allow us to disclose the student's grade?"

Resolution:

If a student has initiated legal action against an institution, FERPA permits an institution to defend itself in court by disclosing to the court the appropriate education records of the student without obtaining the student's written permission, or a subpoena or court order [34 CFR 99.31 (a)(9)(iii)(E)].

7.15 Notifying Students of Grades Received

7.15.1 Posting Grades by Social Security Number

Two professors have inquired about notifying students of their grades. Their questions are:

- Is it okay to post grades by the last four digits of the students' social security numbers?
- If a course is offered via the Internet, could grades be posted on the web using a code such as the last four digits of the students' social security numbers or some other code?

How do you respond?

Resolution:

The Family Policy Compliance Office has determined that grades can be posted by the last four digits of the social security number and the institution will still be in compliance with FERPA. If this is done, it is highly recommended that the posted list not be in alphabetical order.

A more satisfactory strategy, if faculty need to post grades, is to have the faculty member assign a random number to each student in the class that only the student and faculty member know. The grade-posting list should be in random (not alphabetical) order.

7.15.2 Posting Grades on Class Website

Your wife, who is taking an Internet class at the university where you work, tells you she saw her final grade posted on the class website. You, the registrar, watch, as she, using a login id and password, accesses the website. To your dismay, you discover that not only can she see her own grade, but she can see the grades of her classmates as well. What do you do?

Resolution:

The registrar notified the instructor (without tattling on his wife) that it had come to his attention that he (the instructor) had posted grades to his class website that were personally identifiable to specific students; that students in the class could see one another's grades; and that this was a violation of FERPA if the instructor had not first obtained the students' written permission.

The instructor stated that he was aware of FERPA and of the restrictions on posting grades. He explained that he felt he was in compliance since the students needed their login IDs and passwords to access their grades.

The registrar commended the instructor for his attempt to comply with FERPA but explained that since students could see the grades of their classmates and had not given written consent for these grades to be posted, he was in violation of FERPA.

After discussing various options (e.g., segregating the grades so that each student could access only his or her own, sending a letter to each student with his or her grade, making the students wait for their official grade reports), the instructor agreed to remove the grade list from the website.

7.15.3 Leaving Graded Exams for Student Pick-up

First scenario: You receive a phone call from a divisional secretary who needs to know what to tell instructors who want to leave graded exams outside their classrooms/offices for students to pick up.

Similar scenario, same answer: While you are strolling around campus at the end of the semester, after grades are processed, looking for faculty postings of grades on office doors, you come across a group of graded term papers on the table outside of one faculty member's office. The departmental secretary was told by the faculty member before he left for his annual holiday cruise in the Caribbean that some students may come by to pick up their term papers. He told the secretary where they were located and went on his way.

Is this a FERPA violation?

Resolution:

Leaving personally identifiable, graded papers unattended for students to pick through is no different from posting grades in the hallway. If these papers contain "personally identifiable" information, then leaving them unattended for anyone to see is a violation of FERPA if the instructor has not obtained the written permission of each student to do so.

A possible solution would be either to leave the graded papers (exams, quizzes, homework) with an assistant or secretary who would ask students for proper identification prior to distributing them or to leave them in a sealed envelope with only the student's name on it.

Below is an example of a letter that was sent to one faculty member who left papers outside his office prior to leaving for the end-of-semester break:

Memo from the Registrar

To: Hayden Fox
From: Luther Van Damm, Registrar
RE: Papers lying outside your office door
Date: January 17, 1997

Hayden,

I found the enclosed set of papers lying outside your office door in Armstrong last Thursday. I am returning these to you for proper disposal to students.

My reasons are the following: In placing these papers in a public area without any protection against one student seeing another student's grade, a law of Congress (the Family Educational Rights and Privacy Act of 1974, or FERPA for short) is being violated. This law makes it illegal to publicly distribute/display personally identifiable student education records without the students' written permission. These papers are personally identifiable (they have the students' names on them) and are, therefore, education records subject to FERPA. If you obtained the students' written permission to distribute these papers this way, you would be in compliance with FERPA. However, I am assuming that you did not get the students' written permission and, therefore, we are violating students' rights under FERPA.

It would be more proper to request the post office to place the papers in each student's mail box, to have the students see you personally for their papers, or to place each paper in a plain, sealed envelope with only the student's name on it.

I know that you had no intent of violating a law under which our college could be held liable. I encourage you to find a better, legal way of distributing papers in the future. If you have any questions, feel free to contact me.

7.16 ROTC Requests

7.16.1 ROTC Request #1

The ROTC unit at another institution has an agreement with your campus that provides faculty rank for the commander and commits your institution to assisting him in recruiting students for the ROTC program. This has happened in the past. Now the commander wants a list to select students who are receiving GI Bill benefits. Should you comply?

Resolution:

There are two different ways to view this situation, and each way provides a different answer.

1. If the commander can be designated as a "school official," then the question revolves around your institution's policy on what is a "legitimate educational interest." If the commander cannot, by any stretch of the imagination, be included under the institution's definition of "school official," then there is no legal obligation under FERPA to provide any information.

   If the commander falls under the institution's definition of "school official," the request should be treated the same as any other request from any other school official (faculty, staff, president, etc.) using the same criteria to determine whether to release the requested information.

   If the commander can be considered a "school official," it then needs to be determined if there is a legitimate educational interest based on the institutional policy. If the registrar or legal counsel can determine that the request is for a "legitimate educational interest," then any selection criterion can be used to produce the requested information. The selection criteria or information provided do not have to be limited to FERPA directory information. In any case where a "legitimate educational interest" is involved, the registrar can exercise any prerogative on whether to release. In one instance, a request may be approved; in another, it might not, depending on the circumstances involved. Where "legitimate educational interest" is involved, FERPA allows institutions to make decisions based on the individual situation.

2. With the enactment of the Solomon Amendment, institutions are required to comply with requests from representatives of the Department of Defense for "student recruiting information" (according to the definition in the Solomon Amendment). This includes representatives from ROTC units. The Solomon Amendment does not require the institution to use the "legitimate educational interest" criterion to provide the requested information. The institution is required only to provide "student recruiting information," according to the Solomon definition, in a usable format to representatives of the Department of Defense for recruiting purposes (see Chapter 5.41). Because GI Bill benefit status is not currently defined as "student recruiting information," the institution would have no authority under the Solomon Amendment to release the requested information to the ROTC unit commander.

7.16.2 ROTC Request #2

A member of an institution's ROTC unit has requested a list of all students with GPAs of 2.5 or higher. Should you comply?

Resolution:

Because a student's GPA is not identified as "student recruiting information" under the Solomon Amendment, the institution could not comply under its provisions.

Under FERPA, the institution must determine if the ROTC member is designated as a "school official." If not, he has no right of access to this information. If he were considered a "school official," the institution would have to determine if the recruiter has a "legitimate educational interest" in the requested information.

If a biology professor had requested the same information in an effort to recruit new biology majors and/or to award biology scholarships, how would the institution have responded?

If the institution determined the ROTC member was a "school official" with a "legitimate educational interest," it would not be violating FERPA if it released the information requested.

Any "school official" has to understand that any non-directory, personally identifiable information provided in any report must not be released to any third parties without the written permission of the students listed in the report.

7.16.3 ROTC Request #3

The ROTC unit at your institution has requested a list of all students who did not return for the spring semester. After a little sleuthing, you, the registrar, discover that the ROTC unit is requesting the information on behalf of the U.S. Army Recruiting Command in your area. Should you comply?

Resolution:

The ROTC unit should not be acting as an intermediary between the Army Recruiting Command and the registrar's office. It could, however, be considered a recruiting unit under Solomon and be entitled to "student recruiting information." Drop-out lists are not included in the list of items identified as "student recruiting information." Therefore, the request should be denied under Solomon. Additionally, Solomon requires that institutions provide "student recruiting information" to each branch of the armed services only once a semester.

Even if it were determined that the ROTC unit was considered a "school official" with a "legitimate educational interest" in the information, it would have no right or authority to release the material to a third party without first receiving the students' written permission since drop-out status was not identified by the institution as directory information.

Under these circumstances, the registrar's office would be wise not to release the information to the ROTC unit and should inform that unit to have the Army Recruiting Command contact the registrar's office directly.

7.16.4 Request from ROTC for Transcripts/Grades

At your institution, the ROTC staff are being asked by their superiors to provide the mean GPA of students in a particular major and/or department.

Given that this does not include any information that can identify individuals, is this permitted under FERPA?

Resolution:

Yes. You may provide aggregate data as long as no students are personally identified.

Appendix 1

The Family Educational Rights and Privacy Act of 1974 as Amended

United States Code Annotated
Title 20
Education
Ch. 31 Administration Of Programs 20 1232G

1232g. Family educational and privacy rights

Conditions for availability of funds to educational agencies or institutions: inspection and review of education records; specific information to be made available; procedure for access to education records; reasonableness of time for such access; hearings; written explanations by parents; definitions

(a)(1)(A) No funds shall be made available under any applicable program to any educational agency or institution which has a policy of denying, or which effectively prevents, the parents of students who are or have been in attendance at a school of such agency or at such institution, as the case may be, the right to inspect and review the education record of a student includes information on more than one student, the parents of one of such students shall have the right to inspect and review only such part of such material or document as relates to such student or to be informed of the specific information contained in such part of such material. Each educational agency or institution shall establish appropriate procedures for the granting of a request by parents for access to the education records of their children within a reasonable period of time, but in no case more than forty-five days after the request has been made.

(B) The first sentence of subparagraph (A) shall not operate to make available to students in institutions of postsecondary education the following material:

(i) financial records of the parents of the student or any information contained therein;

(ii) confidential letters and statements of recommendation, which were placed in the education records prior to January 1, 1975, if such letters or statements are not used for purposes other than those for which they were specifically intended;

(iii) if the student has signed a waiver of the student's right of access under this subsection in accordance with subparagraph (C), confidential recommendations-

(I) respecting an admission to any educational agency or institution,

(II) respecting an application for employment, and

(III) respecting the receipt of an honor or honorary recognition.

(C) A student or a person applying for admission may waive his right of access to confidential statements described in clause (iii) of subparagraph (B), except that such waiver shall apply to recommendations only if (I) the student is, upon request, notified of the names of all persons making confidential recommendations and (ii) such recommendations are used solely for the purpose for which they were specifically intended. Such waivers may not be required as a condition for admission to, receipt of financial aid from, or receipt of any other services or benefits from such agency or institution.

(2) No funds shall be made available under any applicable program to any educational agency or institution unless the parents of students who are or have been in attendance at a school of such agency or at such institution are provided an opportunity for a hearing by such agency or institution, in accordance with regulations of the Secretary, to challenge the content of such student's education records, in order to insure that the records are not inaccurate, misleading, or otherwise in violation of the privacy or other rights of students, and to provide an opportunity for the correction or deletion of any such inaccurate, misleading, or otherwise inappropriate data contained therein and

to insert into such records a written explanation of the parents respecting the content of such records.

(3) For the purposes of this section the term "educational agency or institution" means any public or private agency or institution which is the recipient of funds under any applicable program.

(4)(A) For the purposes of this section, the term "education records" means, except as may be provided otherwise in subparagraph (B), those records, files, documents, and other materials which-

(i) contain information directly related to a student; and

(ii) are maintained by an educational agency or institution or by a person acting for such agency or institution.

(B) The term "education records" does not include—

(i) records of instructional, supervisory, and administrative personnel and educational personnel ancillary thereto which are in the sole possession of the maker thereof and which are not accessible or revealed to any other person except a substitute;

(ii) if the personnel of a law enforcement unit do not have access to education records under subsection (b)(1) of this section, the records and documents of such law enforcement unit which (I) are kept apart from records described in subparagraph (A), (II) are maintained solely for law enforcement purposes, and (III) are not made available to persons other than law enforcement officials of the same jurisdiction;

(iii) in the case of persons who are employed by an educational agency or institution but who are not in attendance at such agency or institution, records made and maintained in the normal course of business which relate exclusively to such person in that person's capacity as an employee and are not available for use for any other purpose; or

(iv) records on a student who is eighteen years of age or older, or is attending an institution of postsecondary education, which are made or maintained by a physician, psychiatrist, psychologist, or other recognized professional or paraprofessional acting in his professional or paraprofessional capacity, or assisting in that capacity, and which are made, maintained, or used only in connection with the provision of treatment to the student, and are not available to anyone other than persons providing such treatment, except that such records can be personally reviewed by a physician or other appropriate professional of the student's choice.

(5)(A) For the purposes of this section the term "directory information" relating to a student includes the following: the student's name, address, telephone listing, date and place of birth, major field of study, participation in officially recognized activities and sports, weight and height of members of athletic teams, dates of attendance, degrees and awards received, and the most recent previous educational agency or institution attended by the student.

(B) Any educational agency or institution making public directory information shall give public notice of the categories of information which it has designated as such information with respect to each student attending the institution or agency and shall allow a reasonable period of time after such notice has been given for a parent to inform the institution or agency that any or all of the information designated should no be released without the parent's prior consent.

(6) For the purposes of this section, the term "student" includes any person with respect to whom an educational agency or institution maintains education records or personally identifiable information, but does not include a person who has not been in attendance at such agency or institution.

Release of education records; parental consent requirement; exceptions; compliance with judicial orders and subpoenas; audit and evaluation of Federally-supported education programs; record-keeping

(b)(1) No funds shall be made available under any applicable program to any educational agency or institution which has a policy or practice of permitting the release of education records (or personally identifiable information contained therein other than directory information, as defined in paragraph (5) of subsection (a) of this section) of students without the written consent of their parents to any individual, agency, or organization, other than to the following-

(A) other school officials, including teachers within the education institution or local educational agency, who have been determined by such agency or institution to have legitimate educational interests;

(B) officials of other schools or school systems in which the student seeks or intends to enroll, upon condition that the student's parents be notified of the transfer, receive a copy of the record if desired, and have an opportunity for a hearing to challenge the content of the record;

(C) authorized representatives of (I) the comptroller General of the United States, (ii) the Secretary, (iii) an administrative head of an education agency (as defined in section 1221e-3(c) of this title), or (iv) State educational authorities, under the conditions set forth in paragraph (3) of this subsection;

(D) in connection with a student's application for, or receipt of, financial aid;

(E) State and local officials or authorities to whom such information is specifically required to be reported or disclosed pursuant to State statute adopted prior to November 19, 1974;

(F) organizations conducting studies for, or on behalf of, educational agencies or institutions for the purpose of developing, validating, or administering predictive tests, administering student aid programs, and improving instruction, if such studies are conducted in such a manner as will not permit the personal identification of students and their parents by persons other than representatives of such organizations and such information will be destroyed when no longer needed for the purpose for which it is conducted;

(G) accrediting organizations in order to carry out their accrediting function;

(H) parents of a dependent student of such parents, as defined in section 152 of Title 26; and

(I) subject to regulations of the Secretary, in connection with an emergency, appropriate persons if the knowledge of such information is necessary to protect the health or safety of the student or other persons.

Nothing in clause (E) of this paragraph shall prevent a State from further limiting the number or type of State or local officials who will continue to have access thereunder.

(2) No funds shall be made available under any applicable program to any educational agency or institution which has a policy or practice of releasing, or providing access to, any personally identifiable information in education records other than directory information, or as is permitted under paragraph (1) of this subsection unless—

(A) there is written consent from the student's parents specifying records to be released, the reasons for such release, and to whom, and with a copy of the records to be released to the student's parents and the student if desired by the parents, or

(B) such information is furnished in compliance with judicial order, or pursuant to any lawfully issued subpoena, upon condition that parents and the students are notified of all such orders or subpoenas in advance of the compliance therewith by the education institution or agency.

(3) Nothing contained in this section shall preclude authorized representatives of (A) the Comptroller General of the United States, (B) the Secretary, (C) an administrative head of an education agency or (D) State educational authorities from having access to student or other records which may be necessary in connection with the auditing and evaluation of Federally-supported education program, or in connection with the enforcement of the Federal legal requirements which relate to such programs:

Provided, That except when collection of personally identifiable information is specifically authorized by Federal law, any data collected by such officials shall be protected in a manner which will not permit the personal identification of students and their parents by other than those officials, and such personally identifiable data shall be destroyed when no longer needed for such audit, evaluation, and enforcement of Federal legal requirements.

(4)(A) Each educational agency or institution shall maintain a record, kept with the education records of each student, which will indicate all individuals (other than those specified in paragraph (1)(A) of this subsection), agencies, or organizations which have requested or obtained access to a student's education records maintained by such educational agency or institution, and which will indicate specifically the legitimate interest that each such person, agency, or organization has in obtaining this information. Such record of access shall be available only to parents, to the school official and his assistants who are responsible for the custody of such records, and to persons or organizations authorized in, and under the conditions of, clauses (A) and (C) of paragraph (1) as a means of auditing the operation of the system.

(B) With respect to this subsection, personal information shall only be transferred to a third party on the condition that such party will not permit any other party to have access to such information without the written consent of the parents of the student.

Surveys or data-gathering activities; regulations

(c) The Secretary shall adopt appropriate regulations to protect the rights of privacy of students and their families in connection with any surveys or date-gathering activities conducted, assisted, or authorized by the Secretary or an administrative head of an education agency. Regulations established under this subsection shall include provisions controlling the use, dissemination, and protection of such data. No survey or data-gathering activities shall be conducted by the

Secretary, or an administrative head of an education agency under an applicable program, unless such activities are authorized by law.

Students' rather than parents' permission or consent

(d) For the purposes of this section, whenever a student has attained eighteen years of age, or is attending an institution of postsecondary education the permission or consent required of and the rights accorded to the parents of the student shall thereafter only be required of and accorded to the student.

Informing parents or students of right under this section

(e) No funds shall be made available under any applicable program to any educational agency or institution unless such agency or institution informs the parents of students, or the students, if they are eighteen years of age or older, or are attending an institution of postsecondary education, of the rights accorded them by this section.

Enforcement; termination of assistance

(f) The Secretary, or an administrative head of an education agency, shall take appropriate actions to enforce provisions of this section and to deal with violations of this section, according to the provisions of this chapter, except that action to terminate assistance may be taken only if the Secretary finds there has been a failure to comply with the provisions of this section, and he has determined that compliance cannot be secured by voluntary means.

Office and review board; creation; functions

(g) The Secretary shall establish or designate an office and review board within the Department of Health, Education, and Welfare for the purpose of investigating, processing, reviewing, and adjudicating violations of the provisions of this section and complaints which may be filed concerning alleged violations of this section. Except for the conduct of hearings, none of the functions of the Secretary under this section shall be carried out in any of the regional offices of such Department.

Pub.L. 90-247, Title IV, 438, as added Pub.L. 93-380, Title V, 513(a), Aug. 21, 1974, 88 Stat. 571, and amended Pub.L. 93-568, 2(a), Dec. 31, 1974, 88 Stat. 1858.

1988 Supplementary Pamphlet

Education 20 1232g

1232g. Family educational and privacy rights
[See main volume for text of (a)]

(b) Release of education records; parental consent requirement; exceptions; compliance with judicial orders and subpoenas; audit and evaluation of Federal-supported education programs; record-keeping

(1) No funds shall be made available under any applicable program to any educational agency or institution which has a policy or practice of permitting the release of education records (or personally identifiable information contained therein other than directory information, as defined in paragraph (5) of subsection (a) of this section) of students without the written consent of their parents to any individual, agency, or organization, other than to the following [See main volume for text of (A) to (I), closing provisions; (2) to (4)].

(5) Nothing in this section shall be construed to prohibit State and local educational officials from having access to student or other records which may be necessary in connection with the audit and evaluation of any federally or State supported education program or in connection with the enforcement of the Federal legal requirements which relate to any such program, subject to the conditions specified in the proviso in paragraph (3).

[See main volume for text of (c) to (g)]

(As amended Pub.L. 96-46, 4(c), Aug. 6, 1979, 93 Stat. 342.)

Appendix 2

Family Educational Rights and Privacy Act Regulations

34 CFR Part 99

Subpart A—General

Section

99.1 To which educational agencies or institutions do these regulations apply?
99.2 What is the purpose of these regulations?
99.3 What definitions apply to these regulations?
99.4 What are the rights of parents?
99.5 What are the rights of students?
99.7 What must an educational agency or institution include in its annual notification?
99.8 What provisions apply to records of a law enforcement unit?

Subpart B—What Are the Rights of Inspection and Review of Education Records?

Section

99.10 What rights exist for a parent or eligible student to inspect and review education records?
99.11 May an educational agency or institution charge a fee for copies of education records?
99.12 What limitations exist on the right to inspect and review records?

Subpart C—What Are the Procedures for Amending Educating Records?

Section

99.20 How can a parent or eligible student request amendment of the student's education records?
99.21 Under what conditions does a parent or eligible student have the right to a hearing?
99.22 What minimum requirements exist for the conduct of a hearing?

Subpart D—May an Educational Agency or Institution Disclose Personally Identifiable Information from Education Records?

Section

99.30 Under what conditions is prior consent required to disclose information?
99.31 Under what conditions is prior consent not required to disclose information?
99.32 What recordkeeping requirements exist concerning requests and disclosures?
99.33 What limitations apply to the redisclosure of information?
99.34 What conditions apply to disclosure of information to other educational agencies or institutions?
99.35 What conditions apply to disclosure of information for Federal or State program purposes?
99.36 What conditions apply to disclosure of information in health and safety emergencies?
99.37 What conditions apply to disclosing directory information?
99.38 What conditions apply to disclosure of information as permitted by State statute adopted after November 19, 1974 concerning the juvenile justice system?
99.39 What definitions apply to the nonconsensual disclosure of records by postsecondary educational institutions in connection with disciplinary proceedings concerning crimes of violence or non-forcible sex offenses?

Subpart E—What Are the Enforcement Procedures?

Section

99.60 What functions has the Secretary delegated to the Office and to the Office of Administrative Law Judges?
99.61 What responsibility does an educational agency or institution have concerning conflict with State or local laws?
99.62 What information must an educational agency or institution submit to the Office?
99.63 Where are complaints filed?
99.64 What is the complaint procedure?
99.65 What is the content of the notice of complaint issued by the Office?
99.66 What are the responsibilities of the Office in the enforcement process?
99.67 How does the Secretary enforce decisions?

Appendix A To Part 99—
Crimes of Violence Definitions

Subpart A—General

§ 99.1 To which educational agencies or institutions do these regulations apply?

(a) Except as otherwise noted in § 99.10, this part applies to an educational agency or institution to which funds have been made available under any program administered by the Secretary, if-

(1) The education institution provides educational services or instruction, or both, to students; or

(2) The educational agency is authorized to direct and control public elementary or secondary, or postsecondary educational institutions.

(b) This part does not apply to an educational agency or institution solely because students attending that agency or institution receive non-monetary benefits under a program referenced in paragraph (a) of this section, if no funds under that program are made available to the agency or institution.

(c) The Secretary considers funds to be made available to an educational agency or institution if funds under one or more of the programs referenced in paragraph (a) of this section—

(1) Are provided to the agency or institution by grant, cooperative agreement, contract, subgrant, or subcontract; or

(2) Are provided to students attending the agency or institution and the funds may be paid to the agency or institution by those students for educational purposes, such as under the Pell Grant Program and the Guaranteed Student Loan Program (Titles IV-A-1 and IV-B, respectively, of the Higher Education Act of 1965, as amended).

(d) If an educational agency or institution receives funds under one or more of the programs covered by this section, the regulations in this part apply to the recipient as a whole, including each of its components (such as a department within a university).

[Authority: 20 U.S.C. 1232g]

§ 99.2 What is the purpose of these regulations?

The purpose of this part is to set out requirements for the protection of privacy of parents and students under section 444 of the General Education Provisions Act, as amended.

[Authority: 20 U.S.C. 1232g]

Note: 34 CFR 300.560-300.576 contain requirements regarding confidentiality of information relating to handicapped children who receive benefits under the Education of the Handicapped Act.

§ 99.3 What definitions apply to these regulations?

The following definitions apply to this part:

"Act" means the Family Educational Rights and Privacy Act of 1974, as amended, enacted as section 444 of the General Education Provisions Act.

[Authority: 20 U.S.C. 1232g]

"Attendance" includes, but is not limited to:

(a) Attendance in person or by correspondence; and

(b) The period during which a person is working under a work-study program.

[Authority: 20 U.S.C. 1232g]

"Dates of attendance." (a) The term means the period of time during which a student attends or attended an educational agency or institution. Examples of dates of attendance include an academic year, a spring semester, or a first quarter.

(b) The term does not include specific daily records of a student's attendance at an educational agency or institution.

[Authority: 20 U.S.C. 1232g(a)(5)(A)]

"Directory information" means information contained in an education record of a student that would not generally be considered harmful or an invasion of privacy if disclosed. It includes, but is not limited to, the student's name, address, telephone listing, electronic mail address, photograph, date and place of birth, major field of study, dates of attendance, grade level, enrollment status (e.g., undergraduate or graduate; full-time or part-time), participation in officially recognized activities and sports, weight and height of members of athletic teams, degrees, honors and awards received, and the most recent educational agency or institution attended.

[Authority: 20 U.S.C. 1232g(a)(5)(A)]

"Disciplinary action or proceeding" means the investigation, adjudication, or imposition of sanctions by an educational agency or institution with respect to an infraction or violation of the internal rules of conduct applicable to students of the agency or institution.

"Disclosure" means to permit access to or the release, transfer, or other communication of personally identifiable information contained in education records to any party, by any means, including oral, written, or electronic means.

[Authority: 20 U.S.C. 1232g(b)(1)]

"Educational agency or institution" means any public or private agency or institution to which this part applies under § 99.1(a).

[Authority: 20 U.S.C. 1232g(a)(3)]

"Education records" (a) The term means those records that are:

(1) Directly related to a student; and
(2) Maintained by an educational agency or institution or by a party acting for the agency or institution.

(b) The term does not include:

(1) Records that are kept in the sole possession of the maker, are used only as a personal memory aid, and are not accessible or revealed to any other person except a temporary substitute for the maker of the record.
(2) Records of the law enforcement unit of an educational agency or institution, subject to the provisions of § 99.8.
(3)(i) Records relating to an individual who is employed by an educational agency or institution, that:

(A) Are made and maintained in the normal course of business;
(B) Relate exclusively to the individual in that individual's capacity as an employee; and
(C) Are not available for use for any other purpose.

(ii) Records relating to an individual in attendance at the agency or institution who is employed as a result of his or her status as a student are education records and not excepted under paragraph (b)(3)(i) of this definition.

(4) Records on a student who is 18 years of age or older, or is attending an institution of postsecondary education, that are:

(i) Made or maintained by a physician, psychiatrist, psychologist, or other recognized professional or paraprofessional acting in his or her professional capacity or assisting in a paraprofessional capacity;
(ii) Made, maintained, or used only in connection with treatment of the student; and
(iii) Disclosed only to individuals providing the treatment. For the purpose of this definition, "treatment" does not include remedial educational activities or activities that are part of the program of instruction at the agency or institution; and

(5) Records that only contain information about an individual after he or she is no longer a student at that agency or institution.

[Authority: 20 U.S.C. 1232g(a)(4)]

"Eligible student" means a student who has reached 18 years of age or is attending an institution of postsecondary education.

[Authority: 20 U.S.C. 1232g(d)]

"Institution of postsecondary education" means an institution that provides education to students beyond the secondary school level; "secondary school level" means the educational level (not beyond grade 12) at which secondary education is provided as determined under State law.

[Authority: 20 U.S.C. 1232g(d)]

"Parent" means a parent of a student and includes a natural parent, a guardian, or an individual acting as a parent in the absence of a parent or a guardian.

[Authority: 20 U.S.C. 1232g]

"Party" means an individual, agency, institution, or organization.

[Authority: 20 U.S.C. 1232g(b)(4)(A)]

"Personally identifiable information" includes, but is not limited to:

(a) The student's name;
(b) The name of the student's parent or other family member;
(c) The address of the student or student's family;
(d) A personal identifier, such as the student's social security number or student number;
(e) A list of personal characteristics that would make the student's identity easily traceable; or
(f) Other information that would make the student's identity easily traceable.

[Authority: 20 U.S.C. 1232g]

"Record" means any information recorded in any way, including, but not limited to, handwriting, print, computer media, video or audio tape, film, microfilm, and microfiche.

[Authority: 20 U.S.C. 1232g]

"Secretary" means the Secretary of the U.S. Department of Education or an official or employee of the Department of Education acting for the Secretary under a delegation of authority.

[Authority: 20 U.S.C. 1232g]

"Student," except as otherwise specifically provided in this part, means any individual who is or has been in attendance at an educational agency or institution and regarding whom the agency or institution maintains education records.

[Authority: 20 U.S.C. 1232g(a)(6)]

§ 99.4 What are the rights of parents?

An educational agency or institution shall give full rights under the Act to either parent, unless the agency or institution has been provided with evidence that there is a court order, State statute, or legally binding document relating to such matters as divorce, separation, or custody that specifically revokes these rights.

[Authority: 20 U.S.C. 1232g]

§ 99.5 What are the rights of students?

(a) When a student becomes an eligible student, the rights accorded to, and consent required of, parents under this part transfer from the parents to the student.

(b) The Act and this part do not prevent educational agencies or institutions from giving students rights in addition to those given to parents.

(c) An individual who is or has been a student at an education institution and who applies for admission at another component of that institution does not have rights under this part with respect to records maintained by that other component, including records maintained in connection with the student's application for admission, unless the student is accepted and attends that other component of the institution.

[Authority: 20 U.S.C. 1232g(d)]

§ 99.7 What must an educational agency or institution include in its annual notification?

(a)(1) Each educational agency or institution shall annually notify parents of students currently in attendance, or eligible students currently in attendance, of their rights under the Act and this part.

(2) The notice must inform parents or eligible students that they have the right to—

(i) Inspect and review the student's education records;

(ii) Seek amendment of the student's education records that the parent or eligible student believes to be inaccurate, misleading, or otherwise in violation of the student's privacy rights;

(iii) Consent to disclosures of personally identifiable information contained in the student's education records, except to the extent that the Act and § 99.31 authorize disclosure without consent; and

(iv) File with the Department a complaint under § 99.63 and § 99.64 concerning alleged failures by the educational agency or institution to comply with the requirements of the act and this part.

(3) The notice must include all of the following:

(i) The procedure for exercising the right to inspect and review education records.

(ii) The procedure for requesting amendment of records under § 99.20.

(iii) If the educational agency or institution has a policy of disclosing education records under § 99.31(a)(1), a specification of criteria for determining who constitutes a school official and what constitutes a legitimate educational interest.

(b) An educational agency or institution may provide this notice by any means that are reasonably likely to inform the parents or eligible students of their rights.

(1) An educational agency or institution shall effectively notify parents or eligible students who are disabled.

(2) An agency or institution of elementary or secondary education shall effectively notify parents who have a primary or home language other than English.

(Approved by the Office of Management and Budget under control number 1880-0508)

[Authority 20 U.S.C. 1232g(e) and (f)]

§ 99.8 What provisions apply to records of a law enforcement unit?

(a)(1) "Law enforcement unit" means any individual, office, department, division, or other component of an educational agency or institution, such as a unit of commissioned police officers or non-commissioned security guards, that is officially authorized or designated by that agency or institution to—

(i) Enforce any local, State, or Federal law, or refer to appropriate authorities a matter for enforcement of any local, State, or Federal law against any individual or organization other than the agency or institution itself; or

(ii) Maintain the physical security and safety of the agency or institution.

(2) A component of an educational agency or institution does not lose its status as a "law enforcement unit" if it also performs other, non-law enforcement functions for the agency or institution, including investigation of incidents or conduct that constitutes or leads to a disciplinary action or proceedings against the student.

(b)(1) Records of law enforcement unit means those records, files, documents, and other materials that are—

(i) Created by a law enforcement unit;
(ii) Created for a law enforcement purpose; and
(iii) Maintained by the law enforcement unit.

(2) Records of law enforcement unit does not mean—

(i) Records created by a law enforcement unit for a law enforcement purpose that are maintained by a component of the educational agency or institution other than the law enforcement unit; or

(ii) Records created and maintained by a law enforcement unit exclusively for a non-law enforcement purpose, such as a disciplinary action or proceeding conducted by the educational agency or institution.

(c)(1) Nothing in the Act prohibits an educational agency or institution from contacting its law enforcement unit, orally or in writing, for the purpose of asking that unit to investigate a possible violation of, or to enforce, any local, State, or Federal law.

(2) Education records, and personally identifiable information contained in education records, do not lose their status as education records and remain subject to the Act, including the disclosure provisions of § 99.30, while in possession of the law enforcement unit.

(d) The Act neither requires nor prohibits the dis-closure by any educational agency or institution of its law enforcement unit records.

[Authority: 20 U.S.C. 1232g(a)(4)(B)(ii)]

Subpart B—What Are the Rights of Inspection and Review of Education Records?

§ 99.10 What rights exist for a parent or eligible student to inspect and review education records?

(a) Except as limited under § 99.12, a parent or eligible student must be given the opportunity to inspect and review the student's education records.

This provision applies to—

(1) Any educational agency or institution; and

(2) Any State educational agency (SEA) and its components.

(i) For the purposes of subpart B of this part, an SEA and its components constitute an educational agency or institution.

(ii) An SEA and its components are subject to subpart B of this part if the SEA maintains education records on students who are or have been in attendance at any school of an educational agency or institution subject to the Act and this part.

(b) The educational agency or institution, or SEA or its component, shall comply with a request for access to records within a reasonable period of time, but not more than 45 days after it has received the request.

(c) The educational agency or institution, or SEA or its component, shall respond to reasonable requests for explanations and interpretations of the records.

(d) If circumstances effectively prevent the parent or eligible student from exercising the right to inspect and review the student's education records, the educational agency or institution, or SEA or its component, shall—

(1) Provide the parent or eligible student with a copy of the records requested; or

(2) Make other arrangements for the parent or eligible student to inspect and review the requested records.

(e) The educational agency or institution, or SEA or its component, shall not destroy any education records if there is an outstanding request to inspect and review the records under this section.

(f) While an education agency or institution is not required to give an eligible student access to treatment records under paragraph (b)(4) of the definition of "Education records" in § 99.3, the student may have those records reviewed by a physician or other appropriate professional of the student's choice.

[Authority: 20 U.S.C. 1232g(a)(1)(A) and (B)]

§ 99.11 May an educational agency or institution charge a fee for copies of education records?

(a) Unless the imposition of a fee effectively prevents a parent or eligible student from exercising the right to inspect and review the student's education records, an educational agency or institution may charge a fee for a copy of an education record which is made for the parent or eligible student.

(b) An educational agency or institution may not charge a fee to search for or to retrieve the education records of a student.

[Authority: 20 U.S.C. 1232g(a)(1)]

§ 99.12 What limitations exist on the right to inspect and review records?

(a) If the education records of a student contain information on more than one student, the parent or eligible student may inspect and review or be informed of only the specific information about that student.

(b) A postsecondary institution does not have to permit a student to inspect and review education records that are:

(1) Financial records, including any information those records contain, of his or her parents;

(2) Confidential letters and confidential statements of recommendation placed in the education records of the student before January 1, 1975, as long as the statements are used only for the purposes for which they were specifically intended; and

(3) Confidential letters and confidential statements of recommendation placed in the student's education records after January 1, 1975, if:

(i) The student has waived his or her right to inspect and review those letters and statements; and

(ii) Those letters and statements are related to the student's:

(A) Admission to an education institution;

(B) Application for employment; or

(C) Receipt of an honor or honorary recognition.

(c)(1) A waiver under paragraph (b)(3)(i) of this section is valid only if:

(i) The educational agency or institution does not require the waiver as a condition for admission to or receipt of a service or benefit from the agency or institution; and

(ii) The waiver is made in writing and signed by the student, regardless of age.

(2) If a student has waived his or her rights under paragraph (b)(3)(i) of this section, the education institution shall:

(i) Give the student, on request, the names of the individuals who provided the letters and statements of recommendation; and

(ii) Use the letters and statements of recommendation only for the purpose for which they were intended.

(3)(i) A waiver under paragraph (b)(3)(i) of this section may be revoked with respect to any actions occurring after the revocation.

(ii) A revocation under paragraph (c)(3)(i) of this section must be in writing.

[Authority: 20 U.S.C. 1232g(a)(1)(A), (B), (C), and (D)]

Subpart C—What Are the Procedures for Amending Education Records?

§ 99.20 How can a parent or eligible student request amendment of the student's education records?

(a) If a parent or eligible student believes the education records relating to the student contain information that is inaccurate, misleading, or in violation of the student's rights of privacy, he or she may ask the educational agency or institution to amend the record.

(b) The educational agency or institution shall decide whether to amend the record as requested within a reasonable time after the agency or institution receives the request.

(c) If the educational agency or institution decides not to amend the record as requested, it shall inform the parent or eligible student of its decision and of his or her right to a hearing under § 99.21.

[Authority: 20 U.S.C. 1232g(a)(2)]

§ 99.21 Under what conditions does a parent or eligible student have the right to a hearing?

(a) An educational agency or institution shall give a parent or eligible student, on request, an opportunity for a hearing to challenge the content of the student's education records on the grounds that the information contained in the education records is inaccurate, misleading, or in violation of the privacy rights of the student.

(b)(1) If, as a result of the hearing, the educational agency or institution decides that the information is inaccurate, misleading, or otherwise in violation of the privacy rights of the student, it shall:

(i) Amend the record accordingly; and

(ii) Inform the parent or eligible student of the amendment in writing.

(2) If, as a result of the hearing, the educational agency or institution decides that the information in the education record is not inaccurate, misleading, or otherwise in violation of the privacy rights of the student, it shall inform the parent or eligible student of the right to place a statement in the record commenting on the contested information in the record or stating why he or she disagrees with the decision of the agency or institution, or both.

(c) If an educational agency or institution places a statement in the education records of a student under paragraph (b)(2) of this section, the agency or institution shall:

(1) Maintain the statement with the contested part of the record for as long as the record is maintained; and

(2) Disclose the statement whenever it discloses the portion of the record to which the statement relates.

[Authority: 20 U.S.C. 1232g(a)(2)]

§ 99.22 What minimum requirements exist for the conduct of a hearing?

The hearing required by § 99.21 must meet, at a minimum, the following requirements:

(a) The educational agency or institution shall hold the hearing within a reasonable time after it has received the request for the hearing from the parent or eligible student.

(b) The educational agency or institution shall give the parent or eligible student notice of the date, time, and place, reasonably in advance of the hearing.

(c) The hearing may be conducted by any individual, including an official of the educational agency or institution, who does not have a direct interest in the outcome of the hearing.

(d) The educational agency or institution shall give the parent or eligible student a full and fair opportunity to present evidence relevant to the issues raised under

§ 99.21. The parent or eligible student may, at their own expense, be assisted or represented by one or more individuals of his or her own choice, including an attorney.

(e) The educational agency or institution shall make its decision in writing within a reasonable period of time after the hearing.

(f) The decision must be based solely on the evidence presented at the hearing, and must include a summary of the evidence and the reasons for the decision.

[Authority: 20 U.S.C. 1232g(a)(2)]

Subpart D—May an Educational Agency or Institution Disclose Personally Identifiable Information from Education Records?

§ 99.30 Under what conditions is prior consent required to disclose information?

(a) The parent or eligible student shall provide a signed and dated written consent before an educational agency or institution discloses personally identifiable information from the student's education records, except as provided in § 99.31.

(b) The written consent must:

(1) Specify the records that may be disclosed;
(2) State the purpose of the disclosure; and
(3) Identify the party or class of parties to whom the disclosure may be made.

(c) When a disclosure is made under paragraph (a) of this section:

(1) If a parent or eligible student so requests, the educational agency or institution shall provide him or her with a copy of the records disclosed; and
(2) If the parent of a student who is not an eligible student so requests, the agency or institution shall provide the student with a copy of the records disclosed.

[Authority: 20 U.S.C. 1232g(b)(1) and (b)(2)(A)]

§ 99.31 Under what conditions is prior consent not required to disclose information?

(a) An educational agency or institution may disclose personally identifiable information from an education record of a student without the consent required by § 99.30 if the disclosure meets one or more of the following conditions:

(1) The disclosure is to other school officials, including teachers, within the agency or institution whom the agency or institution has determined to have legitimate educational interests.
(2) The disclosure is, subject to the requirements of § 99.34, to officials of another school, school system, or institution of postsecondary education where the student seeks or intends to enroll.
(3) The disclosure is, subject to the requirements of § 99.35, to authorized representatives of—

(i) The Comptroller General of the United States;
(ii) The Attorney General of the United States;
(iii) The Secretary; or
(iv) State and local educational authorities.

(4)(i) The disclosure is in connection with financial aid for which the student has applied or which the student has received, if the information is necessary for such purposes as to:

(A) Determine eligibility for the aid;
(B) Determine the amount of the aid;
(C) Determine the conditions for the aid; or
(D) Enforce the terms and conditions of the aid.

(ii) As used in paragraph (a)(4)(i) of this section, "financial aid" means a payment of funds provided to an individual (or a payment in kind of tangible or intangible property to the individual) that is conditioned on the individual's attendance at an educational agency or institution.

[Authority: 20 U.S.C. 1232g(b)(1)(D)]

(5)(i) The disclosure is to State and local officials or authorities to whom this information is specifically-

(A) Allowed to be reported or disclosed pursuant to a State statute adopted before November 19, 1974, if the allowed reporting or disclosure concerns the juvenile justice system and the system's ability to effectively serve the student whose records are released;or
(B) Allowed to be reported or disclosed pursuant to a State statute adopted after November 19, 1974, subject to the requirements of § 99.38.

(ii) Paragraph (a)(5)(1) of this section does not prevent a State from further limiting the number or type of State or local officials to whom disclosures may be made under that paragraph.

(6)(i) The disclosure is to organizations conducting studies for, or on behalf of, educational agencies or institutions to:

(A) Develop, validate, or administer predictive tests;
(B) Administer student aid programs; or
(C) Improve instruction.

(ii) The agency or institution may disclose information under paragraph (a)(6)(i) of this section only if:

(A) The study is conducted in a manner that does not permit personal identification of parents and students by individuals other than representatives of the organization; and

(B) The information is destroyed when no longer needed for the purposes for which the study was conducted.

(iii) If this Office determines that a third party outside the educational agency or institution to whom information is disclosed under this paragraph (a)(6) violates paragraph (a)(6)(ii)(B) of this section, the educational agency or institution may not allow that third party access to personally identifiable information from education records for at least five years.

(iv) For the purposes of paragraph (a)(6) of this section, the term "organization" includes, but is not limited to, Federal, State, and local agencies, and independent organizations.

(7) The disclosure is to accrediting organizations to carry out their accrediting functions.

(8) The disclosure is to parents, as defined in § 99.3, of a dependent student, as defined in section 152 of the Internal Revenue Code of 1986.

(9)(i) The disclosure is to comply with a judicial order or lawfully issued subpoena.

(ii) The educational agency or institution may disclose information under paragraph (a)(9)(i) of this section only if the agency or institution makes a reasonable effort to notify the parent or eligible student of the order or subpoena in advance of compliance, so that the parent or eligible student may seek protective action, unless the disclosure is in compliance with—

(A) A Federal grand jury subpoena and the court has ordered that the existence or the contents of the subpoena or the information furnished in response to the subpoena not be disclosed; or

(B) Any other subpoena issued for a law enforcement purpose and the court or other issuing agency has ordered that the existence or the contents of the subpoena or the information furnished in response to the subpoena not be disclosed.

(iii)(A) If an educational agency or institution initiates legal action against a parent or student, the educational agency or institution may disclose to the court, without a court order or subpoena, the education records of the student that are relevant for the educational agency or institution to proceed with the legal action as plaintiff.

(B) If a parent or eligible student initiates legal action against an educational agency or institution, the educational agency or institution may disclose to the court, without a court order or subpoena, the student's education records that are relevant for the educational agency or institution to defend itself.

(10) The disclosure is in connection with a health or safety emergency, under the conditions described in § 99.36.

(11) The disclosure is information the educational agency or institution has designated as "directory information," under the conditions described in § 99.37.

(12) The disclosure is to the parent of a student who is not an eligible student or to the student.

(13) The disclosure, subject to the requirements in § 99.39, is to a victim of an alleged perpetrator of a crime of violence or a non-forcible sex offense. The disclosure may only include the final results of the disciplinary proceeding conducted by the institution of postsecondary education with respect to that alleged crime or offense. The institution may disclose the final results of the disciplinary proceeding, regardless of whether the institution concluded a violation was committed.

(14)(i) The disclosure, subject to the requirements in § 99.39, is in connection with a disciplinary proceeding at an institution of postsecondary education. The institution must not disclose the final results of the disciplinary proceeding unless it determines that—

(A) The student is an alleged perpetrator of a crime of violence or non-forcible sex offense; and

(B) With respect to the allegation made against him or her, the student has committed a violation of the institution's rules or policies.

(ii) The institution may not disclose the name of any other student, including a victim or witness, without the prior written consent of the other student.

(iii) This section applies only to disciplinary proceedings in which the final results were reached on or after October 7, 1998.

(15)(i) The disclosure is to a parent of a student at an institution of postsecondary education regarding the student's violation of any Federal, State, or local law, or of any rule or policy of the institution, governing the use or possession of alcohol or a controlled substance if—

(A) The institution determines that the student has committed a disciplinary violation with respect to that use or possession; and

(B) The student is under the age of 21 at the time of the disclosure to the parent.

(ii) Paragraph (a)(15) of this section does not supersede any provision of State law that prohibits an institution of postsecondary education from disclosing information.

(b) Paragraph (a) of this section does not forbid an educational agency or institution from disclosing, nor does it require an educational agency or institution to disclose, personally identifiable information from the education records of a student to any parties under paragraphs (a)(1) through (11), (13), (14), and (15) of this section.

[Authority: 20 U.S.C. 1232g(a)(5)(A), (b)(1), (b)(2)(B), (b)(6), (h), and (i)]

§ 99.32 What recordkeeping requirements exist concerning requests and disclosures?

(a)(1) An educational agency or institution shall maintain a record of each request for access to and each disclosure of personally identifiable information from the education records of each student.

(2) The agency or institution shall maintain the record with the education records of the student as long as the records are maintained.

(3) For each request or disclosure the record must include:

(i) The parties who have requested or received personally identifiable information from the education records; and

(ii) The legitimate interests the parties had in requesting or obtaining the information.

(b) If an educational agency or institution discloses personally identifiable information from an education record with the understanding authorized under § 99.33(b), the record of the disclosure required under this section must include:

(1) The names of the additional parties to which the receiving party may disclose the information on behalf of the educational agency or institution; and

(2) The legitimate interests under § 99.31 which each of the additional parties has in requesting or obtaining the information.

(c) The following parties may inspect the record relating to each student:

(1) The parent or eligible student.

(2) The school official or his or her assistants who are responsible for the custody of the records.

(3) Those parties authorized in § 99.3 1 (a)(1) and (3) for the purposes of auditing the recordkeeping procedures of the educational agency or institution.

(d) Paragraph (a) of this section does not apply if the request was from, or the disclosure was to:

(1) The parent or eligible student;

(2) A school official under § 99.3 1 (a)(1);

(3) A party with written consent from the parent or eligible student;

(4) A party seeking directory information; or

(5) A party seeking or receiving the records as directed by a Federal grand jury or other law enforcement subpoena and the issuing court or other issuing agency has ordered that the existence or the contents of the subpoena or the information furnished in response to the subpoena not be disclosed.

(Approved by the Office of Management and Budget under control number 1880-0508)

[Authority: 20 U.S.C. 1232g(b)(1) and (b)(4)(A)]

§ 99.33 What limitations apply to the redisclosure of information?

(a)(1) An educational agency or institution may disclose personally identifiable information from an education record only on the condition that the party to whom the information is disclosed will not disclose the information to any other party without the prior consent of the parent or eligible student.

(2) The officers, employees, and agents of a party that receives information under paragraph (a)(1) of this section may use the information, but only for the purposes for which the disclosure was made.

(b) Paragraph (a) of this section does not prevent an educational agency or institution from disclosing personally identifiable information with the understanding that the party receiving the information may make further disclosures of the information on behalf of the educational agency or institution if:

(1) The disclosures meet the requirements of § 99.31; and

(2) The educational agency or institution has complied with the requirements of § 99.32(b).

(c) Paragraph (a) of this section does not apply to disclosures made to parents of dependent students under § 99.31(a)(8), to disclosures made pursuant to court orders, lawfully issued subpoenas, or litigation under § 99.31(a)(9), to disclosures of directory information under § 99.31(a)(11), to disclosures made to a parent or student under § 99.31(a)(12), to disclosures made in connection with a disciplinary proceeding under

§ 99.31(a)(14), or to disclosures made to parents under § 99.31(a)(15).

(d) Except for disclosures under § 99.31(a)(9), (11) and (12), an educational agency or institution shall inform a party to whom disclosure is made of the requirements of this section.

(e) If this Office determines that a third party improperly rediscloses personally identifiable information from education records in violation of § 99.33(a) of this section, the educational agency or institution may not allow that third party access to personally identifiable information from education records for at least five years.

[Authority: 20 U.S.C. 1232g(b)(4)(B)]

§ 99.34 What conditions apply to disclosure of information to other educational agencies or institutions?

(a) An educational agency or institution that discloses an education record under § 99.31(a)(2) shall:

(1) Make a reasonable attempt to notify the parent or eligible student at the last known address of the parent or eligible student, unless:

(i) The disclosure is initiated by the parent or eligible student; or

(ii) The annual notification of the agency or institution under § 99.7 includes a notice that the agency or institution forwards education records to other agencies or institutions that have requested the records and in which the student seeks or intends to enroll:

(2) Give the parent or eligible student, upon request, a copy of the record that was disclosed; and

(3) Give the parent or eligible student, upon request, an opportunity for a hearing under Subpart C.

(b) An educational agency or institution may disclose an education record of a student in attendance to another educational agency or institution if:

(1) The student is enrolled in or receives services from the other agency or institution; and

(2) The disclosure meets the requirements of paragraph (a) of this section.

[Authority: 20 U.S.C. 1232g(b)(1)(B)]

§ 99.35 What conditions apply to disclosure of information for Federal or State program purposes?

(a) The officials listed in § 99.31(a)(3) may have access to education records in connection with an audit or evaluation of Federal or State supported education programs, or for the enforcement of or compliance with Federal legal requirements which relate to those programs.

(b) Information that is collected under paragraph (a) of this section must:

(1) Be protected in a manner that does not permit personal identification of individuals by anyone except the officials referred to in paragraph (a) of this section; and

(2) Be destroyed when no longer needed for the purposes listed in paragraph (a) of this section.

(c) Paragraph (b) of this section does not apply if:

(1) The parent or eligible student has given written consent for the disclosure under § 99.30; or

(2) The collection of personally identifiable information is specifically authorized by Federal law.

[Authority: 20 U.S.C. 1232g(b)(3)]

§ 99.36 What conditions apply to disclosure of information in health and safety emergencies?

(a) An educational agency or institution may disclose personally identifiable information from an education record to appropriate parties in connection with an emergency if knowledge of the information is necessary to protect the health or safety of the student or other individuals.

(b) Nothing in the Act or this part shall prevent an educational agency or institution from-

(1) Including in the education records of a student appropriate information concerning disciplinary action taken against the student for conduct that posed a significant risk to the safety or well-being of that student, other students, or other members of the school community;

(2) Disclosing appropriate information maintained under paragraph (b)(1) of this section to teachers and school officials within the agency or institution who the agency or institution has determined have legitimate educational interests in the behavior of the student; or

(3) Disclosing appropriate information maintained under paragraph (b)(1) of this section to teachers and school officials in other schools who have been determined to have legitimate educational interests in the behavior of the student.

(c) Paragraphs (a) and (b) of this section will be strictly construed.

[Authority: 20 U.S.C. 1232g(b)(1)(I) and (h)]

§ 99.37 What conditions apply to disclosing directory information?

(a) An educational agency or institution may disclose directory information if it has given public notice to parents of students in attendance and eligible students in attendance at the agency or institution of:

(1) The types of personally identifiable information that the agency or institution has designated as directory information;
(2) A parent's or eligible student's right to refuse to let the agency or institution designate any or all of those types of information about the student as directory information; and
(3) The period of time within which a parent or eligible student has to notify the agency or institution in writing that he or she does not want any or all of those types of information about the student designated as directory information.

(b) An educational agency or institution may disclose directory information about former students without meeting the conditions in paragraph (a) of this section.

[Authority: 20 U.S.C. 1232g(a)(5)(A) and (B)]

§ 99.38 What conditions apply to disclosure of information as permitted by State statute adopted after November 19, 1974 concerning the juvenile justice system?

(a) If reporting or disclosure allowed by State statute concerns the juvenile justice system and the system's ability to effectively serve, prior to adjudication, the student whose records are released, an educational agency or institution may disclose education records under § 99.31(a)(5)(i)(B).

(b) The officials and authorities to whom the records are disclosed shall certify in writing to the educational agency or institution that the information will not be disclosed to any other party, except as provided under State law, without the prior written consent of the parent of the student.

[Authority: 20 U.S.C. 1232g(b)(1)(J)]

§ 99.39 What definitions apply to the nonconsensual disclosure of records by postsecondary educational institutions in connection with disciplinary proceedings concerning crimes of violence or non-forcible sex offenses?

As used in this part:

Alleged perpetrator of a crime of violence is a student who is alleged to have committed acts that would, if proven, constitute any of the following offenses or attempts to commit the following offenses that are defined in appendix A to this part:

- Arson
- Assault offenses
- Burglary
- Criminal homicide—manslaughter by negligence
- Criminal homicide—murder and nonnegligent manslaughter
- Destruction/damage/vandalism of property
- Kidnapping/abduction
- Robbery
- Forcible sex offenses

Alleged perpetrator of a nonforcible sex offense means a student who is alleged to have committed acts that, if proven, would constitute statutory rape or incest. These offenses are defined in appendix A to this part.

Final results means a decision or determination, made by an honor court or council, committee, commission, or other entity authorized to resolve disciplinary matters within the institution. The disclosure of final results must include only the name of the student, the violation committed, and any sanction imposed by the institution against the student.

Sanction imposed means a description of the disciplinary action taken by the institution, the date of its imposition, and its duration.

Violation committed means the institutional rules or code sections that were violated and any essential findings supporting the institution's conclusion that the violation was committed.

[Authority: 20 U.S.C. 1232g(b)(6)]

Subpart E—What Are the Enforcement Procedures?

§ 99.60 What functions has the Secretary delegated to the Office and to the Office of Administrative Law Judges?

(a) For the purposes of this subpart, "Office" means the Family Policy Compliance Office, U.S. Department of Education.

(b) The Secretary designates the Office to:

(1) Investigate, process, and review complaints and violations under the Act and this part; and
(2) Provide technical assistance to ensure compliance with the Act and this part.

(c) The Secretary designates the Office of Administrative Law Judges to act as the Review Board required under the Act to enforce the Act with respect to all applicable programs. The term "applicable program" is defined in section 400 of the General Education Provisions Act.

[Authority: 20 U.S.C. 1232g(f) and (g), 1234]

§ 99.61 What responsibility does an educational agency or institution have concerning conflict with State or local laws?

If an educational agency or institution determines that it cannot comply with the Act or this part due to a conflict with State or local law, it shall notify the Office within 45 days, giving the text and citation of the conflicting law.

[Authority: 20 U.S.C. 1232g(f)]

§ 99.62 What information must an educational agency or institution submit to the Office?

The Office may require an educational agency or institution to submit reports containing information necessary to resolve complaints under the Act and the regulations in this part.

[Authority: 20 U.S.C. 1232g(f) and (g)]

§ 99.63 Where are complaints filed?

A parent or eligible student may file a written complaint with the Office regarding an alleged violation under the Act and this part. The Office's address is: Family Policy Compliance Office, U.S. Department of Education, 400 Maryland Avenue, SW, Washington, DC 20202-4605.

[Authority: 20 U.S.C. 1232g(g)]

§ 99.64 What is the complaint procedure?

(a) A complaint filed under § 99.63 must contain specific allegations of fact giving reasonable cause to believe that a violation of the Act or this part has occurred.

(b) The Office investigates each timely complaint to determine whether the educational agency or institution has failed to comply with the provisions of the Act or this part.

(c) A timely complaint is defined as an allegation of a violation of the Act that is submitted to the Office within 180 days of the date of the alleged violation or of the date that the complainant knew or reasonably should have known of the alleged violation.

(d) The Office may extend the time limit in this section for good cause shown.

[Authority: 20 U.S.C. 1232g(f)]

§ 99.65 What is the content of the notice of complaint issued by the Office?

(a) The Office notifies the complainant and the educational agency or institution in writing if it initiates an investigation of a complaint under § 99.64(b). The notice to the educational agency or institution-

(1) Includes the substance of the alleged violation; and

(2) Asks the agency or institution to submit a written response to the complaint.

(b) The Office notifies the complainant if it does not initiate an investigation of a complaint because the complaint fails to meet the requirements of § 99.64.

[Authority: 20 U.S.C. 1232g(g)]

§ 99.66 What are the responsibilities of the Office in the enforcement process?

(a) The Office reviews the complaint and response and may permit the parties to submit further written or oral arguments or information.

(b) Following its investigation, the Office provides to the complainant and the educational agency or institution written notice of its findings and the basis for its findings.

(c) If the Office finds that the educational agency or institution has not complied with the Act or this part, the notice under paragraph (b) of this section:

(1) Includes a statement of the specific steps that the agency or institution must take to comply; and

(2) Provides a reasonable period of time, given all of the circumstances of the case, during which the educational agency or institution may comply voluntarily.

[Authority: 20 U.S.C. 1232g(f)]

§ 99.67 How does the Secretary enforce decisions?

(a) If the educational agency or institution does not comply during the period of time set under §99.66(c), the Secretary may, in accordance with part E of the General Education Provisions Act—

(1) Withhold further payments under any applicable program;

(2) Issue a complaint to compel compliance through a cease-and-desist order; or

(3) Terminate eligibility to receive funding under any applicable program.

(b) If, after an investigation under § 99.66, the Secretary finds that an educational agency or institution has complied voluntarily with the Act or this part, the Secretary provides the complainant and the agency or institution written notice of the decision and the basis for the decision.

(Note: 34 CFR Part 78 contains the regulations of the Education Appeal Board.)

[Please note that Part 78 has been removed from the CFR and has been replaced with 34 CFR Part 81.]

[Authority: 20 U.S.C. 1232g(f); 20 U.S.C. 1234]

Appendix A To Part 99—Crimes of Violence Definitions

Arson: Any willful or malicious burning or attempt to burn, with or without intent to defraud, a dwelling house, public building, motor vehicle or aircraft, personal property of another, etc.

Assault Offenses: An unlawful attack by one person upon another.

Note: By definition there can be no "attempted" assaults, only "completed" assaults.

(a) **Aggravated Assault.** An unlawful attack by one person upon another for the purpose of inflicting severe or aggravated bodily injury. This type of assault usually is accompanied by the use of a weapon or by means likely to produce death or great bodily harm. (It is not necessary that injury result from an aggravated assault when a gun, knife, or other weapon is used which could and probably would result in serious injury if the crime were successfully completed.)

(b) **Simple Assault.** An unlawful physical attack by one person upon another where neither the offender displays a weapon, nor the victim suffers obvious severe or aggravated bodily injury involving apparent broken bones, loss of teeth, possible internal injury, severe laceration, or loss of consciousness.

(c) **Intimidation.** To unlawfully place another person in reasonable fear of bodily harm through the use of threatening words or other conduct, or both, but without displaying a weapon or subjecting the victim to actual physical attack.

Note: This offense includes stalking.

Burglary: The unlawful entry into a building or other structure with the intent to commit a felony or a theft.

Criminal Homicide—Manslaughter by Negligence: The killing of another person through gross negligence.

Criminal Homicide—Murder and Nonnegligent Manslaughter: The willful (nonnegligent) killing of one human being by another.

Destruction/Damage/Vandalism of Property: To willfully or maliciously destroy, damage, deface, or otherwise injure real or personal property without the consent of the owner or the person having custody or control of it.

Kidnapping/Abduction: The unlawful seizure, transportation, or detention of a person, or any combination of these actions, against his or her will, or of a minor without the consent of his or her custodial parent(s) or legal guardian.

Note: Kidnapping/Abduction includes hostage taking.

Robbery: The taking of, or attempting to take, anything of value under confrontational circumstances from the control, custody, or care of a person or persons by force or threat of force or violence or by putting the victim in fear.

Note: Carjackings are robbery offenses where a motor vehicle is taken through force or threat of force.

Sex Offenses, Forcible: Any sexual act directed against another person, forcibly or against that person's will, or both; or not forcibly or against the person's will where the victim is incapable of giving consent.

(a) **Forcible Rape** (Except "Statutory Rape"). The carnal knowledge of a person, forcibly or against that person's will, or both; or not forcibly or against the person's will where the victim is incapable of giving consent because of his or her temporary or permanent mental or physical incapacity (or because of his or her youth).

(b) **Forcible Sodomy.** Oral or anal sexual intercourse with another person, forcibly or against that person's will, or both; or not forcibly or against the person's will where the victim is incapable of giving consent because of his or her youth or because of his or her temporary or permanent mental or physical incapacity.

(c) **Sexual Assault with An Object.** To use an object or instrument to unlawfully penetrate, however slightly, the genital or anal opening of the body of another person, forcibly or against that person's will, or both; or not forcibly or against the person's will where the victim is incapable of giving consent because of his or her youth or because of his or her temporary or permanent mental or physical incapacity.

Note: An "object" or "instrument" is anything used by the offender other than the offender's genitalia. Examples are a finger, bottle, handgun, stick, etc.

(d) **Forcible Fondling.** The touching of the private body parts of another person for the purpose of sexual gratification, forcibly or against that person's will, or both; or not forcibly or against the person's will where the victim is incapable of giving consent because of his or her youth or because of his or her temporary or permanent mental or physical incapacity.

Note: Forcible Fondling includes "Indecent Liberties" and "Child Molesting."

Nonforcible Sex Offenses (Except "Prostitution Offenses"): Unlawful, nonforcible sexual intercourse.

(a) **Incest.** Nonforcible sexual intercourse between persons who are related to each other within the degrees wherein marriage is prohibited by law.

(b) **Statutory Rape.** Nonforcible sexual intercourse with a person who is under the statutory age of consent.

[Authority: 20 U.S.C. 1232g(b)(6) and 18 U.S.C. 16]

[These regulations are codified in 34 CFR Part 99 as amended on July 6, 2000 (65 FR 41852).]

Appendix 3

Sample Release Forms

Sample 1: Written Authorization by Student to Send Grades to Parents

Permission to Release Education Record Information

I give permission for ______________________________ to release my
(College/university employee or office)

____
(education record information to be released)

to ____
(name, address)

for (purpose) ____

Signed ____________________________ Date ______________________

Action taken ____
(date) (by whom)

Sample 2: Authorization of Grade Disclosure

OFFICE OF ACADEMIC RECORDS AND SUMMER SCHOOL
SLIPPERY ROCK UNIVERSITY
SLIPPERY ROCK, PA 16057
(724) 738-2010

AUTHORIZATION OF GRADE DISCLOSURE

I hereby authorize Slippery Rock University of Pennsylvania to release my grade reports, both midterm and final, for the ________________ academic year, to my parent(s): (or other named individuals or entitles). If parents live at the same address, please list them both in #1.

1. ______________________________
Name(s)

____
Address

____
City, State, Zip

2. ______________________________
Name(s)

____
Address

____
City, State, Zip

If person(s) named above are not your parent(s), how are they related to you? ______________________

The released reports will be used for the purpose of ______________________________

____

____

I understand that by signing this authorization, I am waiving my rights of nondisclosure of these records under federal law only as to the persons specifically listed. This release does not permit the disclosure of these records to any other persons or entities without my written consent.

____
Date

____
Student's Name (print)

____
Student's Signature

____
Student's Social Security #

7/98

Sample 3: Authorization to Disclose Directory Information/Send Grades to Parents

IMPORTANT -- PLEASE READ CAREFULLY

DISCLOSURE OF DIRECTORY INFORMATION

Central College, in compliance with the Family Educational Rights and Privacy Act of 1974, has designated the following items as DIRECTORY INFORMATION: Student's name, address, telephone number; parents' name, address, telephone number; major field of study; class; enrollment status; anticipated degree date; religious affiliation; participation in officially recognized activities; degree and awards received; most recent previous educational agency or institution attended by the student.

Central College may disclose any of the above listed items without the student's prior written consent, unless the Registrar's Office is notified in writing to the contrary.

All other student academic information is considered confidential and will not be released, with certain exceptions, without the student's written permission.

A student's grades are considered confidential information. Therefore, if you wish to have your grades sent to your parents at the end of each semester, you need to sign this form and return it to the Registrar's Office to authorize the college to do so.

AUTHORIZATION TO SEND GRADES TO PARENTS

______________	______________________	____________
ID#	Student's Name (Please Print)	Date

I authorize Central College to send my grades to my parents at the end of each semester.

____

Student's Signature

Rev. 7/96

Sample 4: Authorization to Disclose Academic Information to Parents/Withhold Directory Information

Student's Name (Please Print) ______________________ Social Security # ______________________

ANNUAL NOTICE TO STUDENTS

THE FAMILY EDUCATIONAL RIGHTS AND PRIVACY ACT OF 1974 (F.E.R.P.A.)

Annually, XXXXXX University informs students of the Family Educational Rights and Privacy Act of 1974, as amended. This Act, with which the institution intends to comply fully, was designated to protect the privacy of educational records, to establish the rights of students to inspect and review the educational records, and to provide guidelines for the correction of inaccurate or misleading data through informal and formal hearings. Students also have the right to file complaints with The Family Educational Rights and Privacy Act Office (FERPA) concerning alleged failures by the institution to comply with the Act.

Local policy explains in detail the procedures to be used by XXXXXX University for compliance with the provisions of the Act. Copies can be obtained from the Office of Student Affairs and Office of the Registrar. It is also printed in the Student Handbook and the University Bulletins. Questions concerning the Family Educational Rights and Privacy Act may be directed to these offices.

****

AUTHORIZATION TO DISCLOSE ACADEMIC INFORMATION TO PARENTS

In accordance with FERPA, the University will disclose to parents information from the academic records of a student provided the University has on file written consent of the student. Please sign below and return to the Office of the Registrar if you consent for the University to release to your parents your educational records.

Student's Signature ______________________ Date ______________________

****

AUTHORIZATION TO WITHHOLD DIRECTORY INFORMATION

The following is considered "Directory Information" at XXXXXX University and will be made available to the general public unless the student notifies the Office of the Registrar in person or in writing before the last day to add classes.

> Student's name, telephone number, date and place of birth, college, major, honors, awards, photo, classification, dates of enrollment, degrees conferred, dates of conferral, graduation distinctions and the institution attended immediately prior to admission.

Under the provisions of the Family Educational Rights and Privacy Act of 1974 you have the right to withhold disclosure of such Directory Information. XXXXXX University will honor your request to withhold Directory Information.

Please consider carefully the consequences of any decision to withhold such Directory Information. Should you decide not to release any of this information, any requests for such information from XXXXXX University will be refused.

This signed request must be received in the Office of the Registrar by 4:45 p.m. on the last day to add classes as listed in the Academic Calendar. This authorization is valid until a written request to rescind is received by the Office of the Registrar.

I hereby request that XXXXXX University not release any Directory Information from my academic records. I have read the above paragraphs and understand the consequences of my action.

Student's Signature ______________________ Date ______________________

Appendix 4

Family Policy Compliance Office Letter Regarding Census Takers

1

April 27, 2000
To Institutions of Postsecondary Education:

The Department of Education has received numerous inquiries from postsecondary institutions regarding the applicability of the Family Educational Rights and Privacy Act (FERPA) to disclosure of information from student education records to the Bureau of the Census for the 2000 Census. This Office administers FERPA and is responsible for providing technical assistance to educational agencies and institutions on the law. 20 U.S.C. § 1232g; 34 CFR Part 99. We are writing to provide you with guidance regarding the disclosure of student information to Bureau of the Census officials.

The attached letter, which this Office prepared for the Census, explains that nothing in FERPA would prevent an institution from disclosing the information being requested by the Census in non-personally identifiable form. That is, an institution may provide census takers with all directory information items except for names of students, provided such information is disclosed on a minimum of several students. This would ensure that the information being disclosed is not personally identifiable to individual students. Thus, institutions could then include the additional information being requested by the Census—race and gender.

Should you have any additional questions, please do not hesitate to call this Office at (202) 260-3887 or email us at FERPA@ed.gov. Additionally, the attached letter is on our newly redesigned Web site at www.ed.gov/offices/OM/fpco/ under "Hot Topics."

Sincerely,
LeRoy S. Rooker
Director
Family Policy Compliance Office

2

April 27, 2000
Mr. Nunzio Cerniglia
Assistant Regional Census Manager
Bureau of the Census
841 Chestnut Street, Suite 5101
Philadelphia, Pennsylvania 19107

Dear Mr. Cerniglia:

This is in follow-up to our telephone conversation yesterday regarding the applicability of the Family Educational Rights and Privacy Act (FERPA) to the disclosure of certain information from student education records by postsecondary institutions to the Census Bureau (Bureau). In our conversation, you explained that, in order to complete the survey on students who have not returned the census form or provided information to census takers, the Bureau would like to receive information on these remaining students from institutions. Specifically, the Bureau would like to ask that institutions provide them with general directory information—without including any student names—as well as the race and gender of those remaining students. As explained more fully below, nothing in FERPA would prevent a school from providing the above-requested information to the Bureau provided that an institution discloses directory information (without the names), race, and gender on a minimum of several students. This Office has historically advised educational agencies and institutions that FERPA does not prohibit them from disclosing information in non-personally identifiable form to an outside party that has requested that information.

FERPA is a Federal law that protects a student's privacy interest in his or her "education records." The term "education records" is broadly defined as:

[T]hose records, files, documents, and other materials, which (i) contain information directly related to a student; and (ii) are maintained by an educational agency or institution or by a person acting for such agency or institution. 20 U.S.C. § 1232g(a)(4). See also 34 CFR § 99.3 "Education records."

FERPA provides that education records, or personally identifiable information from such records, may be disclosed by educational agencies and institutions only after obtaining prior written consent of the eligible student, except in several specified circumstances. 20 U.S.C. § 1232g(b)(1) and (d). See also 34 CFR § 99.30. Section 99.3 of the regulations defines "personally identifiable information" as information that includes but is not limited to:

a. the student's name;
b. the name of the student's parent or other family member;
c. the address of the student or the student's family;
d. a personal identifier, such as the student's social security number or student number;
e. a list of personal characteristics that would make the student's identity easily traceable; or
f. other information that would make the student's identity easily traceable.

As noted above, FERPA generally prohibits the nonconsensual disclosure of personally identifiable information derived from education records, except in certain circumstances. 20 U.S.C. § 1232g(b); 34 CFR § 99.31. Accordingly, if one or more of the exceptions are met, an educational agency or institution may disclose education records, or personally identifiable information from education records, without prior written consent.

One exception to the general prior consent rule is the nonconsensual disclosure of information derived from education records that has been appropriately designated as "directory information" by the educational agency or institution. 20 U.S.C. § 1232g(b)(1); 34 CFR § 99.31(a)(11). FERPA defines "directory information" as information contained in an education record of a student which would not generally be considered harmful or an invasion of privacy if disclosed. 20 U.S.C. § 1232g(a)(5); 34 CFR § 99.3 "Directory information." Directory information could include, but is not limited to, information such as name, address, telephone number, date and place of birth, participation in officially recognized activities and sports, and dates of attendance. However, information such as race, gender, or social security numbers cannot be designated as directory information because disclosure of such information would be considered an invasion of privacy. FERPA provides that a school may disclose directory information if it has given public notice of the types of information which it has designated as "directory information," the student's right to restrict the disclosure of such information, and the period of time within which a student has to notify the school in writing that he or she does not want any or all of those types of information designated as "directory information." 20 U.S.C. § 1232g(a)(5)(B); 34 CFR § 99.37(a).

In our telephone conversation, we discussed ways in which postsecondary institutions could assist the Bureau in completing its survey of students. One way would be for institutions to disclose properly designated directory information to census takers. However, as noted previously, race and gender cannot be designated and thus included in directory information. As we discussed, another way that institutions could assist the Bureau is to provide census takers with all directory information items except for names of students, provided such information is disclosed on a minimum of several students. This could ensure that the information disclosed is not personally identifiable. Institutions could then include information on the students' race and gender. You indicated that providing census takers with the directory information including race and gender in a non-personally identifiable format would provide the Bureau with the information that it needs.

In sum, this Office has advised postsecondary institutions that they may—to the extent allowed by FERPA—provide information to and cooperate with 2000 census takers. This may include disclosing properly designated directory information on those students to census takers, as well as distributing census forms to the student population. In our conversation yesterday, you indicated that the Bureau does not need the students' names from the institutions in order to generate the information necessary to complete the census survey. Therefore, institutions also may disclose directory information items without student names, provided that the institution is disclosing the directory information (without names) of a minimum of several students, and include the additional information on race and gender. We will include this guidance on our Web site (www.ed.gov/offices/OM/fpco/) under "Hot Topics" in a further effort to encourage schools to cooperate with census takers in this manner.

I trust that the above will be helpful in assisting the Bureau in completing the Census 2000.

Sincerely,
LeRoy S. Rooker
Director
Family Policy Compliance Office

Appendix 5

Two Forms for Students to Request Non-Disclosure of Directory Information

Form 1

Alpha University Policy Excerpt Re: Privacy Holds:

"At its discretion Alpha University may provide Directory Information in accordance with the provisions of the Family Education Rights and Privacy Act. Directory Information is defined as that information which would not generally be considered harmful or an invasion of privacy if disclosed. Designated Directory Information at Alpha University includes the following: student name, permanent address, local address, temporary address, electronic mail address, telephone number, dates of attendance, degrees and awards received, participation in officially recognized activities and sports, weight and height of members of athletic teams, theses titles/topics.

Students may withhold Directory Information by notifying the Registrar in writing; please note that such withholding requests are binding for all information to all parties other than for educational purposes. Students should consider all aspects of a Directory Hold prior to filing such a request. Although the initial request may be filed at any time, requests for non-disclosure will be honored by the University until removed by the student."

Please consider very carefully the consequences of any decision by you to withhold any category of "Directory Information". Such designation will call for Alpha University not to release any or all of this "Directory Information"; any future requests for such information from non-institutional persons or organizations will be refused.

Alpha University will honor your request to withhold any of the categories listed below but cannot assume responsibility to contact you for subsequent permission to release them. Regardless of the effect upon you, Alpha University assumes no liability as a result of honoring your instructions that such information be withheld.

Please mark the appropriate boxes and affix your signature below to indicate your disapproval for the institution to disclose the following Directory Information:

______ all directory information listed below
______ student name
______ permanent address
______ local address
______ temporary address
______ electronic mail address
______ telephone number
______ dates of attendance
______ degrees and awards received
______ participation in officially recognized activities and sports
______ weight and height of members of athletic teams
______ theses titles/topics
______ photo

Student Name______________________ Semester/Year ______________________

Student Signature ______________________ Date______________________

Note: requests for non-disclosure will be honored by the University for no more than one academic year. Re-authorization to withhold Directory information must be filed annually in the Office of the Registrar within the first two weeks of the fall semester.

Form 2

Request for Confidential Status of Directory Information

Name ______________________________ Student No ______________________________

Quarter ______________________________ Year ______________________________

At [our university] the following information about a student can, by law, be released to the general public and may be listed in the campus directory: permanent address and telephone number, local address and telephone number, confirmation that you are enrolled here.

No other student information is released to non-university personnel without your written permission. By completing this form, you will be requesting that information NOT be released to non-university personnel or listed in the campus directory.

Some of the effects of your decision to request confidential status will be that you must make all address changes with a signed authorization or in person with a form of ID; friends or relatives trying to reach you will not be able to do so through the University; information that you are a student here will be supressed, so if a loan company, prospective employer, family members, etc., inquire about you, they will be informed that we have no record of your attending here.

Once you have designated a confidential classification, it will not be removed until you submit a signed authorization requesting that it be removed.

Signature______________________________ Date______________________________

Appendix 6

Request for Amendment of Education Records; Description of the Hearing Process at One University

Request for Amendment of Education Records

You have the right to request amendment of your education records if you believe they are inaccurate or misleading. You should write the University official responsible for the specific record, clearly identify the part of the record you want changed, and specify why it is inaccurate or misleading.

That University official will reach a decision and inform you in a reasonable amount of time after receiving the request. If your request to amend the record is denied, the University official will advise you of your right to a hearing on the requested amendment, and provide information on hearing procedures. This hearing will be conducted by a hearing officer or committee appointed by the Vice President for Academic Affairs. The hearing will be held before an officer or committee with no direct interest in the outcome of the hearing. However, the hearing officer or committee may be employed by or exist at the University. The hearing will be held within a reasonable amount of time after the request for a hearing has been made. The hearing officer will notify you, reasonably in advance, of the date, place and time of the hearing.

You will be afforded a full and fair opportunity to present evidence relevant to the issue raised. You may be accompanied by one or more other persons, including an attorney. The hearing officer or committee will make a decision in writing based on the evidence presented at the hearing. The decision will include a summary of the evidence presented and the reasons for the decision.

If the hearing officer or committee supports the complaint, the education record will be amended accordingly and you will be so informed. If the hearing officer or committee decides not to amend the education record, you have the right to place in the education record a statement commenting on the challenged information and/or stating the reasons for disagreeing with the decision. This statement will be maintained as part of the education record as long as the contested portion is maintained, and whenever a copy of the education record is sent to any party, your statement will be included.

Appendix 7

Definition of Dependent

Internal Revenue Code of 1954, Section 152

(Including amendments and applicable sections of the Tax Reform Act of 1976)

Because both the "Final Regulations" and "The Act" make references to the Internal Revenue Code of 1954, Section 152, it is reproduced here in its entirety from the 1976 edition of the Internal Revenue Code of 1954, with permission from Prentice Hall, Inc., Englewood Cliffs, N.J. 07632.

Sec. 152. Dependent Defined.

(a) General Definition—For purposes of this subtitle, the term "dependent" means any of the following individuals over half of whose support, for the calendar year in which the taxable year of the taxpayer begins, was received from the taxpayer (or is treated under subsection (c) or (e) as received from the taxpayer):

(1) A son or daughter of the taxpayer, or a descendant of either,
(2) A stepson or stepdaughter of the taxpayer,
(3) A brother, sister, stepbrother, or stepsister of the taxpayer,
(4) The father or mother of the taxpayer, or an ancestor of either,
(5) A stepfather or stepmother of the taxpayer,
(6) A son or daughter of a brother or sister of the taxpayer,
(7) A brother or sister of the father or mother of the taxpayer,
(8) A son-in-law, daughter-in-law, father-in-law, mother-in-law, brother-in-law, or sister-in-law of the taxpayer.
(9) An individual (other than an individual who at any time during the taxable year was the spouse, determined without regard to section 153, of the taxpayer) who, for the taxable year of the taxpayer, has as his principal place of abode the home of the taxpayer and is a member of the taxpayer's household, or
(10) An individual who—

(A) is a descendant of a brother or sister of the father or mother of the taxpayer,
(B) for the taxable year of the taxpayer receives institutional care required by reason of a physical or mental disability, and
(C) before receiving such institutional care, was a member of the same household as the taxpayer.

Last amendment—Sec. 152(a) appears above as amended by § [1](b) of Public Law 90-78, Aug. 31, 1967, effective (Sec. 2 of Public Law 90-78, Aug. 31, 1967) with respect to taxable years beginning after Dec. 31, 1966.

Prior amendment—Sec. 152(a) was previously amended by Sec. 4(a) of Public Law 85-866, Sept. 2, 1958 (qualified effective date rule in Sec. 1(c)(1) of Public Law 85-866, Sept. 2, 1958). Sec. 152(a) as so amended is in P-H Cumulative Changes.

(b) Rules Relating to General Definition—For purposes of this section—

(1) The terms "brother" and "sister" include a brother or sister by the half-blood.
(2) In determining whether any of the relationships specified in subsection (a) or paragraph (1) of this subsection exists, a legally adopted child of an individual (and a child who is a member of an individual's household, if placed with such individual), or a foster child of an individual (if such child satisfies the requirements of subsection (a)(9) with respect to such individual), shall be treated as a child of such individual by blood.

Last amendment—Sec. 152(b)(2) appears above as amended by Sec. 912(a) of Public Law 91-172, Dec. 30, 1969, effective (Sec. 912(b) of Public Law 91-172, Dec. 30, 1969) with respect to taxable years beginning after Dec. 31, 1969.

Prior amendment—Sec. 152(b)(2) was previously amended by Sec. [1](a) of Public Law 86-376, Sept. 23, 1959, effective (Sec. [1](b) of Public Law 86-376, Sept. 23, 1959) for taxable years beginning after Dec. 31, 1958. Sec. 152(b)(2) as so amended is in P-H Cumulative Changes.

(3) The term "dependent" does not include any individual who is not a citizen or national of the United States unless such individual is a resident of the United States, of a country contiguous to the United States, of the Canal Zone, or of the Republic of Panama. The preceding sentence shall not exclude from the definition of "dependent" any child of the taxpayer—

(A) born to him, or legally adopted by him, in the Philippine Islands before January 1, 1956, if the child is a resident of the Republic of the Philippines, and if the taxpayer was a member of the Armed Forces of the United States at the time the child was born to him or legally adopted by him, or

(B) legally adopted by him, if, for the taxable year of the taxpayer, the child has as his principal place of abode the home of the taxpayer and is a member of the taxpayer's household, and if the taxpayer is a citizen or national of the United States.

Last amendment—Sec. 152(b)(3) appears above as amended by Sec. [1](a) of Public Law 92-580, Oct. 27, 1972, effective (Sec. [1](c) of Public Law 92-580, Oct. 27, 1972) with respect to taxable years beginning after Dec. 31, 1971.

Prior amendments—Sec. 152(b)(3) was previously amended by the following: Sec. 4(b) of Public Law 85-866, Sept. 2, 1958, effective (Sec. 4(d) of Public Law 85-866, Sept. 2, 1958) for taxable years beginning after Dec. 31, 1957.* Sec. 2 of Public Law 333, Aug. 9, 1955 (qualified effective date rule in Sec. 3(b) of Public Law 333, Aug. 9, 1955).*

*Sec. 152(b)(3) as so amended is in P-H Cumulative Changes.

(4) A payment to a wife which is includible in the gross income of the wife under section 71 or 682 shall not be treated as a payment by her husband for the support of any dependent.

(5) An individual is not a member of the taxpayer's household if at any time during the taxable year of the taxpayer the relationship between such individual and the taxpayer is in violation of local law.

Addition—Sec. 152(b)(5) was added by Sec. 4(c) of Public Law 85-866, Sept. 2, 1958 (qualified effective date rule in Sec. 1(c)(1) of Public Law 85-866, Sept. 2, 1958).

(c) Multiple Support Agreements—For purposes of subsection (a), over half of the support of an individual for a calendar year shall be treated as received from the taxpayer if—

(1) no one person contributed over half of such support;

(2) over half of such support was received from persons each of whom, but for the fact that he did not contribute over half of such support, would have been entitled to claim such individual as a dependent for a taxable year beginning in such calendar year;

(3) the taxpayer contributed over 10 percent of such support; and

(4) each person described in paragraph (2) (other than the taxpayer) who contributed over 10 percent of such support files a written declaration (in such manner and form as the Secretary or his delegate may by regulations prescribe) that he will not claim such individual as a dependent for any taxable year beginning in such calendar year.

(d) Special Support Test in Case of Students—For purposes of subsection (a), in the case of any individual who is—

(1) a son, stepson, daughter, or stepdaughter of the taxpayer (within the meaning of this section), and

(2) a student (within the meaning of section 151(e)(4)), amounts received as scholarships for study at an education institution (as defined in section 151(e)(4)) shall not be taken into account in determining whether such individual received more than half of his support from the taxpayer.

(e) Support Test in Case of Child of Divorced Parents, etc.

(1) General rule—If—

(A) a child [as defined in section 151(e)(3)] receives over half of his support during the calendar year from his parents who are divorced or legally separated under a decree of divorce or separate maintenance, or who are separated under a written separation agreement, and

(B) such child is in the custody of one or both of his parents for more than one-half of the calendar year; such child shall be treated, for purposes of subsection (a), as receiving over half of his support during the calendar year from the parent having custody for a greater portion of the calendar year unless he is treated, under the provisions of paragraph (2), as having received over half of his support for such year from the other parent (referred to in this subsection as the parent not having custody).

(2) Special rule—The child of parents described in paragraph (1) shall be treated as having received over half of his support during the calendar year from the parent not having custody if—

(A)(i) the decree of divorce or of separate maintenance, or a written agreement between the parents applicable to the taxable year beginning in such calendar year, provides that the parent not having custody shall be entitled to any deduction allowable under section 151 for such child, and

(ii) such parent not having custody provides at least $600 for the support of such child during the calendar year, or

(B)(i) the parent not having custody provides $1,200 or more for the support of such child (or if there is more than one such child, $1,200 or more for all of such children) for the calendar year, and

(ii) if the parent having custody of such child does not clearly establish that he provided more for the support of such child during the calendar year than the parent not having custody.

For the purposes of this paragraph, amounts expended for the support of a child or children shall be treated as received from the parent not having custody to the extent that such parent provided amounts for such support.

(3) Itemized statement required—If a taxpayer claims that paragraph (2)(B) applies with respect to a child for a calendar year and the other parent claims that paragraph (2)(B)(i) is not satisfied or claims to have provided more for the support of such child during such calendar year than the taxpayer, each parent shall be entitled to receive, under regulations to be prescribed by the Secretary or his delegate, an itemized statement of the expenditures upon which the other parent's claim of support is based.

(4) Exception for multiple-support agreement—The provisions of this subsection shall not apply in any case where over half of the support of the child is treated as having been received from a taxpayer under the provisions of subsection (c).

(5) Regulations—The Secretary or his delegate shall prescribe such regulations as may be necessary to carry out the purposes of this subsection.

Addition—Sec. 152(e) was added by Sec. [1](a) of Public Law 90-78, Aug. 31, 1967, effective (Sec. 2 of Public Law 90-78, Aug. 31, 1967) with respect to taxable years beginning after Dec. 31, 1966.

Tax Reform Act of 1976

[§ 484] Code Sec. 152. Dependent Defined.

* * * * * *

(e) Support Test in Case of Child of Divorced Parents, etc—

* * * * * *

(2) Special rule—The child of parents described in paragraph (1) shall be treated as having received over half of his support during the calendar year from the parent not having custody if—

(A)(i) the decree of divorce or of separate maintenance, or a written agreement between the parents applicable to the taxable year beginning in such calendar year, provides that the parent not having custody shall be entitled to any deduction allowable under section 151 for such child, and

(ii) such parent not having custody provides at least $600 for the support of such child during the calendar year, or

(B)(i) the parent not having custody provides $1,200 or more for the support of such child (or if there is more than one such child, $1,200 or more for1 each of such children) for the calendar year, and

(ii) the parent having custody of such child does not clearly establish that he provided more for the support of such child during the calendar year than the parent not having custody.

For the purposes of this paragraph, amounts expended for the support of a child or children shall be treated as received from the parent not having custody to the extent that such parent provided amounts for such support.

* * * * * *

[Footnote 484] Matter in italics in Sec. 152(e)(2)(B)(i) added by section 2139(a), '76 Tax Reform Act, which struck out (1) "all"

Effective date (Sec. 2139(b), '76 Tax Reform Act)—Applies to taxable years beginning after the date of enactment of this Act.

Title 38, United States Code—Veterans' Benefits

Examination of Records

Section 1790 (c) Notwithstanding any other provision of law, the records and accounts of educational institutions pertaining to eligible veterans or eligible persons who received educational assistance under this chapter or chapter 31, 32, 34, or 35 of this title, as well as the records of other students which the Administrator determines necessary to ascertain institutional compliance with the requirements of such chapters, shall be available for examination by duly authorized representatives of the Government. (Added P.L. 92-540, § 316(2), amended P.L. 94-502, § 510).

Appendix 8

Directory Information Items Identified in a 1988 AAU Survey and a 1991 AACRAO Survey of Member Institutions

Survey of Directory Information Items Identified by 46 AAU (American Association of Universities) Member Institutions, 1988

Number of Schools Identifying Item as Directory Information (Total Schools in Survey = 46)

Name	46
Address	46
Phone	46
Dates of attendance	46
Degree(s) received	46
Major (program)	39 (85%)
Activity and sport participation (plus height and weight)	31 (67%)
Birthdate	26 (56%)
Most recent education institution attended	22 (48%)
Class (year in school)	20 (43%)
Place of birth	20 (43%)
College (unit)	15 (33%)
Full-time/part-time	10 (22%)
Sports participation (height and weight of team members)	5 (11%)
All previous educational institutions attended	5 (11%)
Parent/spouse names/addresses	5 (11%)
Status (graduate, undergraduate, professional, etc.)	4 (9%)
Sex	4 (9%)
Officially recognized activity participation	3 (7%)
Hometown	3 (7%)
Expected graduation date or degree candidacy	3 (7%)
Advisor name	3 (7%)
Campus	3 (7%)
Age	2 (4%)
Theses titles/topics	2 (4%)
Marital status	2 (4%)
Class standing	2 (4%)
Date of admission	1 (2%)
Position on sports teams	1 (2%)
Cumulative credits earned	1 (2%)
Relationship to alumni	1 (2%)
Student publications	1 (2%)
Dates of employment with institution	1 (2%)
Employment as TA/RA	1 (2%)
Secondary school attended	1 (2%)
Type of teacher certification	1 (2%)
Ethnic background	1 (2%)
Arrest records/traffic accident information	1 (2%)
Student parking permit information	1 (2%)
Names and attendance of students in courses	1 (2%)

Directory Information Items Identified in a Survey of 257 AACRAO Member Institutions, 1991

Number of Schools Identifying Item as Directory Information (Total Schools in Survey = 257)

Name	248 (97%)
Dates of attendance	222 (86%)
Degree(s) received	220 (86%)
Major (program)	217 (84%)
Address	213 (83%)
Phone	198 (77%)
Full-time/part-time	152 (59%)
Birthdate	142 (55%)
Sports participation (height and weight of team members)	140 (55%)
Class (year in school)	131 (51%)
Activity and sport participation (plus height and weight)	99 (39%)
College (unit)	96 (37%)
Sex	91 (35%)
All previous educational institutions attended	39 (15%)
Student's current class schedule	36 (14%)
Place of birth	14 (5%)
Parent/spouse names/addresses	4 (2%)
Marital status	2 (1%)

Appendix 9

Sample Compliance Documents

Sample 1: Student Request to Prevent Disclosure of Directory Information

To: All Students Term/Semester/Year _______________

These items listed below are designated as "Directory Information" and may be released for any purpose at the discretion of our institution.

Under the provisions of the Family Educational Rights and Privacy Act of 1974, as Amended, you have the right to withhold the disclosure of any or all of the categories of "Directory Information" listed below.

Please consider very carefully the consequences of any decision by you to withhold any category of "Directory Information." Should you decide to inform the institution not to release any or all of this "Directory Information," any future requests for such information from non-institutional persons or organizations will be refused.

The institution will honor your request to withhold any of the categories listed below but cannot assume responsibility to contact you for subsequent permission to release them. Regardless of the effect upon you, the institution assumes no liability for honoring your instructions that such information be withheld.

Please mark the appropriate boxes and affix your signature below to indicate your disapproval for the institution to disclose the following public or Directory Information.

	Information	Disclose No
Category I	Name, address, telephone number, dates of attendance, class.	______
Category II	Previous institution(s) attended, major field of study, awards, honors (includes Dean's list), degree(s) conferred (including dates).	______
Category III	Past and present participation in officially recognized sports and activities, physical factors (height, weight of athletes), date and place of birth.	______
Category IV	Any item(s) listed above.	______

____

(specify which items listed above you wish not to be disclosed)

Date _______________ Student Signature ____________________

If this form is not received in (campus) office prior to (date), it will be assumed that the above information may be disclosed for the remainder of the current academic year. A new form for non-disclosure must be completed each academic term/semester/year.

Sample 2: Student Request to Prevent Disclosure of Directory Information

OFFICE OF ACADEMIC RECORDS AND SUMMER SCHOOL
SLIPPERY ROCK UNIVERSITY
SLIPPERY ROCK PA 16057
(724) 738-2010

REQUEST TO PREVENT DISCLOSURE OF DIRECTORY INFORMATION

All Students:

The Family Educational Rights and Privacy Act designates certain information related to students as "Directory Information" and gives the University the right to disclose such information to anyone inquiring without having to ask students for permission, unless the students specifically request in writing that all such information not be made public without their written consent. The categories of "Directory Information" are listed in the Slippery Rock University policy statement on privacy rights, a copy of which is available upon request from the Office of Academic Records and Summer School. If you wish to withhold the disclosure of all of the items of "Directory Information," fill out the form below and submit it to the Director of Academic Records and Summer School.

This form must be received in the Office of Academic Records and Summer School within the first two weeks of each semester. If it is not received in that office by that date, all directory information will be disclosed for the remainder of the semester. A new form for non-disclosure must be completed each semester and summer session. This form becomes invalid at the end of the semester identified below.

Please consider very carefully the consequences of any decision made by you to withhold any category of "Directory Information", as any future requests for such information from non-institutional persons or organizations will be refused. Slippery Rock University will honor your request to withhold all of the categories listed below but cannot assume responsibility to contact you for subsequent permission to release them. Regardless of the effect upon you, Slippery Rock University assumes no liability for honoring your instructions that such information may be withheld.

I have carefully read the above and request that all "Directory Information" not be disclosed to non-institutional persons or organizations by the University without my prior written permission:

Term (circle one): Fall Spring Summer 20_____

Student's Printed Name________________________________Social Security #____________

Student's Local/Campus Address____

City________________________________State_______________Zip_______________

Student's Local/Campus Phone _________________________

Today's Date______________________Student's Signature__________________________

Return completed form: Director, Academic Records & Summer School, Room 107, Old Main

6-1-00

Sample 3: Request to Review Education Records

Date: ______________________

NAME OF STUDENT: ____

STUDENT NUMBER: ____

PURPOSE OF REVIEW: ____

____

ITEM(S) OF INFORMATION REQUESTED: ______________________________

____

____

NAME OF REQUESTOR: ____

REQUESTOR'S AFFILIATION: _______________________________________

OFFICE TO WHICH REQUEST WAS MADE: ______________________________

I hereby agree to keep the information disclosed to me confidential according to applicable legislation and regulations.

Signature ______________________________ Date ______________________

....

DISPOSITION OF REQUEST: __________ APPROVED __________ DISAPPROVED

SPECIFY MATERIALS REVIEWED (RECORDS, TYPES OF INFORMATION):

____

____

Signature of Official Approving Request ______________________ Date __________

Name and Title of Official Supervising Review ___________________ Date __________

Sample 4: Student Request to Inspect and Review Education Records

Date submitted: ____________________

To: Record Custodian

I wish to inspect my education record located in the following office(s):

____

____

Print Name (Student) ____

Address ____

Student's Signature ______________________________ Telephone No. ________________________

....

To: Student

Your request for inspection of your record was received on (date).
The requested record will be available at (office) for review on (date).

Date ________________ School Official's Signature ______________________________________

....

To: Custodian

I have inspected and/or have been informed of the contents of the requested education record identified above and am satisfied with its accuracy and completeness.

Date: ________________ Student's Signature ____

....

To: Record Custodian

I have inspected and/or have been informed of the contents of the requested education record identified above and am not satisfied with its accuracy and completeness for the following reason(s):

____

____

Date ________________ Student's Signature ____

....

Observations of the record custodian of disposition of the request:

____

Date ________________ Custodian's Signature ____

....

I hereby agree to keep the information disclosed to me confidential according to applicable legislation and regulations.

Signature ______________________________ Date ______________________________________

Sample 5: Student Request to Inspect and Review Education Records

OFFICE OF ACADEMIC RECORDS AND SUMMER SCHOOL
SLIPPERY ROCK UNIVERSITY
SLIPPERY ROCK, PA 16057
(412) 738-2010

STUDENT REQUEST TO INSPECT AND REVIEW EDUCATION RECORDS

TO: Director of Academic Records & Summer School, Room 107, Old Main., and
Name of Custodian of Record in question: ______________________

I wish to inspect the following education record(s):

____

maintained in the following office(s): ______________________

Print Name (student) ______________________ S. S. # ____________

Local/Campus Address ______________________________

TO: Student

Your request for inspection of your records was received on ____________
The requested record will be available for review on ____________

Date ____________ Record Custodian's Signature ______________________

TO: Record Custodian

I have inspected and/or have been informed of the contents of the requested education record identified above and am satisfied with its accuracy and/or completeness.

Date ____________ Student's Signature ______________________

TO: Record Custodian

I have inspected and/or have been informed of the contents of the requested education record identified above and am not satisfied with its accuracy and completeness for the following reason(s) (use back of sheet if necessary):

____

____

Date ____________ Student's Signature ______________________

Students wishing to have their education records amended must complete a "Request to Amend Education Records" form. This form is available from the University's Office of Academic Records and Summer School, Room 107, Old Main.

Observations of the record custodian of disposition of this request should be written on the back of this sheet.

Date ____________ Record Custodian's Signature ______________________

After completed by the student and Record Custodian, this form should be returned to the Director of Academic Records and Summer School, Room 107, Old Main.

1-19-91

Sample 6: Student Request to Amend or Remove Education Records

OFFICE OF ACADEMIC RECORDS AND SUMMER SCHOOL
SLIPPERY ROCK UNIVERSITY
SLIPPERY ROCK, PA 16057
(412) 738-2010

REQUEST TO AMEND OR REMOVE EDUCATION RECORDS

Date ____________________

Name of student ______________________ Social Security # ____________

City ______________________ State __________ Zip ________

Student's Local/Campus Phone No. ______________________

Student's Signature ______________________ Date ____________

I have reviewed my education records held within the ______________________ office at Slippery Rock University. I am not satisfied with the accuracy and/or completeness of these records. Specifically, I request that these records be amended in the following way(s) (use back of sheet if additional space is needed):

____
____
____
____

I request that the following document(s) be removed from my file: ____________
____

Record Custodian Reviewing Request to Amend Education Record

Name ______________________ Title ______________________

Disposition of Request ________ Approved

________ Disapproved

Reason for Approval/Disapproval (use back of sheet if additional space is needed):

____
____
____
____
____

Custodian's Signature ______________________ Date ____________

Appeals of the Record Custodian's decision may be made by completing a "Student Request For Formal Hearing" form. This form is available in the Office of Academic Records and Summer School, Room 107, Old Main.

The Records Custodian must send a copy of this form to the student making the request and the Director of Academic Records and Summer School.

1-19-91

Sample 7: Student Request for Formal Hearing

OFFICE OF ACADEMIC RECORDS AND SUMMER SCHOOL
SLIPPERY ROCK UNIVERSITY
SLIPPERY ROCK, PA 16057
(412) 738-2010
STUDENT REQUEST FOR FORMAL HEARING

To: Director of Academic Records & Summer School Date ____________________

FROM: Student's Name ______________________________ S. S. #__________________

I request a formal hearing concerning correction of what I believe to be inaccurate or misleading information contained in my education records.

The following Education Record(s) is/are being contested: ____________________

I am contesting the information because: ______________________________________

____

____

________________________(Please use back of sheet if additional space is needed).

Please notify me of the date, time, and place of the hearing. My address and telephone number follows:

____

Local/Campus Address City State Zip

Student's Signature _________________________ Local/Campus Phone #_____________

FIRST ENDORSEMENT

FROM: ______________________________ Chairperson, Hearing Panel, Date __________

TO: Student's Name ____

The decision of the Hearing Panel is as follows (please use back of sheet if additional space is needed)____

____

____

____

Signature: Chairperson, Hearing Panel ____

NOTE: If the student disagrees with the Hearing Panel's decision, he/she has the right to place in his/her record a written statement commenting on the information in the record and/or stating his/her reasons for disagreeing with the decision. This explanation will become part of the student's education record as long as this record is maintained and whenever a copy of this record is sent to any party, the explanation will accompany it.

The Chairperson of the Hearing Panel must send copies of the Panel's decision to the student requesting the hearing, and to the Director of Academic Records and Summer School, Room 107, Old Main.

1-19-91

Sample 8: Student Request for Formal Hearing

To: Chairperson, Hearing Panel Date: ______________

From: (Student's Name)

Subject: Request for Hearing Concerning Student Education Records

I request a formal hearing concerning correction of what I believe to be inaccurate or misleading information, described below, contained in my education records.

Contested Information	Education Record Contested
______________________	______________________
______________________	______________________
______________________	______________________
______________________	______________________

Please notify me of the date, time, and place of the hearing. My address and telephone number follow:

Address ____

____

Student's Signature ____

Telephone No. ____

1st ENDORSEMENT

From: (Chairperson, Hearing) Date: ______________

To: (Student's Name)

The decision of the Hearing is as follows:

____

____

____

____

Chairperson, Hearing ____

Appendix 10

Student Worker Statement of Understanding of the Family Educational Rights and Privacy Act

Sample Form

I understand that by the virtue of my employment with the XXXXXXXX Office at (institution), I may have access to records which contain individually identifiable information, the disclosure of which is prohibited by the Family Educational Rights and Privacy Act of 1974. I acknowledge that I fully understand that the intentional disclosure by me of this information to any unauthorized person could subject me to criminal and civil penalties imposed by law. I further acknowledge that such willful or unauthorized disclosure also violates (institution's) policy and could constitute just cause for disciplinary action including termination of my employment regardless of whether criminal or civil penalties are imposed.

______________ ____

DATE EMPLOYEE'S SIGNATURE

Appendix 11

Institutional Statements on Legitimate Educational Interest

Below are representative statements from institutions which have defined legitimate educational interest as part of their written institutional policy on FERPA.

Statement 1:

"'Legitimate educational interests' means (1) the information or records requested is relevant and necessary to accomplishment of some task or determination; and, (2) the task or determination is an employment responsibility for the inquirer or is a properly assigned subject matter for the inquirer's employment responsibility."

Statement 2:

"For these purposes, 'legitimate educational interests' shall mean an **educationally related** purpose which has a directly identifiable educational relationship to the student involved and underlies the request. More particularly, the following criteria shall be taken into account in determining the legitimacy of a University official's access to student records:

- The official must seek the information within the context of the responsibilities that he or she has been assigned;
- The information sought must be used within the context of official University business and not for purposes extraneous to the official's area of responsibility or to the University;
- The information requested must be relevant and necessary to the accomplishment of some task or to making some determination within the scope of University employment;
- The task must be determined to be consistent with the purposes for which the data are maintained. Requests related to institutional research and studies are subject to this criterion.

Disclosure to a school official having a legitimate education interest does not constitute institutional authorization to transmit, share, or disclose any or all information received to a third party. An unauthorized disclosure of personally identifiable information from the education record of the student is prohibited."

Statement 3:

"'School officials' who have a 'legitimate educational interest.' 'School officials' shall mean any person who is a trustee, officer, agent or employee of the University. 'Legitimate educational interest' shall mean any authorized interest, or activity undertaken in the name of the University for which access to an Education Record is necessary or appropriate to the proper performance of the undertaking. It shall include, without limitation, access by a student, instructor, department or division head, dean, the chief academic and student affairs administrator, the president, a trustee, the custodian of the University records, the alumni administrator, legal counsel, the financial aid administrator, administrators charged with maintaining Education Records, the staff and subordinates of the foregoing, and others authorized by the President, to the extent the foregoing persons are acting within the course and scope of their employment and authority.

1. **School Officials.** School officials with legitimate educational interest in a student's educational records may access those records without the student's consent. School officials are those officials...who act in the student's educational interest within the limitations of their 'need to know.' This includes faculty, administrators, clerical and professional employees. Also included are students serving on university committees where legitimate 'need to know' exists. The demonstrated 'need to know' or the 'legitimate educational interest' must be supported by the institutional responsibilities assigned to an individual and/or to a committee. It is the responsibility of the respective Records Custodian to assess the 'legitimate educational interest' or 'need to know' of the request and to require proper identification, if necessary. When doubt is raised by a Records Custodian about an individual's 'need to know' or 'legitimate educational interest' in having access to specific information the issue shall be decided by the Provost. The Records Custodian will determine whether copies of materials may be made and/or if others need to be present during the examination of the educational records."

Statement 4:

"'Confidential data' includes students' grades, class schedules, and all other nondirectory information contained in a student's records. Confidential student data may only be utilized for official University business and made available to members of the University community who have a 'legitimate educational interest' on a 'need to know' basis. What do we mean by a 'legitimate educational interest'? A demonstrated 'need to know' by those officials of an institution who act in the student's educational interest. It includes faculty, administration, clerical and professional employees, and other persons who need student record information for the effective functioning of their office or position. An example of this is faculty and student members of registered honor societies. They may have access to student records for the sole purpose of determining eligibility for membership on the basis that faculty and students are acting in an official university capacity that is integral to the education function of the University. In such cases, the legitimate educational interest of students and the University has been served."

Appendix 12

Form for Providing Access to Computer Information System

Sample Form

Grand Canyon University
Colleague: SIS (Student Information System)
Access Form: Students Records

Part 1: Please Print

Employee Name: ____________ ____________ ____________
Last First Middle Initial

E-mail: ____________ Phone: (602) 589 - ____________

Position: ____________ Department: ____________

____________ ____________
Immediate Supervisors Signature Required Date

Please sign and date the bottom of this form and return to the Office of the Registrar.

Part 2: Computer Center

Check One: ______ Student Worker Access (Inquiry Only)
______ Advisor Access (Standard Advisor Access)
______ Dean Access (Standard Dean Access)

and/or

Individual Screens: ______ ______ ______ ______ ______ ______ ______
______ ______ ______ ______ ______ ______ ______

Part 3: FERPA (Confidentiality Statement)

Along with the right to access the transcripts of students at Grand Canyon University comes the responsibility to maintain the rights of students particularly as outlined in the Family Educational Rights and Privacy Act (FERPA). The University Catalog, Semester Bulletins and Student Handbook state the policy regarding student records at Grand Canyon University. Student records are open to members of the faculty and staff who have a legitimate need to know their contents; however, you do have a responsibility to maintain confidentiality. Under the terms of FERPA, Grand Canyon University has established the following as directory information: Student's Name, Local Address/Telephone Number, Permanent Address/Telephone Number, E-mail Address, Date and Place of Birth, Hometown, Degrees and Awards Received and Dates, Dates of Attendance (Current and Past), Full or Part-time Enrollment Status, Participation in Officially Recognized Activities, Participation in Officially Recognized Sports, Weight/Height of Member of Athletic Teams, Most Recently Attended Educational Institution, Major Field of Study, Academic Levels, Residency Status, Photographs. All other information may not be released without written consent of the student. Grades, Social Security Numbers, Ethnic, and Student Schedules should not be released to anyone other than the student under discussion and not over the phone.

I have read the above and agree to maintain the confidentiality of student records.

____________ ____________
Employee Signature Date

Part 4: FOR OFFICE USE ONLY

Notes: ____________

Colleague Login ID: ____________

____________ ____________
Registrar's Signature Required Date

Appendix 13

Sample Agreement to Change SSN to Another Personal Identifier

Sample Form

Upon your request, (Institution) will change your current I.D. number which is

______________________ to ______________________
(old number) (new number)

All of the computerized information which (Institution) holds on you in the student records, financial aid, business, housing, and dining service computer systems, whichever are applicable, and any reports generated from those systems which utilize I.D. numbers, will use the new number.

(Institution) will not release your old I.D. number to any outside agencies, but will make a note of what your old I.D. number was on your academic record for internal use only. By signing this form, you also understand and affirm that:

- you will use the new I.D. number in any future transactions involving (Institution) which require an I.D. number;
- certain problems may arise if we receive information requests from outside agencies which only contain your old I.D. number. You will not hold (Institution) responsible for any such problems which may arise due to this change in I.D. numbers.
- you are not receiving any type of financial aid from the State or federal governments.

for (Institution) ______________________ Date ______________________

Student ______________________ Date ______________________

Appendix 14

Model Annual Notification to Students

The Family Educational Rights and Privacy Act (FERPA) affords students certain rights with respect to their education records. These rights are:

1. The right to inspect and review the student's education records within 45 days of the day the University receives a request for access. Students should submit to the registrar, dean, or head of the academic department [or appropriate official] written requests that identify the record(s) they wish to inspect. The University official will make arrangements for access and notify the student of the time and place where the records may be inspected. If the records are not maintained by the University official to whom the request was submitted, that official shall advise the student of the correct official to whom the request should be addressed.

2. The right to request the amendment of the student's education records that the student believes is inaccurate or misleading. Students may ask the University to amend a record that they believe is inaccurate or misleading. They should write the University official responsible for the record, clearly identify the part of the record they want changed, and specify why it is inaccurate or misleading. If the University decides not to amend the record as requested by the student, the University will notify the student of the decision and advise the student of his or her right to a hearing regarding the request for amendment. Additional information regarding the hearing procedures will be provided to the student when notified of the right to a hearing.

3. The right to consent to disclosures of personally identifiable information contained in the student's education records, except to the extent that FERPA authorizes disclosure without consent. One exception, which permits disclosure without consent, is disclosure to school officials with legitimate educational interests. A school official is defined as a person employed by the University in an administrative, supervisory, academic, or support staff position (including law enforcement unit and health staff); a person or company with whom the University has contracted (such as an attorney, auditor, or collection agent); a person serving on the Board of Trustees; or assisting another school official in performing his or her tasks. A school official has a legitimate educational interest if the official needs to review an education record in order to fulfill his or her professional responsibility.

   [*Optional*] Upon request, the University discloses education records without consent to officials of another school in which a student seeks or intends to enroll. [**Note:** FERPA requires an institution to make a reasonable attempt to notify the student of the records request unless the institution states in its annual notification that it intends to forward records on request.]

4. The right to file a complaint with the U.S. Department of Education concerning alleged failures by the University to comply with the requirements of FERPA. The name and address of the Office that administers FERPA is:

   Family Policy Compliance Office
   U.S. Department of Education
   400 Maryland Avenue, SW
   Washington, DC 20202-4605

   [**Note:** In addition, an institution may want to include its directory information public notice, as required by § 99.37 of the regulations, with its annual notification of rights under FERPA.]

Available for download at:
http://www.ed.gov/offices/OM/fpco/psi1.html

Appendix 15

Sample Notice to Student of Intent to Comply with a Subpoena

Sample Letter

January 24, 2000

John Smith
121 Henry Ct.
Anytown VA 24551

Dear Mr. Smith:

Enclosed please find a copy of a subpoena we have received for your records. According to the Family Educational Rights and Privacy Act of 1974, we are required to notify you that we intend to comply with this subpoena on Friday, February 4, 2000.

If you plan to obtain the services of an attorney to attempt to quash this subpoena, we would appreciate notification prior to Friday, February 4, 2000.

Sincerely yours,

James Noe
Registrar

cc: John Henry's Attorney
Law, Law, and Law
344 Willow Lane
Anytown VA 24551

Appendix 16

Final Regulations of July 6, 2000, as Published in the Federal Register, with Introductory Commentary from AACRAO

Introductory Comments from AACRAO Regarding the FERPA Final Regulations of July 6, 2000

Campuses are encouraged to access or download the final regulations, effective August 7, 2000, at http://www.ed.gov/offices/OM/fpco/HotTopics.html.

Text and Adobe Acrobat (.pdf) versions are also posted under the FERPA heading at http://web.aacrao.org/asp_aacrao/govrel/issues.asp.

Background

The Education Department issued final regulations on July 6, 2000, to amend the Family Educational Rights and Privacy Act (FERPA). The amendments implement sections 951 and 952 of the Higher Education Amendments of 1998 (HEA). The final regulations include an analysis of comments and changes made in response to the Notice of Proposed Rulemaking (NPRM) issued June 1, 1999.

The final regulations allow:

- The disclosure of education records to the Attorney General for certain purposes;
- Non-consensual disclosure to courts of a disciplinary proceeding brought by a parent or student against an institution of higher education, or by an institution against a parent or student;
- Non-consensual disclosure of the outcome of a disciplinary proceeding against a student in specified circumstances; and
- Non-consensual disclosure to parents and legal guardians of students under age 21 if the student broke laws or violated policies relating to the use or possession of alcohol or a controlled substance.

Issue-Related Summary

Directory Information—Sec. 99.3: The final regulations provide a definition for "date of attendance" to mean the academic year, semester, or quarter attended and stipulate that the term does not include specific daily records of a student's attendance at the institution.

The Department wrote in its "Analysis of Comments and Changes" that e-mail addresses are now included as examples of directory information since it would not generally be considered harmful or an invasion of privacy if disclosed.

The Department also noted in the Analysis that it was concerned that the inclusion of class rosters and class schedules as examples of directory information "may lead some schools to disclose sensitive information" such as SSN or other identification numbers or enrollment in a remedial or special education course. The Department wrote that it "decided not to include them in the final regulations" as a result and would "reevaluate" its "previous advice that defined these terms as 'directory information.'"

Rights of Students—Sec. 99.5: Regarding student access to admissions files after being accepted but before enrolling at another component of an institution they currently attend or once attended, the Department clarified that students have no FERPA rights until they enroll in and attend that component of the institution.

Attorney General Disclosures—Sec. 99.31(a)(3)(ii): The Department of Education removed the phrase "for law enforcement purposes" from the NPRM language since disclosures to the Attorney General will only be made to investigate or enforce the federal legal requirements applicable to federally supported education programs.

Disclosures to Parents of Dependent Students—Sec. 99.31(a)(8): The final regulations allow institutions to deny access to a student's education record if the parent that claims the student as a dependent does not want his or her financial information disclosed to his or her spouse; the parent who claims the student may ask the institution not to redisclose this information to the spouse or former spouse.

The rule also gives institutions the discretion to determine whether to disclose student information to a parent who is a perpetrator of domestic violence. The Department wrote, "We strongly encourage victims of domestic violence to inform institutions of postsecondary education not to disclose any information from a student's education record to a perpetrator of domestic violence." Schools will not be held liable for releasing a student's education record unknowingly to a perpetrator of domestic violence.

Disclosures to Courts—Sec. 99.31(a)(9)(iii): A section has been added to allow disclosure to a court without consent if a parent or student has initiated legal action against an institution. The Department also deleted the notification requirement that would have required the institution to notify the parent or student before disclosing the student's relevant education records if the institution initiates a legal action against a parent or student.

Campus Disciplinary Proceedings—Sec. 99.31(a)(13) and (14), Sec. 99.39: Regarding campus disciplinary proceedings concerning a crime of violence or non-forcible sex offenses, the Department responded to commenter concerns by providing various definitions, including a list of "crimes of violence" with definitions derived from the FBI's *Uniform Crime Reporting Handbook* definitions.

The regulations reinstate language [see Sec. 99.31(a)(13)] that the Department inadvertently deleted in the NPRM that permits colleges to disclose to the victim the final results of a disciplinary proceeding regardless of the outcome.

Section 99.14(a)(14) of the final regulations, however, provides that the institution may disclose to the public the final results of a disciplinary proceeding only if it has determined that: (1) the student is an alleged perpetrator of a crime of violence or non-forcible sex offense; and (2) the student has committed a violation of the institution's rules or policies with respect to the allegation.

No other students, including a victim or witness, may be named in the proceeding, except for the alleged perpetrator, without prior written consent of the other students involved. Section 99.31 (a)(14) will be effective once an institution reaches its final result in a disciplinary proceeding; since the amendment to FERPA was effective October 7, 1998, only cases decided on or after that date may be disclosed without consent.

Alcohol or Drug Violations—Sec. 99.31(a)(15): The final regulations allow institutions to disclose to parents, without a student's consent, when students under age 21 violate drug or alcohol laws or policies. Institutions may disclose this information to parents "without regard to whether the student is a dependent." Previously, colleges could not inform parents of a student's alcohol violation if he or she was 18 or older, unless the institution could prove that the student was financially dependent on a parent.

Colleges can now establish their own policy and procedures about when parents should be contacted. Colleges are not required to alert students when parents have been notified but are required to maintain a record of the disclosure to the parent and provide it to the student at their request.

Contact: Please contact gourleyj@aacrao.org with comments or questions about the final regulations.

July 6, 2000 Final Regulations Published in the Federal Register

Federal Register / July 6, 2000 (Volume 65, Number 130) / Rules and Regulations [Page 41851-41863]

From the Federal Register Online via GPO Access [wais.access.gpo.gov]

Department of Education

34 CFR Part 99
Family Educational Rights and Privacy

Agency: Department of Education.
Action: Final regulations.

Summary: The Secretary amends the regulations implementing the Family Educational Rights and Privacy Act (FERPA). The amendments are needed to implement sections 951 and 952 of the Higher Education Amendments of 1998 (HEA). These amendments permit postsecondary institutions to disclose certain information to the public and to parents of students.

Dates: These regulations are effective August 7, 2000.

For Further Information Contact: Ellen Campbell, U.S. Department of Education, 400 Maryland Avenue, SW, Washington, DC 20202-4605. Telephone (202) 260-3887. If you use a telecommunications device for the deaf (TDD), you may call the Federal Information Relay Service (FIRS) at 1-800-877-8339.

Individuals with disabilities may obtain this document in an alternative format (*e.g.,* Braille, large print, audiotape, or computer diskette) on request to the contact person listed in the preceding paragraph.

Supplementary Information: On June 1, 1999, the U.S. Department of Education (the Department or we) published a notice of proposed rulemaking (NPRM) in the Federal Register (64 FR 29532). In the preamble to the NPRM, we invited interested persons to submit comments and recommendations, particularly on the proposed regulatory definitions of "crime of violence" and "final results" under Sec. 99.39 and the provisions concerning nonconsensual disclosure of information to parents and guardians under Sec. 99.31(a)(14).

We also proposed the following major changes in the NPRM to incorporate statutory provisions added by the HEA:

- Permit disclosure of education records to authorized representatives of the U.S. Attorney General in specified circumstances.
- Permit non-consensual disclosure of the final results of a disciplinary proceeding against a postsecondary student in specified circumstances.
- Permit non-consensual disclosure to parents and legal guardians of students under the age of 21 of information regarding a student's violation of laws or policies governing the use or possession of alcohol or a controlled substance.

These final regulations have significant changes from those proposed in the NPRM. We have provided more detail regarding the crime of violence provision. Specifically, we have included a list of crimes of violence and non-forcible sex offenses. We have also clarified when results become "final" and what categories of information may be disclosed under this provision. These changes are discussed in more detail in appendix B.

Analysis of Comments and Changes

In response to the Secretary's invitation in the NPRM, 42 parties submitted comments on the proposed regulations. In appendix B, we analyze and summarize these comments and describe changes to the regulations. We discuss substantive issues under the sections of the regulations to which they pertain. Generally, we do not address technical changes and other suggestions that the law does not authorize us to make.

Paperwork Reduction Act of 1995

These regulations do not contain any information collection requirements.

Assessment of Educational Impact

In the NPRM, we requested comments on whether the proposed regulations would require transmission of information that any other agency or authority of the United States gathers or makes available. Based on the response to the NPRM and on our review, we have determined that these final regulations do not require transmission of information that any other agency or authority of the United States gathers or makes available.

Electronic Access to This Document

You may view this document, as well as all other Department of Education documents published in the Federal Register, in text or portable document format (PDF) on the Internet at the following sites:

http://cfco.ed.gov/fedreg.htm
http://www.ed.gov/news.html

To use PDF you must have Adobe Acrobat Reader, which is available for free at either of the previous sites. If you have questions about using PDF, call the U.S. Government

Printing Office (GPO) toll free at 1-888-293-6498, or in the Washington, DC area at (202) 512-1530.

You may also find these regulations, as well as additional information about FERPA, on the following Web site:

http://www.ed.gov/offices/OM/fpco/

Note: The official version of this document is the document published in the Federal Register. Free Internet access to the official edition of the Federal Register and the Code of Federal Regulations is available on GPO Access at:

http://www.access.gpo.gov/nara/index.html
(Catalog of Federal Domestic Number does not apply.)

List of Subjects in 34 CFR Part 99
Administrative practice and procedure, Education, Information, Parents, Privacy, Records, Reporting and record-keeping requirements, Students.

Dated: June 28, 2000.
Richard W. Riley, Secretary of Education.

For the reasons discussed in the preamble and appendix B, the Secretary amends part 99 of title 34 of the Code of Federal Regulations as follows:

Part 99—Family Educational Rights And Privacy

1. The authority citation for part 99 continues to read as follows:

Authority: 20 U.S.C. 1232g, unless otherwise noted.

2. Section 99.1 is amended by revising paragraph (a)(2) to read as follows:

Sec. 99.1 To which educational agencies or institutions do these regulations apply?

(a) * * * * *

(2) The educational agency is authorized to direct and control public elementary or secondary, or postsecondary educational institutions.

* * * * *

3. Section 99.3 is amended by adding the definition of "Dates of attendance", revising the definition of "Directory information", and by revising paragraph (b)(1) of the definition of "Education records" to read as follows:

Sec. 99.3 What definitions apply to these regulations?

* * * * *

Dates of attendance. (a) The term means the period of time during which a student attends or attended an educational agency or institution. Examples of dates of attendance include an academic year, a spring semester, or a first quarter.

(b) The term does not include specific daily records of a student's attendance at an educational agency or institution.

(Authority: 20 U.S.C. 1232g(a)(5)(A))

Directory information means information contained in an education record of a student that would not generally be considered harmful or an invasion of privacy if disclosed. It includes, but is not limited to, the student's name, address, telephone listing, electronic mail address, photograph, date and place of birth, major field of study, dates of attendance, grade level, enrollment status (e.g., undergraduate or graduate; full-time or part-time), participation in officially recognized activities and sports, weight and height of members of athletic teams, degrees, honors and awards received, and the most recent educational agency or institution attended.

(Authority: 20 U.S.C. 1232g(a)(5)(A))

* * * * *

Education records.

* * * * *

(b) * * *

(1) Records that are kept in the sole possession of the maker, are used only as a personal memory aid, and are not accessible or revealed to any other person except a temporary substitute for the maker of the record.

* * * * *

4. Section 99.5 is amended by revising paragraph (c) to read as follows:

Sec. 99.5 What are the rights of students?

* * * * *

(c) An individual who is or has been a student at an education institution and who applies for admission at another component of that institution does not have rights under this part with respect to records maintained by that other component, including records maintained in connection with the student's application for admission, unless the student is accepted and attends that other component of the institution.

* * * * *

5. Section 99.31 is amended by revising paragraph (a)(3), revising paragraph (a)(8), revising paragraph (a)(9)(iii), revising paragraph (a)(13), adding new paragraphs (a)(14) and (a)(15), and revising paragraph (b) and the authority citation to read as follows:

Sec. 99.31 Under what conditions is prior consent not required to disclose information?

(a) * * * * *

(3) The disclosure is, subject to the requirements of Sec. 99.35, to authorized representatives of—

(i) The Comptroller General of the United States;
(ii) The Attorney General of the United States;
(iii) The Secretary; or
(iv) State and local educational authorities.

* * * * *

(8) The disclosure is to parents, as defined in Sec. 99.3, of a dependent student, as defined in section 152 of the Internal Revenue Code of 1986.

* * * * *

(9) * * * * *

(iii)(A) If an educational agency or institution initiates legal action against a parent or student, the educational agency or institution may disclose to the court, without a court order or subpoena, the education records of the student that are relevant for the educational agency or institution to proceed with the legal action as plaintiff.

(B) If a parent or eligible student initiates legal action against an educational agency or institution, the educational agency or institution may disclose to the court, without a court order or subpoena, the student's education records that are relevant for the educational agency or institution to defend itself.

* * * * *

(13) The disclosure, subject to the requirements in Sec. 99.39, is to a victim of an alleged perpetrator of a crime of violence or a non- forcible sex offense. The disclosure may only include the final results of the disciplinary proceeding conducted by the institution of postsecondary education with respect to that alleged crime or offense. The institution may disclose the final results of the disciplinary proceeding, regardless of whether the institution concluded a violation was committed.

(14)(i) The disclosure, subject to the requirements in Sec. 99.39, is in connection with a disciplinary proceeding at an institution of postsecondary education. The institution must not disclose the final results of the disciplinary proceeding unless it determines that—

(A) The student is an alleged perpetrator of a crime of violence or non-forcible sex offense; and

(B) With respect to the allegation made against him or her, the student has committed a violation of the institution's rules or policies.

(ii) The institution may not disclose the name of any other student, including a victim or witness, without the prior written consent of the other student.

(iii) This section applies only to disciplinary proceedings in which the final results were reached on or after October 7, 1998.

(15)(i) The disclosure is to a parent of a student at an institution of postsecondary education regarding the student's violation of any Federal, State, or local law, or of any rule or policy of the institution, governing the use or possession of alcohol or a controlled substance if—

(A) The institution determines that the student has committed a disciplinary violation with respect to that use or possession; and

(B) The student is under the age of 21 at the time of the disclosure to the parent.

(ii) Paragraph (a)(15) of this section does not supersede any provision of State law that prohibits an institution of postsecondary education from disclosing information.

(b) Paragraph (a) of this section does not forbid an educational agency or institution from disclosing, nor does it require an educational agency or institution to disclose, personally identifiable information from the education records of a student to any parties under paragraphs (a)(1) through (11), (13), (14), and (15) of this section.

(Authority: 20 U.S.C. 1232g(a)(5)(A), (b)(1), (b)(2)(B), (b)(6), (h), and (i))

6. Section 99.33 is amended by revising paragraph (c) to read as follows:

Sec. 99.33 What limitations apply to the redisclosure of information?

* * * * *

(c) Paragraph (a) of this section does not apply to disclosures made to parents of dependent students under Sec. 99.31(a)(8), to disclosures made pursuant to court orders, lawfully issued subpoenas, or litigation under Sec. 99.31(a)(9), to disclosures of directory information under Sec. 99.31(a)(11), to disclosures made to a parent or student under Sec. 99.31(a)(12), to disclosures made in connection with a disciplinary proceeding under Sec. 99.31(a)(14), or to disclosures made to parents under Sec. 99.31(a)(15).

* * * * *

7. A new section 99.39 is added to read as follows:

Sec. 99.39 What definitions apply to the nonconsensual disclosure of records by postsecondary educational institutions in connection with disciplinary proceedings concerning crimes of violence or non-forcible sex offenses?

As used in this part:

Alleged perpetrator of a crime of violence is a student who is alleged to have committed acts that would, if proven, constitute any of the following offenses or attempts to commit the following offenses that are defined in appendix A to this part:

- Arson
- Assault offenses
- Burglary
- Criminal homicide—manslaughter by negligence
- Criminal homicide—murder and nonnegligent manslaughter
- Destruction/damage/vandalism of property
- Kidnapping/abduction
- Robbery
- Forcible sex offenses.

Alleged perpetrator of a nonforcible sex offense means a student who is alleged to have committed acts that, if proven, would constitute statutory rape or incest. These offenses are defined in appendix A to this part.

Final results means a decision or determination, made by an honor court or council, committee, commission, or other entity authorized to resolve disciplinary matters within the institution. The disclosure of final results must include only the name of the student, the violation committed, and any sanction imposed by the institution against the student.

Sanction imposed means a description of the disciplinary action taken by the institution, the date of its imposition, and its duration. Violation committed means the institutional rules or code sections that were violated and any essential findings supporting the institution's conclusion that the violation was committed.

(Authority: 20 U.S.C. 1232g(b)(6))

8. Section 99.63 is revised to read as follows:

Sec. 99.63 Where are complaints filed?

A parent or eligible student may file a written complaint with the Office regarding an alleged violation under the Act and this part. The Office's address is: Family Policy Compliance Office, U.S. Department of Education, 400 Maryland Avenue, SW, Washington, DC 20202-4605.

(Authority: 20 U.S.C. 1232g(g))

9. Section 99.64 is amended by revising paragraph (d) to read as follows:

Sec. 99.64 What is the complaint procedure?

* * * * *

(d) The Office may extend the time limit in this section for good cause shown.

10. Appendix A is added to part 99 to read as follows:

Appendix A to Part 99—Crimes of Violence Definitions

Arson: Any willful or malicious burning or attempt to burn, with or without intent to defraud, a dwelling house, public building, motor vehicle or aircraft, personal property of another, etc.

Assault Offenses: An unlawful attack by one person upon another.

Note: By definition there can be no "attempted" assaults, only "completed" assaults.

(a) **Aggravated Assault.** An unlawful attack by one person upon another for the purpose of inflicting severe or aggravated bodily injury. This type of assault usually is accompanied by the use of a weapon or by means likely to produce death or great bodily harm. (It is not necessary that injury result from an aggravated assault when a gun, knife, or other weapon is used which could and probably would result in serious injury if the crime were successfully completed.)

(b) **Simple Assault.** An unlawful physical attack by one person upon another where neither the offender displays a weapon, nor the victim suffers obvious severe or aggravated bodily injury involving apparent broken bones, loss of teeth, possible internal injury, severe laceration, or loss of consciousness.

(c) **Intimidation.** To unlawfully place another person in reasonable fear of bodily harm through the use of threatening words or other conduct, or both, but without displaying a weapon or subjecting the victim to actual physical attack.

Note: This offense includes stalking.

Burglary: The unlawful entry into a building or other structure with the intent to commit a felony or a theft.

Criminal Homicide—Manslaughter by Negligence: The killing of another person through gross negligence.

Criminal Homicide—Murder and Nonnegligent Manslaughter: The willful (nonnegligent) killing of one human being by another.

Destruction/Damage/Vandalism of Property: To willfully or maliciously destroy, damage, deface, or otherwise injure real or personal property without the consent of the owner or the person having custody or control of it.

Kidnapping/Abduction: The unlawful seizure, transportation, or detention of a person, or any combination of these actions, against his or her will, or of a minor without the consent of his or her custodial parent(s) or legal guardian.

Note: Kidnapping/Abduction includes hostage taking.

Robbery: The taking of, or attempting to take, anything of value under confrontational circumstances from the control, custody, or care of a person or persons by force or threat of force or violence or by putting the victim in fear.

Note: Carjackings are robbery offenses where a motor vehicle is taken through force or threat of force.

Sex Offenses, Forcible: Any sexual act directed against another person, forcibly or against that person's will, or both; or not forcibly or against the person's will where the victim is incapable of giving consent.

(a) **Forcible Rape** (Except "Statutory Rape"). The carnal knowledge of a person, forcibly or against that person's will, or both; or not forcibly or against the person's will where the victim is incapable of giving consent because of his or her temporary or permanent mental or physical incapacity (or because of his or her youth).

(b) **Forcible Sodomy.** Oral or anal sexual intercourse with another person, forcibly or against that person's will, or both; or not forcibly or against the person's will where the victim is incapable of giving consent because of his or her youth or because of his or her temporary or permanent mental or physical incapacity.

(c) **Sexual Assault with an Object.** To use an object or instrument to unlawfully penetrate, however slightly, the genital or anal opening of the body of another person, forcibly or against that person's will, or both; or not forcibly or against the person's will where the victim is incapable of giving consent because of his or her youth or because of his or her temporary or permanent mental or physical incapacity.

Note: An "object" or "instrument" is anything used by the offender other than the offender's genitalia. Examples are a finger, bottle, handgun, stick, etc.

(d) **Forcible Fondling.** The touching of the private body parts of another person for the purpose of sexual gratification, forcibly or against that person's will, or both; or not forcibly or against the person's will where the victim is incapable of giving consent because of his or her youth or because of his or her temporary or permanent mental or physical incapacity.

Note: Forcible Fondling includes "Indecent Liberties" and "Child Molesting."

Nonforcible Sex Offenses (Except "Prostitution Offenses"): Unlawful, nonforcible sexual intercourse.

(a) **Incest.** Nonforcible sexual intercourse between persons who are related to each other within the degrees wherein marriage is prohibited by law.

(b) **Statutory Rape.** Nonforcible sexual intercourse with a person who is under the statutory age of consent.

(Authority: 20 U.S.C. 1232g(b)(6) and 18 U.S.C. 16)

Appendix B—Analysis of Comments and Changes

Note: The following appendix will not appear in the Code of Federal Regulations.

Applicability of FERPA to Educational Agencies and Institutions (Sec. 99.1)

Comments: One commenter suggested that examples of an "educational agency and institution" should be provided in the regulations to resolve any confusion caused by the definition. Another commenter asked if the definition applies to State boards of control and governing boards of multi-campus college and university systems.

Discussion: FERPA applies to educational agencies and institutions to which funds have been made available under any program administered by the Secretary. The term "educational agency or institution" is not defined in the statute. Our revision clarifies that FERPA applies only to those agencies that direct or control the public elementary or secondary, or postsecondary educational institutions. These agencies include local schools districts or local school boards. We have deleted the phrase "and performs service functions for" because it is confusing, and have rewritten the definition to make it clearer.

For example, we would not consider a "State educational agency" (SEA) to be an "educational agency" under FERPA unless an SEA is authorized to direct and control public elementary, secondary or postsecondary educational institutions. Likewise, State boards of control and governing boards of multi-campus college and university systems may be educational agencies under FERPA if they are authorized to direct and control the institutions within their jurisdiction and if they receive Departmental funding. This authority to direct and control institutions varies according to State law.

Changes: We have revised Sec. 99.1(a)(2) to apply to an educational agency that is authorized to direct and control public elementary or secondary, or postsecondary educational institutions.

Definitions (Sec. 99.3)

Dates of Attendance

Comments: Several commenters supported our more detailed explanation of the meaning of "dates of attendance."

Discussion: We believe that the clarification of the term "dates of attendance" will provide more detailed guidance to educational agencies and institutions because there has been some confusion over the term.

Changes: Although no substantive changes were made to the term "dates of attendance," we have created a separate paragraph for the definition.

Directory Information

Comments: Four commenters suggested that student e-mail addresses be added to the list of examples of records that may be disclosed as "directory information." One of the commenters noted that e-mail is the preferred method of communication at his institution, and that e-mail is now the primary means of communication with respect to many course-related activities. Another commenter also suggested adding class schedules and class rosters to the list. Two commenters, however, expressed concern about the safety of students if these types of information were made public. Both commenters asked that we discuss the opt-out provision because they felt many parents and students are not aware of this provision.

One commenter noted that "photograph" should not be included as "directory information" because some photographs may be taken involuntarily, such as student identification card photos. The commenter contended that institutions and the Department could be liable in an action for invasion of privacy for misappropriation of a person's likeness. The commenters believed that this could occur where an institution used photos in school catalogs.

Discussion: The examples of "directory information" listed in the regulations are not intended to be exhaustive. Rather, the examples illustrate the types of records that would not generally be considered harmful or an invasion of privacy if disclosed. We agree that as methods of communication and record management continue to evolve, it is useful to list additional categories of information that we believe are directory information, such as a student's e-mail address and photograph.

We do not believe that the disclosure of student e-mail addresses will generally be considered harmful or an invasion of privacy. We think that a student's e-mail address is analogous to a student's mailing address, an item already included as directory information.

The Department also has concluded that a student's photograph is a type of identifying information, like a name and address, that would generally not be harmful or an invasion of privacy if disclosed. Unlike social security numbers (SSNs), we do not believe that disclosure of photographs will allow access to other types of sensitive information such as disciplinary files or grades.

For parents or eligible students who do not wish to have institutions disclose photographs or any other category of directory information, FERPA affords them with an additional protection. FERPA requires schools to provide parents and eligible students with an opportunity to opt out of disclosing "directory information."

In response to the comments we received about class rosters and class schedules, we have decided not to include them in the regulations. We will reevaluate our previous advice that defined these items as "directory information" and further consider the concerns raised by commenters about student safety.

In particular, we are concerned that the inclusion of class rosters and class schedules may lead schools to disclose sensitive information. For instance, we believe a school's disclosure of the class schedule of a student enrolled in a special education or remedial class would be harmful or an invasion of privacy. Additionally, many class rosters include students' SSNs or other identification numbers; a disclosure of this information, even if class roster were designated as directory information, would be a violation of FERPA.

Changes: On the basis of comments that we received, we have revised the definition of directory information by adding student e-mail addresses. Additionally, as proposed in the NPRM, we have added as types of directory information enrollment status and photograph.

Sole Possession Records

Comments: Many commenters noted that the proposed definition of "sole possession records" should be clarified. These commenters were particularly concerned about the proposed phrases in the definition such as "typically maintained by the school official unbeknownst to other individuals" and "information taken directly from a student." The commenters contended that a personal note that is not known to or shared with other staff should be considered a sole possession record, even if the student knows about the note or if the information comes from the student.

One commenter noted that the proposed definition excepted records used to make decisions about the student. The commenter believed that this exception could technically apply to the most minor decision about the student. Another commenter stated that the proposed changes seemed to define "sole possession records" out of existence.

Discussion: We agree that our proposed definition of "sole possession records" requires modification. In the NPRM, we sought to clarify that "sole possession records" do not include evaluations of student conduct or performance. We have decided that some of the requirements in our proposed definition could be confusing.

The main purpose of this exception to the definition of "education records" is to allow school officials to keep personal notes private. For example, a teacher or counselor who observes a student and takes a note to remind himself or herself of the student's behavior has created a sole possession record, so long as he or she does not share the note with anyone else.

Changes: We have decided not to make the revisions we proposed in the NPRM to the definition of "sole possession records" in Sec. 99.3. We have clarified this definition by making minor changes.

Rights of Students (Sec. 99.5)

Comments: Two commenters asked that the provision address whether a student has access to an admissions file after having been accepted for admission but before enrolling.

Discussion: The amendment clarifies that a student attending an education institution who applies for admission to a separate component of the institution and is rejected does not have any FERPA rights with respect to records maintained by that separate component of the institution. That student does not have these rights because he or she has not attended that separate component. Similarly, a student who is admitted to a separate component of an institution does not have FERPA rights with respect to the records of that component until he or she enrolls and becomes a student in attendance there. Each institution may determine when a student is in attendance in accordance with its own enrollment procedures.

Changes: We have revised Sec. 99.5 to clarify that a student does not have FERPA rights with respect to records collected and maintained by a separate component of an education institution, including records concerning the student's application for admission, if the student has not actually attended the other component.

Conditions under Which Prior Consent Is Not Required to Disclose Information (Sec. 99.31)

Disclosures to the U.S. Attorney General (Sec. 99.31(a)(3)(ii))

Comments: A commenter expressed concern that the statutory term "for law enforcement purposes" is confusing and asked for clarification of the term. A commenter asked if "authorized representatives of the Attorney General of the United States" includes only special agents in the Department of Justice or the Federal Bureau of Investigation. This commenter also asked how this provision differs from the exception in FERPA for disclosing education records without consent in compliance with a subpoena. One commenter suggested that the Family Policy Compliance Office (FPCO) work with the Attorney General and educational associations to develop a form to document appropriate demographic information and circumstances supporting the Attorney General's request for education records.

Another commenter was concerned that the amendment may allow the Attorney General to have access to the records of an individual student who is suspected of a crime. The commenter added that this provision should apply only to crimes committed by an institution to defraud the Federal government or Federally funded programs. Another commenter noted that when disclosure is made to another governmental agency without consent, it should be made clear that the agency must protect the information from unauthorized redisclosure.

Discussion: The statutory amendment provides for nonconsensual disclosure of education records to authorized representatives of the Attorney General for law enforcement purposes under the same conditions that apply to the Secretary. In the case of the Attorney General, "law enforcement purposes" refers to the investigation or enforcement of Federal legal requirements applicable to federally supported education programs. For example, under this exception, the authorized representatives of the Attorney General can access education records without consent in order to investigate or enforce Title II of the Americans with Disabilities Act, Section 504 of the Rehabilitation Act of 1973, the Equal Educational Opportunities Act of 1974, Title IX of the Education Amendments of 1972, Title IV of the Civil Rights Act of 1964, or the Civil Rights of Institutionalized Persons Act (CRIPA).

Authorized representatives of the Attorney General include any employee of the Department of Justice, including the Federal Bureau of Investigation, so long as the employee is authorized to investigate or enforce the Federal legal requirements applicable to federally supported education programs.

This exception does not supersede or modify the exception in Sec. 99.31(a)(9) for disclosure in compliance with a judicial order or lawfully issued subpoena. Rather, this new exception permits non-consensual disclosure of education records in connection with the Attorney General's investigation or enforcement of Federal legal requirements of federally supported education programs. Given the limited nature of the allowable disclosures to the Attorney General, we believe that the development of a form to document the Attorney General's request for education records is not needed.

Finally, in response to the commenter seeking clarification about redisclosure provisions, we agree FERPA's redisclosure provisions apply to disclosures made to authorized representatives of the U.S. Attorney General. Section 99.35(b) provides that officials who collect information under this exception must protect the information, unless Federal law specifically authorizes the collection of that information.

Officials must ensure that institutions do not permit personal identification of individuals and that they destroy the records when no longer needed. If another Federal law specifically authorizes the collection of personally identifiable information, then the provisions in that law govern the redisclosure and destruction of information. In addition to the privacy protections afforded parents and students by FERPA, the Privacy Act may afford some protections to some records maintained by Federal agencies. The Privacy Act of 1974 (5 U.S.C. 552a) protects records contained in a system of records maintained by Federal agencies that are retrieved by an individual's name, social security number or some other identifying number.

Changes: We have revised Sec. 99.31(a)(3)(ii) by removing the phrase "for law enforcement purposes." Because disclosures to the Attorney General are subject to Sec. 99.35, those disclosures will only be made to investigate or enforce the Federal legal requirements applicable to federally supported education programs.

Disclosures to Parents of Dependent Students (Sec. 99.31(a)(8))

Comments: Several commenters requested guidance on how to determine dependency status because the Internal Revenue Code definition of "dependent" is based on the student's status during the previous year.

One commenter noted that the NPRM assumed that the use of the words "either parent" implies that only two individuals might be responsible for a student's upbringing. The commenter noted that a guardian or stepparent might also be involved along with the biological parents.

Another commenter asked if a divorced parent might use this process to obtain financial information in the student's record about another parent. The same commenter also asked if the parent who claims the student as a dependent could restrict the kind of information that the institution may disclose to the other parent.

One commenter felt that this provision would harm victims of domestic violence by allowing the disclosure of information in a student's record to a domestic violence perpetrator. The commenter worried that providing educational institutions with the discretion to make these releases would not effectively safeguard victims of domestic violence. The commenter suggested that institutions be prevented from disclosing information in a student's record about one parent to another parent who has committed domestic violence.

A commenter noted that the regulations should clarify whether parents who obtain information about a dependent student under this provision are subject to the limits on redisclosure of information under Sec. 99.33 of the FERPA regulations.

Two commenters wondered whether the provision applies to students who are legally adults and in conjunction with disclosures under Sec. 99.31(a)(14). These commenters stated that this exception should be limited to a dependent student who is also legally a minor. Finally, this commenter also asked whether students may find out if their parents have accessed their education records.

Discussion: This amendment clarifies that if a student is claimed as a dependent for tax purposes and the individual seeking education records meets the definition of the student's "parent" under FERPA, then the institution has the discretion to disclose records to the parent. Under FERPA, a "parent" is defined as "a parent of a student and includes a natural parent, a guardian, or an individual acting as a parent in the absence of a parent or guardian." 34 CFR Sec. 99.3 ("Parent").

We have consistently advised that, in order to determine a student's status as a dependent for tax purposes, institutions should look to the most recent year that the parent filed a return. For example, if the parent of a dependent student seeks access to the student's education records in November 1999, the institution should review the taxpayer's 1998 tax return to determine whether the student is a dependent.

Because eligible students-students attending a post-secondary institution or over the age of 18-retain all rights under FERPA, an educational agency or institution must obtain a reasonable assurance that the student meets the requirements as a dependent for tax purposes. If the educational agency or institution is unable to obtain that assurance, then information from the student's education records may not be disclosed. Once the educational agency or institution obtains that assurance, it has the discretion to, although it need not, disclose the student's education records to a parent of the student.

We received several comments concerning the use of this provision by one parent to access information about another parent. In response to these comments, we note that FERPA provides parents with broad rights of access to their children's education records when a child is under 18 and is not attending an institution of postsecondary education. This provision will have a more limited application because it is typically applied by institutions of postsecondary education.

We agree that a divorced parent could attempt to use this exception to obtain financial information in the student's education records about the other parent if the other parent claims the student as a dependent. However, an institution has no obligation to disclose any financial information about one parent to another. Thus, if a parent claims the student as a dependent, and does not want his or her financial information disclosed to his or her spouse or former spouse, the parent may make that request to the institution. The institution has the discretion not to disclose the information to the spouse or former spouse.

Because this provision provides an institution with discretion regarding what information, if any, it discloses to a parent, we do not believe that institutions will release information to known perpetrators of domestic violence. We strongly encourage victims of domestic violence to inform institutions of postsecondary education not to disclose any information from a student's education record to a perpetrator of domestic violence. We believe that institutions will understand the importance of complying with these requests. If a student or parent does not inform an institution of postsecondary education that a parent is a perpetrator of domestic violence, we do not believe it would be reasonable to expect institutions to be aware of this information. We cannot hold schools responsible for disclosures made unknowingly to a perpetrator of domestic violence.

We agree that the regulations should clarify whether parents who obtain information about a dependent student are subject to the limits on redisclosure of information under Sec. 99.33.

This provision applies to education records of students who are legally adults. The plain language of the statute applies to "dependent students" including students who are adults. This provision is not related to disclosures made under the new drug and alcohol provision, contained in Sec. 99.31(a)(14) of these regulations.

Finally, dependent students can access their own education records. Under FERPA's recordkeeping requirements, the student's records contain, with some exceptions, documentation of every nonconsensual disclosure made by the institution of personally identifiable information.

Changes: We have revised Sec. 99.31(a)(8) to clarify that it applies to a "parent" as defined under FERPA. We have also clarified in Sec. 99.33(c) that parents who obtain information about a dependent student are not subject to these redisclosure limitations.

Disclosures in Response to Legal Actions (Sec. 99.31(a)(9)(iii))

Comments: Several commenters support a new provision that allows an educational agency or institution to disclose education records to a court on a nonconsensual basis, without a court order or subpoena, if a parent or eligible student has initiated legal action against the agency or institution and the records are necessary for the agency or institution to defend itself.

Commenters also noted that the Department has issued letters of finding stating that when a parent or student has filed a complaint with a State or Federal government agency, an accrediting agency, or a third party other than a court, an institution may disclose information to that party without consent in order to defend itself. In particular, one commenter stated that the FPCO reversed its previous position and advised institutions that they could disclose information from a student's education record to a third party if the student alleged wrongdoing by the institution to that third party.

Several commenters suggested that the regulations should address these additional instances of permissible nonconsensual disclosure. Finally, another commenter asked if third party recipients of education records, involved in litigation with a parent or student, may disclose the student's education records without consent during the course of the litigation.

Discussion: FERPA allows agencies and institutions to disclose education records without consent to comply with a judicial order or lawfully issued subpoena. The statute, however, requires that institutions first must make a reasonable effort to notify the parent or eligible student in advance of the disclosure. The purpose of this prior notification is to give the parent or eligible student an opportunity to object to the issuance of the judicial order or to move to quash the subpoena.

In 1996, the Department revised Sec. 99.31(a)(9) to allow an educational agency or institution that initiated legal action against a parent or student to disclose relevant education records without consent and without a court order or subpoena, provided that the agency or institution had complied with the notification requirements contained in Sec. 99.31(a)(9)(ii).

We also noted in the 1996 final regulations that we interpreted FERPA to allow an educational agency or institution to infer the parent's or student's implied waiver of the right to consent to the disclosure of information from education records if the parent or student had sued the institution. (61 FR 59292, 59294 (November 21, 1996). This interpretation allowed an educational agency or institution to disclose a student's education records to a court without consent, and without a court order or subpoena, in cases where a parent or the student had sued the agency or institution. While we discussed this interpretation in the preamble, we did not include it in the 1996 regulations.

For two reasons, we have concluded that an educational agency or institution may disclose education records to a court without consent and without a court order or subpoena if a parent or student has sued the agency or institution. First, an agency or institution should not be required to subpoena its own records or seek a judicial order in order to defend itself in a lawsuit initiated by a parent or student.

Second, we believe that when a parent or eligible student sues an agency or institution, the parent or eligible student understands that the agency or institution must be able to defend itself. In order to defend itself, the agency or institution must be able to use relevant education records of the student. Thus, we believe that the parent or eligible student waives their FERPA protections under a theory of implied consent.

We have also concluded that the notification requirements contained in Sec. 99.31(a)(9)(ii) are not necessary in any litigation between an educational agency or institution and a parent or student. For this reason, we have deleted the notification requirement in former Sec. 99.31(a)(9)(iii) and have not included it in Sec. 99.31(a)(9)(iii)(B) of these regulations.

The notification requirement is intended to provide a parent or student with an opportunity to object to an order or to move to quash a subpoena before an educational agency or institution discloses education records in compliance with the court order or subpoena.

However, there is no such reason to require notification of a parent or student if an educational agency or institution sues a parent or student because the parent or student must be served with the lawsuit.

Similarly, if a parent or student sues an educational agency or institution, the parent or student will not need to be notified of the lawsuit.

When an educational agency or institution files a lawsuit against a student or parent, the complaint is likely to disclose personally identifiable information from the student's education records. It does not make sense to require that an educational agency or institution inform a parent or student that it plans to disclose personally identifiable information from a student's education records in a complaint because a parent or student cannot do anything to prevent the complaint from being filed. Further, after a complaint has been filed, we do not think that notification of a parent or student is necessary.

A parent or student who has been sued by an educational agency or institution should realize that personally identifiable information from the student's education records might be disclosed in the lawsuit.

If the parent or student wants to ensure the student's privacy, the parent or student may petition the court to take measures to protect the student's privacy, such as sealing the court's records.

When a student or parent files a lawsuit against an educational agency or institution, the student or parent should realize that the educational agency or institution might need to disclose personally identifiable information from the student's education records in order to defend itself. We also feel that it is overly burdensome to require that an educational agency or institution notify the parent or student every time that it wants to disclose personally identifiable information from the student's education records in the lawsuit.

Notification is also unnecessary because a parent or student who sues an educational agency or institution may petition the court to take measures to protect the student's privacy, such as sealing the court's records.

Several commenters asked the Department to extend the theory of implied waiver of the right to consent to a non-litigation context. Specifically, they alluded to the Department's ruling that when a student has taken an adversarial position against the institution, made written allegations of wrongdoing against the institution, and shared this information with third parties, the institution must be able to defend itself. While we offered this interpretation in a previous letter of finding, we did not propose to regulate on this issue in the NPRM. As a result, we cannot include these guidelines in our final regulations.

Finally, in response to the commenter who asked if third party recipients of education records may release student education records if the student or parent sues the third party, we did not address this issue in the NPRM. Thus we cannot regulate on this issue at this time.

Changes: We have added Sec. 99.31(a)(9)(iii)(B) which allows an educational agency or institution to disclose education records to a court without consent, and without a court order or subpoena, if a parent or eligible student has initiated legal action against an educational agency or institution. We have also deleted the notification requirement in Sec. 99.31(a)(9)(iii)(A) so that an educational agency or institution that has initiated legal action against a parent or student does not have to notify the parent or student before disclosing the student's relevant education records.

Disclosure of the Final Results of a Disciplinary Proceeding (Sec. 99.31(a)(13), Sec. 99.31(a)(14), and Sec. 99.39)

Comments: We received numerous comments about these provisions. The comments fell into four general categories: scope of the provision; the meaning of its terms; its effective date; and the applicability of FERPA's redisclosure provisions. Specifically, with respect to the second category, commenters sought clarification of the terms "alleged perpetrator," "crime of violence," "non-forcible sex offense," and "final results."

Scope of the Provision

Commenters asked whether postsecondary institutions are now required to disclose the final results of a disciplinary proceeding conducted against an alleged perpetrator of a crime of violence or a non-forcible sex offense or whether the disclosure is discretionary. Commenters added that many public institutions are subject to State open records laws that require the release of records unless that release is contrary to Federal law. Thus, one commenter contended that an institution's discretion to release the final results of specified disciplinary proceedings is an illusion because the amendment eliminated the protection that FERPA had provided against disclosure.

Some commenters asked whether institutions may disclose the final results of a disciplinary proceeding to anyone or to just the victim.

One commenter also noted a change to Sec. 99.31(a)(13). He noted that, as proposed, Sec. 99.31(a)(13) would have limited the disclosure of final results to proceedings in which the institution determines that the student committed the violation. The commenter noted, however, that the Department requires notification of the final results of a disciplinary proceeding, regardless of the outcome, to the victim in a sexual assault case.

Definitions: "Alleged Perpetrator"

We received many comments about the definitions used in this provision. Many comments concerned the term "alleged perpetrator of a crime of violence." These commenters noted that this term is confusing. Several commenters asked who is responsible for making the determination that a student is an "alleged perpetrator" of a crime of violence. Specifically, one commenter wondered whether the complainant, the requester, or the institution determines that a student is an "alleged perpetrator."

Commenters also asked when a student becomes "an alleged perpetrator." One commenter wondered if this determination is made when formal criminal charges are brought or sometime earlier in the criminal process. This commenter also wondered what would happen if the charges were dropped or if the student were found not guilty in a court of law. Several other commenters felt that a student should only become an "alleged perpetrator" of a crime of violence after formal criminal charges have been brought. In contrast, some other commenters suggested that Congress intended to cover disciplinary charges whether or not police or other law enforcement officials are involved. They added that the institution must determine whether a student is an "alleged perpetrator" of a crime of violence through the institution's disciplinary process.

Finally, some commenters expressed concern about libel or slander claims if institutions label a student an "alleged perpetrator of a crime of violence," because institutions do not use the terms "alleged perpetrator" or "crime of violence" in their disciplinary codes.

"Crime of Violence"

Many commenters suggested that the regulations should identify more specifically what offenses constitute "crimes of violence." For example, educational institutions asked whether petty property crimes, technical batteries, and other offenses are crimes of violence. College administrators indicated that they must be free to exercise discretion in categorizing incidents as "crimes of violence" without fear of losing institutional funding. Another commenter liked our proposed use of the Federal Bureau of Investigation's (FBI) Uniform Crime Reporting Program definitions.

One commenter asked that the Secretary remove confusing language and permit the disclosure of information for any student who commits a violation of institutional policies involving behavior that includes an element of violence or physical force. This commenter suggested that the term "felony" (which is used in the statutory definition of "crime of violence") should be replaced with "other serious offense." This commenter also asked that we provide examples of what constitutes a "serious" offense. Finally, this commenter asked that the Department recognize the difference between criminal prosecutions and student disciplinary proceedings by changing the term "student charged" to "student found responsible."

"Non-Forcible Sex Offense"

Many commenters wondered whether the new disclosure provisions apply to disciplinary proceedings against alleged perpetrators of a "non-forcible sex offense." The commenters were concerned that if the regulations do not apply to non-forcible sex offenses, postsecondary institutions could continue to keep proceedings secret, even matters involving such offenses as date rape. In short, these commenters were concerned that the term "crime of violence" may not encompass offenses such as date rape and asked that we include and define the term "non-forcible sex offense." One commenter contended that, without a clear definition of "nonforcible sex offense," the institution would be able to manipulate its disciplinary code in order to shield offenses from disclosure.

A commenter stated that the regulations did not define or include the term "non-forcible sex offense" because such an offense is considered a "crime of violence." Another commenter noted that the FBI's Uniform Crime Reporting (UCR) Program defines non-forcible sex offense as statutory rape and incest. However, one commenter contended that Congress did not intend the term "non-forcible sex offense" to include only statutory rape and incest.

"Final Results"

Many commenters stated that the regulations should define when a result is final. They noted that at many institutions a student has a right to appeal or seek review of a decision before a result is truly final. The commenters suggested that "final results" should be defined as that point when all internal institutional appeals have been exhausted. However, another commenter felt that "final results" should be defined earlier in the disciplinary process so that the public can be informed if there is institutional favoritism in the appeals process.

Several commenters also noted that the proposed definition of "final results" was unclear because it did not offer sufficient guidance as to the type of information that may be released. Because the proposed definition of "final results" includes disclosure of the violation committed, these commenters specifically requested that we define the term "violation committed."

One of these commenters contended that the term "violation committed" calls for a plain language description of the behavior that formed the basis of the disciplinary violation. Another commenter suggested that "violation committed" should be defined to include the nature of the offense, including both the institution's categorization or description of the offense and any criminal offenses to which that categorization corresponds, and the date, time and location of the offense. If the term "violation committed" is not defined, commenters believed that institutions could release vague summaries of offenses, such as describing an assault as "disorderly behavior."

Commenters also noted that the definition of the term "final results" calls for the "sanction imposed." Consequently, these commenters requested that we define the term "sanction imposed" to include a description of the disciplinary action, the date of imposition and duration, and definitions of any terms used, such as `disciplinary probation.'

Several commenters had suggestions about the methods that institutions should use to disclose the final results of disciplinary proceedings. The commenters suggested that we should permit disclosure of the final determination, or the updated crime log required under 20 U.S.C. 1092(f), rather than requiring institutions to create a new, one-line record that constitutes final results. The commenters stated that any crime of violence or non-forcible sex offense should have a related entry on the campus crime log, including the nature, date, time, and general location of each crime and the disposition of the complaint, if known. (20 U.S.C. 1092(f)(4)(A)(i) and (ii)). One commenter noted that new information pertaining to a crime or offense, such as the final results of a disciplinary proceeding, must be included in the campus crime log within two business days. (20 U.S.C. 1092(f)(4)(B)(ii)). He stated that the regulations should also clarify that everything other than the final results of the disciplinary process, such as transcripts of proceedings and other documents, remains protected by FERPA as part of a student's education record.

In contrast, one commenter argued that the statute clearly defines final results. The commenter stated that the statute lists the types of information that may be disclosed as part of the final results of the disciplinary proceeding-the student's name, the violation committed, and any sanction imposed. The commenter noted that any amendment to FERPA that takes away the privacy rights of students should be construed narrowly to protect the intent of the law. Under this reasoning, he stated, the proposed regulatory language should not be modified.

Redisclosure

Some commenters asked that the regulations clarify that redisclosure limitations in Sec. 99.33 do not apply to disclosures under Sec. 99.39. Because the statute provides that final results may be disclosed to anyone, these commenters reasoned that limitations on redisclosure are inappropriate.

Effective Date

Several commenters asked us to address the issue of the effective date of the regulations. In particular, they asked us if the statute applies to determinations of the final result reached after October 7, 1998, or to requests dated after October 7, 1998. These commenters explained that students subject to disciplinary proceedings conducted prior to October 7, 1998 had a legitimate belief that Federal confidentiality laws protected their education records generated during these proceedings. The commenters requested that we continue to ensure that these records remain confidential. In contrast, one commenter felt that the statute should apply to any requests dated after October 7, 1998, regardless of when the records were created. Finally, one commenter asked the Secretary to clarify how institutions should handle requests that were made after October 7, 1998, but before the effective date of the final rule.

Discussion:

Scope of the Provision

This new exception to the prior written consent rule does not require postsecondary educational institutions to disclose the final results of disciplinary proceedings to anyone. The disclosure is permissive. Thus, the effect of the amendment is that institutions are now free to follow their own policies regarding disclosure of this information. Institutions should consult with their own counsel or State officials regarding whether their State open records law requires disclosure of the final results of disciplinary proceedings in which a student is found to be an alleged perpetrator of a crime of violence.

In response to the commenter who was concerned about State open records laws that require disclosure, FERPA does not prevent that disclosure.

Inadvertent Deletion

In section 99.31(a)(13) of the NPRM, we inadvertently deleted a provision that permits postsecondary institutions to disclose to the victim the results of a disciplinary proceeding against the alleged perpetrator of a crime of violence, regardless of the outcome. We have reinstated that provision, designated as Sec. 99.31(a)(13). Sections 99.31(a)(13) and 99.31(a)(14) differ significantly. Victims may be informed of the final results of a disciplinary proceeding against an alleged perpetrator under Sec. 99.31(a)(13), regardless of the outcome of that proceeding. In contrast, under Sec. 99.31(a)(14), the institution may disclose to the public the final results of a disciplinary proceeding only if it has determined that:

(1) The student is an alleged perpetrator of a crime of violence or non-forcible sex offense; and
(2) The student has committed a violation of the institution's rules or policies with respect to the allegation.

Definitions: "Alleged Perpetrator" and "Crime of Violence"

We have reviewed the numerous comments we received on these terms. In particular, we have considered the comments from school officials that contend that student codes of conduct are not generally written using criminal terms. We agree that the statutory definition of "crime of violence," as defined in 16 U.S.C. 18, is difficult to apply.

Therefore, we have re-written the provision to define "crime of violence." The definition consists of an all-inclusive list of "crimes of violence." This list consists of:

- Arson
- Assault offenses
- Burglary
- Criminal homicide-manslaughter by negligence

- Criminal homicide-murder and nonnegligent manslaughter
- Destruction/damage/vandalism of property
- Kidnapping/abduction
- Robbery
- Forcible sex offenses.

We define these crimes according to the Federal Bureau of Investigation's Uniform Crime Reporting (UCR) Handbook (1984) and the UCR Reporting Handbook: National Incident-Based Reporting System (NIBRS), Volume I (Data Collection Guidelines) (1996). We have listed these definitions in appendix A following these regulations. We have used the same definitions of murder and nonnegligent manslaughter, manslaughter by negligence, forcible sex offenses, non-forcible sex offenses, robbery, aggravated assault, burglary and arson, that are used in the Student Assistance General Provisions, 34 CFR Part 668, because institutions of postsecondary education already are familiar with these definitions. We have taken from the UCR Reporting Handbook: NIBRS the definitions for those crimes of violence that are not defined in the Student Assistance General Provisions regulations. Copies of these UCR publications are available from: Programs Support Section, Criminal Justice Information Services Division, Federal Bureau of Investigation, 1000 Custer Hollow Road, Clarksburg, West Virginia 26306-0154.

We believe that this list will be easier to apply for institutions and that a standard set of definitions will allow for more uniform application. In response to the commenter who wondered if a petty property crime or a technical battery would constitute a crime of violence, those incidents are crimes of violence if they fall within the definitions of one of the crimes listed above.

We also agree with commenters that the term "alleged perpetrator" is not clear, and should be clearly defined. We define an "alleged perpetrator" as a student who is alleged to have committed acts that would, if proven, constitute any of the offenses that we have stated are crimes of violence or non-forcible sex offenses. As this definition suggests, we believe that institutions will have to use their judgment on a case-by-case basis about whether certain alleged acts constitute a crime of violence or non-forcible sex offense.

In order to determine if someone is an alleged perpetrator, institutions should look at allegations made as part of the disciplinary proceeding. These allegations can be made by a victim, a third-party witness, or by the institution. These allegations can be made at any time during the disciplinary proceeding, beginning from the time that an initial complaint or a charge is filed, until the final result is reached. This disciplinary process is not related to criminal proceedings. The institution does not need to refer the matter to the police or await any criminal proceedings in order to consider a student an alleged perpetrator of a crime of violence or non-forcible sex offense.

In response to the commenters who expressed concern about possible defamation claims if an institution labels a student "an alleged perpetrator of a crime of violence," we note that the provision merely calls for the school to determine that a student has been alleged to have committed a crime of violence. In short, such a determination does not mean that the student committed a crime of violence, but that an allegation was made that the student engaged in the type of behavior that rises to the level described in the definitions of a crime of violence. We do not believe that a school can be found liable on a defamation claim for this type of determination.

"Non-Forcible Sex Offense"

We agree with the commenters who argued that Congress intended to cover the crimes of date rape and acquaintance rape. However, these two crimes fall within the statutory definition of "crime of violence," specifically within the meaning of "forcible sex offense" as defined in the UCR Reporting Handbook: NIBRS. We have clarified that the definition of "an alleged perpetrator of a crime of violence" includes forcible sex offenses such as date rape and acquaintance rape.

However, in an effort to avoid any confusion caused by not including a definition of "non-forcible sex offense," we also define the term "alleged perpetrator of a non-forcible sex offense" in the regulations. "Alleged perpetrator of a non-forcible sex offense" is defined as "a student who is alleged to have committed acts that, if proven, would constitute statutory rape or incest." This definition is based on the FBI's definition of "non-forcible sex offense." The definition is listed in appendix A, which follows these regulations.

"Final Results"

The Department is concerned about violence on campus. We recognize the need for students to be aware of how an institution responds to these incidents. Therefore, we have defined "final results" to allow institutions to disclose the results of disciplinary proceedings before all internal reviews and appeals have been exhausted. We define "final results" to mean a decision or determination, made by an honor court or council, committee, commission, or other entity authorized to resolve disciplinary matters within the institution. We believe that this definition will benefit students who have been victims of violent crimes and non-forcible sex offenses. Institutions will not be able to claim that FERPA allows them to release results of disciplinary proceedings only after all internal reviews and appeals have been exhausted.

We agree that the regulations should provide additional guidance regarding how much and what type of information may be provided in the final results. We have defined the term "violation committed" and "sanction imposed" in order to help institutions understand what information may be released. We define "violation committed" as the institutional rules or code sections that were violated and any essential findings supporting the institution's conclusion that the violation was committed. We agree with the commenter that "sanction imposed" should be defined as a description of the disciplinary action taken by the institution, the date of its imposition, and its duration.

We believe that institutions generally will be able to disclose the final results of the disciplinary proceeding without creating new records. An institution may disclose its letter of final determination provided that the institution redacts all personally identifiable information in the letter except those portions that contain the student's name, the violation committed, and the sanction imposed. In other words, the institution must not disclose, without consent, any other portions of the letter of final determination that contain personally identifiable information that is directly related to the accused student or to any other student. If, however, the letter of final determination does not contain the violation committed or the sanction imposed, then the institution has discretion to create a new document in order to disclose this information.

Several commenters suggested that the final results of disciplinary proceedings be released in the form of an updated crime log. Because the release of this information is discretionary under FERPA, we agree with these commenters that the release of an existing crime log, as required by the campus security regulations (34 CFR Sec. 668.46(f)), may be a satisfactory way to disseminate this information. It is worth noting that a crime log contains any crime reported to campus police or a campus security department, rather than only crimes of violence or non-forcible sex offenses.

The release of a campus crime log, however, will not disclose some information that is permitted to be disclosed under FERPA. Specifically, a campus crime log does not contain the names of alleged perpetrators of crimes of violence or non-forcible sex offenses. Rather, a campus crime log includes the nature, date, time and general location of each crime and the disposition of the complaint, if known. (20 U.S.C. 1092(f)(4)(A)(i) and (ii).) Final results that can be disclosed under FERPA, however, concern the name of the student, the disciplinary violation that the student committed, and the disciplinary sanction imposed on the student.

Redisclosure

The redisclosure limitations in Sec. 99.33 do not apply to disclosures made under Sec. 99.31(a)(14) because information about the final results of a disciplinary proceeding concerning a crime of violence or a non-forcible sex offense may be disclosed to anyone, including the media. Thus, we have revised Sec. 99.33.

Effective Date

This amendment to FERPA was effective October 7, 1998. We interpret the effective date to mean the date that an institution reaches its final result in a disciplinary proceeding. This result preserves the expectation of students regarding confidentiality of disciplinary proceedings occurring before the effective date of the statute. Thus, institutions may disclose the final results of a disciplinary proceeding under Sec. 99.31(a)(14) so long as the final results are reached on or after October 7, 1998.

With regard to requests for education records received between October 7, 1998, and the effective date of these final regulations, we will not find that institutions violated FERPA for disclosing the final results of disciplinary proceedings, regardless of when these results were reached. We previously had interpreted the effective date as being the date an institution received a request for records, rather than the date that an institution reached its final results. We will not find that institutions that followed our advice regarding this issue violated FERPA.

Changes: We have reinserted Sec. 99.31(a)(13) in the regulations. This provision permits institutions of postsecondary education to disclose to the victim the final results of a disciplinary proceeding conducted against the alleged perpetrator of a crime of violence or a non-forcible sex offense regardless of the outcome of the proceedings.

We have explained that an alleged perpetrator of a crime of violence or non-forcible sex offense should be determined by looking at the allegation that a student has committed a crime of violence or non-forcible sex offense. We have revised the definition of crime of violence to reflect an all-inclusive list of crimes. The list includes forcible sex offenses, such as date rape and acquaintance rape, and non-forcible sex offenses.

We have revised the definition of "final results." The definition means a decision or determination, made by an honor court or council, committee, commission, or other entity authorized to resolve disciplinary matters within the institution. We have also defined "violation committed" and "sanction imposed."

We have clarified that the redisclosure provisions do not apply to disclosures made in connection with a disciplinary proceeding under Sec. 99.31(a)(14).

We have also explained that only final results determined on or after October 7, 1998, may be disclosed without consent under Sec. 99.31(a)(14).

Disclosures to Parents about Drug and Alcohol Violations (Sec. 99.31(a)(15))

Comments: Many commenters were confused that Sec. 99.31(a)(15) did not address a student's status as a dependent. They asked that we address the relationship between this exception and Sec. 99.31(a)(8).

One commenter felt that using 21 as a dividing line will result in students being treated differently depending on their age. For example, if the institution disciplines the same student before and after the student turns 21, the institution may only disclose the earlier disciplinary determination. The commenter also believed that parents will not understand why they may be notified in the first instance and not in the second.

Another commenter pointed out that is it not clear how an institution should determine a student's age under the exception. The commenter wondered whether the institution should use the student's age when the incident occurs, when the institution determines that a disciplinary violation occurs, or when the institution makes a disclosure. He argued that the institutions should be able to disclose records to parents about violations if the student is under 21 at the time of the drug or alcohol incident.

Another commenter stated that the statute permits disclosure without consent to a "parent" or "legal guardian" but noted that the FERPA regulations define "parent" to include legal guardian, as well as an individual acting as a parent in the absence of a parent or a legal guardian. The commenter asked that the Department clarify the regulations by using only the term "parent," because use of "legal guardian" is confusing and repetitive. Alternatively, he contended that the regulations should use a special, narrower term such as "natural or adoptive parent" because FERPA is a privacy statute and should be construed narrowly. The commenter stated that the Department should also change the definition of "parent" in Sec. 99.3 specifically to include individuals who adopt children.

Another commenter requested that we clarify that the statute does not apply to determinations of disciplinary violations that were made before October 7, 1998. Similarly, a commenter questioned what rule would apply to disclosures made under this exception after the passage of the statute and prior to the promulgation of these regulations.

A commenter stated that this provision, like the statute, is unclear because the term "disciplinary violation" is not defined. The commenter stated that without a regulatory definition of "disciplinary violation," FERPA will not be implemented uniformly throughout the 50 states, as required under 20 U.S.C. 1232g(c), and will vary based on the whims of campus administrators.

A commenter asked if there is any significance in using the term "determination" in Sec. 99.31(a)(15), while using the term "disciplinary proceeding" in Sec. 99.31(a)(14). He also asked if an institution must make a determination in a disciplinary proceeding, or if an institution can make a determination that there has been a violation of its disciplinary code in some other way. For example, the commenter wondered if an institution could determine that a disciplinary violation has been committed and send information to a parent under this provision if a video camera simply recorded an intoxicated student walking around campus. The commenter expressed concern that the threshold could be set so low as to eliminate the phrase "disciplinary violation" from the statute.

Finally, a commenter asked us to explain that students can find out when their parents have been notified of a drug or alcohol violation.

Discussion: This provision applies only to students under the age of 21 at the time of the disclosure to the parent. We clarify that an institution may disclose information under this exception without regard to whether the student is a dependent for tax purposes.

We have concluded that the student must be under 21 years of age at the time that the institution discloses to the student's parent that the student has committed a disciplinary violation with respect to alcohol or drug use or possession. We reach this conclusion because the statute links the institution's option to disclose with the age of the student and the institution's determination that the student committed a disciplinary violation. The Secretary has no statutory authority to allow institutions to disclose alcohol and drug violations of students after they have turned 21.

We agree with the commenter that the use of the term "legal guardian" is repetitive and unnecessary. The statutory term "parent and guardians" is covered by our regulatory definition of the term "parent." Likewise, it would be redundant to include the term "adoptive parents."

In response to the comment about disciplinary violations occurring before October 7, 1998, we conclude that institutions are not permitted to disclose any determinations of disciplinary violations reached before October 7, 1998. This conclusion protects the legitimate expectation of confidentiality that students had regarding drug or alcohol disciplinary violations before October 7, 1998.

With regard to institutional disclosures to parents under this exception occurring after October 7, 1998, but prior to the promulgation of these final regulations, we will not find that institutions violated FERPA so long as the disclosure was based on a reasonable interpretation of the statutory amendment.

We recognize that there is confusion over the terms "determination" and "disciplinary violation." Commenters sought guidance on the meanings of these terms and the responsibilities of postsecondary institutions under this exception.

We note that an institution may make a determination under this exception without conducting any sort of disciplinary proceeding. We reached this conclusion for two reasons. First, we compared the language used by Congress in this exception and the "crime of violence" exception. The "crime of violence" exception permits the disclosure of final results of a disciplinary proceeding conducted by the institution. This statutory provision clearly indicates that, before making any disclosures under this exception, an institution must first conduct some type of hearing or proceeding.

However, the drug and alcohol provision is worded very differently. That statutory provision does not use the term "disciplinary proceeding," and we believe Congress' choice of words was deliberate.

Therefore, we do not have the authority to require schools to conduct a disciplinary proceeding in order to determine that a student has committed a disciplinary violation with respect to drug or alcohol use.

Institutions may establish and follow their own procedures for making these types of determinations.

The limited nature of this disclosure supports our interpretation that this exception does not require institutions to conduct any sort of formal disciplinary proceeding. This exception permits disclosures only to parents. In contrast, disclosures made in accordance with Sec. 99.31(a)(14) can be made to the public. Thus, we believe that Congress intended to make it easier for institutions to inform parents of drug and alcohol violations by allowing the institution to release the information without conducting a formal disciplinary hearing.

Although we recognize that commenters sought a definition of the term "disciplinary violation," we decline to define this term. We recognize that institutions have different codes of conduct. If we imposed a specific standard for a "disciplinary violation," we would be placing a large burden on institutions to conform their codes of conduct to our regulatory definition. We will not impose such a burden.

In response to the concern that an institution could set the threshold so low as to read the phrase "disciplinary violation" out of the statute, we do not believe that institutions will act irresponsibly when making disclosures under this provision. We also emphasize that this disclosure, as with other permissible disclosures under Sec. 99.31(a), is discretionary. Furthermore, the statutory amendment also provides that this new exception does not supersede any provision of State law that prohibits an institution of postsecondary education from making the permitted disclosure.

Finally, FERPA does not require institutions to notify students each time the institution discloses information from their education record. Institutions, however, are required, with some exceptions, to maintain a record of each disclosure of personally identifiable information from an education record along with that education record.

Students at postsecondary institutions have the right under FERPA to access and view their own education records which should include a record of any disclosures made. Postsecondary students who wish to know if their parents have been notified of drug or alcohol violations should seek access to their own education records.

Changes: We revised Sec. 99.31(a)15 by removing the term "legal guardian." We have also specified that a student must be less than 21 years of age when the institution discloses to the parent that the institution has determined that a disciplinary violation has occurred.

[FR Doc. 00-17058 Filed 7-5-00; 8:45 am]

BILLING CODE 4000-01-P

Appendix 17

Letter from LeRoy S. Rooker to Daniel Boehmer Regarding the Role of the National Student Loan Clearinghouse in Verifying Current Enrollments of Students, August 2, 1999

August 2, 1999

Mr. Daniel R. Boehmer
President
National Student Loan Clearinghouse
2191 Fox Mill Road, Suite
Herndon, VA 20171-3019

Dear Mr. Boehmer:

This responds to your letter of June 2, 1999, in which you asked this office whether operation of a new EnrollmentSearch program by the National Student Loan Clearinghouse (Clearinghouse) would comply with the requirements of the Family Educational Rights and Privacy Act (FERPA), 20 U.S.C. § 1232g. The Family Policy Compliance Office (FPCO) is responsible for investigating complaints and providing technical assistance to ensure compliance with FERPA and its implementing regulations found at 34 CFR Part 99. We find that the proposed operation of the new EnrollmentSearch program, as described in your June 2 letter, would not violate the requirements of FERPA.

In particular, under the proposed EnrollmentSearch Addendum to the Clearinghouse's participation agreement, member institutions that wish to obtain information on the current enrollment or graduation status of students who have left the institution (Requester Institutions) will submit the following directory information to the Clearinghouse: the student's name, date of birth, and date of last attendance at the Requester Institution. Institutions may not submit this information for students who have blocked the release of directory information under FERPA.

The Clearinghouse will use the student's name, date of birth, and date of last attendance to search its existing database. The existing database is composed of both directory and non-directory information submitted by institutions in order to meet certain reporting requirements of the Federal student loan process. If there is a match, and if the student has not blocked the release of directory information by the institution that submitted the information to the Clearinghouse, the Clearinghouse will provide the following directory information to each Requester Institution: the student's name; whether a transfer record was found (Y/N); the student's new name, if any; the name of the school of first transfer; the Office of Postsecondary Education Indentification (OPEID) code of the transfer school; and the starting date for the transfer term. The release of information under the EnrollmentSearch program is separate and distinct from the release of information for purposes of meeting student status confirmation and other enrollment status requests under the Federal Family Educational Loan (FFEL) and other student financial assistance programs.

FERPA provides that an educational agency or institution that receives Federal education funds may not have a policy or practice of releasing education records, or personally identifiable, non-directory information from education records, unless the parent or eligible student has provided prior written consent for the disclosure, except in several statutorily specified circumstances. 20 U.S.C. § 1232g(b)(1); 34 CFR §§ 99.30; 99.31. An institution may designate certain information as "directory information" and then disclose or release the information without first obtaining written consent. See 34 CFR § 99.31(a)(11). "Directory information" includes the following:

> the student's name, address, telephone listing, date and place of birth, major field of study, participation in officially recognized activities and sports, weight and height of members of athletic teams, dates of attendance, degrees and awards received, and the most recent previous educational agency or institution attended by the student.

20 U.S.C. § 1232g(a)(5)(A). FERPA regulations explain further that directory information means information contained in an education record of a student which would not generally be considered harmful or an invasion of privacy if disclosed.

34 CFR § 99.3 ("Directory information").

In accordance with these provisions, FPCO has advised that certain types of information not listed in the statute, such as a student's social security account number (SSN) or other student identification number, may not be designated and disclosed on a nonconsensual basis as directory information because of the relative ease with which it can be used to access other information about the student that would be considered harmful or an invasion of privacy if disclosed. Accordingly, EnrollmentSearch is structured so that the information released or disclosed by participating institutions and the Clearinghouse does not identify students by SSN or other identification numbers. Rather, it is our understanding that the program uses only information that falls clearly within the scope of "directory information" as specified in both statute and regulation.

The student's name, date of birth, and dates of attendance at an institution are listed as examples of directory information in the statute. As explained in your letter, these are the primary data fields used by Requester Institutions and the Clearinghouse to identify students in the Enrollment Search program. An indication whether a transfer record has been found merely identifies the student's enrollment status in an institution. Similarly, the starting date of a transfer term merely indicates dates of attendance, which may be designated and disclosed as directory information. The institution's OPEID code contains only information about the transfer institution itself and does not contain information from a student's education record. As described above, all information from education records released by the Requester Institution and the Clearinghouse under the EnrollmentSearch program is directory information under FERPA.

FERPA regulations also provide that an educational agency or institution may disclose directory information only if it has given public notice to parents or eligible students in attendance at the institution of:

1. The types of personally identifiable information that the agency or institution has designated as directory information;
2. A parent's or eligible student's right to refuse to let the agency or institution designate any or all of those types of information about the student as directory information; and
3. The period of time within which a parent or eligible student has to notify the agency or institution in writing that he or she does not want any or all of those types of information about the student designated as directory information.

34 CFR § 99.37(a).

You explained that in order to comply with this FERPA provision on blocking the release of directory information, the EnrollmentSearch program requires modification of institutional databases to include a "data block indicator" for those students who have exercised their FERPA right to opt out of disclosure of directory information. Under the basic participation agreement, institutions must now include this data block indicator for the information that is submitted every four to six weeks as part of confirmation of enrollment status process for current students. This will ensure that the Clearinghouse does not release directory information for student's who have blocked the release of directory information, even if there is a match with information submitted by a Requester Institution. You also indicated that the Clearinghouse will ask participating institutions to complete a data block indicator for former students, and that if the institution is unable or unwilling to provide that information for former students, the Clearinghouse will not release enrollment status information for those students.

In summary, FERPA prevents an institution from requesting EnrollmentSearch information for students who have blocked the release of directory information under FERPA, and the Clearinghouse will not release EnrollmentSearch information for those students who have blocked the release of directory information. Based on these conditions, we find that the EnrollmentSearch program complies with the requirements of FERPA regarding the release or disclosure of personally identifiable information from education records on a nonconsensual basis. Please note that other terms and conditions for the release of information about students under the Federal Family Educational Loan (FFEL) and any other student loan programs remain as set forth in our April 19, 1993, letter to the Clearinghouse.

Sincerely,

LeRoy S. Rooker
Director
Family Policy Compliance Office

Appendix 18

Final Rule on the Solomon Amendment, January 13, 2000

Military Recruiting and Reserve Officer Training Corps Program Access to Institutions of Higher Education

Department of Defense
Billing Code 5000-04
Office of the Secretary
32 CFR Part 216
RIN 0790-AG42

Agency: Department of Defense
Action: Final rule

Summary: The Department of Defense promulgates the rule addressing military recruiting and Reserve Officer Training Corps program access at institutions of higher education. This rule implements the National Defense Authorization Act for Fiscal Year 1995, the National Defense Authorization Act for Fiscal Year 1996, and the Omnibus Consolidated Appropriations Act, 1997 (the Acts).

The Acts state that no funds available under appropriations acts for any fiscal year for the Departments of Defense, Transportation (with respect to military recruiting), Labor, Health and Human Services, Education, and Related Agencies may be provided by contract or grant (including a grant of funds to be available for student aid) to a covered school that has a policy or practice (regardless of when implemented) that either prohibits, or in effect prevents, the Secretary of Defense from obtaining, for military recruiting purposes, entry to campuses, access to students on campuses, access to directory information on students, or that has an anti-ROTC policy.

Effective Date: (Date of publication)

For Further Information Contact: William J. Carr, (703) 697-8444.

Supplementary Information:

On April 8, 1997 the Department of Defense published an interim rule to implement the Acts, and invited public comments by July 7, 1997 (62 FR 16691). Consistent with the Acts, the interim rule took effect on March 29, 1997. Public comments were received and appropriate adjustments were made as reflected in this final rule.

The Secretary is committed to establishing sound procedures to implement current statutes, while keeping the regulatory burden to the minimum necessary to carry out the congressional intent. To that end, the Department has finalized this rule in consultation with other Federal agencies, including the Departments of Education, Labor, Transportation, and Health and Human Services. Agencies affected by this rule will continue to coordinate as they implement its provisions.

This rule defines the criteria for determining whether an institution of higher education has a policy or practice prohibiting or preventing the Secretary of Defense from maintaining, establishing, or efficiently operating a Senior ROTC unit; or has a policy of denying military recruiting personnel entry to campuses, access to students on campuses, or access to directory information on students. The Acts establish that institutions of higher education having such policies or practices are ineligible for certain Federal funding.

The criterion of "efficiently operating a Senior ROTC unit" refers generally to an expectation that the ROTC Department would be treated on a par with other academic departments; as such, it would not be singled out for unreasonable actions that would impede access to students (and vice versa) or restrict its operations.

This rule also defines the procedures that would be followed in evaluating reports that a covered school has not met requirements defined in this rule. When a component of the Department of Defense (DoD component) believes that policies or practices of an institution of higher education might require such an evaluation, that component is required to confirm the institution's policy in consultation with the institution. If that exchange suggests that the policy or practice could trigger a denial of funding, as required by the Acts, the supporting facts would be forwarded through Department of Defense channels to the decision authority, who is the Assistant

Secretary of Defense for Force Management Policy [ASD(FMP)].

The Department of Defense received and considered comments relating to this rule. One recommendation urged that the DoD Grant and Agreement Regulations (DoDGARs) be modified to comport with the rule, and the proponent office of DoDGARs is moving to adopt necessary adjustments. One commenter expressed a conviction that an institution of higher education should be ineligible for funds under the rule when any of its subelements [see §216.3(d)] has been determined to be in violation—a position that the Department believes to be incompatible with Congressional intent. The vast majority of public comments related to the interplay between the Acts and Family Educational Rights and Privacy Act of 1974, as amended (FERPA), 20 U.S.C. 1232g. Commenters have inquired whether release of student information in response to a request from a military recruiter would violate FERPA. Commenters pointed out that "directory information" is a term of art under FERPA that triggers particular responsibilities of the institution regarding the confidentiality of student information. Depending on the policy of a particular institution, that term may not necessarily refer to the same information that may be requested by a military recruiter.

Commenters also pointed out that FERPA provides a mandatory opportunity for a student to object to release of "directory information" designated by an institution, and questioned whether the same opportunity to object must be provided to a student if a request is received from a military recruiter.

In response to the basic question of whether providing information in response to a request from a military recruiter would violate FERPA, the Department of Education has informed the Department of Defense that it will not consider provision of responsive student information as required under the Acts and this rule to violate FERPA. Institutions must take care, however, to release only that information specifically required under the Acts and this rule.

The Department of Defense appreciates the comments received regarding possible confusion from the use of the term "directory information" in the interim rule. Because the term is not synonymous under FERPA or the Acts, and to avoid possible conflict or confusion, the final rule substitutes the term "student recruiting information" for "directory information" as that term was used in the interim rule.

Regarding the opportunity for a student to "opt-out" of or object to release of "directory information" under FERPA, the Department of Defense provides the following clarification. If an institution receives a request for student recruiting information, and that request seeks information that the institution has included in its definition of "directory information" that is releasable under FERPA, and a student has previously requested that the "directory information" not be disclosed to any third party, the Department of Defense agrees that information for that student will not be provided to the Department of Defense. If an institution declines to provide student recruiting information because a student has "opted-out" from the institution's policy of disclosing "directory information" under FERPA, the Department of Defense will not consider that institution to have denied access under the Acts. The Department of Defense will honor only those student "opt-outs" from the disclosure of directory information that are even-handedly applied to all prospective employers seeking information for recruiting purposes. The Department of Defense will also honor the "opt-out" in cases where the institution's "directory information" definition does not include all of the student recruiting information requested by the recruiter.

If an institution does not release all of the requested student recruiting information as part of its "directory information" policy under FERPA (or has a policy of disclosing no "directory information"), the institution must nevertheless honor the request from a military recruiter for student recruiting information on students who have not "opted-out", even if that information would not be available to the public under FERPA. Because this information is requested exclusively for military recruiting, a special opportunity for a student to decline the release of student recruiting information is not necessary or appropriate.

Summary of Rule:
In carrying out their customary activities, DoD components must identify any institutions of higher education that, by policy or practice, denies military recruiting personnel entry to the campus(es) of those schools, access to their students, or access to student recruiting information. When repeated requests to schedule recruiting visits or to obtain student recruiting information are unsuccessful, the DoD component concerned must seek written confirmation of the school's present policy from the head of the covered school through a letter of inquiry, allowing 30 days for response. If written confirmation cannot be obtained, oral policy statements or attempts to obtain such statements from an appropriate official of the school shall be documented. A copy of the documentation shall be provided to the covered school, which shall be informed of its opportunity to forward clarifying comments to accompany the DoD component's submission to the

ASD(FMP), and shall be provided 30 days to offer such clarifying comments. When that 30-day period has elapsed, the DoD component will forward the case for disposition.

Similarly, in carrying out their customary activities, DoD components also must identify any institutions of higher education that, by policy or practice, deny establishment, maintenance, or efficient operation of a unit of the Senior ROTC, or deny students permission to participate, or effectively prevent students from participating in a unit of the Senior ROTC at another institution of higher education. The DoD component concerned must seek written confirmation of the school's policy from the head of the covered school through a letter of inquiry, allowing 30 days for response.

If written confirmation cannot be obtained, oral policy statements or attempts to obtain such statements from an appropriate official of the school shall be documented. A copy of the documentation shall be provided to the covered school, which shall be informed of its opportunity to forward clarifying comments to accompany the DoD component's submission to the ASD(FMP), and shall be provided 30 days to offer such clarifying comments. When that 30-day period has elapsed, the DoD component will forward the case for disposition.

The recommendation of the DoD component then must be reviewed by the Secretary of the Military Department concerned, or designee, who shall evaluate responses to the letter of inquiry and other such information obtained in accordance with this part, and submit to the ASD(FMP) the names and addresses of covered schools that are believed to be in violation of current law. Full documentation must be furnished to the ASD(FMP) for each such covered school, including the school's formal response to the letter of inquiry, documentation of any oral response, or evidence showing that attempts were made to obtain either written confirmation or an oral statement of the school's policies.

Following any determination by the ASD(FMP) that policies or practices of an institution of higher education require ineligibility for certain Federal funding, as required by the Acts, the ASD(FMP) shall:

Disseminate to Federal entities affected by the decision, including the DoD components and the General Services Administration (GSA), the names of the affected institutions. The ASD(FMP) also shall notify the Committee on Armed Services of the Senate and the Committee on National Security of the House of Representatives; Publish in the Federal Register each such determination, and publish in the Federal Register at least once every six months a list of all institutions currently determined to be ineligible for contracts and grants by reason of such determinations; and Inform the affected institution that its funding eligibility may be restored if the school provides sufficient new information to establish that the basis for the determination no longer exists.

This rule contains procedures under which funding may be restored. Not later than 45 days after receipt of a school's request to restore funding eligibility, the ASD(FMP) must determine whether the funding status of the covered school should be changed and notify the applicable school of that determination. Pursuant to that determination, entities of the Federal government affected by the decision, including the DoD components and the GSA, shall be notified of any change in funding status.

Other Matters

In the event of any determination of ineligibility by the ASD(FMP), Federal agencies concerned shall

determine what funds provided by grant or contract to the covered school are affected and take appropriate action. As a result of this division of responsibility and the large number of Federal agencies affected, this rule does not detail what specific funds are affected by any determination of ineligibility.

The Department of Education provided information on the impact of the Acts on the programs of student financial assistance under Title IV of the Higher Education Act of 1965, as amended, in a January 1998 "Dear Colleague Letter" (NO. GEN-98-3). That letter is available by request by calling 800-4FEDAID, or through the Department of Education's website at "http://www.ifap.ed.gov".

The Secretary of Education has determined that funds under the following programs are covered by this rule: the Federal Supplemental Educational Opportunity Grant Program (Title IV, Part A, Subpart 3), the Federal Work-Study Program (Title IV, Part C), and the Federal Perkins Loan Program (Title IV, Part E). Collectively referred to as the campus-based programs, these three programs depend on institutional applications for funding. Once funds are received, the institution determines which students will receive allotted funds, within statutory and regulatory guidelines. Thus, for the purposes of this rule, these funds are considered to be grants to the institution.

The Secretary of Education has determined that funds under the Federal Pell Grant Program (Title IV, Part A, Subpart 1), the Federal Family Education Loan Program (Title IV, Part B), the Federal Direct Student Loan Program (Title IV, Part D), the William D. Ford Federal Direct Loan Program (Title IV, Part D), the State Student Incentive Grant Program (Title IV, Part A, Subpart 4), the Robert C. Byrd Honor Scholarship Program (Title IV, Part A, Subpart 6), and the National

Early Intervention Scholarship and Partnership (NEISP) Program (Title IV, Part A, Subpart 2) are not covered by this rule. States that receive NEISP Program grants may continue to award student scholarships to be utilized at institutions that have been determined to be ineligible by the DoD. States may not, however, award sub-grants or contracts for NEISP services to such institutions.

Executive Order 12866, "Regulatory Planning and Review"

This final rule is a significant regulatory action that OMB has approved for publication.

Public Law 96-354, "Regulatory Flexibility Act" [5 U.S.C. 601]

The Secretary certifies that these proposed regulations would not have a significant economic impact on a substantial number of small entities since recent history indicates that its provisions are not applicable to the vast majority of institutions of higher education.

Public Law 96-511, "Paperwork Reduction Act" [44 U.S.C. Chapter 35]

This final rule will not impose any additional reporting or record keeping requirements under the Paperwork Reduction Act.

List of Subjects in 32 CFR Part 216

Armed forces; Colleges and universities

Accordingly, 32 CFR part 216 is revised to read as follows:

Part 216—Military Recruiting and Reserve Officer Training Corps Program Access to Institutions of Higher Education

Sec.

216.1 Purpose.
216.2 Applicability.
216.3 Definitions.
216.4 Policy.
216.5 Responsibilities.
216.6 Information requirements.
Appendix A of part 216—Military Recruiting Sample Letter of Inquiry
Appendix B of part 216—ROTC Sample Letter of Inquiry

Authority: 10 U.S.C. 983.

§216.1 Purpose.

This part:

(a) Implements the National Defense Authorization Act for Fiscal Year 1995 (108 Stat. 2663),
(b) Implements 10 U.S.C. 983, and
(c) Implements the Omnibus Consolidated Appropriations Act, 1997 (110 Stat. 3009).
(d) Updates policy and responsibilities relating to the management of covered schools that have a policy of either denying, or effectively preventing military recruiting personnel entry to their campuses, access to their students, or access to student recruiting information.
(e) Updates policy and responsibilities relating to the management of covered schools that have an anti-ROTC policy.

§216.2 Applicability.

This part applies to the Office of the Secretary of Defense, the Military Departments, the Chairman of the Joint Chiefs of Staff, the Combatant Commands, the Defense Agencies, and the DoD Field Activities (hereafter referred to collectively as "the DoD components"). The policies herein also affect the Departments of Transportation, Labor, Health and Human Services, Education, and Related Agencies. The term "Military Services," as used herein, refers to the Army, the Navy, the Marine Corps, the Air Force, and the Coast Guard, including their Reserve or National Guard components.

The term "Related Agencies," as used herein, refers to the Armed Forces Retirement Home, the Corporation for National and Community Service, the Corporation for Public Broadcasting, the Federal Mediation and Conciliation Service, the Federal Mine Safety and Health Review Commission, the National Commission on Libraries and Information Science, the National Council on Disability, the National Education Goals Panel, the National Labor Relations Board, the National Mediation Board, the Occupational Safety and Health Review Commission, the Physician Payment Review Commission, the Prospective Payment Assessment Commission, the Social Security Administration, the Railroad Retirement Board and the United States Institute of Peace.

§216.3 Definitions.

(a) Anti-ROTC policy. A policy or practice whereby a covered school prohibits or in effect prevents the Secretary of Defense from maintaining, establishing, or efficiently operating a unit of the Senior ROTC at the covered school, or prohibits or in effect prevents a student at the covered school from enrolling in a Senior ROTC unit at another institution of higher education.
(b) Covered School. An institution of higher education, or a subelement of an institution of higher education, subject to the following clarifications:

(1) In the event of a determination (§216.5) affecting only a subelement of a parent institution (see §216.3(d)), the limitations on the use of funds (§216.4 (a) and (b)) shall apply only to the subelement and not to the parent institution as a whole.
(2) The limitations on the use of funds (§216.4 (a) and (b)) shall not apply to any individual institution of

higher education that is part of a single university system if that individual institution does not prevent entry to campus, access to students, or access to student recruiting information by military recruiters, or have an anti-ROTC policy, even though another campus of the same system is affected by a determination under §216.5 (a).

(c) Student Recruiting Information. For those currently enrolled, the student's name, address, telephone listing, age (or year of birth), level of education (e.g., freshman, sophomore, or degree awarded for a recent graduate), and major.

(d) Institution of Higher Education. A domestic college, university, or other institution (or subelement thereof) providing postsecondary school courses of study, including foreign campuses of such domestic institutions. The term includes junior colleges, community colleges, and institutions providing courses leading to undergraduate and post-graduate degrees. The term does not include entities that operate exclusively outside the United States, its territories, and possessions. A subelement of an institution of higher education is a discrete (although not necessarily autonomous) organizational entity that may establish policies or practices affecting military recruiting and related actions (e.g., an undergraduate school, a law school, a medical school, or other graduate schools). For example, the School of Law of XYZ University is a subelement of its parent institution (XYZ University).

(e) Student. An individual who is 17 years of age or older and is enrolled at a covered school.

(f) Enrolled. Registered for at least one credit hour of academic credit at the covered school during the most-recent, current, or next term.

(g) Military Recruiters. Personnel of DoD whose current assignment or detail is to a recruiting activity of the DoD.

(h) Pacifism. Opposition to war or violence, demonstrated by refusal to participate in military service.

§216.4 Policy.

It is policy that:

(a) Under 108 Stat. 2663 and 110 Stat. 3009, no funds available under appropriations acts for any fiscal year for the Departments of Defense, Transportation (with respect to military recruiting), Labor, Health and Human Services, Education, and Related Agencies may be provided by contract or by grant (including a grant of funds to be available for student aid) to a covered school if the Secretary of Defense determines that the covered school has a policy or practice (regardless of when implemented) that either prohibits or in effect prevents the Secretary of Defense from obtaining, for military recruiting purposes, entry to campuses, access to students on campuses, or access to directory information on students (student recruiting information).

(b) Under 110 Stat. 3009, no funds available under appropriations acts for any fiscal year for the Departments of Labor, Health and Human Services, Education, and Related Agencies may be provided by contract or grant (including a grant of funds to be available for student aid) to a covered school that has an anti-ROTC policy or practice (regardless of when implemented). Additionally, under 10 U.S.C. 983, no funds appropriated or otherwise available to the Department of Defense may be made obligated by contract or by grant to a covered school that has such a policy or practice.

(c) The limitations established in paragraph (a) of this section, shall not apply to a covered school if the Secretary of Defense determines that the covered school:

(1) Has ceased the policies or practices defined in paragraph (a) of this section;

(2) Has a long-standing policy of pacifism based on historical religious affiliation;

(3) When not providing requested access to campuses or to students on campus, certifies that all employers are similarly excluded from recruiting on the premises of the covered school, or presents evidence that the degree of access by military recruiters is at least equal in quality and scope to that afforded to other employers;

(4) When not providing any student recruiting information, certifies that such information is not maintained by the covered school; or that such information already has been provided to the Military Service concerned for that current semester, trimester, quarter, or other academic term, or within the past four months (for institutions without academic terms);

(5) When not providing student recruiting information for specific students, certifies that each student concerned has formally requested the covered school to withhold this information from third parties;

(6) Permits employers to recruit on the premises of the covered school only in response to an expression of student interest, and the covered school;

(i) Provides the Military Services with the same opportunities to inform the students of military recruiting activities as are available to other employers; or

(ii) Certifies that too few students have expressed an interest to warrant accommodating military recruiters, applying the same criteria that are applicable to other employers; or

(7) Is prohibited by the law of any State, or by the order of any State court, from allowing Federal military recruiting on campus. Such exemption does not apply to funds available to the Department of Defense, in accordance with 108 Stat. 2663 (note: this exemption terminated effective March 29, 1998, in accordance with 110 Stat. 3009).

(d) The limitations established in paragraph (b) of this section, shall not apply to a covered school if the Secretary of Defense determines that the covered school:

(1) Has ceased the policies or practices defined in paragraph (b) of this section;
(2) Has a long-standing policy of pacifism based on historical religious affiliation;
(3) Is prohibited by the law of any State, or by the order of any State court, from allowing Senior Reserve Officer Training Corps activities on campus . Such exemption does not apply to funds available to the Department of Defense, in accordance with 10 U.S.C. 983. (note: this exemption terminated effective March 29, 1998, in accordance with 110 Stat. 3009).

(e) A covered school may charge for actual costs incurred in providing military recruiters access to student recruiting information, provided such charges are reasonable and customary; in this case, the school must explain to the military recruiter, within 15 days of a request by the recruiter, its method for determining costs, and its basis for concluding that such charges are reasonable and customary.

(f) An evaluation to determine whether a covered school maintains a policy or practice covered by paragraph (a) of this section shall be undertaken when:

(1) Military recruiting personnel cannot gain entry to campus, cannot obtain access to students on campus, or are denied access to student recruiting information (however, military recruiting personnel shall accommodate a covered school's reasonable preferences as to times and places for scheduling on-campus recruiting, to the same extent such preferences are applicable to employers, generally);
(2) The costs being charged by the school for providing student recruiting information are believed by the military recruiter to be excessive, and the school does not provide information sufficient to support a conclusion that such charges are reasonable and customary; or
(3) The covered school is unwilling to declare in writing, in response to an inquiry from a DoD component, that the covered school does not have a policy or practice of denying, and that it does not effectively prevent, the Secretary of Defense from obtaining for military recruiting purposes entry to campuses, access to students on campuses, or access to student recruiting information.

(g) An evaluation to determine whether a covered school has an anti-ROTC policy covered by paragraph (b) of this section shall be undertaken when:

(1) A Secretary of a Military Department or designee cannot obtain permission to establish, maintain, or efficiently operate a unit of the Senior ROTC; or
(2) Absent a Senior ROTC unit at the covered school, students cannot obtain permission from a covered school to participate, or are effectively prevented from participating, in a unit of the Senior ROTC at another institution of higher education.

§216.5 Responsibilities.

(a) The Assistant Secretary of Defense for Force Management Policy, under the Under Secretary of Defense for Personnel and Readiness, shall:

(1) Not later than 45 days after receipt of the information described in paragraph (b)(3) of this section:

(i) Make a final determination under 108 Stat. 2663, 10 U.S.C. 983; and 110 Stat. 3009 and/or this part, and notify any affected school of that determination along with the basis, and that it is therefore ineligible to receive prescribed funds as a result of that determination.
(ii) Disseminate to Federal agencies affected by 110 Stat. 3009, to the DoD components, and to the General Services Administration (GSA) the names of covered schools identified under paragraph (a)(1)(i) of this section, and the basis of the determination.
(iii) Disseminate the names of covered schools identified under paragraph (a)(1)(i) of this section, to the Secretary of Education and to the Committee on Armed Services of the Senate and the Committee on National Security of the House of Representatives.
(iv) Inform the applicable school identified under paragraph (a)(1)(i) of this section, that its funding eligibility may be restored if the school provides sufficient new information that the basis for the determination under paragraph (a)(1)(i) of this section no longer exists.

(2) Not later than 45 days after receipt of a covered school's request to restore its eligibility:

(i) Determine whether the funding status of the covered school should be changed, and notify the applicable school of that determination.

(ii) Notify the parties reflected in paragraphs (a)(1)(ii) and (iii) of this section when a determination of funding ineligibility (paragraph (a)(1)(i) of this section) has been rescinded.

1. Publish in the Federal Register each determination of the Assistant Secretary of Defense for Force Management Policy that a covered school is ineligible for contracts and grants made under 108 Stat. 2663, 10 U.S.C. 983, and 110 Stat. 3009 and/or this part.
2. Publish in the Federal Register at least once every six months a list of covered schools that are ineligible for contracts and grants by reason of a determination of the Secretary of Defense under 108 Stat. 2663, 10 U.S.C. 983, and 110 Stat. 3009 and/or this part.

(b) The Secretaries of the Military Departments shall:

(1) Identify covered schools that, by policy or practice, deny military recruiting personnel entry to the campus(es) of those schools, access to their students, or access to student recruiting information.

(i) When requests by military recruiters to schedule recruiting visits or to obtain student recruiting information are unsuccessful, the Military Service concerned shall seek written confirmation of the school's present policy from the head of the school through a letter of inquiry. A letter similar to that shown in Appendix A of this part shall be used, but it should be tailored to the situation presented. If written confirmation cannot be obtained, oral policy statements or attempts to obtain such statements from an appropriate official of the school shall be documented. A copy of the documentation shall be provided to the covered school, which shall be informed of its opportunity to forward clarifying comments to accompany the submission to the ASD(FMP), and shall be provided 30 days to offer such clarifying comments.

(ii) When a request for student recruiting information is not fulfilled within a reasonable period, normally 30 days, a letter similar to that shown in Appendix A shall be used to communicate the problem to the school, and the inquiry shall be managed as described in 216.5.(b)(1)(i). Schools may stipulate that requests for student recruiting information shall be in writing.

(2) Identify covered schools that, by policy or practice, deny establishment, maintenance, or efficient operation of a unit of the Senior ROTC, or deny students permission to participate, or effectively prevent students from participating in a unit of the Senior ROTC at another institution of higher education. The Military Service concerned shall seek written confirmation of the school's policy from the head of the school through a letter of inquiry. A letter similar to that shown in Appendix B of this part shall be used, but it should be tailored to the situation presented. If written confirmation cannot be obtained, oral policy statements or attempts to obtain such statements from an appropriate official of the school shall be documented. A copy of the documentation shall be provided to the covered school, which shall be informed of its opportunity to forward clarifying comments to accompany the submission to the ASD(FMP), and shall be provided 30 days to offer such clarifying comments.

(3) Evaluate responses to the letter of inquiry, and other such evidence obtained in accordance with this part, and submit to the ASD(FMP) the names and addresses of covered schools that are believed to be in violation of policies established in §216.4. Full documentation shall be furnished to the ASD(FMP) for each such covered school, including the school's formal response to the letter of inquiry, documentation of any oral response, or evidence showing that attempts were made to obtain either written confirmation or an oral statement of the school's policies.

(c) The Heads of the DoD components shall:

(1) Provide the ASD(FMP) with the names and addresses of covered schools identified as a result of evaluation(s) required under §§216.4(f) and (g).

(2) Take immediate action to deny obligations of DoD Funds to covered schools identified under paragraph (a)(1)(i) of this section, and to restore eligibility of covered schools identified under paragraph (a)(2) of this section.

§216.6 Information requirements.

The information requirements identified at §§216.5 (b) and (c)(1) have been assigned Report Control Symbol P&R-(AR)-2038 in accordance with DoD 8910.1-M. (See Note 1.)

Note 1: Copies may be obtained, at cost, from the National Technical Information Service, 5285 Port Royal Road, Springfield, VA 22161

Appendix A of Part 216— Military Recruiting Sample Letter of Inquiry

(Tailor letter to situation presented)

Dr. John Doe
President
ABC College
Anywhere, USA 12345-9876

Dear Dr. Doe:

I understand that military recruiting personnel [are unable to recruit on the campus of ABC College] [have been refused student recruiting information[1] on ABC College students for the purpose of military recruiting] by a policy or practice of the College. Current law[2] prohibits funds by grant or contract (including a grant of funds to be available for student aid) from appropriations of the Departments of Defense, Transportation (with respect to military recruiting), Labor, Health and Human Services, Education, and Related Agencies to schools that have a policy or practice of denying military recruiting personnel entry to campuses, access to students on campuses, or access to student recruiting information. Implementing regulations are codified at 32 Code of Federal Regulations, Part 216.

This letter provides you an opportunity to clarify your institution's policy regarding military recruiting on the campus of ABC College. In that regard, I request, within the next 30 days, a written policy statement of the institution with respect to access to campus and students, and to student recruiting information by military recruiting personnel. Your response should highlight any difference between access for military recruiters and access for recruiting by other potential employers.

Based on this information, Department of Defense officials will make a determination as to your institution's eligibility to receive funds by grant or contract. That decision may affect eligibility for funding from appropriations of the Departments of Defense, Transportation, Labor, Health and Human Services, Education, and Related Agencies. Should it be determined that ABC College is in violation of the aforementioned statutes, such funding would be stopped, and the school would be ineligible to receive such funds in the future.

I regret that this action may have to be taken. Successful recruiting requires that Department of Defense recruiters have reasonable access to students on the campuses of colleges and universities, and at the same time have effective relationships with the officials and student bodies of those institutions. I hope it will be possible to [define the correction to the aforementioned problem area(s)]. I am available to answer any questions.

Sincerely,

Notes:

1. Student recruiting information refers to a student's name, address, telephone listing, age (or year of birth), level of education (e.g., freshman, sophomore, or degree awarded for a recent graduate), and major.
2. 108 Stat. 2663 and 110 Stat. 3009.

Appendix B of Part 216—ROTC Sample Letter of Inquiry

(Tailor letter to situation presented)

Dr. Jane Smith
President
ABC College
Anywhere, USA 12345-9876

Dear Dr. Smith:

I understand that ABC College has [refused a request from a Military Department to establish a Senior ROTC unit at your institution][refused to continue existing ROTC programs at your institution][prevented students from participation at a Senior ROTC program at another institution] by a policy or practice of the College. Current law[1] prohibits funds by grant or contract (including a grant of funds to be available for student aid) from appropriations of the Departments of Defense, Labor, Health and Human Services, Education, and Related Agencies to schools that have a policy or practice prohibiting or preventing the Secretary of Defense from maintaining, establishing, or efficiently operating a Senior ROTC unit. Those statutes also bar agency funds for schools that prohibit or prevent a student from enrolling in an ROTC unit at another institution of higher education. Implementing regulations are codified at 32 Code of Federal Regulations, Part 216.

This letter provides you an opportunity to clarify your institution's policy regarding ROTC access on the campus of ABC College. In that regard, I request, within the next 30 days, a written statement of the institution with respect to [define the problem area(s)].

Based on this information, Department of Defense officials will make a determination as to your institution's eligibility to receive funds by grant or contract. That decision may affect eligibility for funding from appropriations of the Departments of Defense, Labor, Health and Human Services, Education, and Related Agencies. Should it be determined that ABC College is in violation of the aforementioned statutes, such funding would be stopped, and the school would be ineligible to receive such funds in the future.

I regret that this action may have to be taken. Successful officer procurement requires that the Department of Defense maintain a strong ROTC program. I hope it will be possible to [define the correction to the aforementioned problem area(s)]. I am available to answer any questions.

Sincerely,

L. M. Bynum
Alternate OSD Federal Register Liaison Officer
Department of Defense

Note:

[1] 10 U.S.C. 983 and 110 Stat. 3009

Bibliography

American Association of Collegiate Registrars and Admissions Officers. 1991. "1991 Survey of AACRAO Member Institutions on FERPA Policies and Practices." Washington, DC: AACRAO.

American Association of Collegiate Registrars and Admissions Officers. 2000. *Retention of Records: Guide for Retention and Disposal of Student Records*. Washington, DC: AACRAO.

American Association of Collegiate Registrars and Admissions Officers and National Association of College and University Attorneys. 1984. *Legal Guide for Admissions Officers and Registrars*. Washington, DC: AACRAO and NACUA.

American Jurisprudence. 1991 (2d ed.). Volume 81. Rochester, NY: Lawyers Cooperative.

Ault, R.L. 1993. "To Waive or Not to Waive? Students' Misconceptions about the Confidentiality Choice for Letters of Recommendation," *Teaching of Psychology*: 20:44–45.

Baker, M.G. 1987. "The Teacher's Need to Know versus the Student's Right to Privacy," *Journal of Law and Education* (Winter) 16:71–91.

Baker, Thomas R. 1997. "Inaccurate and Misleading Student Hearing Rights under FERPA," *West's Education Law Reporter* (February 6) 114:72–.

Burd, Stephen. 2000. "College Allowed to Tell Parents about Alcohol Use," *Chronicle of Higher Education* (July 14) 46: A31.

"Colleges Say Privacy Laws Hinder Class-Rank Admissions Plans," 2000. *Chronicle of Higher Education* (October 3) 47: A47.

Curran, R. 1988. "The Law, Computers, and Student Privacy," *CUPA Journal* (Fall) 39:37–45.

Davis, T. E., et al. 1987. "Writing Letters of Recommendation: The Struggle Continues," *The Teacher Educator* (Spring) 22:27–30.

Dobbins, K. W. 1987. *Student and Administrator Knowledge and Perception of the Buckley Amendment at Kent State University*. Doctoral dissertation, Kent State University.

Ericson, J. L. 1993. "Real World, Pretend Universities," *Educational Record* (Winter) 74: 43–48.

Essex, Nathan L. 2000. "Confidentiality and Student Records: Ten Ways to Invite Legal Challenges," *The Clearing House* (May/June) 73: 259–61.

Federal Civil Judicial Procedures and Rules, Title 28—Judiciary and Judicial Procedure. 2000 (rev. ed.). The West Group.

Fry, Bobbye G. 1999. *An Academic Dilemma: Student Records, Faculty Access, and the Family Educational Rights and Privacy Act*. Doctoral dissertation, Texas Tech University.

Fulkert, Ronald F., and Konnie G. Kerstron. 2000. "Limiting Your Liability in the Classroom," *Business Education Forum* (October) 55:42–45.

Garfinkel, S. L. 1987. "An Introduction to Computer Security, Part I." *Practical Law* (September) 39–48.

__________. 1987. "An Introduction to Computer Security, Part II". *Practical Law* (October) 57–67.

Holder, H. 1990. *Buckley Amendment—Help or Hindrance for Post-secondary Institution Admissions Officers*. Doctoral dissertation, George Washington University.

Hollander, P. A. 1992. "Student Records," *New Directions in Student Services* (Fall) 59:49–59.

Johnson, T. P. 1993. "Managing Student Records: The Courts and the Family Educational Rights and Privacy Act of 1974," *West's Education Law Reporter* (February 11) 79:1–18.

McDonald, Steven J., (ed.). 1999. *The Family Educational Rights and Privacy Act: A Legal Compendium*. Washington, DC: National Association of College and University Attorneys.

McIntyre, Gregory N. 1989. *Post-1974 Trends in Students' and Teachers' Rights to Control Information about Themselves*. Doctoral dissertation, University of Georgia.

Mawdsley, Ralph D. 1996. "Litigation Involving FERPA," *Education Law Reporter* (September 6) 675–692.

Morley, Robert. 1996. "Killing the Electronic Messenger," *CAUSE/EFFECT* (Spring) 43, 53.

Nolan, J. and Nolan-Haley, J. 1990. *Black's Law Dictionary* (6th ed.). St. Paul, MN: West Publishing.

Pechman, Ellen, and O'Brien, Eileen. 1994. "Issues in Educational Data Confidentiality and Access." Paper prepared for the National Center for Education Statistics and the National Forum on Education Statistics Steering Committee on Technology (January 6).

Pennsylvania Rules of Court. 1991. St. Paul, MN: West Publishing.

"Privacy and the Handling of Student Information in the Electronic Networked Environments of Colleges and Universities, A White Paper." 1997. *CAUSE*.

Quann, C. James et al. 1997. "An Argument for and a Case Study of Recording Significant Disciplinary Actions on Student Transcripts," *College and University* (Summer) 73: 2–6.

Rapp, James A. 1995. *Education Law, Volume 3: Student Records*. New York: Matthew Bender and Co.

Rooker, LeRoy S. 1989–2000. "Family Educational Rights and Privacy Act (FERPA)." Papers presented at the Annual Meeting of the American Association of Collegiate Registrars and Admissions Officers.

Rothenberger, J. 1994. "Transmission Security and Acknowledgment." Paper presented at the AACRAO SPEEDE Workshop, October, Madison, Wisconsin.

Schuerman, William C. 1980. *A Model Institutional Policy on the Privacy of Student Records in Compliance with the Family Educational Rights and Privacy Act of 1974 as Amended.* Doctoral dissertation, American University.

Siegler, Gregory E. 1996. "What Should Be the Scope of Privacy Protections for Student Health Records? A Look at Massachusetts and Federal Law," *Journal of Law and Education* (Spring) 25: 237–66.

Tanaka, Paul. 1995. "The Permissibility of Withholding Transcripts Under the Bankruptcy Law." Washington, DC: National Association of College and University Attorneys.

Tener, M. 1992. "The Buckley Amendment: Student-Athlete 'Privacy,'" *Scholastic Coach* (Fall) 61:13.

Tidwell, J. A. 1986. "Educator's Liability for Negative Letters of Recommendation," *Journal of Law and Education*: 15: 479–83.

Trubow, G. B. *Law Enforcement Information and the Family Educational Rights and Privacy Act*, American Bar Association.

Turner-Dickerson, Madalyn. 1997. *The Family Educational Rights and Privacy Act of 1974 as Amended: Knowledge, Practices and Perceptions.* Doctoral dissertation, University of Pittsburgh.

United States Department of Education. 1993. *SPEEDE/ExPRESS: An Electronic System for Exchanging Student Records.* National Center for Education Statistics. Washington, DC: NCES.

"Universities Wield Privacy Law in Clashes with T.A. Unions," 2000. *Chronicle of Higher Education* (October 27) 47: A12–A13.

Van Tol, J. (ed.) 1989. *College and University Student Records: A Legal Compendium.* Washington, DC: National Association of College and University Attorneys.

Index